Thomas Bradbury

The Mystery of Godliness, Considered in Sixty-One Sermons

Wherein the Deity of Christ is Proved upon no Other Evidence....: Vol. II.

Thomas Bradbury

The Mystery of Godliness, Considered in Sixty-One Sermons
Wherein the Deity of Christ is Proved upon no Other Evidence....: Vol. II.

ISBN/EAN: 9783337116842

Printed in Europe, USA, Canada, Australia, Japan

Cover: Foto ©Lupo / pixelio.de

More available books at **www.hansebooks.com**

THE MYSTERY OF GODLINESS,

CONSIDERED IN

SIXTY-ONE SERMONS.

WHEREIN

The DEITY of CHRIST is proved upon no other Evidence than the *Word of GOD*, and with no other View than for the *Salvation of Men*.

IN TWO VOLUMES.

BY THE REVEREND
THOMAS BRADBURY.

Know that for THY SAKE I have suffered rebuke. Thy Words were found, and I did eat them, and thy Word was unto me the joy and rejoicing of my heart; for I am called by THY NAME, O Lord God of Hosts. JER. XV. 15, 16.

VOL. II.

EDINBURGH:

PRINTED BY ADAM NEILL AND COMPANY,
AND SOLD BY JOHN OGLE,
PARLIAMENT-SQUARE.

M.DCC.XCV.

CONTENTS

OF

THE SECOND VOLUME.

SERM. **XXXII**, XXXIII, XXXIV, XXXV, XXXVI, XXXVII, XXXVIII, XXXIX.

	Pag.
Believed on in the World.	1
To BELIEVE *on Christ, is*	3
To receive his testimony,	4
To look on him as the only Saviour,	9
To rely upon his righteousness,	12
To derive a new life from him,	14
To grow up in him,	15
To depend on him as a Comforter,	16
To obey him universally,	19
To worship him in our religion,	21
To trust him for protection,	25
To own him as the Finisher of faith.	27
If he is not GOD,	28
The New Testament only proclaims a creature,	32
We cannot take him for the only Saviour,	36
Or rely on his merit as our righteousness,	40
Or expect a derivation of grace from him,	44
Or draw down daily supplies to it,	45
Or depend upon him as a Comforter,	50
Or obey him in all conversation,	53
Much less give him religious worship,	54
Or trust him for a future protection,	58
Or think that he will finish our faith.	59
This is a MYSTERY:	67
That there should be any believing at all,	68
It is acting without the direction of reason,	ib.
Nay, sometimes against it,	ib.
And in opposition to example,	71
It is purely personal.	72
That this should be in the world,	73
In this world, and not in heaven,	74

In

	Pag.
In a world where he had been refused,	77
Where the greatest evidence seemed ineffectual,	80
In a world where he appears no longer,	82
In a world full of prejudice,	83
And under the power of Satan,	85
And where nothing is got by it.	86
It is a mystery of GODLINESS: *as that signifies*	87
Our subjection and conformity to Christ,	88
As God he is the object of this duty,	89
As God the author of this change:	90
Our compliance with the rule of his word,	93
As God he demands a duty to himself,	94
As God he directs a duty to men:	95
Our profession of faith; His deity	96
Makes us act upon a certainty,	ib.
Grow up to a confidence:	100
Our joys and satisfaction in him; as God	101
He pardons our sins,	103
This is the act of Christ, and yet	ib.
It is the peculiar of God,	107
He gives the hopes of glory.	109
Hence see the necessity of preaching Christ,	111
The opposition of Satan,	112
The wickedness of those who hinder faith,	113
The need of prayer,	114
The necessity of our believing in Christ,	115
And regarding all his perfections.	ib.

SERM. XL, XLI, XLII, XLIII, XLIV, XLV, XLVI, XLVII, XLVIII, XLIX, L, LI.

Received up into glory.	116
His GLORY *may be considered three ways:*	118
As he is Man, he has	119
The imperfection of our nature,	121
Complete rest from all his labours,	125
A glory and reputation in his Person;	128
His soul is satisfied with joys,	129
His body is independent on all supplies,	134
Because it is a glorious body,	137
It is received into an immortal life,	139
And an eternal settlement,	141
He has the office of Judge; but the greatest glory is	143
The union of the human nature to the Divine.	147

THE CONTENTS.

As he is Mediator, *his glory appears in*	Pag. 151
The stupendious union of the two natures,	153
His separation to the work of a Saviour,	155
His discharge of the trust,	156
His acquittance from the Father;	161
The union between the two *natures is confirmed,*	165
In this union he receives the praises of heaven,	166
He continues the mediation between God and man.	168
As he is God, *he has the glories of the Deity,*	169
Spirituality,	178
Omniscience,	183
Omnipotence,	191
Truth,	198
Holiness and goodness,	204
Eternity,	209
Chief agency in nature and grace,	217
Right to universal homage.	221
Being received *into this glory, may be considered with reference to*	223
His human nature:	
A cloud received him,	225
Angels attended him,	229
He abides in heaven,	230
He has received the reward.	233
His mediatorial office: *in the union of natures,*	234
He is owned by the Father,	235
Recognised by Saints and Angels,	237
Declares his resolution to continue so,	242
Proceeds in this character through all his works,	243
Of nature,	ib.
Of grace,	245
Of providence,	246
He rules the Church,	ib.
He will judge the world.	248
His Divine Nature: *the glory of this appears in*	249
Throwing off the vail that was upon it,	255
And laying that aside for ever,	259
A fresh exposing himself to the worship of Angels,	261
Speaking the language of a God in heaven,	263
And thus revealing himself on earth.	268
Therefore, he will keep his glory,	271
In his authority over the Church,	273
In his full and proper Deity,	274
And expects we should keep it.	276

SERM.

SERM. LII, LIII, LIV, LV, LVI, LVII.

The opposition made to this doctrine is various, Pag.	280
By Samosatenus, *the* Aetians, Eunomians, Arians Ebionites, Macedonians, Noetians, Praxeans, Sabellians, Socinians, *and the new scheme,*	283
None of them delivered in Scripture-words,	ib.
Never was charity more limited.	284
The question in debate fairly stated ;	290
They own Christ is called God; but	ib.
They deny that he is underived,	291
They are divided about his worship,	292
Their distinction from Arianism *is vile and foolish,*	293
Their arguments against the Deity of Christ answered,	295
His inferiority to the Father,	ib.
That his Deity makes him the same person with the Father, &c. answered,	297
The nature of God is incomprehensible,	ib.
We always assert a distinction of persons,	299
They allow no medium between Sabellianism *and* Tritheism,	300
Christ did give satisfaction to himself,	301
That their scheme is philosophical, answered,	ib.
Never the better for that, if it were so, but	ib.
It is rather irrational,	303
It runs into the Egyptian *folly,*	304
Makes a wrong distribution to the Son and Spirit,	307
It is vain deceit.	309
That Christ is the begotten of the Father, answered,	310
Infinite Nature is not to be measured by finite,	311
The word need not signify derivation of nature,	312
But rather expresses an identity,	313
In many places it cannot signify derivation.	314
Their methods to oppose the truth :	315
They disguise the question in the following ways,	317
Trifling with the word God,	318
Distinguishing between supreme and subordinate worship,	320
Pretending that the matter is all speculation.	322
They pretend that we have only human creeds, answered,	325
This was professed at the Reformation,	326

And

And re-asserted by the Divines at Westminster, Pag. 327
They did all this upon Scripture authority, 329
And so have I done quite through this work. 330

They make a boast of free-thinking, *answered,* 331
This vanity is an ill mark upon the cause, ib.
The charge of Enthusiasm *may be retorted,* 333
This very argument is a downright slander. 335

They impose upon us with false quotations, 337
This practice will be fatal to them, 339
It is an instance of their impudence, ib.
This injury on the memories of good men ought to be resented. 342

They would confine us to Scripture-words, ib.
Which was never their own practice, ib.
It is what a Papist *may do,* 344
They know we plead nothing but Scripture. ib.

They glory in their charity : 345
This should not be opposed to faith, 347
But is always founded on an union in faith, 348
Charity is to go by Scripture rule. 351

They despise mysteries and church-communion, 354
The opinion is bad that makes people worse, 355
Beware of trifling with the Lord's day, 356
Arguments should be answered, not bantered, 357
The laugh will be turned upon them, 358
Our cause abhors such methods. ib.

SERM. LVIII, LIX, LX, LXI.

Great is the Mystery,——God received into Glory,

An account of mysteries in general, 359
Of this in particular :
  He who was destitute below, has all fulness above, 363
  The object of God's wrath lives in his favour, 366
  He was deserted of men and Angels, and is now their head, 368
  A suffering nature is united with an eternal. 370

A vindication of this mystery, 371
  Denying of mysteries is universally exploded, 372
  Explaining of mysteries is nonsense. ib.

THE CONTENTS.

This is a doctrine of GODLINESS : *it promotes*   Pag. 373
  Faith, by which   375
    We rest on the bare word of God,   376
    We make an honest profession of him,   379
    We live with duty to him.   383
  Hope, by owning his Deity,   385
    We rest upon his righteousness,   ib.
    We trust him for protection,   386
    We resign to him at death.   387
  Charity, the several senses of the word,   **388**
    A belief of Christ's Divinity teaches
    Forbearance of one another,   398
    Union in the faith the foundation of charity,   401

Advice to those who do not believe the truth,   403
  Do not deride it,   404
  Shun profane babblings, viz.   407
    Denying a certainty in faith,   408
    Deriding the work of the Spirit,   409
    Curtailing revelation,   ib.
    Despising good men,   ib.
    Neglecting practical religion.   410
  Be open to conviction,   ib.
  Beg the Divine teachings.   411

Exhortation to such are convinced.   412
  Feel what you believe,   413
  Own what you have felt.   414

Some account of my engaging in this subject,   416

SERMON XXXII.

July 19. 1719.

1 TIM. iii. 16.

———*Believed on in the World.*

THESE words carry our thoughts into the fifth branch of the Christian religion, or, as the Apostle calls it, *the record that God has given of his Son.* And it is like all the rest, a Mystery of Godliness: That God should be *manifest in the flesh;* and after all the scandal that he met with there, *justified in the Spirit:* That when he was refused of men, he should be *seen of Angels;* and upon the contradiction of the *Jews, preached unto the Gentiles;* and this so very effectual to their advantage, and his reputation, that he is *believed on in the world.* I shall here proceed by that method which I have observed all along in the other parts of this glorious subject; that is,

1. Shew you the sense of the phrase, or what it is for the world to *believe on Christ.*

2. Open

2. Open this as an argument of his true Divinity; that He who is so believed on can be no other than the Most High God.

3. Consider it as a *mystery*, that bears a place among those many things that are too wonderful for us; such as are high, and we cannot attain unto.

4. Let you see the benefit of such a doctrine: it is a Mystery of *Godliness*, and helps on the religion that ought to be our concern and practice.

I. We must enquire what is farther said of Him, concerning whom we have heard so much already: and the branch that I am now upon gives us *glad tidings* indeed. They tell us of a *glory to God in the highest;* they introduce a *peace upon earth*, and proclaim a *good will towards men*. We have heard before that he was preached unto the Gentiles, among people who *sought him not*, and were *not called by his name*, but continued *without Christ* for several generations, *strangers and foreigners*. Now, it is a natural enquiry, To what purpose is the report carried among the Gentiles, which had so little influence on the Jews? Is Christ any gainer in his revenue, or they in their salvation? What is the advantage of it? We may answer, much every way, because he was *believed on in the world*.

This part of our religion tallies exactly to the other, that we were last upon. There is no proportion between his being *manifest in the flesh*, and *justified in the Spirit*. Thousands saw him, and heard him, to whom the Spirit gave no such testimony. The witnesses to his incarnation were saints and sinners, Jews and Greeks, good and bad, friends and enemies. *Jesus of Nazareth was a man approved of God among them by signs and miracles, which God did by him in the midst of them, as they themselves also knew*. But when he is justified, admired, approved of, and heartily chosen, this was only done by those to whom the Spirit had
glorified

glorified him. Now, though there is no proportion between his being manifest and his being justified; yet there is something that looks like it between the *fourth* and *fifth* branches of our religion. His being preached unto the Gentiles is answered by this, that he was believed on in the world. Not but that several would hear the former, who are eternal strangers to the latter; for *death and destruction say, We have heard the fame of him with our ears.*

But there is a harmony between these parts of the Christian Doctrine in two particulars. *First,* The success or result of his being *preached,* is, that he is *believed on.* To this end did he receive gifts for men, and *gave some Apostles, Prophets, Evangelists, pastors, and teachers.* And, *secondly,* The place where this attempt was made, is that where no such event could be expected: he is preached *among the Gentiles;* those parts where grace and revelation had employed no culture; the unprepared regions of the earth. Well, he is believed on *in the world,* in these unlikely countries. As the day-star had arisen upon the people that sat in darkness and saw no light, so it did not shine out in vain, but made known to them *a salvation by the remission of their sins, through the tender mercy of our God, and guided their feet into the way of peace.* In opening out this head of Divinity, I shall observe both the things now mentioned.

1. What it is for any people to *believe* on Christ.
2. That thus he was believed on *in the world.*

1. What is it for him to be *believed on?* you know this is a word of great repute in the New Testament, and very often expresses the whole of our religion, as it takes in both the duty and the expectation of a Christian. And though sometimes it signifies only a bare assent to the truth of what he said, yet the more usual meaning is of a greater latitude. It may be considered several ways.

As

As regarding the *doctrine* that Christ has revealed, there believing is being satisfied that it is all true. As regarding his *Person*, there believing is closing with him as the anointed of God. In respect to our *hope*, believing is that dependence by which we receive the benefits that he gives, and wait for those that he has promised. With respect to our *duty*, believing goes out into life and practice. It bears all these interpretations in the book of God. And as in our text we are called to consider the success of his Gospel among the Gentiles, so when it is said he was *believed on in the world*, I think we may take the expression in its whole latitude, and you will find that they who do indeed believe on Him, may have the following characters affirmed of them.

They receive the *testimony* that he has given of himself: they look upon him as the only *Saviour* of a lost race: they rely upon the *righteousness* that he has brought in for their acceptance with God: they derive from his *fulness* the graces of the Holy Spirit: they *increase* in the life of God by supplies from Him: they regard him as their great *Comforter* in every time of need: they *obey* him in all manner of conversation; in particular, they live in the acts of religious *worship* to him: they trust in him for a *protection* to the end of life: they look to him as the *Finisher* of their faith. All these things go by the name of believing: and though a good man may not have them in an equal evidence, yet there is such a connection among them, that where there is one, there are all.

(1.) I begin with that which seems to be the lowest act of faith: and that is receiving the testimony he has given of himself; believing that *his doctrine is of God*, that it came from above. This takes in not only what he said in person to his disciples, whom he had chosen, but what he has since told them by the Holy Ghost, and with which revelations

velations he has completed the rule of faith and hope. So that no man can make any additions to the words of the prophecy of this book: he has *sealed up the sayings*. Believing in this case is depending upon the authority of the Scriptures, that they are given by *inspiration of God, and that by them the man of God may be perfect, thoroughly furnished to every good work*. He that sets up any other rule besides the Bible, either for our practice or comfort, is no believer; because in the revelation that a Saviour gives of himself, he has struck off our regard from every one else. Our faith is never to *stand in the wisdom of men.*

<small>SERM. 32.

2 Tim. iii. 16, 17.

1 Cor. ii. 5.</small>

And, ' whatever insinuations are given about, ' there is nothing that my soul does more abhor, ' than to set up the decrees of men as the grounds ' of believing.' That is rather to deny the faith than to promote it. We do not believe in creeds, catechisms, and confessions, much less in those persons who compiled them. All the profession that can be made upon these heads is, that we take the doctrine as it is there expressed, to agree with the revelation contained in the Scriptures: *We write no other things unto you, than what you read and acknowledge, and I trust you shall acknowledge even to the end. Evil men and seducers wax worse and worse, deceiving, and being deceived:* in opposition to whom, *we continue in the things that we have learned and been assured of, knowing of whom we have learned them; and that from children we have known the Scriptures, which are able to make us wise to salvation, through faith which is in Christ Jesus.*

<small>2 Cor. i. 13.

2 Tim. iii. 13, 14, 15.</small>

You may think that such a believing as this, is no great matter: that we grow into it by time; it is only the manufacture of education, and is established by the laws of the country. And indeed if we are believers to no other purpose than this, it is far from being the faith I am speaking of.

But

SERM. 31. But nevertheless, the Scripture has placed our receiving the testimony of Christ Jesus a great deal higher than some are apt to imagine. What a noble account does John the Baptist give of such a believer? What Christ *had seen and heard, that he declared; and——he that received his testimony has set to his seal that God is true.* He has given a sort of assurance to all the promises that are upon record. He is a voucher to the Divine faithfulness in the midst of an unbelieving world; and therefore our Saviour makes it no small matter to be *received* even in this sense: *We speak that we do know, and testify that we have seen, and ye receive not our witness.* His enemies came with a snare, if not with a scorn, saying, *Master, we know thou art righteous, and teachest the way of God in truth.* But it is what they were not satisfied in, though, as he saith, none could convince him of evil.

Joh. iii. 32, 33.

ver. 11.

And indeed there is a great difference between a man's being able to run down the evidence that is given of the Christian Religion, and his receiving *the love of that truth.* Many a one dare not deny it, who yet cannot be said to believe it. We read of some Jews *who believed on him,* of whom he saith afterwards, *Ye are of your father the devil, and the lusts of your father ye will do:——because I tell you the truth, ye believe me not: none of you convinces me of sin, and if I say the truth, why do not ye believe me? He that is of God, hears God's words: ye therefore hear them not, because ye are not of God.* I am apt to think it is with revealed religion as it is with natural. There are thousands who cannot get over the arguments they meet with for the being of a God, and yet are fools enough to *say in their hearts, There is no God. Their minds and consciences are defiled: they profess that they know God, but in works they deny him; being abominable, disobedient, and to every good work reprobate.* When these people are converted, their
believing

Joh. viii. 31. 44, 45, 46, 47.

Pf. xiv. 1
Tit. i. 15, 16.

believing is to quite another purpofe; which fhews it to be from quite another principle. Juft fo it is with the authority of Chrift in the things that he has faid of himfelf: Though a perfon may not know how to difpute againft them, yet there is a great deal more goes to a thorough conviction.

SERM. 31.

When our Saviour had fent the difciples of John back to their mafter, with that which would confirm *him,* and might perfuade *them,* that *the dead are raifed, the deaf hear, the blind fee, the lame walk, and the lepers are cleanfed,* he adds, *Bleffed is he whofoever fhall not be offended in me; q. d.* notwithftanding all the evidence that makes you converts, yet the work muft be afcribed to a Divine power as well as a moving argument; for that which abundantly fatisfies you, will be of no weight to millions of other people. We may complain, after all our pains to eftablifh a doctrine that is called the wifdom of God, *Who has believed our report!* people rather take the Chriftian Religion for granted, than look into it; and the confequence of this is, that they will be *carried away with every wind of doctrine.* Though the miniftration of the Spirit is glorious, though they who are employed in it ufe *great plainnefs of fpeech,* though they renounce the hidden things of difhonefty, *not walking in craftinefs, nor handling the word of the Lord deceitfully, but by manifeftation of the* truth commend themfelves to every man's confcience in the fight of God; yet after all this, *our Gofpel is hid, and many are loft.* We have need therefore not only to look into the book of God, but at the time of doing it, to waft up the fame defire with David, *Lord, open thou mine eyes, that I may behold wonders out of thy law.* And there is the more occafion for this, when *the god of this world has blinded the eyes of them that believe not, left the light of the glorious Gofpel of Chrift, who is the image of the invifible God, fhould fhine into their hearts.*

Mat. xi. 6.

Ifa. liii. 1

2 Cor. iv. 2, 3, 4.

What

SERM. 32. What is it that makes a believer, and gives him a right persuasion, that the testimony we have of Jesus Christ is true? I answer, there is a great deal of what we call *moral evidence.* We have a consistence in the parts, a harmony in the whole, a strain of piety running through, and a demonstration of miracles bearing witness. But all this will not do, till *He who caused the light to shine out of darkness, shines into our hearts, to gives us the light of the knowledge of the glory of God, in the face of Jesus Christ.* Peter told our Lord what men said of him: some that he was Elias, some John the Baptist, others that one of the old Prophets was risen again. All the opinions proclaimed him to be a wonderful person: and had he been any of these, no manner of doubt, *mighty works would have shewn themselves in him.* I cannot say, but that one raised from the dead might have been able to do as many miracles. But this was not believing him to be what he really was. Though in these imaginations they supposed a great deal, yet not enough.

2 Cor. iv. 6.

Now the question is, upon what grounds any could say, he was more than a prophet returned into the world, and no less than the Christ of God? Our Saviour saith to him, *Blessed art thou Simon Barjona, flesh and blood has not revealed this to thee, but my Father who is in heaven.* Flesh and blood, *i. e.* human reason, employed upon these observations, might prove him to be more than a man; but here is another evidence given to him, that can proceed from none but God.—Well, thus he was believed on in the world; his Gospel was approved of. The word that they heard of the Apostles, was *not received as the word of man, but as it is in truth the word of the living God, that works effectually in those that believe.* He takes notice of this to the Thessalonians: *Our testimony among you was believed.* This is the ground of all: we do well to take

1 Thes. ii. 13.

take heed to the sure word of prophecy: if we cease to take heed to that, no doctrines of the Christian revelation will ever imprefs us. They are recommended to us, as *not coming by the will of man, but that holy men of God spake as they were moved by the Holy Ghost.*

SERM. 32.
2 Pet. i. 19, 20, 21.

(2.) They that believe on Christ, look upon him as *the only Saviour* of a lost world. This was the great matter of his testimony, when the Jews asked, *What shall we do, that we may work the work of God?* The meaning of the question seems to be this: What is that particular duty which above all others God expects from us? What is the obedience that may be called *working the work of God?* He answers, *This is the work of God, that ye believe on Him whom he has sent.* Here the matter stuck. His enemies could not deny him to be richly furnished; but his being the Christ, the anointed of God, the Messiah, the Interpreter, who is one among a thousand, the feed of the woman, the Son of Abraham, is what they could not imagine: *They stumbled at that stumbling-stone; as it is written, Behold, I lay in Sion a stumbling-stone, and a rock of offence, and whoever believes on him shall not be ashamed.*

Rom. ix. 32, 33.

Therefore it is said, that *he was in the world, and the world was made by him, and the world knew him not;* that is, they knew not what they were chiefly to have known. *He came to his own, and his own received him not:* not but that they followed him with esteem and wonder, but they did not receive him as *the gift of God,* as the great appointment of infinite wisdom, as *the hope of Israel,* and the substance of those promises that were made to the fathers: to them that thus *received him, gave he power to become the sons of God:* it was a sort of Divine act, *even to them that believe on his name.* Their believing is not put upon the clearness of the evidence, and their own studious impartial searches,

Joh. i. 10, 11, 12, 13.

Joh. iv. 10.

searches, but upon a higher nature: they were *born not of blood, nor of the will of man, nor of the will of the flesh, but of God.*

This is what he all along insisted on: to this John bare witness, saying, *Behold the Lamb of God who takes away the sins of the world.* And John's disciples who were sent to him, gave this confession, *Rabbi, thou art the Son of God, thou art the King of Israel.* Thus the woman of Samaria speaks, *Come, see a man that told me all things that ever I did, is not this the Christ?* And so say the men of the city to her again, *Now we believe, not because of thy saying, for we have heard him ourselves, and know that this is indeed the Christ, the Saviour of the world.* Thus they speak of him to others, *We have found him, of whom Moses in the law and the prophets did write.* By which way of arguing, you see how they understood the Scriptures of truth. They were delivered *at sundry times, and in divers manners;* they had laws, promises, types, and histories; but, like so many lines, they were all tending to one point. Thus our Saviour speaks of himself, in such language as no prophet ever used: *He stood in the last and great day of the feast, and cried, If any man thirst, let him come unto me and drink.*

It would have been in vain for any to plead then as some do now, that this was merely a speculation. Let but people mind their duty, live honestly, and carefully, and they shall never be condemned for *not believing* what they cannot understand. This vain talking is what the Scripture has left us no room for. Our Lord tells them plainly, *If ye believe not that I am he, ye shall die in your sins.* He saith again, *All that came before me are thieves and robbers: I am the door; by me if any man enter in, he shall find pasture.* And it was a proper question that John's disciples came with, *Art thou be that should come, or do we look for another?* Several had appeared in different ages, to make known the will,

will of God, and in particular their own great ma- *Serm. 32.*
fter, but there was no more than *One* that should
come as Mediator between God and man: *It was* Joh. xvii. 3.
*life eternal to know the only true God, and Jesus
Christ whom he had sent.*

Cornelius was a person who gave alms, and had
a good report of all men, and prayed always; that
is, devotion was his habit and his practice; and yet
God bids him send to Joppa for Peter, who would
tell him words whereby he should be saved. And Acts x. 6.
what are these words, but a report of Jesus Christ?
for, as he had observed to the Jews before, *There
is salvation in no other, neither any other name given under heaven among men.* So he does the same
again: *The word,* faith he, *which God sent to the* ver. 36, 37,
children of Israel, preaching peace by Jesus Christ, 38.
*that word which was published through all Judea,
and begun from Galilee, how God anointed Jesus
Christ with the Holy Ghost. To Him give all the* ver. 43.
*prophets witness, that through his name, whoever
believes in him shall receive remission of sins.* Thus
it was foretold he should be preached, agreeable to
what he faith himself, *Look unto me, and be ye saved all the ends of the earth; for I am the Lord,
and there is none else.* The Apostle gives it as a
maxim, that *other foundation can no man lay, be-* 1 Cor. iii.
sides that which is laid, who is Jesus Christ. 11.

So that believing in him is collecting and cen-
tring all our hopes here, rejecting all other mediat-
ors as physicians of no value; looking upon him
as *the way, the truth, and the life, that no man can* Joh. xiv. 6.
come unto the Father but by him. He is, as the very
devils confessed him to be, *The Holy One of God.*
The New Testament has made so great an account
of this, that certainly it must be of the last importance to our salvation. If mere doing justice, loving mercy, and walking humbly with God, which
some people set in opposition to faith, if these
would have done, there was no need to have puzzled

zled the world with the claims of a person who was set *for the fall and the rising again of many in Israel, and a sign that should be spoken against.* Paul touching the righteousness of the law *was blameless,* and yet at that time *the chief of sinners.* He therefore desires to be found in none of that righteousness, but only in one that came from God by faith. But this leads me to shew,

(3.) Believing in Christ is relying upon the *righteousness,* that he has brought in for our acceptance with God. This is easily talked of, but the soul that ever knew what it meant, finds it the hardest thing in the world. It is easier to *perform* a hundred duties than to *deny* one of them. It is what every good man is most jealous of himself about. He may hope that he loves Christ, there are several arguments of this, but he is afraid that something else is stealing into his soul as the matter of his rejoicing. The pleasures that flow into a duty, and the reflection that afterwards he makes upon it, are not so easily kept out of his hopes of justification. It is a very hard thing, after we have done all, to sit down with patience and say, We are unprofitable servants. This was the misery of the Jews; they had a zeal of God, *they went about to establish a righteousness of their own, and would not submit themselves to the righteousness of God.* Now *Christ is the end of the law for righteousness to every one that believes.*

And this is believing, not neglecting our duty, but looking beyond it to something else as the great atonement. *To him that works is the reward reckoned not of grace, but of debt; but to him that works not,* that is, not with any expectation of being pardoned for it, *but believes on him that justifies the ungodly, to him his faith is imputed for righteousness.* This is believing, and before a soul is brought to it, the Holy Spirit has been thoroughly at work with him. It may be supposed of every one who relies

relies on the merits of Christ, that he owns, he feels the pollution of his nature, according to that cry of the Church, *Our righteousnesses are as filthy rags, and ourselves as an unclean thing.* He sees the terrors of the law, *When the commandment comes, sins revives, and he dies.* He beholds the justice of God, who *will by no means clear the guilty,* and *in whose sight no flesh living can be justified.* He confesses the vanity of all his own endeavours, to answer the demands of a righteous Creator. *How shall man be just with God, or how shall he be pure who is born of a woman?* And oh! how desirable to such a one will *Jesus the Mediator of the new covenant* be, and *the blood of sprinkling, that speaks better things than the blood of Abel!*

^{SERM. II.}

Rom. vii. 9.

Heb. xii. 24.

The more you value the death of Christ, the greater evidence do you give of believing. The Apostle wanted to *know the fellowship of his sufferings, and to be conformed to his death. Him has God set forth as a propitiation for our sins through faith in his blood.* He in his own person is the great Propitiation, the Paschal Lamb, *Christ our passover is sacrificed for us.* But the particular notice that our faith takes, is of his blood. He was *delivered for our offences, and rose again for our justification.*

Phil iii. 10.

Rom. iii. 25.

1 Cor. v. 7.

Rom. iv. 25.

Those people that deny the infinite evil of sin, (by which *we* mean its being directed against an infinite Majesty, and deserving an eternal punishment), these are *enemies to the cross of Christ;* they make it a needless thing, and what the world might have done without: But whatever arguments persons may have against the satisfaction made to divine justice, one shake of an uneasy conscience will set them to rights; they will then see, that *without shedding of blood, there could be no remission.* This is believing; our persons, our duties, or as they are called, *our garments, are washed in the blood of the Lamb.* It is here that faith takes a fast hold, that Christ has *loved us, and given himself*

Rev. i. 5.

self for us, having washed us from our sins in his own blood. A poor convinced soul finds he is undone, and that there is no *standing in God's sight when once he is angry;* and it is only owing to him from whom *we have received the atonement,* that we have *access by faith into the grace wherein we stand.*

Ps. cxxx. 3.

Rom. v. 2.

(4.) Believing in Christ is deriving from his fulness the principles of *a new life.* The satisfaction that he has made, was with a view to this. *He loved the church, and gave himself for it, that he might sanctify it with the washing of water by the word.* Conversion is a looking to him as the *Author of our faith.* Then is *Christ formed in us;* from that time we are his people, and feel his power. He sends out his servants to *open our eyes, to turn us from darkness to light;* not that they can do it, for *who is sufficient for these things?* But the *Son quickens whom he will.* Thus he speaks to Paul in a vision at Corinth, *I have much people in this city.* He sees us in our bondage as well as in our guilt, and if from both these the Son makes us free, *then are we free indeed.* In which words he is to be understood of spiritual liberty, having stated the opposite condition in these terms: *He that commits sin is the servant of sin.*

Eph. v. 25, 26.

Heb. xii. 2.
Gal. iv. 19.

John v. 21.
Acts xviii. 10.

John viii. 36.

This is believing, then we begin to live, or rather *Christ lives in us, and the life we live in the flesh is by faith in the Son of God;* so that when it is said, that he is preached among the Gentiles, and believed on in the world, the meaning is, he has made them alive. *He is the Head over all things unto the church, and has the fulness of him who fills all in all. And you has* HE *quickned who were dead in trespasses and* SINS. The scripture has represented him as an agent in our conversion. *When I am lifted up,* saith he, *I will draw all men unto me.* 'The mountain of this Lord's house is exalted above

Gal. ii. 20.

Eph. i. 23.

—— ii. 1.

John xii. 32.

Isa. ii. 2, 3.

above the tops of the mountains; He *will teach us of his law, and we will walk in* his *way.* The believer has not only a new state, having passed from death to life, but a new nature, he is brought *from the power of Satan to the living* God. Christ who pleads *for* him, does also plead *with* him, his own cause; and he does it in such a way, as to make all opposition flee. *The strong man armed, has kept his goods in peace; but here is a stronger than he, who takes from him his armour wherein he trusted.* This is the Apostle's account of his own conversion. *It pleased God to call him by his grace, and reveal his Son in him,* and with that begun his hopes of glory. *This faith is of the operation of God.*

(5.) Believing in Christ, is *growing* in the spiritual life. We are *preserved in Christ Jesus, and called: As ye have received Christ Jesus the Lord, so walk ye in him: Rooted and built up in him, established in the faith, as ye have been taught, and abounding therein with thanksgiving. I am come,* saith he, *that ye might have life, and that ye might have it more abundantly.* To this purpose we read of his *dwelling in our hearts by faith.* This agrees to the language of his own prayer to the Father, *I in them, and thou in me, that they may be made perfect in one.* This will be thoroughly understood in the visions of another state, *In that day ye shall know, that I am in the Father, and the Father in me, and I in you.* He told his disciples, *I go away and come again, because I live, ye shall live also. He that has begun a good work is to perform it to the day of Christ Jesus.*

So that believing is a continued rest of soul upon him. Your faith must be often looking thither. *Who is this that comes up out of the wilderness leaning on her beloved?* Thus he advises, *Abide in me, and I in you. As the branch cannot bear fruit of itself, except it abide in the vine; no more can ye,*

Serm. 31.

Gal. i. 15, 16.

Jude 1.
Col. ii. 6, 7.

Joh. x. 10.

Eph iii. 17.

John xvii. 23.

——— xiv. 20.

ver. 19.

Phil. i. 6.

Cant. viii. 5.
Joh. xv. 4, 5.

except

SERM. 32. *except ye abide in me. I am the vine, ye are the branches: He that abides in me, and I in him, the same brings forth much fruit, for without me ye can do nothing.*

August 2.
1719.

SERMON XXXIII.

(6.) WHEN we believe in Chriſt, we regard him as our great *Comforter* in every time of need. There is a diſtinction that you ought to obſerve in this caſe, which will keep you out of a miſtake that many people run into. I do not aſſert that faith always takes into it the joys of the Holy Ghoſt, for we know there are perſons
Iſa. l. 10. who *ſit in darkneſs and ſee no light*, and yet *fear the Lord and hearken to the voice of his ſervant.*
Pſ. xxxiv. 5 But you muſt own, that even theſe are *looking* to Jeſus that they may be *lightened*. They have no
— lxi. 2. other friend to truſt to. This is a *rock* that is *higher than themſelves*, where they ſeek a ſhelter *when their ſouls are overwhelmed within them;* and therefore they are exhorted to *truſt in the Lord, and ſtay themſelves upon their God.*

I do not mean that the believer always has theſe comforts from a Saviour, but that he flies to HIM for them, and is encouraged by that gracious pro-
Mat. xi. clamation, *Come unto* ME, *all ye that are weary and*
28, 29, *heavy laden, and I will give you reſt.* It is he that
30. ſaith, *Take* MY *yoke upon you, and learn of* ME, *and*

ye

ye shall find rest unto your souls; for MY *yoke is easy,* and MY *burden is light.* And thus he was promised: He is *the root of Jesse, who shall stand for an ensign of the people, to which the Gentiles shall seek; and his rest shall be glorious.* Our lot is cast into a rolling world, which like the troubled sea cannot rest, but *sends up mire and dirt.* Here we are floating, tossing, heaving, and cannot expect a full rest till we come to that which *remains for the people of God, when a sea* of waters shall be changed into one *of glass,* and instead of being unsettled any longer, we shall have crowns on our heads, and harps in our hands, *to sing the song of Moses and the song of the Lamb.*

SERM. 33.

Isa. xi. 10.

Heb. iv. 9.

Rev. xv. 2.

John xiv. 18.

But even in this life our Redeemer does not leave us *comfortless,* or, as the word signifies, he does not leave us orphans. We are not fatherless, though our Head is gone up to heaven, and we see him no more; or if we are so, yet our hope is in Him with whom *the fatherless find mercy. I will see you again,* saith he to his disciples, *and your heart shall rejoice, and your joy shall no man take away from you.* And that he told them in maintenance of a kind promise, *Verily, verily, I say unto you, ye shall weep and lament, and the world shall rejoice, and ye shall be sorrowful, but your sorrow shall be turned into joy.* This he illustrates by a similitude that is very common, and yet very powerful. He takes the chief instance of nature to shew the efficacy of grace, *A woman when she is in travail, has sorrow, because her hour is come; but as soon as she is delivered of a child, she remembers no more the anguish, for joy that a man is born into the world.* And that unaccountable transition, from a sadness to a serenity of mind, was to be brought about by his coming again.

— xvi. 22.

ver. 20, 21.

The meaning of that I take to be twofold. Both these senses are included in it: *First,* It immediately refers to his conversation with the disciples

SERM. 33. after his passion, by which he gave *infallible proofs* of his rising again ; this was a delightful interview to those who ran from his cross and wept over his grave. *He shewed them his hands and his feet, and then were the disciples glad when they saw the Lord:* But, *secondly,* Surely the promise is more extended, and reaches farther than to the blessings of those *forty days.* It belongs to all those upon whom he has bestowed the other Comforter, *The Spirit of truth who shall abide with us for ever.* And he mentions this as a mystery, that this Spirit is one *whom the world cannot receive, because it sees him not, neither knows him ; but ye know him, for he dwells with you, and shall be in you.* And by those words he has prepared you to understand what follows, *I will not leave you comfortless, I will come unto you ; yet a little while and the world sees me no more, but ye see me,* i. e. by a faith that others have not ; *because I live, ye shall live also.* There is a connection in the parts of that promise, that shall reach through all the ages of time, whilst there is a believer upon earth, and from it he deduces another gracious promise : *He that has my commandments, and keeps them, he it is that loves me ; and he that loves me, shall be loved of my Father, and I will love him, and will manifest myself to him.* This he repeats and enlarges, *If any man love me, he will keep my words ; and my Father will love him, and we will come unto him, and make our abode with him.* Certainly though these phrases are to be guarded against any gross and impure exposition, yet they mean something.

There is a joy that is struck from a communion with Christ, whether a carnal world will allow it or no. *He stands at the door and knocks, and if any man hears his voice, he comes in and sups with him.* He knew the toil that his people were like to meet with, and therefore as they *lacked nothing* whilst he was among them, so they shall be as well furnished

John xx. 20.

— xiv. 16, 18, 19.

ver. 21.

— 23.

Rev. iii. 20.

furnished when he went away. Bidding them *go* <small>SERM 33.</small>
and disciple all nations, was throwing them into a <small>Mat. xxviii. 19, 19, 20.</small>
duty of the greatest compass; ordering them to
*baptize into the name of the Father, Son and Holy
Ghost*, was engaging against them all the disdain
of the earth; but what signifies that, when he
saith, that *he will be with them to the end of the
world?*

We find they used to set *his* promise over a-
gainst all their troubles. As the Apostle argues, <small>2 Tim. i. 12.</small>
*Though I suffer these things, nevertheless I am not
ashamed, for I know in whom I have believed*, q. d.
he has already accounted for all that. Good people will have their sorrows; *without are fightings,
within are fears;* and what must they flee to?
Here is a plain way for their hope, *In the world* <small>John xvi. 33.</small>
*ye shall have tribulation, but in me ye shall have
peace; be of good cheer, I have overcome the world.*
Thus he arises, not only with life and virtue, but
with healing under his wings. He is the consola- <small>Mal. iv. 2.</small>
tion of Israel. *His love is better than wine, and* <small>Cant. i. 4.</small>
*the smell of his garments than all spices. We sit un-
der his shadow with great delight, and his fruit is
sweet unto our taste. He that believes on him, out* <small>John vii. 38.</small>
of his belly shall flow rivers of living waters. We
believe that Jesus is the Christ, the Son of God,
and *believing, we have life in his name. The God of* <small>—— xx. 31.</small>
hope fills us with all joy and peace in believing, that <small>Rom. xv. 13.</small>
*we may abound in hope through the power of the
Holy Ghost.*

(7.) They that believe in Christ, are obedient to
him in all manner of conversation. I know that
a severe accuracy will not let this go by the name
of faith; but as it always is the fruit of it, I shall
not separate what God has joined together. It is
certain, that they who depend upon a Saviour are
devoted to him; he is their *law-giver*, they serve
the Lord Christ. *One is their Master, that is Christ.* <small>Mat. xxiii. 10.</small>
He purifies to HIMSELF *a peculiar people, zealous of* <small>Tit. ii. 13.</small>
good

good works. And it is so much in vain to make a profession without this, that he reasons upon the folly of it, *Why call ye me Lord, Lord, and do not the things that I say? I have ordained,* saith he, *that ye should go and bring forth fruit, and that your fruit should remain: hereby is my Father glorified, that ye bring forth fruit; so shall ye be my disciples.*

This is sometimes called the will of his Father, and sometimes he gives out the command in his own name. *The word that I speak is not mine, but the Father's who has sent me.* And in his last prayer he saith, *I have manifested thy name to the men whom thou gavest me out of the world; thine they were, and thou gavest them me, and they have kept thy word: Now they have known that whatever things thou hast given me are of thee, for I have given unto them the words that thou gavest me.* And again afterwards, *I have given unto them thy word, and the world has hated them.* Besides these, there are scriptures that assert the doctrine to be his own, though not exclusive of the Father; but yet he represents himself as the fountain of light and truth. Hence we read of those who not only know not God, but *obey not the Gospel of his Son; and of our adorning the doctrine of* GOD *our Saviour in all things. He that abides in the doctrine of* CHRIST, *he has the Father and the Son.* We are not *without law to God, but under the law to Christ.* It was for HIM that Paul suffered the loss of all things; he was so entirely devoted to him, that *as always, so now, this was his earnest expectation and desire, that* CHRIST *should be magnified in his body whether by life or death;* as if he had no other end above or beyond the magnifying of Christ; and this he grounds upon a principle that is of the greatest extent, *For to me to live is Christ.* In preaching CHRIST, *they warned every man, and taught every man, that they might present every man perfect in Christ, striving according to his working, who wrought*

in

in them mightily. *In the name of Jesus every knee is to bow, of things in heaven, earth, and under the earth.* SERM. 33.
Phil. ii. 10.

(8.) In particular, they that believe in Chrift, live in the acts of religious *worſhip* to him. They endeavour to walk worthy of him: He is *the King of Saints.* It is he who *loved us, and waſhed us from our ſins in his own blood, and has made us to be kings and prieſts to God and his Father.* We are to *grow in grace, and in the knowledge of our Lord and Saviour Jeſus Chriſt; to whom be glory both now and for ever, Amen.* They come to his footſtool, they bow before his throne, and worſhip towards the place where his honour dwells. Rev. i. 5, 6.

2 Pet. iii. 18.

To this did the providence of God give an early teſtimony. Wiſe men came from the eaſt to Jeruſalem, ſaying, *Where is He who is born King of the Jews, for we have ſeen HIS ſtar, and are come to worſhip HIM.* It is making very little of that word to ſuppoſe that it means no more than the preſents they brought him; for *when they ſaw the ſtar, they rejoiced with exceeding great joy.* Was this only for an opportunity to pay him a civil compliment? When they came into the houſe, *they ſaw the young child and his mother, and fell down and worſhipped HIM; and when they had opened their treaſures, they preſented unto HIM gifts, gold, frankincenſe and myrrh.* Theſe I take for granted were the methods of adoration in their country. It was foretold of Chriſt, that *the kings of Tarſhiſh and of the iſles ſhall bring preſents: The kings of Sheba and Seba ſhall offer gifts. Yea, all kings ſhall fall down before him, and all nations ſhall ſerve him.* They meant by what they did, a great deal more than homage to a temporal prince, becauſe ſuch a carriage was all a ſuperfluity to an Infant who could not receive it. Mat. ii. 1, 2.

ver. 11.

Pſal. lxxii. 10, 11.

If it is ſaid that theſe were heathens and idolaters, and therefore nothing ought to be concluded from

from their practice as a rule to ours: the answer is very easy; they were now under a particular conduct from the great God; Providence brought them in as witnesses to Him who was to be *the desire of all nations;* there was a star to guide them thither, an extraordinary dream to direct them back again; and can we think he would suffer them to pollute the first honours that were paid to our Saviour with rank idolatry? Is it not natural to suppose, that these men were brought from afar with greater thoughts than merely because *a child was born, and a Son was given?* They do not speak of his miraculous conception, that he was the Son of a Virgin, but regard him in a quality of which there was no visible appearance, as one *born King of the Jews,* and as such a one they came to worship him. A king of the Jews had no relation to them, they were in no subjection to a prince of that country; but under this name they enquire for a Saviour, who being the object of their worship, must be conceived to have another nature besides the human. *All the ends of the world shall remember and turn to the Lord, and all the kindreds of the nations shall worship before* THEE. *All they that be fat upon earth, shall eat and worship: All they that go down to the dust shall bow down before* HIM; *A seed shall serve* HIM, *it shall be accounted to the Lord for a generation. He shall live, and to him shall be given of the gold of Sheba; prayer also shall be made for him continually, and daily shall he be praised.* HIS *name shall endure for ever: his name shall be continued as long as the sun: Men shall be blessed in* HIM, *and all nations shall call him blessed.*

To this agrees the practice of his own followers, whom he would no more suffer to call him good, and fall down before him, than he would the young man in the Gospel, if they had not been persuaded of another nature besides what came into to the imaginations of that person. But when the *Word was made flesh and dwelt among them, they beheld his glory as the glory of the only begotten of the Father.* What a strange acknowledgment does he receive from Nathanael, upon his telling him, *Before Philip called thee, whilst thou wast under the fig-tree I saw thee.* Upon which he cries out, *Rabbi, thou art the Son of God, thou art the King of Israel.* A Prophet might have said as much as this. Elisha told the king of Israel what the king of Syria said in his bed-chamber, and therefore the conclusion from his seeing Nathanael under the fig-tree, could be no more than that of the Samaritan woman, *Sir, I perceive thou art a Prophet:* But as soon as ever he receives the knowledge of the truth, he professes another sort of regard. Though Christ *did* no more in that case than some Prophets had done, yet he *was* much more than any prophet had been. The confession goes out in such language as was never used to any other, *Thou art the Son of God, thou art the King of Israel.* And our Lord is so far from correcting or holding in the zeal of the man, that he opens out the argument there was for it, *Ye shall see heaven opened, and the Angels of God ascending and descending on the Son of man.*

We find that as the Apostles were better instructed, they went to greater examples of adoration. Peter fell at his feet, and cried out, *Depart from me, for I am a sinful man, O Lord.* This he was led into by a surprise at the draught of fishes. It is a strange way of addressing one who had both given him a miracle and a favour. Why should he upon that talk of his *departing from him,* and why must that lead him into a confession of his being a *sinful man?* I take it for an impression of the same nature with that upon Isaiah, when he saw *his glory* in person as Peter did in fact, *Wo is*

SERM. 33. *me, for I am undone, a man of unclean lips, for mine eyes have seen the* King, *the* Lord of Hosts.

It was a very proper motion made by the Pharisees, when the children and the multitude were singing *Hosannah* before him, *Master, rebuke thy disciples:* That he ought to have done, if he had not looked upon himself as the great object of worship. For we find of whom these things were to be said, *Blessed is he that comes in the name of the Lord:* God *is the Lord who has shewn us light.*

Pf. cxviii. 26, 27.

After his resurrection he gave way to the same practice, and that in a higher degree. We read that *when they saw him, they worshipped him; but some doubted.* That the term of worship does not always signify a religious adoration, is certain; but that it sometimes does so, is as certain; and therefore the question is not what sense it may bear in other places, but what is more likely in *this:* Here we read of some that worshipped him, and of others that doubted. Doubted what? whether they should pay him an external civility? If he was *not* their Saviour, there could be no harm in bowing to him. If *that* was all that the others meant by their worship, there need be no great dispute between them: But it is plain these doubts were about the truth of his resurrection. They who were satisfied of that, shew it in a way that the rest durst not, and that is, by acts of religious worship. Nay more than that, we read of his taking them as far as to Bethany, *and blessing them, and whilst he blessed them, he was parted from them, and taken up to heaven;* and yet THEN it is said *they worshipped him.*

Mat. xxviii. 17.

Luke xxiv. 51, 52.

Was *this* only an external compliment too? We pay such things to a creature, but never to an absent one. What can worshipping him, when he was gone, include less than their belief, that he is the Lord who *fills heaven and earth?* Had they regarded no more than his body, all respects to that were over; but we read their thoughts in their

carriage,

carriage, and it muſt not be ſaid of them, that *they* SERM. 33.
worſhipped they knew not what.

Nay, the great badge of the Chriſtian Religion, that which his diſciples wear, is *the name of the* Mat. xxviii. *Father, Son, and Holy Ghoſt.* Into this they are 19. baptiſed; and what an odd character would it be to ſay, that we are reſigned to one ſupreme and two ſubordinate Gods? that we are as much devoted to a higher and a lower creature, as we are to *the Father of Spirits?* The notion that baptiſm is not an act of worſhip, is ſuch a degrading of that ſolemnity, that it only ſhews the people will ſay any thing to maintain their ſcheme. Is it not worſhip for me to give up myſelf to be the Lord's? To have his name called upon by me? To enter into his covenant, and proclaim this to the world? Ought not my ſoul to go along with that ſurrender? Do I not then avouch the Lord to be my God, and depend upon the bleſſings that he has promiſed, and is not this worſhipping? *One ſhall* Iſa. xliv. 5, *ſay, I am the Lord's,—and another ſhall ſubſcribe* 6. *with his hand to the Lord.* What Lord is this? He gives the anſwer himſelf, *Thus ſaith the Lord the King of Iſrael, and his Redeemer the Lord of hoſts, I am the firſt, and I am the laſt, and beſides me there is no god.*

(9.) Believing in Chriſt is truſting him for *protection* to the end of life. Our inheritance is reſerved, our principles are imperfect. It does not appear either what we ſhall *be*, or what we ſhall *have*. Our great life is not revealed, but *hid with Chriſt* Col. iii. 3, *in God; and he who is our life* is hid too. We are 4. waiting for the day when *he ſhall appear, and we appear with him in glory.* The grace that is to be brought to us, comes *at the revelation of Jeſus* 1 Pet i. 13. *Chriſt.* No ſecurity of the covenant, no ſtanchneſs of the promiſes, can ſet the Chriſtian above his fears; and therefore he muſt look to One who can ſecure him till he gets home.

Vol. II.   D   And

SERM. 33. And for this, he has his eyes upon that Saviour,
Jude 24. who is *able to keep him from falling, and to present him faultless before his glory, with exceeding joy.* We are *preserved in Christ Jesus, and called.* The perseverance of the saints is as true as it is comfortable; but it has been much opposed. Now, if the dispute is upon man's ability to save himself, and the sufficiency of those principles that are put into a believer to work through, and work out a salvation, we must give it up. *There is no just man upon earth that does good, and sins not: a just man falls seven times a day.* And if we had no other security than this, we must never affirm any thing of that nature.

But you know the truth hinges upon something else; and that is, whether Christ *can* save to the uttermost those that come to him, and whether he
Phil. i. 6. has not said that he *will.* Our confidence is in *this very thing, that he who has begun a good work, will perform it till the day of Christ.* So that, believing is depending upon him for what is behind.

Every Christian finds himself engaged in an unequal *war:* there is no fair match between the confederate powers of darkness, and the poor frail resolutions of a man. But the battle is the Lord's,
Heb. v. 9. and so our confidence is in One, who *being made perfect from his sufferings, is become the author of eternal salvation to as many as obey him.* This
Rom. i. 17. makes it needful that *the just* should *live by his faith; the righteousness of God is revealed from faith to faith.* Believing is a continual rest of soul upon Christ: We in this wilderness are *leaning on*
Heb. vi. 18, *our beloved.* Here is *a hope set before us; and to*
19. *that we flee for a refuge, to lay hold upon it. This hope we have as an anchor sure and stedfast, and it enters into that within the vail.* The anchor takes *its hold* above, we have ours below, and keep pulling, and drawing, and bringing ourselves to. Thus we are pleading his righteousness afresh, that our
God

God may *multiply to pardon. The life we live in* SERM. 33.
the flesh, is by faith in the Son of God. Living in Isa. iv. 7.
holiness is a renewed or a continued believing. Gal. ii. 20.
We have never done with that faith till our life is
at an end in the flesh, and we gone up to the world
of Spirits.

(10.) Believing in Christ is looking to him as the
finisher of our faith; as one that is to give the
completing stroke to his own work. *His hands* Zech. iv. 9.
laid the foundation, as it was said of Zerubbabel, in
the building of the temple, *and his hands shall lay
the top-stone with shouting.* And what are they to
shout? but *Grace, grace unto it?* that is the grace
of our Lord Jesus Christ. We are to be *complete* Col. ii. 10.
in HIM. It is he that saves εἰς τὸ παντελὲς to the last
perfection, to the end of the work, to the giving
in all that is meant by it. Our proficiency is by
degrees, and God knows, very slow ones. *The* Job xvii. 9.
*righteous holds on his way, and he that has clean
hands grows stronger and stronger.* But the perfection comes all at once; one moment will give
us the fulness of grace and purity, that here we
have sought in vain.

Now, this comes from Christ: *he is the head of
principality and power.* Every man is to be *presented perfect in him:* he is called *the finisher of our
faith.* And, with respect to this great happiness,
we *die in faith,* knowing that when we are *absent* 2 Cor. v. 8.
from the body, we shall be present with the Lord.
To be *with Christ* is far better; it is that which Phil. i. 23.
gives us a *desire to depart.* In this we have an eye
to the full felicity of the soul, that in leaving one
house of an earthly tabernacle, we shall be *cloathed upon with another house which is from heaven,*
and *so mortality is swallowed up of life.*

But besides this, with Christ we trust our bodies,
our *flesh shall rest in hope;* and, *if we believe that* Psal. xvi. 9.
Jesus died and rose again, even them also that sleep 1 Thess. iv. 14.
in Jesus will God bring with him. *He is the resur-* Joh. xi. 25.
rection

rection and the life; and whoever believes in him, though he were dead, yet shall he live. They are called *the dead in Christ*, who shall rise first. His resurrection is considered two ways: *First*, as the pattern of ours; he being raised, is become *the first-fruits of them that sleep. Every man in his own order; Christ the first-fruits, and then they that are Christ's at his coming.* And, *secondly*, He is the author of that great work: He *changes and fashions these vile bodies like unto his glorious body, by a power that subdues all things to himself.* They that are in their graves shall *hear the voice of the Son of man; and they that hear shall live. Our Redeemer lives, and he shall stand at the latter day upon the earth.* So that, *though after our skin worms destroy this body, yet in our flesh we shall see* God, *whom we shall see for ourselves, and not for another, though our reins be consumed within us.*

    This it is to believe; and for these several benefits does our faith regard Him, who was manifest in the flesh, and justified in the Spirit. He is seen of Angels, and he is believed on in the world. We walk by faith, and they by sight. They behold him *as he is;* and though we at this distance do not *see him, yet we love him; and in whom, though now we see him not, yet believing, we rejoice with a joy unspeakable, and full of glory.* This is *the faith of God's elect*, the employment that it is in, and the application that it makes. It is a faith in the Son of God, as well as in the Father. We believe in God, we believe also in him. This gives a virtue to all our religion: the Scriptures are no farther able to make us wise to salvation, than through the faith which is in Christ Jesus.

    II. I am now to open this account that is given of Him, as an argument of his Divinity; that He in whom the world are to believe, can be no other than the Most High God. You plainly find a distinction between the two natures in our
blessed

blessed Lord. Sometimes he is represented as the medium, rather than the *object* of our faith: for faith being an act of worship, it ought to fix upon none but the supreme cause: *He that comes unto God must believe that he is;* and there is a consideration that we may have of our Saviour, wherein he cannot be the object of it. The Apostle is very particular, and speaks with all the guard that could be desired. He saith, *Christ was manifest in these last times for us, who by him do believe in God that raised him from the dead, and gave him glory, that our faith and hope may be in God.*

SERM. 33.

Heb. xi. 6.

1 Pet. i. 20, 21.

Here you find two things. *First*, That as Mediator we do not believe *in him*, but *by him.* He does not receive our faith, but direct it and convey it. And, *secondly*, That the faith and hope of a Christian can be in no other than a God; and therefore, if we are not to have a higher consideration of a Redeemer, than as a middle person between God and us, we can never be said to believe *in him.* What care does the Apostle take to tell us, that this is too much for a creature? And if there had not been scriptures of another import, that reveal him to us as the proper object of our faith in the same way that the Father is, we could never have said so much of him. Now, these texts are not to be dashed against one another; there is no manner of contradiction between them.

We may, and ought to regard our Saviour in his two limited characters: *First*, As true and proper man; one *made of a woman.* Thus he was frail in his body, and imperfect in the qualifications of his soul: he *grew in knowledge* as well as *stature.* There were things that he *knew not.* He came to a fig tree, if he might find fruit on it. The hour of judgment is what no man knows, nor the Angels, nor *even the Son,* but the Father. On this account he would not be called good, because there is none good but one, that is God.

Secondly,

SERM. 33. *Secondly*, Even as Mediator he is to be considered in a lower station. For though that character takes into it a Divine Nature, yet he is situated between God and man; below the one, and above the other; or rather, as high as the one, and as low as the other. Thus he was *made under the law,* and came not to do his own will, but the will of him that sent him. And *when all things are subject, the Son himself must give up the kingdom to the Father, and be subject, that God may be all in all.* In this respect *the Father is greater than he.* But neither of these are a contradiction to those other accounts that we have of him. As man he was not equal to God in *nature;* as Mediator, he was not equal to him in *place,* but appeared *in the form of a servant.* But in the existence that he had before he took upon him our nature, *he thought it no robbery to be equal with God.* Nor can we believe in him the several ways that I have opened to you, if he is not *the only living and true God.*

1 Cor. xv. 28.

Joh. xiv. 28.

Aug. 16. 1719.

SERMON XXXIV.

AFTER this preliminary distinction, into which we are led by a cloud of witnesses, I may reassume my argument, That He who is thus believed on in this world, deserves the name that is given him in this text, of the Most High God. By that expression I do not mean a titular deity. Those shuffling arts of language are unworthy of a minister, and scandalous to the Gospel that he preaches:

preaches: *We have renounced the hidden things of dishonesty, not walking in craftiness, nor handling the word of the Lord deceitfully.* As our exhortation is not of *uncleanness*, so neither is it of *deceit or of guile; but as we are put in trust with the Gospel, so we preach, not as pleasing men,* who may easily be imposed on, *but* that God who searches the hearts, and knows what we mean in every disguise of speech. For *there is not a word in our mouths, but lo, he knows it altogether.* We are not sent to trifle with mankind. If Christ is not God, it would be dangerous to call him so; and I should never dare to do it without a guard. But if he is, we need not be afraid of owning his title, against all the learning and violence that are brought into the quarrel; for it will be found, *that the wisdom of this world is foolishness with God.*

SERM. 34.
2 Cor. iv. 2.
1 Thef. ii. 3.
1 Cor. i. 20.

I have already shewn you what it is for him to be believed on; and as I think that account agrees with the whole current of the Bible, so I shall go over every one of those particulars again, and let you see that they can be true of none but *the Most High God.* You have heard that believing in him is, 1. Receiving the *testimony* that we have concerning him. 2. A *looking* upon him as the only Saviour of the world. 3. *Relying* upon the righteousness that he has provided. 4. *Deriving* from him a principle of grace. 5. Being *supplied* by him with an increase. 6. *Regarding* him as the great comforter of our souls. 7. *Obeying* him in all manner of conversation. 8. Giving him religious *worship*. 9. *Trusting* him for a protection; and, 10. *Looking* to him as the finisher of our faith. That these are things comprehended in our believing, I doubt not, will be plain enough to all that look into the Scriptures; he that runs may read it. Now, I see no danger in affirming, that every one of these particulars suppose Him to be

SERM. 34. be truly and eternally God, or otherwise our preaching is in vain, and your faith in vain.

1. As believing signifies our receiving the testimony that is given concerning him, it concludes him to be a God, or otherwise, we must look upon the New Testament as a strange book, if it does no more than proclaim the coming of a creature. They that bring good tidings, are ordered to *lift up their voice with strength, to lift it up, and not be afraid, saying to the cities of Judah, Behold your* GOD. *Behold, the* LORD GOD *shall come with a strong hand, and his arm shall rule for him. Behold, his reward is with him, and his work before him.* And this is He, who shall *feed his flock like a shepherd.* Why must there be warnings given, Prophets raised up in every age, wonders and miracles wrought, and above all, the *Holy Ghost sent down,* merely to make way for a derived being, who, notwithstanding all his glory, is infinitely below *the Father of Spirits?*

Isa. xl. 9, 10, 11.

It has been the design of God, ever since he made the world, to be worshipped in it. And he has taken ways to display himself for that very purpose. Thus it pleased him to write out his perfections upon the heavens, which *are the work of his fingers.* He has added to these arguments the methods of his providence, by which a man is brought to say, *Verily there is a reward for the righteous; verily, he is a God who rules in the earth.* And these are so clear and valid, that *the heathen are without excuse, because what may be known of God is manifest in them; for he has revealed it to them.* But there are still more eminent ways of making him known to the world. A Redeemer appears with a greater evidence than can ever be fetched out of the works of creation: he has something better than sun, moon, and stars, to tell mankind what he is. And,

Pf. lviii. 11.

Rom. i. 19, 20.

Must the Supreme God be discovered with these lower and feebler methods? and shall a creature
shew

shew himself to the world in ways more divine and glorious? Are we directed to find out the Father by the growth of the earth, and the beauty of the heavens? and can there be no revelation of the *Son*, but by sending him among us, with a train of miracles, signs, and wonders, and last of all, by the effusion of the Spirit? Is the Holy Ghost sent down to glorify the Son, and are we directed to the lowest parts of the creation, in our searches after the Father? *Ask the beasts of the field, and they will tell thee, and the birds of the air will declare to thee.* In these cases the honour is no way proportioned, we worship and serve the creature more than the Creator.

The greatest testimony that ever the world received was by the Holy Spirit. This is above all thunders, voices, ministers, prophets, and miracles. He was sent down from heaven; and what is he a witness to? What is his errand among us, both in forming the scripture, and working upon the conscience? Christ tells us, *He shall glorify* ME, *for he shall take of mine, and shew it unto you.* We, saith the Apostle, *are witnesses of these things, and so is the Holy Ghost, whom God has given to them that obey him.* The dispensation of the Spirit is to lead us to a Saviour. And is our way to *Him* under greater directions than ever that to a *God* was? Is there something in making *him* known more divine and glorious, than any methods that the Father himself has taken for several generations? what! shall the greater Person be talked of with lower discoveries? and shall a creature, a derived dependent being, have more train and retinue to his reputation, than ever was heard of for the Supreme Majesty of heaven and earth?

Certainly you must conclude, that He who shines into our hearts, does it to give us *the light of the knowledge of the glory of God, in the face* or person *of Jesus Christ.* We see in him the glory

John xvi. 15.
Acts v. 32.

2 Cor. iv 6.

of a God; and on purpose that we may see it, more is done for us, and more in us than making a world: *To him give all the Prophets witness*; and it was *the Spirit of Christ* in those Prophets that bare this witness: *They searched diligently into this salvation*, namely, *the sufferings of Christ, and the glory that should follow.* These are prophecies of the most early date; and these are matched with the testimony of the Holy Ghost in after ages. Now, what could be done more for a God?

And is all this profusion of evidence a tribute to one who is a creature? No; the Scripture has never given us an account so unequal and monstrous as that must have been. We are not directed to the creation, to things that *do appear*, for the proofs of an *eternal power and godhead;* and to things that do *not appear*, that from them we may have our conviction of a Saviour. This would be too much for him if he was not God; and therefore we are expressly told, when he was in the world, that *the world was made by him.*

There are two interpretations given of these words, which are very different from one another, though they are both of them directed against the truth as it is in Jesus. Sometimes we find one of them insisted on, and sometimes another; for Satan is resolved to drive the nail that will go.

Some tell us, that the world made by him is the Gospel-church, which is a sort of a new world. But to such expositors we may cry out with the Apostle, *O foolish people, who has bewitched you?* Do but see what confusion it brings into the text: *He was in the world;* that is, in the church; *and the world was made by him;* that is, he is the author of the church; but then it is added, *and the world knew him not.* Can this be understood of the church? Did not *they* know him? Yes, the very thing that made them his people, or rather proved them so, was their *seeing his glory, as the*

glory

glory of the only begotten of the Father, full of grace and truth. He himself diftinguifhed between the world and his people: *O righteous Father, the world has not known thee, but I have known thee, and thefe have known that thou haft fent me.* But this fhews that *the legs of the lame are not equal.* It is with the adverfaries of his Divinity, as it was with thofe of his Innocence, that their *witnefs agrees not together.*

Another interpretation which people are now driven to, is, that he made the world as an *inftrument*. But did ever true language fay that an inftrument made any thing? Is it not enough that we talk error, but muft we talk nonfenfe? *Shall the ax boaft itfelf againft him that heweth therewith? or fhall the faw magnify itfelf againft him that fhakes it? as if the rod fhould fhake itfelf againft him that lifts it up, or as if the ftaff fhould lift up itfelf, as if it were no wood.* The world was made by *Him*, who was then *in it, i. e.* when he was made flefh, and dwelt among us. And, if this may be faid of an inftrument, how can any words go higher to the honour of the fupreme Agent, than thefe we have of *him*, that *all things were made by him, and without him was not any thing made that was made.*

What is the report that we have of him? John the Baptift was the greateft of his meffengers, and he proclaims, *Prepare ye the way of the Lord, and make ftraight in the defart a high-way for our God.* This paffage in the Old Teftament cannot without fraud and force be applied to a creature. *Comfort ye, comfort ye my people, faith your God.* And is not this to be underftood of the Supreme Being? How is the comfort to flow or be revealed, but by the voice of him that cries in the wildernefs? This is what John the Baptift faid of himfelf, that he was the perfon defcribed in that prophecy. He was, as his father Zacharias faid of him, *fent before*

fore *the face of the Lord, to prepare the way before him.* Now this is called by the Prophet preparing the way *for our God,* for the God of Ifrael, who was known by his relation to that people; for *the Lord alone did lead him, and there was no ſtrange god with him.* Thus it is farther faid of John, that *he was the Prophet of the Higheſt,* of the Moſt High: which is a name fit for none but Him, who is *over all bleſſed for evermore. The Lord ſhall reign for ever, even thy God, O Zion, unto all generations. Jeſus is the ſame yeſterday, to-day, and for ever.*

Pf. cxlvi. 10.

Heb. xiii. 8.

2. In believing we look upon him as the only Saviour of the world; and this cannot be affirmed of one that is not God: *We know that the Son of God is come, and has given us an underſtanding that we may know him that is true; and we are in him that is true, even in his Son Jeſus Chriſt. This is the true God, and eternal life.* You will find a great deal of difference between Him and other good men, who have ſerved their generation according to the will of God.

1 John v. 20.

I take Moſes to be the firſt in that character; a perſon honoured with the fulleſt commiſſion, and the cleareſt credentials: *There aroſe not a Prophet ſince in Iſrael, like to Moſes, whom the Lord knew face to face.* It was needful that the people ſhould believe his being ſent from God, that he did not thoſe things of his own mind. Of him we have this character in the New Teſtament, *that he was faithful to him that appointed him in all his houſe.* But then, it is there obſerved, that he was only ſo faithful *as a ſervant, and in teſtimony of things that were to be ſpoken after.* There was no fear of miſtaking him for a God; the diſtinction was always plain and full between himſelf and the Divine Majeſty whom he repreſented. He was *made a god to Pharaoh;* but that ſentence does not deſerve a place in the objection. The man muſt be very

Deut. xxxiv. 10.

Heb. iii. 2.

very ignorant indeed, who concludes his deity from that. He all along told them, that *their murmurings were not against him, but the Lord.* He did every thing according to the pattern shewed him in the mount ; and therefore saith himself in that song: *He* (i. e. God) *loved the people; all his Saints are in thine hand; they sat down at thy feet; every one shall receive of thy words: Moses commanded us a law:* he always directed them to a greater than himself.

Deut. xxxiii. 3, 4.

The people once made choice of him for a *Mediator: Go thou near, and hear all that the Lord our God shall say, and speak thou unto us all that the Lord our God shall speak unto thee, and we will hear it and do it.* But did he take this honour to himself? No ; he makes an advantage of the peoples desire to have a middle person between God and them, and upon that tells them of our blessed Saviour. You find the prophecy connected to that very case. *The Lord thy God will raise up to thee a Prophet from the midst of thee, of thy brethren, like unto me ; unto* HIM *shall ye hearken: According to all that thou desiredst of the Lord thy God in Horeb, in the day of the assembly, saying, Let me not hear the voice of the Lord my God, neither let me see this great fire any more, lest I die. And the Lord said unto me, They have well spoken, in that they have spoken, I will raise them up a Prophet from among their brethren, like unto thee.* This is a passage that the New Testament makes great use of. The Apostle Peter pleads from it, that God *had sent Jesus, who before was preached unto you; whom the heavens must receive till the times of the restitution of all things, which God has spoken of by the mouth of all his holy Prophets since the world began: For Moses truly said unto the fathers, A Prophet shall the Lord your God raise up unto you, of your brethren, like unto me ; him shall ye hear in all things, whatever he shall say unto you.* So the Martyr

xviii. 15, 16, 17.

Acts iii. 20, 21. 22.

tyr Stephen, when he had given an account of the great things that Moses had done, by how many changes, and through how many contradictions he was formed to the deliverance of the people out of Egypt, he fixes on that one point, *This is that Moses who said unto the children of Israel, A Prophet shall the Lord your God raise up unto you.*

So that upon the whole you find though Moses had such a commission as was never equalled, and those credentials that were never exceeded, yet still he referred the people to one above and beyond himself, one that was their God, and who in the fulness of time would be their Prophet. Now you will observe, though the Apostle gives it as a noble character of Christ, that *he was faithful to him that appointed him, even as Moses was faithful in all his house;* yet he adds, *This man was counted worthy of more glory than Moses;* not upon account of faithfulness, for that an inferior may have equally with a superior. A man whom you trust with twenty shillings is as honest as one that manages a concern of ten thousand pounds; as Moses is said to be faithful in all things, so *in that* he could not be exceeded.

But Christ is *worthy of more glory* upon another account, from the dignity of his person, *inasmuch as he that builded the house has more honour than the house.* By his house is meant his people, his Church, the whole family, both in heaven and earth. Moses was only a servant to these, and therefore could have no more than his particular share with them; but Christ having built the whole house, has more honour than all of it put together, than the whole assembly of Saints and Angels, whose names are written in heaven. And can this be conceived of a creature? No; *Every house is built by some man, but he that built all things is* God. Christ is said to be this *builder* in the former verse; and to shew us of *what nature* that is

to

to be understood, he calls him *a God* in this. Mo-ses *was very faithful in all his house as a servant,* *i. e.* he fulfilled his orders; he did every thing according to the pattern shewed him in the mount, but this was *for a testimony of those things that were to be spoken after.* Now *Christ is a Son over his own house, whose house we are.* It could not be said of Moses that the Israelites were his. When God tells him, *Thy people whom thou broughtest out of Egypt have rebelled,* he returned the relative term back again, *Lord, they are* THY *people and thy inheritance whom* THOU *hast purchased for thyself:* and so he saith in another place, *Have I conceived all this people at once?* But Christ calls the house *his own,* and who must this be?

Well, the Apostle applies to him that passage out of the 95th Psalm, *Harden not your hearts in the provocation, and the day of temptation in the wilderness,* as they did who are said to tempt Christ; and then concludes thus, *Take heed, brethren, lest there be in any of you an evil heart of unbelief, in departing from the living God.* I take these characters to be joined, or otherwise I can see no force in his argument, and no propriety in his quotation. He who is said to be the *builder of all things,* the *builder of his house,* the *Son over his own house,* is at last called *the living God,* not by obscure and uncertain consequences, but in the plain and natural language of Scripture.

Let none say that we affirm this without the authority of the Bible, or that it comes in among the things that man's wisdom teaches. It is as plainly a doctrine that *the Holy Ghost teaches* as any can be, and appears so to every one who will compare spiritual things with spiritual. Do we call him your only Saviour who is not your God? No, we dare not. The work that he has done *for* you, and must do *in* you, is too great and good for any thing but Divinity, and therefore the titles are joined;

joined; he is *a juſt God, and a Saviour, and there is none beſides him.* David's defence was of God, which may be underſtood of a temporal deliverance; and is *our* greateſt happineſs from a creature? No; we have very noble notions of a Deity from our intereſt in him; for *our God is the God of ſalvation, and to God the Lord belong the iſſues from death.*

Pſal. lxviii. 20.

Compare ſuch titles as theſe with what is ſaid of Chriſt, that *there is ſalvation in no other;* upon which account he goes by that name, for all the ends of the earth ſhall ſee *the ſalvation of our God!* So good old Simeon ſaith, *Now letteſt thou thy ſervant depart in peace; for mine eyes have ſeen thy ſalvation; which thou haſt prepared before the face of all people: A light to lighten the Gentiles, and the glory of thy people Iſrael.* Your ſalvation is of that Lord who made heaven and earth; and who is this, but the ſame, who being made perfect from his ſufferings, *became the author of eternal ſalvation to as many as obey him?* Thus he is placed as *the ſalvation in Zion for Iſrael his glory.* What is got by talking of a Saviour who is not a God? We loſe our hope, and He his praiſe: But I truſt *you have not ſo learned Chriſt.* You may ſay of him in whom your confidence is placed, *This is our God for ever and ever, and he ſhall be our guide even until death.*

Iſa. lii. 10.
Luke ii. 29, 30, 31.

Pſal xlviii. 14.

3. Believing in Chriſt Jeſus, is relying upon the *righteouſneſs* that he has brought in. We find that none can ſtand in God's ſight *when once he is angry,* and *marks iniquity,* and this we are ſure he does. *Thou ſetteſt our iniquities before thee, our ſecret ſins in the light of thy countenance.* Here we have nothing to flee to but *the blood of ſprinkling.* It is called ſo from that which was typical of it under the Old Teſtament, Heb. ix. 19. 21. You there ſee how far the virtue of it was extended; *When he had ſpoken every precept, he took the blood*

Pſal. xc. 8.

of

of calves and goats, and sprinkled both the book and all the people. He sprinkled the book to bring the law within the covenant of grace, to take away the curse that was in it, and continues upon all those that are under it. He sprinkled the people to take off their guilt, that they might be purified from an evil conscience. Nay, it is said, he sprinkled with blood the *tabernacle and all the vessels of the ministry;* and in particular we read, that he threw some of this blood upon the *mercy-seat,* which was supposed to be the throne of God, and upon the *tabernacle,* which was his house, and upon the *vessels of the ministry,* which were his furniture,—to shew that heaven itself must be rendered propitious by an atonement or satisfaction; and these, as the Apostle tells us, were *patterns of things in the heavens:* But saith he, *The heavenly things themselves,* the real happiness, and all the grace that leads to it, *were to be purified with better sacrifices than these.* And what are they? Christ has by his own blood *gone into the holiest of all, to appear in the presence of God for us.*

That he who died was a man, a partaker of flesh and blood, is true enough; for that reason he was *in all things made like unto his brethren, that by death he might subdue him who had the power of death, that is, the devil.* Our nature was needful to make his dying a *reality,* but whence did it derive the merit to make it a *satisfaction?* This supposes another nature that is without any robbery *equal to God.* And his obedience to death, even the death of the cross, could be only valid to his own glory, and our happiness, from the antecedent dignity of his person. *Being the brightness of his glory,* Heb. i. 3. *and the express image of his person, and upholding all things by the word of his power, he did by himself purge away our sins.*

So that when we read of his sufferings in the most pathetic terms, that he was broken, grieved,

SERM. 34. *taken from prison, and from judgment,* there is this
Isa. liii. 8. thrown in, *Who shall declare his generation?* It was
an easy matter to trace his family, that he was of
the seed of David, according to the flesh; and
therefore that is not the generation which the Prophet speaks of as a matter not to be declared. For
he would say himself, *Ye know who I am, and
whence I came, but He who sent me is true, whom ye*
Pro. xxx. 4. *know not. Who has ascended up into heaven, or descended? who has gathered the wind in his fists? who has bound the waters in a garment? who has established all the ends of the earth? what is his name, and what is his son's name, declare if thou canst tell?*

What would the smiting of the shepherd have signified, if the sword had not been directed by God against *the man that was his fellow?* and why should he be called God's *righteous servant* at the time that it *pleased the Father to bruise him, and put him to grief?* Why should it be said, *By his knowledge shall he justify many,* when the way of his doing it, is *bearing their iniquity?* His death was soon over, and how came he in that to bring in *an everlasting righteousness?* The virtue was not in his sufferings, but in his person, and therefore it is
Jer. xxiii. said, *This is the name whereby he shall be called,*
6. *Jehovah our Righteousness.* As Jehovah he must live for ever, as our righteousness he was obliged to die; for *he put away sin by the offering of himself.* He who was crucified must be a man; He who by *that* brought in a righteousness must be Jehovah. It appears by this, that he who paid the price was equal to him that received it.

That objection is only a found, That if He who made the satisfaction was a God, then the same person both gave it and took it. This proves that what we speak of is a *mystery,* but it does not for that cease to be a *truth;* for the same argument lies almost against every thing in religion. Is our
grace

grace and duty any thing else but what God both gives and receives? *All things come of thee, and of thine own have we given thee.* Is it not said as plainly as it can be in words, that Christ *presents us to himself?* and therefore the objection that some are so proud of, is but a flash of powder that makes a blaze, but does no execution. There is no more contradiction in this than there is in all the other articles of religion, that he who gives the satisfaction is also to take it. *God reconciles us to himself;* he is both the reconciler and the person reconciled. Be not driven away *from the hope of the Gospel* by the vain splutter of men. This is a poor *wind of doctrine* indeed, and none but mere *children* can be carried away with it. But, to return to my argument, SERM. 34. 1 Chron. xxix. 14. Eph. v. 27. 2 Cor. v. 18.

Why should He who is our righteousness be called Jehovah? The name is incommunicable, and belongs to none but the Most High. Angels are called gods, and so are magistrates, *There are lords many, and gods many;* but *thou whose name alone is* JEHOVAH *art the Most High over all the earth.* If this is given to a creature, we cannot say that his name *alone* is Jehovah. And the Scripture by throwing about titles with so much confusion, has left us no distinction between God and a creature. But you may be sure, as God will not hold him guiltless who takes his name in vain, so the Holy Spirit would not be guilty of that crime. Though in bringing in a righteousness, Christ submitted to death, yet he did it in the quality of Jehovah, the great original, the fundamental life and being. 1 Cor. viii. 2. Ps. lxxxiii. 18.

There is an answer, such a one as it is, to this argument, That the church is called *the Lord our righteousness.* She is so indeed, and I need do no more than read you the passage, and leave you to judge with what propriety it is pleaded. *In those days, and at that time, I will cause the Branch of righteousness to grow up unto David, and he shall* Jer. xxxiii. 15, 16.

execute

execute judgment and righteousness in the land. In those days Judah shall be saved, and Jerusalem dwell safely; and this is the name wherewith she shall be called, The Lord our righteousness. I ought to make an apology for giving an answer to this argument. It is obvious to every one, that the title must be understood of Christ, and can only be applied to his people on the account of their relation to him. As he is called *Israel*, and God is called *Jacob*, so they are called the Lord our righteousness. But there is one thing more that I shall observe from these words, and that is, the New Testament Church is here described by the profession they were to make of their faith in one who is Jehovah, and one who is their righteousness; and therefore when people shuffle with his divinity, and deny his satisfaction, they are not that Judah and Jerusalem who are called by the name.

Isa. xlix. 3.
Pf. xxiv. 6.

4. Believing is *deriving* from him a principle of grace. *Christ dwells in our hearts by faith.* He *quickens those who were dead in trespasses and sins,* and how should he do this, if he had not *the fulness of him who fills all in all?* This is all along represented as the chief creation, compared to the *exceeding greatness of God's power in raising Christ from the dead,* and would never be attributed to any agent but one who does according to his pleasure. And the Apostle, who writes to a people that had this experience, lets them know, that their friend is no less than the Most High. They *are born of the uncorruptible seed, the word of God, who lives and abides for ever.* Whether you understand this of Christ the personal Word, or of the everlasting Gospel, it is all one to the argument: That which he puts the advantage upon, is their having *tasted that the* LORD *is gracious.*

Eph. iii. 17.
——ii. 1.

1 Pet. i. 23.

——ii. 3.

This you know is an Old Testament phrase, a way of speaking that God's people have always used. *O taste, and see that the Lord is good,* Da-

Pf. xxxiv. 8.

vid

vid cannot be supposed to design by this Lord any other than Him whom he had in heaven alone, and besides whom he could desire none upon earth. And what Lord is that whom the Apostle saith they had tasted to be gracious? One whom they were still to *come to as a living stone, disallowed of men, but chosen of God and precious.* These latter words make it evident, that it can be understood of none but Christ, as the former make it equally evident, it can be understood of none but God. Now why are these scriptures laid so near, and the connection made so strong, if one sentence refers to the Supreme Being, and the other to a person that is derived and dependent?

[SERM. 34.]

[1 Pet. ii. 4.]

These arguments have swelled beyond my first design, but I could not baulk them: I bless God my soul is in this cause, which is so dear, that I hope no reproaches will ever move me; and if I should *suffer the loss of all things,* divine grace can teach me to despise them, for *the excellency of the knowledge of Christ Jesus my Lord.*

SERMON XXXV.

August 30. 1719.

5. YOU have also heard, that believing in Christ is drawing down farther supplies of grace and holiness from him. *I am come,* saith he, *that ye might have life, and that ye might have it more abundantly;* so that your advance in religion sometimes goes by the name of conversion;

[John x. 10.]

it is called Christ's being *formed in you.* For this the Apostle *travailed in birth* over those who were his children before. The thing that he desired with so many throws and wishes was, that *Christ might be formed in them;* which would not be understood of their first religion, for that was begun already; but he speaks of the improvements they were to make in it as if it was a new conversion. When David begs to be restored to the use of his graces, he does it by a word that might signify the first implanting of them, *Create in me a clean heart, O God.*

Thus was Christ to be formed in these people. Every communication that he made of himself to them was like beginning the work over again. We are still to be *transformed by the renewing of our minds;* we ought daily to *put off the old man, and be renewed in the spirit of our minds.* Now it shews us the necessity of a dependence upon him, that we do not only receive from him the principles of a divine life, but it is he that gives it all the enlargement that it can have. *Unto those that fear his name does the Sun of righteousness arise with healing in his wings, that they may go forth and grow up as calves of the stall.* From him we have the perfecting of the saints and the edifying of the body.

And what can this proclaim him to be, but a God? We can say it of none besides an infinite nature, *With thee is the fountain of life.* This was one of the noblest apprehensions that could be conveyed into the minds of men, and what the Apostle opens as superior to all the doctrines of idolatry, that *in God we live, and move, and have our being;* that it was He who *made of one blood all nations of men that dwell upon the face of the earth;* that *we are his offspring.* Now there is a greater life than this derived from our Saviour, that which is more glorious in itself, and more important to those

those that have it, as we are told by the Evangelist, *In him was life, and that life was the light of men.* It led them to the knowledge of the truth, it breathed into them the principles of an heavenly joy; and this life is said to be in *him* as the fountain where it sprung and from whence it came. It is not enough to say, that this life was *by him* as a friend who took care to give it, in pursuance of a commission; no, he is infinitely more than a trustee, for it is *in him*. Thus the same writer tells us in his epistle, *This is the record, that God has given to us eternal life; and this life is* IN HIS SON: *He that has the Son has life.*

Let us compare these accounts of a Redeemer with the sermon to the Athenians about the great God. The Apostle Paul took it for granted, that he had no better argument for the worship of a Deity than this, that *he gives life, and breath, and all things.* By doing that, he was distinguished from all creatures both in heaven and earth. This could never be affirmed of any but the Supreme Being. And can a *natural* life have no other author than a God, and shall that which is *spiritual* be produced by a deputy deity? No, *This is the true God, and this is eternal life.* When Christ tells us that we must *abide in him*, and that *without him we can do nothing*, he mentions greater obligations and a more intimate dependence than we can have for the life that we live in the flesh.

He is the head of the body, and from him all the members, deriving the nourishment that is ministred to them *increase with the increase of God.* This phrase tells us the author of the increase as well as the nature of it. For though the name of God in a Hebraism very often signifies no more than what is great and noble, yet it is a mere fraud and shift to bring such an exposition into this place. Suppose we should use the same device in speaking of the righteousness of God, and the grace of God,

what

SERM. 35. what murdering work should we make in the chief articles of our religion? But as the righteousness of God is a righteousness that God brings in, and stands in opposition to that which is our own; and as the grace of God is a principle that God' implants, and of which he is the author, so this *increase of God* is what he gives. He from whom it is derived can be no other than a God, Eph. iv. 15. and yet we *grow up unto him in all things who is the head, even Christ*. As in one place Christ is said to begin a good work in you, so in another you are expressly told, that *he who has wrought you for the self same thing is God*.

What creature could say, as our Lord did to the John iv. woman of Samaria, *If thou hadst known who said unto thee, Give me to drink, thou wouldest have asked of him, and* HE *would have given thee living water?* Though that was a metaphorical expression, yet what he says afterwards is open enough: *The water that I give is a well of water springing up to everlasting life.* If all the Angels in heaven cannot give wings to a fly, or breath to a worm; if it is purely the work of a God to *quicken the dead;* if he is our life, and the length of our days,—is there any room to suppose that the concerns of a life more divine and glorious will be lodged with a creature?

And yet all the advance that a believer makes in holiness is ascribed to Jesus; as the Apostle, who was both a minister and a witness of the Christian Gal. ii. 20. religion, says, *The life I live in the flesh, I live by faith in the Son of God, who loved me, and gave himself for me.* His faith was that by which he maintained this life; and Christ being the object of this faith, was the Person from whom he had all supplies given him. It is only a God who *holds our souls in* a natural *life;* and what must He be who can answer all the cries and demands of a Pro. viii. 21. spiritual life? who *causes those that love him to inherit*

herit substance, and fills all their treasures? The eyes of all things wait on the Supreme Being, to be *upheld by the word of his power.* It is He that hears the young ravens when they cry; *the lions roar after their prey, and seek their meat from God.* And does the believer seek the bread that endures to everlasting life from one that is less than a God? Is grace maintained by a lower friend than nature? Is our *breath in the hands of God,* for a life that is but a span? and can one, who by nature is no God, be sufficient for a life that is eternal? No; when you read of your being built up on your most holy faith, and that the body *makes increase to the edifying of itself in love,* though these blessings come from Christ, you may be sure that *the builder and maker* is no other than God.

Serm. 35.

Dan. v. 23.

Eph. iv. 16.

One of the greatest notions that we can have of the Father, is that *he has life in himself,* and we are told in the same verse, that *he has given to the Son to have life in himself;* and *as the Father raises up the dead, and quickens them, so the Son quickens, whom he will.* There is nothing in the expression of *giving this to him,* that can diminish the thing of *having life in himself.* It signifies as much in one part of the verse as it does in the other. Either He that has life in himself is God, or otherwise it gives us but a lower conception of the Father. It declares an independence on any superior. He that has one above him, cannot have *life in himself:* and therefore by giving it to him here, we must understand no more than his proclaiming that Christ should have it in his union to our nature, that he would have us to know the Son of man is no less than God. There is no creature in heaven or earth, but as they are receivers and possessors of life, so they cannot be said to have it *in themselves*; for that is peculiar to an author, and we can apply it to no other than the great *Preserver of men:* and yet

John v. 26.

yet here it is affirmed of Christ, which proves that he is the *brightness of his Father's glory, and the express image of his Person, because he upholds all things by the word of his power.* He has, more especially in the religious world, created all things, and for his pleasure they are and were created.

6. Believing in Christ is regarding him as our *Comforter* in every time of need. This is sometimes applied to the Father: *Blessed be the God and Father, of our Lord Jesus Christ, the Father of mercies, and the God of all consolations, who comforteth us in all our tribulation, that we may be able to comfort them who are in any trouble, by the comfort wherewith we ourselves are comforted of God.* Sometimes it is represented as the work of the Spirit, *I will pray the Father,* faith Christ, *and he will give you another Comforter, who shall abide with you for ever, even the Spirit of truth.* Hence we read of *a joy in the Holy Ghost. We are sealed with the good Spirit of promise;* and, as you have already heard, our Lord takes it to himself.

Now, whoever it is that can set the believer above his fears, and give him a peace and joy, does by that proclaim a Divine Nature. It is *God who comforts them that are cast down.* Elihu admires this power of a Deity, *When he speaks quietness, who can give trouble;* and David cannot be supposed to beg it from any other, *Make me to hear joy and gladness, that the bones which thou hast broken may rejoice. The Lord raises up them that are bowed down, He heals the broken in heart, and binds up their wounds.* This *Lord shall reign for ever, even thy God, O Zion.*

Now, upon all occasions, our Saviour tells the disciples, that HE *would not leave them comfortless. In the world they shall have trouble, but in* HIM *they must have peace.* There was something in his way of dealing out this favour, that shewed him to be God :

God: *Peace I leave with you, my peace I give unto you; not as the world gives, give I unto you.* He is known to his people by these distributions; they that receive his kindness, are able to distinguish it from all that creatures can do; *for he has made his wonderful works to be remembered.* {SERM. 35. John xiv. 27. Pf. cxi. 4.}

From this the Apostle John argues all along for the support of Christians under the rage of enemies, and the treachery of apostates, when many Antichrists had gone out into the world. You see, that he leads them to a sense, and an improvement of their union to Christ. Thus he pleads, *Now we are the sons of* GOD, *and it does not appear what we shall be; but when he shall appear, we shall be like* HIM, *for we shall see him as he is*: Him, that is, the God whose sons we are. To this he adds, *Every one who has this hope in him purifies himself even as* HE *is pure*, *i. e.* the God of all purity, to whom they are related. And who this is you find afterwards, *Ye know that* HE *was manifest to take away our sins*. These words bring it to our Saviour, and agree to the language of my text, *that God was manifest in the flesh.* So again, in the next chapter he joins these two together, *Ye are of* GOD, *little children, and have overcome them*, *i. e.* the false prophets who are gone out into the world; *for greater is* HE *that is in you, than he that is in the world*. He that is said to be in them, is our blessed Saviour, who had overcome the world. His being *in them*, agrees to all the language of Scripture, *I in them, and thou in me, Christ in you the hope of glory.* {1 Joh. iii. 2. ver. 3. 1 Joh. iv. 4. John xvii. 23. Col. i. 27.}

Now this is true of the Divine Nature; for *God dwells in us, and we in him*. Certainly this phrase of a Being that dwells in men, ought not to be used without any distinction, and given out promiscuously both to God and a creature. David means no other than a Deity, when he says, *In the multitude of my thoughts within me,* THY *comforts delight* {Psal. xciv. 19.}

SERM. 35. *delight my soul.* And does the Apostle derive it
2 Cor. i. 3, from any lower hands? No; these were *comforts*
4, 5. *wherewith they were comforted of* GOD; and yet
in the very next verse he tells us, that as *the sufferings of Christ abound in us, our consolation abounds
by* CHRIST: And afterwards saith, *The people were
his rejoicing, as he was theirs in the day of the Lord
Jesus.*

Isa. ix. 6, 7.   Our Saviour has *the government upon his shoulder, and of the increase of his government and
peace, there shall be no end.* He gave Saul his
Acts xxvi. commission, with a promise that he would *deliver
17. him from the people and the Gentiles, to whom he
sent him.* And as he met with a long experience
ver. 22. of this protection, he tells Agrippa, *Having therefore obtained help from God, I continue to this day.*
The word *therefore* refers us to the former promise. It was Christ that told him, that HE would
deliver him: well, he had done so, and this the
Apostle calls an obtaining help from God. Christ
appeared to him at Corinth, and gave him an assurance, *No man shall set on thee to hurt thee.* And
Acts xviii.
10. there is nothing in Paul's language that obliges us
to exclude Christ from the account we have of his
— xxvii. deliverance at sea: *There stood by me,* saith he, *the
23. Angel of God, whose I am, and whom I serve.* All
the Angels are ministring Spirits to our Lord, and
by him sent forth to the heirs of salvation.

But the comforts that he gives to his people are
of a more inward kind; and these can be no other
than the work of a God. It is the *joy of the Lord
that must be our strength.* It is He who, when the
outward man decays, *renews us in the inward man*
2 Cor. iv. *day by day. We always bear about with us the
10. dying of Jesus, that the life of Jesus may be manifest
in our body:* that made them, when they were
*troubled on every side, not to be distressed, when they
were perplexed, they were not in despair;* because,
say they, *We who live are always delivered to death
for*

for Jesus' sake, that the life also of Jesus may be manifest in our mortal flesh. Now this is more than a creature can do; for, as he tells us there, *the excellency of the power was to be of God, and not of them.*

How could our Lord say to the disciples, *Yet a little while, and ye see me no more; and again, Yet a little while, and ye shall see me.* In the former sentence, he plainly refers to their losing of his body; they were to know Christ no more after the flesh, but the latter is understood of a Divine presence. And was this fit for any to say but the Supreme Being? *Do not I fill heaven and earth, saith the Lord?* How should he say the world sees me no more, *but ye see me, and because I live, ye shall live also?* This is more than any of the saints can say: As the world does not see them, so neither do they see the church; they live, and we live also, but the one is not the cause of the other. Does not this argue an omnipresence? that heaven is not only the place from whence we *look* for a Saviour to judge the world, but from whence we *feel* one? And how can it be said of any less than a God, *that he went far above all heavens, that he might fill all things.*

SERM. 35.

John xvi. 16.

Eph. iv. 10.

7. If we believe in Christ, we shall declare it by an *obedience* to him in all manner of conversation. *To me,* saith the Apostle, *to live is Christ.* And is it not too much to have this said of a creature? The notion we have of religion is this, that a man *lives his time in the flesh, not to the lusts of men, but to the will of God. The Lord made all things for himself; of him, and to him, and through him, are all things.* And more especially in the nobler work of redemption he has declared himself to be the great end of the whole contrivance: *We are to the praise of the glory of his grace, wherein he has made us accepted in the beloved. None of us lives to himself, and no man dies to himself; but whether*

Phil. i. 21.

1 Pet. iv. 2.

Rom. xi. 36.

Eph. i. 6.

Rom. xiv. 7, 8.

we

we live, we live unto the Lord, or whether we die, we die unto the Lord; whether therefore we live or die, we are the Lord's. Can there be any words that express so full a surrender as this? and must it be made to any besides the great God? and yet you see what Lord he means in the next words, *For to this end Christ both died and rose again, and revived, that he might be the Lord both of dead and living.* Where can you find expressions of duty that are more significant? *What can David say more to thee, O Lord God?*

Nothing farther can be said of our obedience to the Most High. The Apostle tells them, *Whether we are besides ourselves, it is to* God, *i. e.* for his service; *or whether we be sober,* it is for your cause. What God is it, that all their zeal is directed to? You will learn his meaning from the next words that come in as an argument, *for the love of* Christ *constrains us, who died for all, that they who live should not live unto themselves, but to* him *that died for them and rose again.* What David may be supposed to say to the Father, these Apostles say to the Son: *Truly I am thy servant, I am thy servant.* And can the profession be directed to any but the same infinite Nature? *One shall say I am the Lord's, and another shall subscribe with his hand to the Lord. Thus saith the Lord the King of Israel, and his Redeemer the Lord of Hosts, I am the first, and I am the last, and besides me there is no God.*

8. They that believe in Christ give him a religious *worship:* and as that is the greatest thing we can do in this world, so let it not be said that *we worship we know not what. Heaven and earth shall pass away before one tittle* of the law does, and especially *that* in the first and second commandment: *Thou shalt have no other gods before me;*—it is no matter for a creature's having the name of a god: *Thou shalt not make to thyself the likeness of any*

Serm. 35.

2 Cor. v. 13.

ver. 14, 15.

Psal. cxvi. 16.

Isa. xliv. 5, 6.

Mat. v. 18.

Exod. xx. 3, 4.

any thing in heaven above, as well as in the earth beneath; thou shalt not bow down thyself unto them: not only to the likeness that thou makest of them, for that must be a stupid idolatry indeed; but there is *none in heaven above*, before whom thou must bow down and worship; *for I the Lord thy God am a jealous God*.

If the Gospel had not represented Christ as a God, I should never have dared to get over the prohibition of this law. He himself gives no answer but this to Satan, *It is written, Thou shalt worship the Lord thy God, and him only shalt thou serve*. [Mat. iv. 10.] So that he refuses to fall down before him, not merely because he is a devil, but because he is a creature. And what he saith to him, would have been as proper to the brightest Angel in heaven. The Angel forbid John to do it upon this very ground, *Worship thou God*. [Rev. xxii. 9.] No excellency of nature, no engagement of kindness, can make any person the object of our devotion. When we are called to *fall down and worship*, it is *before the Lord our Maker*. [Pf. xcv. 6.] And

Upon no other consideration could we read of worshiping the Son: the Angels of God are charged to *worship him*; [Heb. i. 6.] and the reason is plain, because *by him were all things created, whether they be in heaven or on earth; thrones, principalities, dominions and powers, all are created by him and for him*. [Col. i. 16.] The world below is called to do it, because *the world was made by him*: [Joh. i. 10.] His people to do it, because *he is the Author and Finisher of their faith*. [Heb. xii. 2.] The church of the First-born, whose names are written in heaven, fall down before Him who sits on the throne, and before the Lamb, because they are *his house, and he that has built them is God*. ——[iii. 4.]

The Scripture has put a great value upon your doing any thing in the name of God: *All people will walk every one in the name of his god, and we will walk in the name of the Lord our God for ever* [Mic. iv. 5.]
and

and ever. Chrift ufes the fame language in a gracious promife: *Where two or three are met together in my name, there am I in the midft of them.* That phrafe *in my name* is ufed about the greateft folemnities in religion. This, I think, is too much for a creature, according to that profeffion of the Church, *Other lords befides thee have had dominion over us, but by thee only will we make mention of thy name. The defire of our foul is to thy name, and to the remembrance of thee.* But not to force the word beyond the neceffary meaning, who could make fuch a promife, *That where two or three are met together, there am I in the midft of them?* Here obferve two things:

Firft, This comes in as the reafon of what he had told them before; that *if two of you fhall agree on earth as touching any thing that they fhall afk, it fhall be done for them of my Father who is in heaven, for I am in the midft of them.* Does not this prove that he and the Father are one? Why is *his* being in the midft of them an argument that the Father will hear them? But befides that,

Secondly, He here talks in the language of a God. He does not fay *I will* come down to them, *I will* bow the heavens, and come down; no, but *I am* in the midft of them, antecedent to their defire. It is true, thefe words do not *mention* an omniprefence, becaufe his being among them fignifies more than his being with the wicked; but they *fuppofe* it. How can it be true that he fhould be prefent with fo many thoufands of their affemblies? or you may call them conventicles if you pleafe; a good thing is never the worfe for a hateful word. How fhall he make good his promife to the vaft numbers that are met together in his name, if it was not He of whom David faith, *Whither fhall I flee from thy Spirit, or go from thy prefence?* He is called indeed *the branch of the Lord*, that fhould be *beautiful and glorious*, and we read *of the fruit of the earth that shall be excellent and comely for them that are escaped of Israel.* This supposes his taking upon him the human nature; but nothing less than a Divine Nature can make good what we read afterwards, that *the Lord will create upon every dwelling place upon Mount Zion*, let there be never so many thousands of them, *and upon all her assemblies, a cloud of smoke by day, and the shining of a flaming fire by night;* that is, he will be as actually and effectually present with every church under the New Testament, as he was with *the church in the wilderness.* And how is this possible, if his name was not *excellent in all the earth, and his glory above the heavens?* [Isa. iv. 5.] [Pf. viii. 1.]

It is in vain for any to deny the truth of his being among us, because we cannot explain it. Nothing has more the air of darkness and arrogance, than to object, against the *reality* of a thing, the difficulty there is in the *manner* of it. Thus the doctrine of the Trinity is used. The men that oppose it do not demand of you a proof, but an explication, and imagine with contempt enough, that because you are at a loss in the one, so you must be in the other. The presence of Christ with his assemblies is one of those *mysterious certainties* that we are to believe, though we cannot unfold the way of it.

I need not lead you into Divinity for several matters which have the greatest evidence that they are so, and yet the greatest obscurity how they come to be so. *Dost thou know the balancings of the clouds? Canst thou tell how thy garments are warm when he quiets the earth with his south wind? Hast thou entered into the springs of the sea, or hast thou walked in the search of the depth? Knowest thou the ordinances of heaven, or canst thou set the dominion thereof upon the earth?* and yet, can you deny these things? *Thou knowest not the way of the spirit,* [Job xxxvii. 16. 17.] [—xxxviii. 16. 33.] [Ecclef. xi. 5.]

spirit, *nor how the bones do grow in the womb of her that is with child;* and yet thou muſt be a very aukward creature to ſay there is no ſuch thing. But ſo it is, that perſons who are puzzled with a worm, are impatient to be told that they cannot know a God!

9. Believing in Chriſt is truſting him for a future protection, to carry us through all our dangers: *The Lord ſhall preſerve us from every evil work, and bring us to his heavenly kingdom.* And who is this Lord? I anſwer, *You are preſerved in Chriſt Jeſus, and called.* He *that loved the church, and gave himſelf for it, is to preſent it to himſelf, as a holy church, without ſpot or wrinkle, or any ſuch thing.* David expected this from no other than God: *Thou wilt guide me by thy counſel, and afterwards receive me to thy glory.* And to ſhew that there was but One who could do this, he adds, *Whom have I in heaven but Thee, and there is none upon earth whom I deſire beſides Thee. My fleſh and my heart fails; but God is the ſtrength of my heart, and my portion for ever.*—*We commit the keeping of our ſouls to a faithful Creator.*

And yet the Apoſtle directs our hopes to the great Redeemer: *We look for the mercy of the Lord Jeſus to eternal life.* And having ſpoken of that, he concludes with this doxology: *Now unto him that is able to keep us from falling, and to preſent us faultleſs before the preſence of his glory, with exceeding joy; to the only wiſe God our Saviour, be glory and majeſty, dominion and power, both now and ever, Amen.* His ability to keep us from falling is what the Scripture has abundantly teſtified: *He is able to ſave to the uttermoſt.* His preſenting us before his own glory agrees to what is ſaid of him in ſeveral other places, *Behold I, and the children whom God has given me.* And the Apoſtle calls him that does it, by the name of the only wiſe God our Saviour.

God *believed on in the* World.

viour. He reprefents thefe things as fit for none but a God to do; and therefore as they belong to Chrift, he is the only wife God our Saviour,—to whom be glory for ever, *Amen.*

SERMON XXXVI.

Sept. 13. 1719.

10. BELIEVING in Chrift Jefus is LOOKING to him as the *Finifher* of our faith, who will give a completenefs to his own work. I choofe to exprefs this great act of the foul upon a death-bed, in the language that God has cloathed it with; and it agrees to all thofe phrafes by which good people have delivered their notions of a true Gofpel-faith. Thus in the Old Teftament, believing in Chrift was for *all the ends of the earth to look to him and be faved.* And the converfion of the Jews is laid down in thefe terms: *They fhall look unto him whom they have pierced.*

Ifa. xlv. 22.

Zech. xii. 10.

It is true, we read of an oppofition between faith and fight; the former, by which we walk, gives us the limitations we are under in this world, and the latter opens out the liberty and glory of the next. But yet faith has in it the nature of vifion, though it is here diftinguifhed from it. It is faid of thofe that received Chrift, which is explained by their *believing in his name,* that *they beheld his glory, the glory of the only begotten of the Father.* The faith of Mofes is delivered to us in thefe words: *He endured as feeing him who is invifible.*

Joh. i. 12, 14.

Heb. xi. 27.

So that, you obferve this is the language both of the Old and New Teftament; and what they are

ufed

SERM. 36. used to, who build upon the foundation of the Apostles and Prophets. Though believing is distinguished from seeing, yet it is very often expressed by it. To which end we read, that *as Moses lifted up the serpent in the wilderness, so must the Son of man be lifted up,* that, as by looking at the one, so by believing in the other, they might find an healing virtue: *They looked to him, and were lightened. Him has God set forth to be a propitiation for our sins.* The first act of our faith is a closing with that call, *I said, Behold me, behold me.* And the last look we take, is to One who will give the great perfection to his own image, and *present us without spot or wrinkle, or any such thing, before his glory, with exceeding joy.* Now, it is to Jesus that we thus look, *as the Author and Finisher of our faith.* We consider the cloud of witnesses with which we are encircled and encompassed about, as so many examples; but our eyes are upon HIM as the efficient of what we *are* and what we *shall be.*

Joh. iii. 14.

Pf. xxxiv. 5.
Rom. iii. 25.
Isa. lxv. 1.

Eph. v. 27.

And who can this be but the Most High *God?* The Scripture has directed us to no other than an Almighty Agent, either for the working of faith in us, or carrying it on *with power,* or raising it to felicity and vision. We read of the *exceeding greatness of his power towards them that believe.* David saith, *The Lord will perfect that which concerns me, and not forsake the work of his own hands, because his mercy endures for ever.* The Apostle saith in the most positive terms, *He that has wrought us for the self-same thing, is God: He that establisheth us in Christ, and has anointed us, is God, who has also sealed us, and given us the earnest of the Spirit in our hearts.* It is *God who fulfils in us all the good pleasure of his goodness, and the work of faith with power.* They that believe in Christ, are *born of God;* and he who has begun this good work, will perform it to the day of Christ Jesus. *All things are of God, who has reconciled us*

Eph. i. 19.

Pf. cxxxviii. ult.

2 Cor. v. 5.
—i. 21, 23.

2 Thes. i. 11.

1 Joh. v. 1. 4.

2 Cor. v. 18.

to

to himself; that is, all those things that make us new creatures.

Now, what is performing the thing that he has begun, but that He will be the *Finisher,* who has been the *Author* of our faith? that he will fulfil the work of faith with power, *that the name of our Lord Jesus Christ may be glorified in you, and ye in him?* 2Thes.i,12.

Christ is the Governor both of grace and nature; *he has the keys of death,* and of the invisible state. Rev. i. 18. It is by the turn of his hand that we are let out of one world into another; and it is also by him, that the better life, which is here begun, rises into that life that was its pattern, and will be its end. And is not this too much for a creature to do?

Can a believer have his last confidence in one who is not God, and go out of the world under the hazard and appearance of idolatry? David durst trust himself with none but an infinite Being, *In-* Pf. xxxi. 5. *to thy hands do I commit my spirit, Lord God of truth, for thou hast redeemed it.* This is the employment of faith, in which every good man is to follow him. They are to die in that way, who *die in the Lord;* for they *all die in faith.* And I can never think that a true believer will stop at any thing short of what they depended on; our faith and hope are to be in a God, as well as David's. We have *none* in heaven but God; it is He who Pf. lxxiii. 25. made with the sweet Psalmist of Israel *a new and everlasting covenant,* which was *all his salvation.* 2Sam. xxiii. 5. Stephen's faith was thus employed: he *called on God, saying, Lord Jesus receive my spirit.* Acts vii. 59.

There are two answers given to the argument that arises out of this scripture. *First,* That the word *God* is not in the original, but supplied by our translators; and their doing so has been insulted as a trick or a fraud*. But the persons, who can be triumphant upon that observation, shew
they

---

* See a discourse of Free-thinking.

SERM 36.
Isa. lvii. 4.

they are very ready for it; and I must tell them it is a little too soon for people to boast at the girding on of the harness: *Sporting and making a wide mouth, and drawing out the tongue*, are given as a mark to know the *children of transgression, and the seed of falsehood*. That the word was thrown in by our translators, is plain enough; but apparently without any design to steal upon us the doctrine of Christ's divinity; for this truth receives no advantage at all from that reading, but stands in fuller force, and in a better light without it. Because it is evident, that Stephen, who *saw heaven opened, and the glory of God, and Jesus at the right hand of God*, found it was now his duty to commend a departing soul to One who could take care of it; and whoever this was, he called upon *Him*. His last prayer and *recumbence* was on Him; for the word signifies both these. He has nothing farther to say about himself, than to beg that the Person he spoke to would *receive his spirit*.

Now the question is, whether his faith was at this time dealing with the same that David's did? or whether the Jewish religion taught people to think that none but the Supreme God was fit to be their friend in a dying hour, but that Christianity has made us dependent on one who is dependent himself? It is but a sorry compliment to the Gospel, to suppose that it makes that to be the work of a creature, of which none but God is capable. They of old used to deal with the principal Agent, and are we to believe in a deputy? The accusation had been true, that Stephen spake blasphemous words *against Moses and against God*, if he taught people such a dependence upon Christ, as all good men used to have upon a faithful Creator.—Strike the word *God* from this text, and read it thus, that *they stoned Stephen, calling upon, and saying, Lord Jesus receive my spirit*, and does it not appear that the Person he called upon was Jesus,

and

and the petition that he made to him was, that he would *receive his spirit?* the best thing that HE could do, and the last resignation that he could make. {SERM. 3.}

This agrees to the promise that our Saviour left with his disciples, *I will come again, and* RECEIVE YOU *to myself, that where I am, there ye may be also.* {Joh. xiv. 3.} Can we think that He who said this was any less than the benefactor upon whom the Psalmist had his whole dependence? *Thou wilt guide me by thy counsel, and afterwards receive me to thy glory.* {Pf. lxxiii. 24.} Are there two of these friends; and is one of them not a God? Thus he revealed himself to his people, and thus they received him: *The Lord God of the holy Prophets sent his Angel to shew to his servants the things that must shortly be done.* {Rev. xxii. 6.} And who is he? *I Jesus have sent my Angel to testify to you.* {ver. 16.} *He that testifies these things says, Surely I come quickly.* {—20.} We see of whom they understood it by their answer, *Amen, even so, come, Lord Jesus.*

When God spake at sundry times, and in divers manners, by types, prophecies, visions, voices, miracles, and signs, he still led up the people through those things to himself: The faith of men did not centre in the figure or the prophet, but in Him that appointed them. And does he speak in these last days *by his Son,* to drop his own name, that we should have less concern with a God now, than they had formerly? and yet this is plainly the case, if Christ and the Father are not one. But that is a doctrine which he has proclaimed: *If ye had known me, ye should have known my Father; and henceforth ye know him, and have seen him. Believest thou not that I am in the Father, and the Father in me. The words that I speak unto you, I speak not of myself, but the Father that dwells in me does the works. Believe me, that I am in the Father, and the Father in me, or else believe me for the very works sake.* {John xiv. 7. 10, 11.}

Moses

SERM. 36. Moses was a faithful servant to the Most High: he never stood as a skreen between the people and their God, but still directed them higher and further; and it is very unhappy that Christ was more furnished than he, and that by his coming into the world, our faith has less to do with a God than theirs had; which it certainly must have, if we do not *see the light of the glory of God in the face of Jesus Christ*. David had a great opinion of Moses; but he durst not say to him, *Into thy hands do I commit my spirit*. No; there are two reasons for this surrender to God, that can never be applied to a creature. 1*st*, That *he had redeemed it*; and certainly Stephen meant no less, when he said, *Lord Jesus receive my spirit*, he looked upon him to be *the holy One of Israel, and his Redeemer.* 2*dly*, David calls him *the God of truth*, which may either be understood of his nature, that he is the true God, in opposition to idols, or of his covenant, that this is *ordered in all things, and sure*.

Now, both these reasons are equally good in the petition of Stephen: In calling upon Jesus, he had to do with Him who is full of grace and *truth*, the way, *the truth* and the life; *the Amen*, the faithful and *true* witness: He that is holy, and he that is *true*; that holy and *just* One, as he is called, and by whom grace and *truth came* to the world, who came to bear witness to the *truth*, and to whom it is said in the praises of heaven, *Just and true are all thy ways, thou King of Saints*. Thus we are built on the foundation of the Apostles and Prophets, Jesus Christ himself being the chief corner-stone.

John i. 14.
—— xiv. 6
Rev. i. 5.
—— xv. 3.
Eph. ii. 20.

Secondly, Another answer to this expression of the Martyr's faith, is what I have met with in a late book, where the author is very full of a profession, that he is *Christianus*, but not *Christicola*; a Christian, but not a worshipper of Christ. He says, the case of Stephen was extraordinary; that he he had such a vision as none can expect, and that therefore he is no more an example to us, than Paul was in his being caught up to the third heavens. This is a mighty thought indeed, and may be numbered rather among the *perverse* than the cunning *disputings* of men of corrupt minds, who are destitute of the truth.

That his discoveries were unusual I grant, but his sentence is no other than the last profession of every believer. They are all *looking to Jesus*, as the Finisher of their faith. What he said was either right or wrong: If it was right for him to put his soul into the hands of Jesus, I must tell you, it is impossible he should do any more to the great God, who has said so plainly, *My Son, give me thy heart:* If it was wrong, and stands not for your example, but your caution, I think the favour of God to his Martyrs has rather proved a snare than a benefit to the church. If the first man who ever suffered for the Christian religion made such an unhappy use of the testimony that was given him from above, as to bequeath *that* to a creature, which is the most noble present that can be made to a God, we must not say that the blood of the Martyrs is the seed, but rather the stain and the scandal of the church.

But when he said it, *he was full of the Holy Ghost,* whose office it was not to delude, but to *guide them into all truth.* Now, here is the choice that is left us, either to condemn Stephen for an *idolater,* or this author for an *infidel;* either the one made a prostitute of his conscience, or the other has done it of his reason. And though I hope I shall ever admire charity as the glory of my religion, yet I must profess I have a greater esteem for that Martyr, than I have for such writers, who confess themselves to be out of the number of those that *in every place call on the name of the Lord Jesus Christ.* Well, my brethren, this is like to be the

Acts vii. 55.
John xvi. 13.

1 Cor. i. 2.

SERM. 36. the case of every one of us in a little time. Die we must; and as long as nature and grace are capable of acting, we shall be putting ourselves into some hands or other. The Scripture has directed us by many a precept, as well as this noble example, thus to look unto Jesus; which is more than I shall dare to do, if I do not think him to be a God. 'Unto thee, O Lord, do I lift up my soul.

Pf. xxv. 1.

' Whenever my soul used this language, I knew in
' whom I have believed, and was persuaded that
' He is able to keep what I have committed to him
' against that day. I always understood it of Christ.
' It is to him the consignments have been made
' many a time; and therefore, as soon as ever I
' come to find that he is no God, my religion will
' be all a draw-back, a fetching of things out of
' his hand.' Whatever value I may have for him,
(as I owe a great deal to the Angels who are below him) ' yet my faith and hope must be in a
' God; and more especially in the last and greatest
' concern that I can have.'

I cannot dismiss this head, though I have been a long while upon it, without telling you a story that has some relation to it. A very good friend and most intimate acquaintance, told me several years ago what scruples he had about the Divinity of Christ. I could not but observe in the frequent conversation I had with him, that he was far from the length that some have arrived at, to have no pleasure in the truth, but a pleasure in unrighteousness. I could see the objections gave him a great deal of pain, and he strove to reconcile the Arian and Socinian doctrine with what is opposite to them. I remember I once plied him with this particular instance of the Martyr Stephen, and told him how dreadful it would be in a dying hour for a man not to know where to look, or upon whom to have a dependence as the last friend of his soul: and that if the Scripture directs my faith only to

Jesus,

Jesus, and reason tells me he is not God, I shall SERM. 36. take believing in that case to be a disconsolate venture. I desired him not to strive against inward evidence, or treat the mysteries of religion as if he was sure they were either a falsehood, or the craft of designing men. And I the rather did this, because he had been for some time in a languishing state of health. After these things, he more than once told me, how earnestly he had desired, that God would not let him go out of the world uncertain about that matter. And though he had continued long ill, yet his death was so far sudden, that a few moments before, he declared himself something better than he had been for several weeks, and so had just time and strength enough to say no more than these words, *Lord Jesus receive my spirit.*—Thus have I gone through both the explication of the text, and the argument that it gives us, that He who is believed on in the world, is no other than the Most High God. I am now to take this doctrine in another view.

III. As it is a MYSTERY. Indeed we have lived to see and hear this very name treated as if it was only a jest; and that by *mystery* you are to understand either a contradiction or an imposture. Thus are *high thoughts exalting themselves against the* 2 Cor. x. 3. *knowledge of the Son of God.* I am sure in using the phrase we do not depart from the *words* of Scripture. *There* we often have it; and certainly the Holy Spirit did not scatter it about in *his* book, to have it bantered and exposed in *ours.* Such profaneness will end in universal trembling: it makes those tremble now who are serious; and it will do the same in those that are not so: *There-* Isa xxviii. *fore be not mockers, lest your bands be made strong.* 22. For my part, I shall consider it in the way that my text has presented it. And you will find that believing on Christ in the world is a Mystery, if you do but attend to these two things.

1. The

1. The nature of the work.
2. The nature of the place: that there should be any *believing* at all, and that it should be *in the world*.

1. *Believing* itself is a myftery; as it is acting without the direction of fenfe and reafon, and very often againft them; and therefore in oppofition to the example and practice of others. So that it muft proceed from fomething that we feel only in ourfelves.

(1.) Believing is acting without the direction of fenfe and reafon: it is *depending* upon what we do not fee, and *admiring* what we cannot underftand:

John iii. 6. *That which is born of the flesh is flesh, and that which is born of the Spirit is spirit.* We look at

2 Cor. iv. 18. *the things that are not seen, which are eternal.*

1 Pet. i. 8. *Whom having not seen, ye love; and in whom, though now ye see him not, yet believing, ye rejoice with a joy unspeakable, and full of glory.* And is not this wonderful to thofe whofe fouls get no far-

Phil. iii. 19. ther than their bodies, who *mind earthly things?* Their great enquiry is, Who will *shew* us any good?

Ecclef. xi. 9. They walk in the *fight of their eyes*; their portion, bufinefs, and hearts, are in this life; they know nothing what believing is; and perfons who are thus diftinguifhed from them, make an unac-

Ifa. viii. 13, 14. countable figure in their opinion: *The Lord of Hosts, whom believers sanctify in their hearts, is for a stone of stumbling, and rock of offence;* and

ver. 18. both *he and the children whom God has given him are for signs, and for wonders in Israel.*

(2.) Believing is oftentimes acting *againſt* thefe two principles, by which we are to be conducted in other things. We are called to believe what reafon cannot explain, and to perform what fenfe

1 Cor. vi. 8, 9. will abhor: *By honour and dishonour, by evil report and good report; as dying, chastened, sorrowful, poor, and having nothing.* I know that this very defcription of faith makes it the contempt of the world;

but

but it is never the worse for that: a minister is to be *patient to all men;* but it is carrying the complaisance a great deal too far, if they who are enemies to the Gospel of Christ can persuade him either to give it up, or to keep it in. The Apostle begged that *utterance might be given him, that he might open his mouth boldly, to make known the mystery of the Gospel, for which he was an ambassador in bonds, that therein he might speak boldly as he ought to speak.*

SERM. 36.

Eph. vi. 19, 20.

I look upon human reason to be no more a judge of doctrine than it is of practice. It is employed indeed about the rule, it receives the evidence upon which I believe. This is revelation; but it has nothing to do to determine about the matters revealed: *We have received, not the spirit of the world, but the Spirit which is of God, that we may know the things that are freely given to us of God. The natural man receives not the things of the Spirit of God, for they are foolishness to him; neither can he know them, because they are spiritually discerned.*

1 Cor. ii. 12.

ver. 14.

I will give you an instance of this in duty. Abraham's reason told him, that the command to offer his son Isaac came from God; that it was truly the Lord who tempted him, and said those cutting things that led him into an unheard of practice; but he never enquired of reason whether he should obey or no. He never measured this command by the law of nature, which obliged him to shed no blood, and to take care of his child; or even by the promise of the covenant, that *in Isaac shall thy seed be called.* I am sure that precept, *Go take thy son, thy only son Isaac whom thou lovest, and offer him for a burnt-offering,* is as unintelligible, and liable to as many objections, as that text can be: *There are three that bear record in heaven, the Father, the Word, and the Holy Ghost, and these three are one.* Our reason may with equal justice

Gen. xxii. 2.

1 Joh. v. 7.

call

call this nonsense, and endeavour to prove it spurious, and go about hunting into copies with as much speed as a wild ass runs in the wilderness; for indeed both these works are but *snuffing up the wind at pleasure*.

Let not any say, God cannot be supposed to tell me, that *three are one* by revelation, because he has before-hand told me, that three cannot be one in nature; and I must not imagine that he gives me a new light to contradict the old one. Abraham's love to his son, and his abstaining from shedding innocent blood, was as much rooted in nature, and established by all the principles of religion, as that one cannot be three. He was as sure of those practical maxims, as we are of this mysterious notion. Had all the Angels in heaven given him that command about Isaac, and sent him to Moriah upon so dreadful an errand, you may be sure he would have stuck by the principles that God had implanted already, of justice to human nature, and affection to his child, and especially a regard to the promise, *In Isaac shall thy seed be called*, and not a hair of his head must have perished.

1 Pet. iii. 15.
1 Cor. xv. 52.
Isa. vii. 14.

No more should we ever say that *three are one*, or that *the just dies for the unjust*, or that *the body shall rise incorruptible*, or that *a Virgin shall conceive and bring forth a Son*, or that *God could be manifest in the flesh;* these things cannot be explained by reason: they are *spiritually discerned*, and therefore not to be *received* but upon report; and upon no report but that of a God, who cannot lie.

1 Cor. ii. 14.

If he has said them they must be, though we are at a loss to conceive how they can be. So it was with Abraham: he had no more to do than to enquire whether this command came from God or no; and when that difficulty is over, his reason is under a bar. The objections that would have prevailed, had the exhortation been given by a creature,

ture, are not allowed to stir, or move a tongue. He knew the promise would hold, he knew the command must be answered, he knew the one was destructive of the other; but he leaves that to God. His faith was to ask no questions, but to believe the good old way, *in hope and against hope*, because it depended upon *him who raises the dead, and calls the things that are not, as though they were.* _{Rom. iv. 17.}

Now, we go no greater lengths in receiving a doctrine that we cannot understand, than in doing a duty that we cannot account for. Do not say that God will not put you upon *believing* against reason; you see he may put you upon *acting* against it. What principle of nature is more early, more internal and perpetual with us, than that of self-preservation? and therefore what can be more abominable than a religion that destroys it? and yet it is notorious that this is the great demand of Christianity: *If any man,* saith our Lord, *hate not his own life, he cannot be my disciple.* It is observed of some of his people, that they *loved not their lives unto the death.* He has hung a dreadful punishment over the contrary disposition, *He that saves his life shall lose it.* It is as reasonable to embrace a mystery as a martyrdom; they are both unaccountable. Human reason is laid aside, or plainly over-ruled in each of them, and shews that *God's ways are not our ways,* nor his thoughts our thoughts. Therefore, _{Rev. xii. 11.} _{Isa. lv. 8.}

(3.) Believing is acting in opposition to the practice and example of others; and it is no easy matter to get thus high. Nay, perhaps your discouragement will arise from men of great names, from particular friends, from such as *call themselves of the holy city.* Your faith will be loaded with all the scandalous insinuations of enthusiasm, persecution, conceit and folly. Arguments against you will be said to rise from a zeal for liberty, the honour _{Isa. xlviii. 2.}

SERM. 36. nour of the Christian religion, and a prospect of making it go down with infidels.

Some profess to believe the doctrine of the Gospel, and take a Christian name only as they took a civil one, because they found it where they were born; these will not endure the trial. In a day of temptation mere forms of speaking are what they may be driven from; and if they make a Creed, which is but the *language* of faith, to be the *ground* of it, it will never do. These, rather than be the jest of an adversary, will be their captives, and prove treacherous to the cause which they cannot maintain; and when they leave you, it will be with the destruction of all modesty, humility, and tenderness. Though they cannot lift up their heads, they will lift up their *heels* against you.

Now, is it not a wonder, when the roads are so lined and guarded, that there is any believing in the world? and yet *faith is of the operation of God;* as men do not plant it, so men shall not root it up. Christ has always raised up some who have a concern for those doctrines which the world reckon a trifle, and many professors have dropped as an error. There is a principle that carries us through all the snares of friendship, and all the terrors of shame; Jam. iv. 4. that makes us know *the friendship of the world to be emnity with God,* and sets things out to our choice in this fair distinction, that *the friend of the world is the enemy of God.*

(4.) This proceeds from something within ourselves. We have several arguments for the doctrine, that may be pleaded with others; as a clear revelation, the comparing spiritual things with spiritual, the known sense of words, the frequent testimony of Scripture; and some of a lower nature, the concurrence of God's people in all ages; I do not only mean those who were witnesses in a *council,* but those who were so at a *stake.* These, I say, are

are confiderations that will have their weight with such as are seeking after the truth. *[SERM. 36.]*

But the principle of believing is incommunicable, and cannot be conveyed in an argument. *No man can say that Jesus is the Lord, but by the Holy Ghost.* *[1 Cor. xii. 3.]* Peter and the rest of the Apostles had much evidence of our Lord's being the Son of God from his doctrine, his miracles, and his conformity to all the prophetical characters; and yet flesh and blood did not reveal this to them, but *our Father who is in heaven.* Saul had heard great reasonings for the Christian Religion at the trial and the death of Stephen; but that faith and love which he found at last came along with *the exceeding abundant grace of God in Christ Jesus our Lord.* *[1 Tim. i. 14.]*

SERMON XXXVII.

Sept. 27. 1719.

2. TO what is said of believing in general, we may add the circumstance of *place where* men are to look for it, which leads us farther into the mystery. It is a wonder there should be any such principle as faith, but it is more so that Christ is believed on IN THE WORLD: In this world, and not in heaven; in a world where he had been refused; where the greatest evidence had proved in vain; where he was no longer to appear; where people were possessed with prejudice against him; under the power of his most obstinate enemy, and where nothing was to be got by it.

VOL. II. K (1.) You

SERM. 37. (1.) You will observe the mystery of believing in Christ, if you regard it as a thing to be met with *in this world*, and not in heaven. Had it been said of him now, that he is received up with glory, that the vast multitudes who hear his voice admire his person, we could easily come into the report, because there he is revealed with a brightness unconfined: There is no vail upon his face, no limitation to their eyes. *Now we see through a glass darkly, but then face to face; now we know in part, but then we shall know even as ourselves are known.* And this is so much above all our experience here, that he is supposed to be in a sort of obscurity till that time comes. *That is the revelation of Jesus Christ. He who is our life shall appear.* He is now our life, we have a life that is hid with Christ in God; but in all the present manifestations of him, there is the *hiding of his power*.

1 Cor. xiii. 12.

1 Pet. i. 13.
Col. iii. 4.

His appearing is always spoken of as a thing that is future, and belongs to the felicities of another state. It is said of them that are before the throne of God, that *they see his face, and his name is in their foreheads.* The will of Christ was, that his people should be *with him where they are to behold his glory.* There the disguise is off both from him and them, and no wonder that in broad day-light they should *see the King in his beauty,* because they are got into the land which to us is *afar off.* There is no danger that any of those above should be offended in him. The Angels that proclaim his perfections, and the saints that live upon his merit, have not one unbeliever to say any thing against them; but the whole assembly and church of the first-born, whose names are written in heaven, *ascribe honour, and glory, and salvation, and power, to him that sits upon the throne, and to the Lamb for ever.* They are got up to the *fountain of life*, to the spring-head where life runs clean, and full, and eternal; and so *in his light they see light.* They

Rev. xxii. 4.

Joh. xvii. 24.

Pf. xxxvi. 9.

see him as he is. He appears to them, as he appears to himself, in the brightness of his person, and the express declaration of his glory. *They are before the throne of God, and serve him day and night in his temple, and He that sits upon the throne dwells among them.* {SERM. 37. Rev. vii. 15.}

But the mystery is, that he is believed on in a world where all this is hid; that he has a people, *who having not seen him, do love him, and though now they see him not, believing in him, do rejoice with a joy unspeakable and full of glory.* This is more than Thomas would do. He insisted upon external evidence as the condition and guide of his faith, *Except I see in his hands the print of the nails, and put my finger into the print of the nails, and thrust my hand into his side, I will not believe;* and perhaps this is what he was led into by the account that the other disciples gave of an interview in his absence, that he *shewed them his hands and his side.* All this advantage they have in heaven, for *he is in the midst of the throne as a Lamb that has been slain. He is clothed with a vesture dipt in blood.* — Our Saviour, who pitied their frame, condescended to one who was so weak in the faith, and therefore saith to Thomas, *Reach hither thy finger, and behold my hands, and reach hither thy hand, and thrust it into my side, and be not faithless, but believing.* But he closes the conversation with that remark, *Thomas, because thou hast seen me thou hast believed, but blessed are they that have not seen and yet believe.* {1 Pet. i. 6. Joh. xx. 25. Rev. v. 6. —xix. 13.}

Now what is it for them to believe? What is that act of the soul which goes by this title? You will be able to answer the question by comparing the two parts of this story. *These things are written, that ye might believe, that Jesus is the Christ the Son of God, and that believing ye might have life in his name.* I take the faith that is here described to be of the same nature and extent with that which Thomas had before professed in those words, {Joh. xx. 31.}

My

SERM. 37. *My Lord and my God.* Believing him to be the Chrift the Son of God, and believing that you may have life in his name, is believing him to be *your Lord and your God.* As your Lord he is the Chrift, and as your God he is the author of that life that you are to have in his name. Do not put it, as fome people ftrive to do, upon the confufion that Thomas was in, and that the words fignify not his fentiments but his furprife; for fuch exclamations and profane interjections are what the Scripture would teach us rather to abhor than to imitate. This was the language of a believer, and not of an affrighted man, and it is in vain to divert the force of the argument by another interpretation, *viz.* that Thomas declared *Chrift* to be his Lord, and the *Father* to be his God. This is againft all the laws of reading; it is making any thing of every thing; and at that rate there is not a fentence in the Bible that comes within a determinate meaning. It is plain our Saviour calls this the language of Thomas's faith, and of a faith *in him:* He had been *faithlefs* before, not in the Father, for that was not the queftion, but in the reality of Chrift's refurrection; and what he calls believing, was the root of that good profeffion, *My Lord and my God.*

And fuch a faith was to obtain, through the preaching of the Gofpel, among thofe that had never feen what Thomas did. For it is remarkable, that his faith went beyond the evidence. All that he could fee in his fingers and his fide, proved no more than that he was that very man who had fuffered upon the crofs, and that the fame body was rifen indeed, that had been crucified and flain. But when he is fure of that, he fpeaks of him not merely as one dead and alive again, but as the fame that he always took him for, *his Lord and his God.* The wounds in his fide, the prints of nails and fpears, are no marks of a God; it had been

been blasphemy to give him the title upon that ac-   SERM. 37.
count; these proved no more than a human na-
ture; but you see the office of a true faith: *If thou*   Rom. x. 9.
*believest that Jesus died, and that God raised him
from the dead, thou shalt be saved.* This is not to
be struck off from a regard to his Deity; for Thomas, who questioned his resurrection, is no sooner
convinced of *that*, but he declares his opinion of
the *other*, that he was his Lord and his God. Thus
the *kingdoms of this world are to become the king-*   Rev. xi. 15.
*doms of our Lord and of his Christ, and he shall
reign for ever and ever. The earth is* this *Lord's,*   Ps. xxiv. 1.
and the fulness thereof.

(2.) It is mysterious that he is believed on in a
world where he had been refused. When *the Son
of man came, he found* little or *no faith in the earth.
He was in the world, and the world was made by*   John i. 10,
him, and the world knew him not. He came to his   11.
own, and his own received him not. This was needful on several accounts, and an honour to God's
justice, that the Jews, who had killed the Prophets
and stoned those who were sent unto them, should
fill up the measure of their iniquity; upon this
account *their house was left unto them desolate.*
Nor is this proceeding void of a regard to his mer-
cy; for *by their fall salvation is come unto the Gen-*   Rom. xi.
tiles; the middle wall of partition, which had con-   11.
tinued so long between the one and the other, was
to be *broken down* at his death, as the veil of the   Eph. ii. 14.
temple was at that time rent asunder. And in-
deed the project of God's wisdom, the design of his
mercy to mankind in general, made it needful that
a Saviour should not be known: *For had the princes*   1 Cor. ii. 8.
*of this world known him, they would not have cru-
cified the Lord of glory;* and without the shedding
of his blood there could be no remission. The A-
postle gave that soft account of it to the Jews,
I wot that through ignorance ye did it, and so did   Acts iii. 17,
your rulers, but those things which God before had   18.
shewn

SERM. 3I *shewn by the mouth of all his Prophets that Christ should suffer, he has so fulfilled.* We might, from a flood of Scripture arguments, prove, that Christ Luke xxiv. *must needs have suffered and enter into his glory.* 46. But,

I am now to consider the wonder that arises out of the case, that after such an usage he should ever have a people to receive him. How strangely are the parts of the xxiid Psalm put together! At the Pf. xxii. 1, beginning he complains of God's *forsaking him,* 2. and being so *far from the words of his roaring;* that his enemies had acted like *greedy dogs,* given him *vinegar to drink, and gaped upon him with their mouths as a ravening and a roaring lion,* which describes with a great deal of propriety the very manner of his sufferings so many ages after; and yet when all this is over, *the kingdom shall be the Lord's;* this Lord's who before was *a worm and no man.* Nothing after that is said of him, but what shews him to be a God. He is to be *the Governor among the nations,* not merely by the force and ways of Providence, but *a seed shall serve him, and be accounted to the Lord for a generation; they shall arise and declare his righteousness to a people that shall be born, that the Lord has done this,* i. e. his name, and the righteousness that he has brought in, shall be handed down through all ages. As they that are *gone down to the dust* have hoped for his truth, so they who are not yet come out of the womb shall be instructed to do the same. His glory is to run parallel with time. He will have a church as long as he has a world.

Who could have expected this after he was *despised and rejected of men?* We usually say at the blasting of a new project, that it is nipt in the bud, the very blossom goes up as dust. To speak in the language that God himself has taught us, he had made several experiments, and all in vain. He is compared to a King, who sent out many servants to to his subjects; some they stoned, others they killed, and all of them they refused; he has but one way more, I will send them, saith he, my well-beloved Son, *when they see him, they will reverence him.* He speaks there after the manner of men, all the reason in the world would give it that they should do so; but instead of that they cry out, *This is the heir, come let us kill him.*

Now, after such a treatment, might he not have said, 'As I can send no *better* than my Son, I will send no *more?* And yet in that world where he was so little known, that they despised him, they hated him, they killed him, there is he to be admired, *Kings shall fall down before him, and all nations shall serve him; he shall live; and to him shall be given of the gold of Sheba,* though he died so poor and necessitous: *Prayer shall be made for him continually, and daily he shall be praised; his name shall endure for ever, his name shall continue as long as the sun, men shall be blessed in him, and all nations shall call him blessed.* He who was *a servant of rulers, whom men despised and abhorred, was to sprinkle many nations.* His doctrine would not conquer like thunder, but like rain. *Kings were to shut their mouths at him:* He that had been the reproach of men was to become *the desire of all nations;* and he that poured out his soul unto death. was to have *a portion with the great, and divide the spoil with the strong.*

Little did the Jews imagine that their hour was his hour, *when the Son of man should be glorified;* and that the power of darkness should prove *the womb of the morning.* They did not understand, and could not believe the propriety of that comparison, that his interest would be like *a grain of wheat thrown into the ground.* Whilst it was entire, it abode alone, but by dying it was to be multiplied. This the Apostle tells them: *It was needful that the word of God should be first preached un-*

SERM. 37. *to you; but seeing ye have put it far from you, and judged yourselves unworthy of everlasting life, lo we turn to the Gentiles.* And he speaks with af-
Acts xxviii. 28. surance upon another occasion, *The salvation of God is sent to the Gentiles, and they will hear it.*

Agreeable to which, a prophetic rapture is put in-
Isa. xlix. 5, 6. to the mouth of Christ, *Thus saith the Lord that formed me from the womb to be his servant, to bring Jacob again to him, Though Israel be not gathered, yet shall I be glorious in the eyes of the Lord, and my God shall be my strength. And he said, It is a light thing that thou shouldest be my servant to raise up the tribes of Jacob, and to restore the preserved of Israel; I will also give thee for a light to the Gentiles, and thou shalt be my salvation to the ends of the earth.*

(3.) To this you may add another consideration, which heightens the wonder, that he is believed on in a world where the greatest evidence has al-
John iii. 32. ready proved in vain. *What he has seen and heard he testified, and no man received his testimony.* If we are to judge of things by the gross reasoning of mankind, the Jews had a thousand times more to make them Christians than we have. Our Lord was among the blameless, by their own confession, *A Lamb without blemish, and without spot;* whereas the Gospel is preached to you by sinners; we have this *treasure in earthen vessels*, made of clay and tinged with guilt; and yet our ministry succeeds more than his, in accomplishment of that
— xiv. 12. promise, *He that believeth on me, shall do the things that I do, yea greater things than I do shall he do, because I go to my Father.*

Again, he spake as never man did; his enemies wondered at *the gracious words that proceeded out of his mouth;* as no guile, so no error ever came from his lips: but your conversion is by the means of such as are but of yesterday, and know no-
1 Cor. xiii. 9. thing: They who *know but in part*, must *prophecy in part.*

And

And chiefly you may observe the miracles that he wrought were in a way that never any person ought to pretend to, I mean at his own pleasure. He had it always in his power to ruffle nature and surprise the world, and he still did it in a testimony to himself, which was going higher than ever Moses did, or any creature ought to do. Moses told them, he would give them a *sign that the Lord had sent him;* but the works that Christ refers to, are a proof that *he is in the Father, and the Father in him.* They were arguments to prove more than a divine commission; he pleads from them such an union, as it would have been prophane for him to speak of if he was not God.

SERM. 37.

John xiv. 10.

How much of this evidence was thrown away? As he saith, *I have done among them such works as no other man did, yet they have hated both me and my Father.* Now, could it ever be expected, that things should mend when miracles ceased? Was it not in vain to hope that an effusion of the Spirit would convince those whom the resurrection of Lazarus had left impenitent? I do not look upon this wonder to be greater than the other; but as an argument of that power that our Saviour had above, he sent the Spirit upon his Apostles for an evidence, and the Spirit upon his enemies for a conviction: *We are witnesses to these things, and so also is the Holy Ghost, whom God hath given to them that obey him.*

xv. 24.

Though there were so few in his own nation that had any regard to him, and they had lately in an outrage wished his blood upon themselves and their children, yet we read of three thousand converted at one sermon; to let us see that the success of the Gospel does not arise from a virtue in the person who delivers it, but from the blessing which God is pleased to convey by it. The Jews *saw no form or comeliness in him, that they should desire him. He was despised and rejected of men, a man*

Isa. liii. 2, 3.

VOL. II. L of

of sorrows and acquainted with grief, they hid their faces from him; and yet he was *fairer than the sons of men, his countenance is as Lebanon, excellent as the cedars.*

(4.) He is thus believed on in a world where he appears no longer. If he had so little influence when he was here, what can be expected from the distance of heaven? Now that we are to know him no more after the flesh, God has closed our hopes of an intercourse with him in his glorified state. The stories that the Papists tell upon this head deserve to be laughed at as ridiculous, and abhorred as prophane; and yet, though he is no more with us in person, I mean in his body, we find the truth of that promise, *I will be always with you to the end of the world. Amen,*

They that deny his Deity have also the rancour to slander his love; and as they had rather be without a happiness than allow him to give it, they take pains to empty these words of the kind assurance they are so full of, and tell us, that the promise signifies no more than a presence with his disciples as long as they lived; that the end of the world was the end of that age. But what?— Does the possession *of all power in heaven and earth,* with which he introduced this promise, reach no further than the lives of these Apostles? Was the duty of *discipling all nations, baptizing them into the name of the Father, Son, and Holy Ghost, and teaching them to observe all things that he had commanded,* limited to them in person? Was the Gospel no more than so much apostolical breath, that went forth when they returned to their dust? Yes surely, *They were to be enlarged according to their rule abundantly; to preach the Gospel in the most distant regions.*

And if he was present with *them,* is he not capable of being so with *us?* The argument why he is not present with *us,* is, that he is now in heaven:

so

so he was a long while after he parted with *them*. They were *witnesses of the sufferings of Christ, and partakers of the glory that should be revealed.* They served him many years; and if being in heaven destroyed his presence with a people on earth, the words of Christ must not be understood of the end of the Apostles lives, but the end of his own: and so here is a promise for the present time, I am *always* with you, that is, I am so *now*, and the word *always* must comprehend no more than a few days. These men of Galilee saw him go up to heaven, *a cloud received him out of their sight;* and yet after that, they knew he would be with them, and found it so upon all occasions, for *Jesus is the same yesterday, to-day, and for ever.*

(5.) He is thus believed on in a world possessed of the greatest prejudice against him. Both the things and the persons in it are his enemies; it all lies under a curse. *If the world,* saith he, *hate you, ye know that it hated me before it hated you.* As for the men of the world who have their portion in this life, they have no Bible-character but that of *God's sword.* They hate those who are chosen out from among them; and as they do not believe themselves, they rise with a perpetual anger against them that do. The Apostle desires to be *delivered from wicked and unreasonable men,* and gives this as the ground of it, *that all men have not faith.* You may conclude from his way of arguing, that though the men who have not faith pretend to the greatest moderation and to the brightest reason, yet really they are cruel and absurd, and such as the people of God had need pray to be delivered from. With what affection does he recommend himself to them upon this head? *Now I beseech you, brethren, for the Lord Jesus Christ's sake, and for the love of the Spirit, that ye strive together with me in your prayers to*
God

SERM. 37. *God for me, that I may be delivered from them that do not believe in Judea.*

He that looks into a world that is unseen, and depends upon a world that is future, has much such a life as Noah had, by which he became an Heb. xi. 7. *heir of the righteousness that is by faith, and condemned the world.* They laughed at his preparing the ark, he was in vain *a preacher of righteousness* among them; and the dispute between them held till the flood came and decided it. Nay, as Enoch walked with God by faith, he was the jest of those whom he lived amongst; and therefore from him we have a prophecy concerning Christ, and the vengeance he will take on unbelievers at the last day. It is above five thousand years since he foretold the scornful usage that ministers of the Gospel Jude 14, should have; for *he prophecied of these, saying,* 15. *Behold, the Lord comes with ten thousands of his saints to execute judgment upon all, and to convince all that are ungodly among them, i.e.* in their communions, *of their ungodly deeds which they have committed, and of the hard speeches which they have spoken against him.*

Now when there is such a run against revealed religion, it must be the mighty power of God that makes a Christian resolved not to be laughed 1 Pet. ii. 4. or threatened out of it. Here is *a stone disal-* 7. 8. *lowed indeed of men, but chosen of God, and precious, and to them that believe, he is precious; though others stumble at the word, being disobedient.* That is no right faith that does not conquer repu- John v. 44. tation, and over-rule what may be said for it. *How can ye believe,* saith Christ, *who receive honour from one another, and neglect the honour that comes from God only?* It is too often that popularity steps in between us and our duty; hence we are told, that Rom. x. 9. thou must not only *believe in thine heart the Lord Jesus, but confess* WITH THY MOUTH *that God raised him from the dead.* It was here that the argument

gument stuck with many of the Jews and Phari- | SERM. 37.
sees, of whom we are told, that *they believed in* | John xii.
him, but did not CONFESS *him, lest they should be put* | 42, 43.
out of the synagogue; for they loved the praise of men
more than the praise of God. The faith of Moses
was just the reverse to what is said of these men,
that *he esteemed the reproach of Christ*, that is, the | Heb. xi. 26.
reproach that he endured for him, *to be greater*
riches than all the treasures of Egypt, for he had
respect to the recompence of reward. He that is
for present pay, and cannot trust a promise, is not
fit to deal with our God in his covenant.

Nay, the THINGS of this world are enemies to
our faith; *riches enter in and choak the word;* and
therefore they that are rich in this world are
charged with a particular caution, *not to trust in* | 1 Tim. vi.
uncertain riches, but in the living God: as if their | 17.
trust could not be in both; if it is in riches, it is
not in the living God. The faith that is right
gives us a victory over the present world; *we shall*
sell as though we sold not, and buy as though we | 1 Cor. vii.
possessed not, and use these things as not abusing | 30, 31.
them. And is not this a mystery that there should
be such a person as a believer upon earth? One,
who *though he walks in the flesh, does not war af-* | 2 Cor. x, 3.
ter the flesh? whose body is upon earth, and his
conversation in heaven? because his heart is upon | Phil. iii. 20.
things above, *where Jesus sits at the right hand of* | Col. iii. 1.
God. Ye are of God, little children, and have over- | 1 John iv.
come them; for greater is he that is in you, than he | 4, 5, 6.
that is in the world: They are of the world, there-
fore speak they of the world, and the world hears
them. We are of God; he that knows God, hears
us; he that knows not God, hears not us: Hereby
know we the Spirit of truth, and the spirit of error.

(6.) It is farther strange that he is believed on
in a world that is under the power of his most
obstinate enemy. The influence of the evil spirit
is declared in the very pride that denies it. There
are

SERM. 37. are no greater examples of this truth than among
Eph. ii. 2. those who have it in contempt. He is *the prince of the power of the air, the spirit that now works in the children of disobedience.* From the fulness of his command, and the efficacy of his tempta-
2 Cor. iv. 4. tions, he is called *the god of this world;* as such, he *blinds the eyes of them that believe not, lest the light of the glorious Gospel of Christ, who is the image of God, should shine into their hearts.* He
Jam. ii. 19. himself *believes and trembles,* and if sinners believed, they would tremble too; therefore, on purpose to hinder *a godly sorrow that works repentance,* he keeps them as stupid as he can.

Nor can I account for the opposition that is made to the Gospel any other way. Where is the temptation for men to be angry that their Saviour is their God, that his death is their atonement, that his grace is their fund, and his righteousness their plea? If these are errors, they are very delightful ones. I am sure they lay things out for our hope, and yet men are enraged that their Redeemer is so great, their happiness so good, and the covenant so certain. What can this be owing to, but as the
Jam. iii. 6. Apostle saith, that they are *set on fire of hell?* When a man strives to believe against himself, takes pains not to be settled on his lees, but to be unsettled, and not to know what he shall trust to, it is an unnatural way of sinning. Well might
Prov. viii. 36. our Saviour say, *He that sins against me, wrongs his own soul; all they that hate me love death.* Now believing gives us a victory over him who leads so many thousands captive at his pleasure. He loseth a soul, when that soul gets a right faith: there is one of the strongest creatures baffled, and one of the craftiest outwitted.

(7.) It is strange that people should believe on Christ in a world when nothing is to be got by it. I do not affirm this in the strict sense of the words,
1 Tim. iv. 8. for you know *godliness has the promise of all things;*
but

but my meaning is, that the soul, in the recumbence of his faith upon Christ Jesus, looks above all riches, honours, and every endearment of life. A life that is carried on by faith in the Son of God, is a life that is *hidden*, obscured and reserved. It is not looking at things that are seen, but *at those that are not seen; for the things that are seen are temporal, but the things that are not seen are eternal.* And how great must that principle be, that foils the senses in their own kingdom? that takes off the soul from them when they have all their arguments about them? *We that are in this tabernacle do groan, being burdened; not for that we would be unclothed, but that mortality might be swallowed up of life.*

_{SERM. 37.}

2 Cor. iv. 18.

2 Cor. v. 4.

SERMON XXXVIII.

Oct. 11. 1719.

IV. I AM now to shew, that for the world to believe in Christ Jesus as GOD who was manifest in the flesh, is a means of promoting that Religion that ever was and ever will be the ornament of any profession. It is a Mystery of GODLINESS. There is no necessity of opposing revelation to duty, as if they who preached up one were careless about the other. They are joined together: *Your faith groweth exceedingly, and the charity of every one of you all towards each other aboundeth.* We have no dry speculations, nor any doctrine which is not *according to godliness*. The believer has not received and admired a set of unmoving opinions, but the grace of God that brings salvation

2 Thes. i. 3.

tion

SERM. 38. tion has taught him to *deny ungodliness and worldly*
Tit. ii. 12. *lusts, and to live soberly, righteously, and godly, in*
―― 10. *this present world.* You are to *adorn the doctrine of God your Saviour in all things*, by filling up every relation.

Nor are there any better examples of those works that are *good and profitable to men*, than among
1 Thef. i. 6, them that *believe in Christ Jesus. Ye became fol-*
7, 8. *lowers of us, and of the Lord, having received the word in much affliction, with joy of the Holy Ghost: So that ye were examples to all that believe in Ma-cedonia and Achaia; for from you sounded out the word of the Lord, not only in Macedonia and Achaia, but in every place your faith to Godward is spread abroad.*

This will appear if you do but confider with impartial thoughts, what the great business of religion is, and to what purposes it is both recommended as a practice, and promised as a blessing. I take it to consist in these four things: 1*st*, A *sub-jection* to Christ's authority, and a *conformity* to his image; this may be called inward religion, and thus I shall consider it in the principle. 2*dly*, There arises from this a duty both to God and man, which is commanded in the two tables of the moral law. 3*dly*, It is a branch of this religion to make a *profession* of Christ, to own him in the world, and shew forth his praises. 4*thly*, The *joys* and satisfaction that Christ gives to his people who thus wait upon him, may come into the general notion that we have of *godliness*. Now all these are begun, advanced and extended by the belief of those mysteries that we meet with in the faith, and in particular that he is a GOD who was *manifest in the flesh.*

1. You will see how the doctrine of incarnation is a Mystery of Godliness, if you do but consider that it is thus we come by our principle of subjection to Christ's authority, and conformity to his image.

image. He has made us for his *service*, and be- SERM. 3⁹.
lieving in him is obeying him. He has also made
us for his *delight*, and thus believing in him is
growing like unto him. We have both these notions of holiness conveyed to us in Scripture. He
is equally the Sovereign and the Original of every
good man. *Whom God foreknew, them did he pre-* Rom. viii.
destinate to be conformed to the image of his Son, 29.
that he might be the first-born among many brethren.
Now each of these supposes your receiving him *as*
God; for without this there is no duty to his empire, and there can be no resemblance of his purity.

(1.) It is as he is *God* that we believe in him to
all the purposes of subjection and duty. The Gospel is *made known for the obedience of faith;* the —xvi. 26.
obedience that flows from faith as a consequence,
and is included in it as a property; for the very
act of believing is a homage to his sovereignty,
who gave us the revelation. It is our allegiance
to his truth, that we depend upon his word, and
surrender every thought that would make an opposition to his command and pardon. That we
are to have this regard of him in our approaches
to him is plain, owning him as *Lord of all;* and
therefore *the weapons of our warfare that are
mighty through God*, through his appointment and
his blessing, are *to pull down strong holds*, to this
purpose. *In casting down imaginations, and every* 2 Cor. x. 5.
*high thing that exalteth itself against the knowledge
of God, and bringing every thought in obedience to
Christ.*

Here you may observe a divine appointment of
the ministry, we do *not war after the flesh.* Here
is also that which renders it effectual, it is *mighty
through God.* And can we suppose that all this
while God is working for a creature? that he
sends out his great power in the preaching of the
Gospel to advance any less than himself: No, it is
not to be imagined; and therefore those *high things*

SERM. 38. that exalt themselves against the knowlege of God, must be brought into captivity to the obedience of *Christ*. The knowledge of *God*, and the obedience of *Christ*, are the same thing; it is but one opposition that is offered to them both, and the moment that a person is cured of his ignorance and pride, he comes into a state of duty; so that you see an obedience to *Christ* is the great end of our ministry, the thing for which we preach, and which is carried on with a divine blessing.

Rom. xi. 36. And again, He that is the efficient is also the final cause of our salvation. As *of him*, and *through him*, so *to him* are all things. But if Christ is not God, we may say, here is an almighty power inspiring the word, merely for the sake of a creature. And what an unaccountable imagination must it give us, to think that God alone is the great end of every other work, all things are done that he may be glorified, but that Christ is to be the principal gainer in the chief design? If the graces of the Holy Spirit are given to fill you with a reverence to the Mediator, to make him the object of your fear, and love, and hope, and to throw you into a state of communion with him, you must either conclude that he is a God, or that religion makes you exceed in your apprehensions of him.

Pl. xlv. 11. *He is thy Lord*, saith David to the Church, *and worship thou him*; and as the sceptre of his kingdom is a right sceptre, he is the God whose *throne is for ever and ever*.

(2.) It is only from a sense of his Deity that our believing in him can give us a conformity to him. Good men have no other author than God, unless you will suppose that the new life is not so well made as the old one, and that grace is of a lower original than nature. At first God made man in his own image, and after his own likeness; and when he is created anew in Christ Jesus, is it after one who is not divine? Shall the better life be af-

ter

ter the model of a creature, whilst the lower and worse is taken from the Deity itself? for *the new man is renewed in holiness after the image of him that created him.* {SERM. 38. Col. iii. 10.}

Consider this transform upon the believers both ways, either in its principle, as it is infused and implanted in him, or in its progress, as it is carried on by acts of faith; the author of the former, and the object of the latter, can be no other than God. Now, we are said to be made holy by Christ Jesus in each of these respects. You find them in one verse, *Both he that sanctifies, and they that are sanctified, are both of one, and therefore he is not ashamed to call them brethren.* {Heb. ii. 11.} It is plain this is not said of the Father, but of Him who was made *perfect from his sufferings;* and we here read of this Person as one that *sanctifies:* he is the author of all that purity that his people receive. Their religion is given, as well as conducted by him. This cannot be affirmed of him as a man; for though in that respect he is a noble *example* of sanctification, yet he cannot be the author of it. As a man, he is of the same original with believers; they are *both of one,* and therefore he is not ashamed to call them brethren. This supposes him to be sanctified himself; but as a sanctifier, he cannot be said to call them brethren. They are his creation, the work of his hands, the effect of his holiness and love.

And he cannot be conceived of as doing this for them, unless he is God; the Sanctifier must be the Creator: *He that has wrought us for the self-same thing, is God,* and he can be no other. David begs for it under a proper title, and from a proper hand: *Create in me a clean heart, O God. I will sprinkle clean water upon you, and you shall be clean,* {Pf. li. 10. Ezek. xxxvi. 25.} saith he in the Old Testament. *It is God that works in us both to will and to do,* saith the Apostle in the New. *Of his own will has he begotten us* {Phil. ii. 13. Jam. i. 18.}

again

SERM. 38. *again by the word of truth, that we might be the first-fruits unto his creatures.* Can we think, after so many claims of the Divine Nature to the work of sanctification, that it should ever be attributed to a creature? Must it be said of one who is not God, that it is *He who sanctifies?* Is he not only the object, but the author of your faith? Well, if he has made you believers, as he certainly has, then there is in you the exceeding greatness of an *Almighty power;* no less than that which raised himself from the dead, and set him on the right hand of the Majesty on high.

And besides, how can any act of faith produce such a turn within us, that whilst we see him, we are *changed from glory to glory by the Spirit of the Lord,* unless the object on which it fixes be God? We are *to the praise of his glory, who have trusted in Christ, after we have heard the word of truth, the Gospel of our salvation; in whom, after we have believed, we are sealed with the Holy Spirit of promise.* The resembling virtue is not in the principle, but in the object. We see a thousand things and believe them, that do not make us like themselves: and how comes it to pass, that when we see Christ as he is, *we shall be like him,* but only that he has a power of creation in himself? To this purpose he is proposed to our faith. For this end we are to believe *in him;* not only believe him, that he is the Messiah, the Person appointed by God to treat with men, but we believe *in him*, that *by him* we may have the life begun, *in him* we may have it continued, and *with him* we may have it perfected.

2 Cor. iii. 18.

Eph. i. 11, 13.

It is a very poor and low notion of Christianity, to think that it requires no more than an assent that Christ is the Messiah, the anointed of God, and that they that thus believe shall be saved; as if it was enough, that a man's sentiments kept him from being either a Jew or a Mahometan. I dare say

say *the devils believe* in this sense, and they *tremble* SERM. 38.
at it. But if we are to talk of faith as the Scrip- Jam. ii. 19.
ture does, we must make a great deal more of it.
It is a principle that does not only pay an homage,
but draw a life and virtue from him with whom it
corresponds; and such a one can be no less than
God. *In him was life, and that life was the light* John i. 4.
of men, is an expression that imports a Deity, as
full as any words can do: *The life was manifest,* 1 Joh. i. 2.
*and we have seen it, and bear witness, and shew to
you the eternal life that was with the Father, and
was manifested unto us.*

But now, if people do not look upon him as
God, who is thus believed on in the world, as I do
not see how they can pay a proper veneration to
him, so there is no resemblance that they can desire to have of him. It is in vain to hope that
looking to him will make you like him, unless
there is a creating virtue either in the act or the
object. Either faith itself must have the power of
changing you, or it must be in Him whom you thus
contemplate. *He will at last change your vile bodies,* Phil. iii. 21.
like unto his glorious body; and for that he must
have *a power that subdues all things to himself.* And
does he speak of any less when he tells Paul, *That* Acts xxvi.
He will open their eyes, and turn them from dark- 18.
*ness to light, and from the power of Satan to God,
that they may receive forgiveness of sins, and an inheritance among them who are sanctified by the faith
that is in him?* Their sanctification is begun by
him in opening their eyes, and it is always considered in him. This then is the first account that
you may take of godliness, that it is a principle of
subjection and conformity to Christ; and it could
not be either of these, if he was not God.

2. This godliness does also take into it the duty
that we have so good a rule for in the word of
God. He that has this esteem for Christ, and this
resemblance of him, *must himself walk as he also
walked.*

94 *The Mystery of* GODLINESS,

SERM. 38. *walked.* He that believes in Chriſt muſt be careful to maintain good works, which are good and profit-
Tit. iii. 8. able *to men. This is a faithful ſaying ; and theſe things I will,* faith the Apoſtle, *that thou affirm conſtantly.* What I now mean takes into it the whole
Acts xxiv. 16. compaſs of duty. Herein are we to *exerciſe ourſelves, to have* always *a conſcience void of offence towards God and man.* But I do not ſee how either we are capable of regarding Chriſt in ſuch an authority as to obey him, or be thus uſeful to others upon that ground, if we do not believe his Deity.

(1.) Without this there muſt be an end of all our duty to him. As a Prophet he might declare it; but if he is not God, it is wrong for him to receive it. It involves *him* in the guilt of uſurpa-
Iſa. xxxiii. 22. tion, and *us* in the danger of idolatry. *The Lord is our Judge, the Lord is our Law-giver, the Lord is our King, and he will ſave us,* was the free profeſſion of the Church in the Old Teſtament; and I can never be of opinion that we ought to talk
Jam. iv. 12. any lower language in the New: *There is but one*
Iſa. xxvi. *law-giver, who is able to ſave and to deſtroy.* Lord,
12, 13. ſay they, *thou wilt ordain peace for us, for thou haſt wrought all our works in us. O Lord our God, other lords beſides thee have had dominion over us, but by thee only will we make mention of thy name.* Are not theſe declarations too great a tribute for any creature? and yet in an equal ſtrain are we taught by the New Teſtament, to ſpeak both *of* Chriſt, and *to* him. He will ordain peace for us, in him we muſt have *peace.* He has wrought our works in us,
John xvii. 23. every branch in him *bears fruit: I in them,* faith he to the Father, *and thou in me. We name the name of Chriſt,* we are called by it, we look upon him as *Lord of all.* It is he that has ordained a religion for the world, and having all power both
Mat. xxviii. 20. in heaven and earth, has appointed us to *teach all things that he hath commanded.*

(2.) That

(2.) That part of duty which has a regard to others supposes that he by whose authority we do it can be no less than God. Thus saith the Apostle, *We preach not ourselves, but Christ Jesus the Lord, and ourselves your servants for Jesus' sake.* He was ready to be spent among them; but the end of all this was for advancing the glory of a Redeemer. And can we think he intends any lower Person in that sentence than Nehemiah did, who professes that he durst not act as other rulers had done, *because of the fear of God?* Was he under an awe from his Maker? and has a Christian all his motive and restraint from a creature?

SERM. 38.

2 Cor. iv. 5.

Neh. v. 15.

Servants are directed to keep up the duty of their relation with a decency that will recommend a good profession, that they may *adorn the doctrine of* God *our Saviour in all things*. What God and Saviour is this who claims a propriety in the doctrine they are to adorn? It is easy to see he understands it of a doctrine peculiar to Christians. They lived among those of *a contrary part*, as you read a few verses before. There were among them *unruly and vain talkers and deceivers, especially they of the circumcision, who subverted whole houses, teaching things that they ought not, for filthy lucre's sake.* They are bid *not to give heed to Jewish fables, and commandments of men.* This opposition was all against the Christian doctrine. The Jews were no enemies to the revelation of the Old Testament. But besides, he speaks of a word *manifested in due time, through preaching committed to him according to the commandment of God our Saviour*. This is the title under which he declares him; for he has made us sufficiently acquainted what this commandment of God our Saviour was, by telling us that the Gospel he preached was *not taught of man, but by the revelation of Jesus Christ.* This is the doctrine of God our Saviour, which servants are to adorn in all things.

Tit. ii. 10.

chap. i. 10, 11.

14.

And

And we may carry the same interpretation through the next words, *that the grace of God* (of this God who was manifest in the flesh) *that brings salvation, has appeared unto all men,* and *in looking for the blessed hope,* we also expect *the glorious appearing of the* GREAT GOD *and our Saviour Jesus Christ;* or, as the words may be read, of our Great God and Saviour Jesus Christ. This agrees to the directions he gives about relative duties in other places: *Servants be obedient to them that are your masters according to the flesh, with fear and trembling, in singleness of heart, as unto* CHRIST: *Not with eye-service, as men-pleasers, but as the servants of* CHRIST, *doing the will of* GOD *from the heart; with good will doing service as to the* LORD, *and not to men: Knowing that whatsoever good thing any man does, the same shall he receive of the* LORD, *whether he be bond or free.* So we read, that *one is our Master, even* CHRIST.

Eph. vi. 5, 6, 7, 8.

Mat. xxiii. 10.

3. This godliness demands from us a *profession* of what we believe. There must be *an acknowledgment of the truth which is after godliness.* Christ tells Ananias concerning Saul. *He is a chosen vessel to* ME, *to bear* MY *name before the Gentiles, and kings, and the children of Israel.* Our light is to shine before men; we are every way to *hold forth the word of life, and shew the praises of him that hath called us.* And I do not see there is any doing this, unless we are persuaded of his Divinity, because it is thus we come first to a *certainty*, and then to a *confidence* in our profession.

Tit. i. 1.

Acts ix. 15.

Phil. ii. 15.
1 Pet. ii. 9.

(1.) In believing Christ to be God, we act upon a certainty: we tell mankind in plain words what our souls think of him, and do not go about with a company of uncertain sounds: *Seeing we have such hope we use great plainness of speech.* *He that hath a dream let him tell a dream; but he that hath my word let him speak my word faithfully. What is the chaff to the wheat, saith the Lord?* It is not

2 Cor. iii. 12.

Jer. xxiii. 28.

to

to be thought that Chrift, who fealed the doctrine of the Gofpel with his blood, and fent it abroad with fuch an effufion of his Spirit, ever defigned that preachers fhould cover their opinions with fcandalous ambiguities: *Having this miniftry, we renounce the hidden things of difhonefty, not walking in craftinefs, nor handling the word of the Lord deceitfully.* [SERM. 38.] [1 Cor. iv. 2.]

A notion that will not endure plain language, is a notion that cannot bear the light, and fitter for *wizards that peep and mutter*, than the fervants of the God of truth. When he bids us *blow the trumpet in Zion, and found an alarm in his holy mountain*, he did not mean a broken trumpet, that gives out a double or a confused and a grating found. There is no taking the note; for, as you find by the argument, *even things without life giving found, whether pipe or harp, except they give a diftinction in the founds, how fhall it be known what is piped or harped? So likewife you, except ye utter by the tongue words eafy to be underftood, how fhall it be known what is fpoken, for ye fhall fpeak into the air? If I know not the meaning of the voice, I fhall be to him that fpeaks a Barbarian, and he that fpeaks fhall be a Barbarian to me.* [1 Cor. xiv. 7, 8, 9. 11.]

In faying Chrift is *the mighty God, the everlafting Father*, you know the meaning of the words: in faying that *his goings forth are of old from everlafting*, that *he is the fame yefterday, to-day, and for ever*, that *of his kingdom there fhall be no end*, that *all things were made by him, and without him was not any thing made that was made;* thefe are open and undifguifed expreffions: whatever difficulty there is in the doctrine, there is none in the words. We refer you for arguments to plain Scripture. We fay not thefe things as men, but the Gofpel faith the fame alfo; and we cannot fuppofe that God fpeaks unintelligibly in matters of the greateft concern to our faith and practice. [Ifa. ix. 6.] [Mic. v. 2.] [Luke i. 33.] [John i. 3.]

SERM. 38. But it is making the whole revelation in vain, to give the expressions such a sense when they are used of Christ, as would be harsh and improper if applied to any other occasion. It is easy to see, that God speaks of himself as he does of no one else. Nothing can be plainer, than that though divine titles are given to Angels and men, there is no danger of confounding them with him, or supposing that the name God signifies *that* in the one, that it does in the other. But if the account he gives us of Christ is to be understood with such limitations, it is pity that he has not been a great deal more distinct, and let us see that though the *words* he uses for himself and our Saviour are exactly the same, yet the *sense* is so widely different, especially when he has said, *I am the Lord or Jehovah; that is my name, and my glory will I not give to another*.

Isa. xlii. 8.

It is unhappy that we read of him as the *mighty God*, who is not self-sufficient, or, as they rather choose to rumble it out, not self-originated. We are confounded in these words, that *he is before all things, in the beginning with God, and from everlasting*. Such characters of the Father are always understood of a proper eternity; but when applied to the Son, they lose their meaning, and signify not the thousandth part so much as they used to do; but instead of being an instruction to lead our faith, become great swelling words of vanity to confound it.

So again, we are apt to think when we read that *in the beginning God created the heavens and the earth*, that it means no more than another sentence, *All things were made by him, and without him was not any thing made that was made:* or, that *by him all things consist;* that *he has laid the foundations of the earth, and the heavens are the work of his hands*. This is talking plainly, and tells the world what we have received; that the same things are said

Gen. i. 1.
John i. 3.
Col. i. 17.
Heb. i. 10.

with

with equal force of words of the Father and the Son; and, according to our *good Confession*, they are the same in substance, equal in power and glory.

But if creation signifies in some of these scriptures what is peculiar to the Deity, and in others what may be done by a creature, our faith is entangled by the very book that should set it at liberty; and we must look upon Revelation as that which our God would not have to be understood, whereas *he has not spoke in secret, or a dark place of the earth*. ^{Isa. xlv. 19.}

Our preaching and your profession are neither of them such frivolous uncertain things. We are bid in *doctrine to shew uncorruptness, gravity, sincerity, sound speech that cannot be condemned*. Certainly he does not mean speech that cannot be understood. We are not to talk of a dependent God, of an eternity that had a beginning, of an Omnipotence that is derived, of a subordinate Creator, of a Person that has all the titles of Divinity, and not one of them just and proper. You who are bid to *give a reason for the hope that is in you*, are not left to any of these shuffling ways. Mankind are to know what you would be at: error needs a disguise, but truth will not bear it. You are neither to *run*, nor to talk *uncertainly*, and we are neither to fight nor to preach as those that beat the air, who make a noise and a brushing, but no mortal knows what they strike at.

Let us speak the mystery of Christ boldly, and not persuade people by deceitful words one day to believe that we are with them, and after that explain it all away again. These two arts are as dishonourable to human nature, as they are to the Gospel of Christ: confessions that hide the truth, and explications that darken the sense. But though error will always have the wriggle of its author, who is a winding crooked serpent, yet blessed be God,

God, truth will be *a shining light that shines more unto a perfect day.*

If Christ is not God, the case is clear, we ought not to call him so, or do any thing to delude people into a persuasion that we think so. If he is God, we may speak it out without any drain to the expression, and let mankind see that we are not leading them to mean more by what we say, than we do ourselves. But *the words of the Lord,* those that relate to himself, must have a *free course,* unclogged, unlimited, and so be *glorified.* It is by this honest profession that we shall stand our ground: *Our exhortation is not of uncleanness, nor of deceit, nor of guile; but as we are allowed of God to be put in trust with the Gospel, even so we speak, not as pleasing men, but God that searches the hearts.*

1 Thes. ii. 3, 4.

(2.) This gives us a confidence in our profession, we take it to be a duty, according to that rule, *Watch ye, stand fast in the faith, quit yourselves like men, be strong.* A faith that is not to be declared belongs neither to the Old Testament nor the New. As the Apostle saith, *We having the same spirit of faith, according as it is written, I have believed, and therefore have I spoken; we also believe, and therefore speak.* This was his way of arguing, as it had been David's before him, that they who do believe it are to speak it. But ' what a spirit of faith is
' that, which is bold for concealment, and makes
' a stand against professing, and turns the reason-
' ing quite otherwise; we believe, and therefore
' we will *not speak;* that reproaches a good con-
' fession, and calls it by all the odious names that
' are given to the vilest actions in the world?
' May it not be said upon a comparison between
' these examples of the Bible, and those of later
' ages, David I know, and Paul I know; *their*
' *believing led them into a necessity of speaking,*
' *but*

1 Cor. xvi. 13.

2 Cor. iv. 13.

'but who are *these* dumb believers that muzzle <small>SERM. 38.</small>
'their faith with a pretence of charity?'

There is such a thing as being ashamed of God's words before an adulterous and sinful generation. In opposition to which, our Saviour has made a noble promise to those that *confess him before men:* Such as these will *the Son of man confess when he comes in the glory of his Father.* He has a particular regard to them now, *Because thou hast kept* <small>Rev. iii. 10.</small> *the word of my patience, I also will keep thee from the hour of temptation that is coming upon the world to try all them that are upon the earth.* They that have *sought righteousness and meekness, shall be hid* <small>Zeph. ii. 2, Ch. iii. 11. 13.</small> *in the day of the Lord's anger:* when such as rejoice in their pride, and are haughty because of God's holy mountain, are taken away from the midst of us: *the remnant of Israel who do not tell lies, nor suffer a deceitful tongue to be found in their mouths, shall lie down, and have none to make them afraid.* But this is little in comparison of the great reserves in another world; *for he shall come to be glorified in* <small>2 Thes. i. 10.</small> *his saints, and admired in them that believe,* because, saith the Apostle, *our testimony among you was believed in that day.* Then will the name of our Lord Jesus Christ be glorified in you, (that name which you have confessed before men), and ye shall be glorified in him.

SERMON XXXIX. <small>Oct. 25. 1719.</small>

4. UNDER this name of Godliness we may include what is peculiar to it; I mean, the joys and satisfaction that Christ gives to his own people.

people. These are sometimes called *a hope in God*, sometimes *a rejoicing in Christ Jesus*, and sometimes *a comfort in the Holy Ghost*. They are mentioned under several names quite through the Scriptures, to convince us of these two things, *first*, That there is a delightful part in religion; and *secondly*, That this is of such a nature, that it cannot be the experience of any but a good man. *He is satisfied from himself*; Christ puts it upon faith in him, that *if a person believes, out of his belly shall flow rivers of living water*.

Now, you will soon perceive that faith in the great mystery of godliness (God manifest in the flesh) is the way to these consolations; and to that purpose I need remind you of no more than that it is *He who pardons your iniquities*. The peace that I speak of is the fruit of your acceptance, *Being justified freely by his grace, we have peace with God through our Lord Jesus Christ*. Again, it is He who gives you a security of the great things that are laid up for those that love him. You are glad of the change that is begun in a reconciliation to God *through the death of his Son*. And these joys are drawn out and swelled up from the prospect of another change, when you shall be *saved through his life*; that is, as he himself has called it, *saved to the uttermost*. These are what the Apostle brings together within our thoughts, that *we have access by faith into the grace wherein we stand, and then rejoice in hope of the glory of God*.

Now, as it is our faith that tells us of a pardon here, and assures an arrival at heaven hereafter, and for that fixes upon Christ Jesus, so it must regard him in his Deity. Without such a consideration of Him there can be none of this peace, and joy, and hope in believing, as you will see in the two particulars I have now mentioned: 1*st*. It is as God that he forgives our iniquities; 2*dly*, As a God he takes us into his glory, and therefore the satisfaction that arises from a sense of the former, and a hope of the latter, supposes our belief of his Deity. {SERM. 39.}

(1.) One reason of our rejoicing in Christ Jesus is, because he pardons our sins. The Scripture has given us this truth in several views: *first*, Christ as a Mediator places himself between God and man. He was *the days-man between us, and laid his hand upon us both; he is our peace.* {Job ix. 33.} *Secondly*, Christ as man, made of a woman, and made under the law, became a curse for us. {Eph. ii. 14.} In the former character, he *procured* our pardon; in the latter, he *deserved* it: *He made peace through the blood of his cross.* {Col. i. 20.} *Thirdly*, He may also be said to *give* it, as we often find he does. Now, where he speaks in that language, he appears to be no less than the great God. Laying down the price of our pardon, gives him no right to *bestow* it; that belongs to him who *receives* the satisfaction, not to him that *makes* it. Our debt was to the Divine Nature, and our discharge must be from it. The human nature could suffer, but it could not forgive; and therefore he does this, not in the form of a servant, but as one who *thought it no robbery to be equal with God.* {Phil. ii. 6.} In order to present this argument in a proper light, I will do these two things: *first*, Shew you that he who is believed on in the world, does and can forgive our iniquities; and, *secondly*, That this is altogether the prerogative of a God.

[1.] It is plain from the whole story of our blessed Saviour, that he *pardons iniquity, transgression, and sin*. There are several passages both in the Old and New Testament, which tell us that the God who went before the Israelites from Egypt to Canaan, was he who should afterwards be manifest in the flesh. Both Jews and Christians understand it of a Redeemer, the second of those three that bear record

SERM. 39.
Heb. xi. 26.
1 Cor. x. 9.
Isa. lxiii. 1, 2, 3. 9.

record in heaven. Moses suffered the *reproach of Christ;* they who died in the wilderness *tempted Christ.* He that came from Edom *with his dyed garments from Bozrah, glorious in his apparel, and travelling in the greatness of his strength,* is one who has *trodden the wine-press alone: in all their affliction he was afflicted.* That passage, of Moses's seeing God, is better applied to One who was to be incarnate, than to the Father, *whom no man has seen at any time.* When he proclaimed the name of the Lord, and made his goodness to pass before him, it was in these terms: *The Lord God, merciful and gracious, long-suffering, and abundant in goodness and truth, forgiving iniquity, transgression and sin.* And when after this, we read of the Angels going before them, it is added, *He will not pardon your iniquities, for my name is in him.* The expression signifies a power that he has in himself of condemning or absolving.

Exod. xxxiv. 6, 7.

Jam. iv. 12.
Num. xiv. 14.
ver. 17, 18, 19, 20, 21.

Now there is but *one law-giver who is able to save and to destroy.* Moses says to him, *Thou Lord art seen of us face to face,* and prays, *I beseech thee, let the power of my Lord be great, according as thou hast spoken, saying, The Lord is long-suffering and of great mercy, forgiving iniquity, and transgression. Pardon I beseech thee, the iniquity of this people, according to the greatness of thy mercy; and as thou hast forgiven this people from Egypt until now. And the Lord said, I have pardoned according to thy word, but as truly as I live, all the earth shall be filled with the glory of the Lord.*

Isa. ix. 6.

Thus it was foretold, that one of his names whereby he should be called, was *the Prince of peace;* and that this did not only signify that he should proclaim it as a minister, and procure it as a sacrifice, but give it as a proprietor, is evident from the situation of that title. It stands upon a level with the other four, *Wonderful, Counsellor, the mighty God, the everlasting Father.* To these

is added a fifth, that he is *the Prince of peace. Of* SERM. 39.
the increase of his government and peace there shall
be no end; so that our peace comes from him as a
Governor. *Dominion and fear are with him, he* Job xxv. 2.
maketh peace in his high places.

He was *born King of the Jews*, as the wise men Mat. ii. 2.
were taught to say by the star that appeared to
them in their own country. And how did he
open his empire? Not in the gross way that his
own nation expected, but by *giving salvation to his* Luke i. 77.
people in the remission of their sins. His greatness
appeared in doing away iniquity. *He finished*
transgression, and made an end of sin in a twofold
capacity, *first*, As one who had a power to do it;
and, *secondly*, As one that had the merit to claim
it. Messiah is called *the Prince*, though he was to Dan. ix. 25,
be *cut off*. 26.

Antecedent to his suffering of death, by which
he brought in an everlasting righteousness, he used
to join those two things together which David admires in the Most High God: *It is he who forgives* Psal. ciii. 3.
thine iniquities and heals thy diseases; and thus in
a double sense *redeems thy life from destruction.*
How common was it for him to say, Son or
daughter be of good chear, *thy sins are forgiven*
thee? And again, *Go thy way, thy faith has made*
thee whole.

Do but consider, that in such language he must
design a great deal more than to work a miracle.
All that was *visible* to the world, and upon which
he was to raise the reputation of a Messiah, was
doing a wonder. If they saw that the sick were
cured in this extraordinary way, it was enough to
establish the argument, that *a great Prophet was*
come among them, and God had visited his people.
But he speaks of things which they *could not see*,
and to which the miracles that he wrought were
to carry on their meditations, a pardon of sins to

Vol. II.   O   the

the recovered person as what his faith had depended on.

The prophets that performed several wonders never talked of either of these. As for instance, Elisha did not insist upon *faith* in Naaman the Syrian, but the cure was wrought whilst the patient was an unbeliever. It is quite otherwise in the story of Christ Jesus. He used very often to ask the question of those that came to him, *Believe ye that I am able?* And in some places *he did not many mighty works, because of their unbelief.* Thus he said to the man whose prayer was wavering, *if thou canst do any thing for us, help us; If thou canst believe, all things are possible to him that believes.*

So that, you see, it was not enough that they were to be convinced of his having a Divine commission, but there must be a faith *in himself.* This lay secret to the eyes of the world, but he that knew the heart, gave testimony to it, sometimes in these words, *Thy faith has saved thee;* sometimes, *According to your faith be it unto you.* He shewed himself more than the Sovereign of nature, one who could discharge the miseries of poor creatures; he does at the same time take upon him a much greater character, as the Lord of grace; and from the fulness of the Godhead, that dwelt in him bodily, he says to them that their sins are forgiven.

To his own practice he has formed the ministry of his servants. They are to *preach the Gospel of repentance for the remission of sins. Repentance and remission of sins were to be preached among all nations in his name.* He tells Saul, that the success of the Gospel should be *the turning people from darkness to light, and from the power of Satan to God, that they might receive forgiveness of sins, and an inheritance among them who are sanctified by faith that is in him:* as if he would set his mark upon faith, he does not think it enough to say, *faith in me,* but *the faith that is in* ME, because there it
is

is to fix; and if it does so, I must tell you, it re- *gards him as more than a Mediator; for under that notion it is* BY *him that we believe in God, who raised him from the dead, and gave him glory, that our faith and hope may be in God.* But by the faith that is IN him we have the forgiveness of our sins, and an inheritance among all them that are sanctified. We do not only believe that he died for us, that forgiveness comes by him, by him as a procurer, and by him as a price, but it is *in him,* as the original disposer. Thus the Apostles preached and acted. *In the name of Jesus Christ of Nazareth,* saith Peter to the lame man, *rise up and walk.* And he is also *a Prince and a Saviour, to give repentance and remission of sins.*

SERM. 39.

1 Pet. i. 21.

Acts iii. 6.

——v. 31.

2. I must observe to you, that this belongs to none but God. That though as man he *gave himself for our iniquities, and rose again for our justification,* that is, in order to deserve and procure the blessing, yet the giving it is a glory that the Most High will never transfer to another. *Who is a God like unto thee, that pardons our iniquity, and passes by the transgression of the remnant of thine heritage?* And when the promise runs so full and free, *Let the wicked forsake his way, and the unrighteous man his thought, and turn unto the Lord, and he will have mercy on him, and to our God who will abundantly pardon;* on purpose both to assure the believer and to glorify himself, he adds, *For my ways are not your ways, neither are your thoughts my thoughts, saith the Lord;* q. d. ' When I talk of ' abundant pardon, and of having mercy, it is the ' language of a God; I speak of that which crea-
' tures may admire, but can never imitate.' Thus saith he in another place, *I, even I am he that blots out your iniquities for my name's sake.* And the New Testament carries the matter as high: *Who shall lay any thing to the charge of God's elect? it is God that justifies;* and therefore it must be very assu-

Rom. iv. ult.

Mic. vii. 18.

Isa. lv. 7, 8.

——xliii. 25.

Rom. viii. 33.

ming

ming for any to speak in such a manner, as the Most High has made it peculiar to himself.

It gave the Jews great offence whenever they heard our Saviour pronounce those words, *Thy sins are forgiven thee.* People that were astonished at the miracle lost all the benefits of what they saw, by an opinion that the man spake blasphemies, *because none could forgive sins but God only.* Here was an opportunity for Christ to have shewn them that this was not peculiar to the Deity, that it might be communicated to a creature; and if he had meant no more than *declaring* them pardoned, there had been no room for the objection of the Pharisees. No doubt of it, they could remember what Nathan said to David, *The Lord has done away thy sin, thou shalt not die.* And had Christ said no more than that, though they might question his commission, they would never have charged him with blasphemy. Now what way does he take to answer the accusation? Not by contradicting their maxim, and the foundation they went upon, (that none could forgive sins but God only), no, he leaves them in possession of that sentiment, as what was true and very dutiful to the Divine Nature.

But he goes on to assert his own right of forgiving sins, in maintenance of what he had often said, that he and the Father were one, and that whatever the Father does, the same does the Son likewise. His argument deserves your attention, *That ye may know that the Son of man has power upon earth to forgive sins, he saith to the sick of the palsy, Arise.* This gift of healing never proved a power to forgive sins in any other. When Elisha recovered Naaman, and restored a dead man to life, he did not pretend to pardon either of them; and therefore how can our Saviour make the one an evidence of the other, but by taking upon him a character that no Prophet ever had? All their virtue

tue was in a commission, but his was his own. They might be directed to pronounce the sentence, but he had *power even upon earth to forgive sins,* and he appeals to a miracle as the argument of it. A miracle was to witness *that* in his case, which it never had done in any other.

[2.] It is as a God that we have any hope of glory from him. He saith, *They are my sheep, and I give to them eternal life.* Now we know that *the gift of God is eternal life;* and surely he would never have us expect from him the greatest bounty and evidence of the Deity if he was only a creature. *He that is our God, is the God of salvation;* and thus *the Author of eternal salvation to all that obey him.* He may well say, *All that the Father has is mine,* when he pretends to the disposal of our everlasting inheritance.

As Mediator we have this life for his sake, and by his means: *He leads us to the fountains of living waters;* but as God he *gives* them, and wipes away all tears from our eyes. There must be an infinite distance between *deserving* this eternal life, and *bestowing* it, dying for it, and presiding over it. Our dear Lord sustains both these characters, though the notion that some would give us of him, that he is the First-born of the creation, made greater, and better, and older than all the world, comes within neither of them; and that this super-angelical Spirit became the soul of that body which he received of the virgin.

In this representation he is neither low enough to be a sacrifice, nor high enough to be a Saviour. They have neither made him capable of suffering for the procurement of this life, nor of being glorious in bestowing it. For in order to dying, he must have all the infirmities of a man, a soul subject to terrors, as well as a body to pain; and in order to the giving of heaven, he must have *the fulness of him that fills all in all.* Do not err, my beloved

SERM. 39. beloved brethren, *every good gift, and every perfect gift comes down from the Father of lights, in whom there is no variableness or shadow of turning.* Therefore, whatever lower names he takes upon him to signify the reality of his humiliation, yet he always speaks up to the dignity of a God, when he mentions those things that are gifts of the Divine Nature:

Jude 24, 25. *He that is able to keep you from falling, and to present you faultless before the presence of his glory with exceeding joy, is the only wise God our Saviour.*

You must understand such an expression as Peter uses in a twofold construction, when he says to

Acts iii. 15. the Jews, *Ye have killed the Prince of life;* as man he was not the Prince of life, and as the Prince of life he could not be killed. They stumbled for want of distinguishing right, when he tells them,

Joh. xii. 32. *I, if I be lifted up, will draw all men to me.* They
34. knew not what to make of it: *We have heard out of the law that Christ abides for ever; how sayest thou then, the Son of man must be lifted up?* So that though they killed him, he had an eternal life within his empire, and what must ever be the matter of his donation. But by dying he appeared to be in all things like unto his brethren, and when he is called the Prince of life, it supposes *that* to be his property, which is the greatest and best argument that we can have of a God.

Do but examine into that peace which a believer has from Christ, without any regard to his Deity: Think that he is forgiven by one who is not the Sovereign, not the principally offended party.

Psal. li. 1, Whereas David prays, *Have mercy upon me, O God,*
2. 4. *according to thy loving kindness, according to the multitude of thy tender mercies, blot out my transgressions: For against thee, thee only have I sinned.* According to the modern notions, our remission comes from one who is no more than a servant. We cannot conclude from hence, that *whom the Son makes*

makes free, he is free indeed, if the Son is not supreme over his own house. If he has a superior over him, then, as the Apostle says, *he differs nothing from a servant, though he be Lord of all*.

But it is from this that the peace of a believer flows; he knows that *God is judge of all*, and that he has *reconciled us to himself, not imputing our trespasses*. He also knows, that the Person *in whom we have forgiveness through his blood*, was in the beginning with God, and that Spirit by whom we are sealed to the day of redemption, as he does the work, so he has the attributes of the Most High.

I will now discharge my thoughts of this branch in the Christian Religion with a short APPLICATION. If it is part of the Mystery of Godliness, that Christ is believed on in the world, then,

1. You see how both ministers and people do best fall in with the design of Christianity; the one by preaching up this faith, and the other by receiving it. That believing in Christ Jesus will be more than a name, that it will fill the hearts and form the lives of his peculiar people is very true; but certainly the faith that we are promoting is something more than mere morality. Either there is to be a receiving of this report that we go about the world with, and an esteem of something that we could never have known by the light of nature, or otherwise I do not see why Christ should have come amongst us. If living with justice and mercy had been all that religion expected from you, our Redeemer might have purchased you at a cheaper rate than with the expence of his blood. We need never have heard of God manifest in the flesh, in order to be justified in the spirit, but might have shifted as they did in those ages and generations to whom these things were hid.

God has distinguished us in a way that has been expressive of his condescension, and if it was not necessary to our happiness, it might much better have

SERM. 39. have been spared. But if he is believed on in the world, it supposes there are doctrines to be received which nothing but revelation could declare; and therefore when we set morality *against* these doctrines it is unnatural, and when we set it *above* them it is ungrateful. Christ calls himself *the*
Joh. xii. 36. *light*, and tells them that they must *believe in the light, that they might be children of light.*

We should never have known there was any more than one person concerned in our redemption: The very name of Father, Son, and Holy Ghost, would have been an eternal secret, had not God given us the Bible; and as this opens to us what must have been hid for ever, so certainly it
—xvii. 3. becomes us to receive the testimony. *It is life eternal to know Jesus Christ.* He manifested the name of God to the men who were given him out of the world, and they kept his word. By refusing the great mysteries of religion, we throw ourselves back again into rude nature, and uncultivated humanity; it is a scorn returned upon all the benevolence of Divine wisdom; it is chusing darkness rather than light; it is striking at the eternal
1 Joh. v. 10. veracity of God, *For he that believes not the record has made him a liar.*

2. If that is one branch of religion, that Christ is believed on in the world, no wonder that Satan
2 Cor. iv. 4. sets himself in opposition to it: *He blinds the*
5. *eyes of them that believe not, lest the light of the glorious Gospel of Christ should shine into their hearts.* In Popery he converted the doctrines of Christianity into *old wives fables*, things that were unworthy of reason and revelation too. Now that the folly of that part is made manifest, he varies the malice, and works in another form; as before he hurried on the reverence of the people for *human mysteries*, so now he teaches them to growl against those that are *divine*. If he can but any way engage you against the truth, either by denying

ing

ing a doctrine, or deriding a solemnity, he refuses no degrees of service. But as the testimony of Jesus calls us to oppose the *man of sin*, so it gives us the same concern that our religion be not run away with by the *men of sense*. For this also is a character that we find among the enemies of the truth. *The natural man receives not the things of the Spirit of God;* and there be some who *separate themselves, being sensual and not having the Spirit.*

^{SERM. 39.}

^{1 Cor. ii. 14. Jude 19.}

They that would not be ashamed of Christ and his words, will have a trial of their courage. Certainly if he is believed on in the world, he must be preached to the world: *How shall they believe in him of whom they have not heard, and how shall they hear without a preacher?* Supposing that Paul had never insisted on more than he did to Felix, *righteousness, temperance, and a judgment to come,* would that have been *declaring the whole counsel of God?* Were these *the unsearchable riches of Christ, and the fellowship of the mystery that from the beginning was hid in God?* Had any authority or *advices* endeavoured to confine his ministry to these subjects, *whose* interest would those people have been pursuing? They that *withstand our words*, when they are words of truth and soberness, are acting under the enemy; they that oppose themselves, and who do not *acknowledge the truth, are in the snare of the devil, and led captive by him at his pleasure.*

^{Rom. x. 14.}

^{Eph. iii. 8, 9.}

^{2 Tim. ii. 25, 26.}

3. How great a wickedness must theirs be who would hinder the faith of Jesus in the world! I have shewn you under the former head that it has in it the spirit of Satan; and though some people may think it no great matter that preachers are restrained from insisting upon the heads of pure revelation, yet the impiety that this leads to is the greatest that we are capable of. When the Spirit of grace comes, who is to *convince the world of sin,* he sets his particular mark upon this, that *they believe*

^{John xvi. 9.}

VOL. II.   P

believe not in Christ; as if there was something in that viler than all immortality. The Apostle calls himself *the chief of sinners;* not that he was scandalous in his conversation, lewd and filthy in his behaviour; but *a blasphemer, a persecutor, and injurious,* which were all the fruits of his *ignorance and unbelief.* No wonder then that they who set themselves against the Deity of Christ, have such low thoughts of the Holy Spirit who is charged to exalt him. But one serious touch of his hand is enough to divide the clouds of darkness, as well as to break a course of impiety: *The mystery that in other ages was not made known to the sons of men, is now revealed to the holy Apostles and Prophets by the Spirit.*

4. What need have we to be very earnest for that faith which is of the operation of God? *No man can say that Jesus is Lord, but by the Holy Ghost.* We have lived to see that no liberties of worship can secure the Gospel we profess from the contempt of men. *Beware therefore lest any man spoil you through philosophy and vain deceit, after the rudiments of the world, after the commandments of men, and not after Christ.* Pray for that Spirit who will lead us into all truth. His testimony will be a victory over others, and a security to yourselves. There are some that would seduce you, but the *anointing which ye have received of him abides in you; it teaches you all things, and is true, and is no lie; and as it has taught you, ye shall abide in him.* Endeavour to go out in his strength. There is a wisdom and a spirit which none of your adversaries will be able to gainsay or resist. Desire that he will *open your understandings, that ye may know the Scriptures,* that the word of God may dwell richly in you; that you may not be as *children tossed to and fro with every wind of doctrine by the craft of men, who lie in wait to deceive;*

but

but grow up unto him in all things who is the head of the body, even Christ Jesus.

5. See that this end is answered upon your souls. *We preach Christ Jesus, warning every man, and teaching every man, that we may present every man perfect in him.* But how vain will it be upon your account to have it said, that this foundation which is laid in Zion, is to you *a stone of stumbling, and rock of offence?* We may say, as Christ did, notwithstanding all the evidence that is given to the glory of his person, and the nature of his design, *Blessed is he whoever is not offended in him.* This faith which I am recommending to you goes deeper than a bare assent to the doctrines of the Gospel. If you are no more than proselytes or disputants after you have been teachers of others, yourselves may be cast away. But shew by a good conversation that this is a doctrine according to godliness; let your duty be an argument that you take it, not as *a vain thing,* but as *your life;* that you feel it in experience, and deliver it out in practice, *holding forth the word of life;* and then whatever your poor ministers meet with here, in *the day of Christ Jesus we shall rejoice together, that we have not run in vain, nor laboured in vain. Yea, if we be offered upon the sacrifice and service of your faith, we will rejoice with you all.*

6. Be sure that in believing on him you regard all his perfections. There is no equivalent to his Deity. If he is a God, this cannot be denied with any possible reparation. The Socinians said that he was a man, only more enriched with a divine power than any other. The Arians allowed his pre-existence, but yet made him a creature, by saying, there was a time when he was not. The bladder is now a little more blown, but the finer it is the thinner it is. They tell us of an *eternal emanation* to which he owes his being. This is a word

SERM.

Col. i. 28.

Mat. xi. 6.

Phil. ii. 16, 17.

SERM. 39. word contrived on purpose to confound us between beginning and no beginning, a creature and no creature, as I may shew you at large from the next and last head of our religion, that *he was received into glory.*

SERMON XL.

Nov. 3. 1719.

1 Tim. iii. 16.

—— *Received up into Glory.*

THESE words give us the last part of our religion; concerning the whole of which we may say, Great without controversy is the Mystery of Godliness. The Person spoken of has his name continued quite through the story; that as it is God who was manifest in the flesh, justified in the Spirit, seen of Angels, preached unto the Gentiles, and believed on in the world, so he is no other than God, *who is received up into glory.*

This branch is placed in a good light, and receives a proper advantage from what was said before. He was *manifest in the flesh,* with all the simplicity and contempt of human nature, *as a root out of a dry ground, with no form or comeliness in him*: but it is otherwise in the next world, for there he appears in *glory.* Or, you may take the several parts of the text in this relation to one another; that though Christ was to be low and despised,

despised, yet there were honours of two sorts designed for him.

First, Some on earth, where he is *justified in the Spirit*, approved, admired, and adored by his own people: to which purpose he is *preached to the Gentiles*, that he might widen his kingdom, and carry it beyond the limits that for several ages had been set to the true religion. The success of this is agreeable to the design; for he is *believed on in the world;* the entrance of the Gospel was not in vain. The Spirit who had the custody of a Redeemer's honour, and was to *justify* him, did his office, *first*, by giving the Gospel, and, *then*, by attending it.

This was a better balance to all the troubles that he met with, than any external pomp could have been. It was more glorious in itself, and more desirable to him, to have converts bowing to his authority, than princes waiting at his gate. When Satan offered him the kingdoms of the world, and the glory of them, it was too little. He has more satisfaction from *the travail of his soul*, in one sinner that repents, than in all the monarchies and empires of the universe. It was in this sense that he is spoken of, as one *lifting up the head*, after he had *drunk of the brook that ran in the way*. Not that he was to have an outward greatness; but *the rod of his strength he sends out of Zion*, and his way of *ruling among enemies* is by making them *a willing people in the day of his power*. That is one sort of honour designed for him, with regard to which *the kingdom was to be the Lord's, and he the Governor among the nations*. But then, the mystery of godliness tells us things of another nature; that as he was manifest and justified, preached and believed on; so,

Secondly, Our thoughts are called after him into the place whither he is gone. It was before observed that he is seen of Angels; the object of their

their care as he is a man, of their wonder as he is a Mediator, and of their adoration as he is the God of *their* nature as well as the friend of *ours*. Now, as there were *three* branches of the Christian doctrine that relate to his advancement upon earth in a religious empire; so there are *two* that your meditations may apply to heaven; that which I have now mentioned, his being *seen of Angels*, and this that closes up the whole account, that he was *received into glory*. You know the method in which I have considered all the other parts of this subject, and I see no reason to change it in the last. I shall therefore,

1. Open to you the meaning of this sentence, that Christ was *received into glory*.

2. Make good this character that runs through the whole text, and shew you that this, as well as the rest, belongs to him as GOD.

3. Let you see that this is one of those *mysteries* that the natural man receives not; but the Spirit of truth sets it home with a mighty and useful evidence upon the hearts of believers. And that,

4. From this principle we are led into the *godliness* that Christianity is to promote in this world, on purpose to work us up for a better.

I. I begin with the first of these, and that is to open the meaning of the sentence; or, how we are to understand it, that our Saviour was *received into glory*. Here are two words made use of, which must be considered apart.

[1.] The *glory* that he went into.

[2.] The manner of his being *received* thither.

[1.] We read of a *glory* that He is now in, who was once manifest in the flesh; and that agrees to the whole stream of the Bible, both in the Old and New Testament. These two things are always the doctrine that God revealed concerning a Redeemer:

First,

First, That he should be very mean and misera- ble, *the seed of the woman*, and therefore born in sorrow; the reproach of men, the abhorence of his own nation; punished and forsaken by the God that sent him; accused and tortured, under the curse of his own law, as a worm, and no man, crawling upon the earth, trampled on without any care or pity. Such an unhappy life, such a wretched death, was all along described as the lot appointed for him, by *the determinate counsel and fore-knowledge of God*.

[SERM. 40.]
[Acts ii. 23]

Secondly, There was also another character under which he is spoken of from the beginning of the promise. He is slain from the foundation of the world; and as early was he triumphant, to *bruise the serpent's head:* notwithstanding that *his visage was marred more than any man, and his form more than the sons of men*; yet he is a conqueror, he *leads captivity captive*. And these are not to be dashed against one another, as so many contradictions, but there is a harmony, a consistence in the whole story. His poverty is not to be pleaded against his fulness, but was the way to it, and the ground of it. His pain and vexation were things from which he passed over to the joy that was set before him. The *powers of darkness*, to which he was subject, had but *their hour*. After a little while, it was *his* turn to *divide the portion with the great, and the spoil with the strong*. Now, the glory of our Saviour is mentioned in the Scripture with a great variety, to suit the different apprehensions that the Holy Spirit has given us of him.

[Isa. lii. 14.]
[Ps. lxviii. 18.]
[Isa. liii. 12.]

(1.) Consider him as *a man*, and then his glory is the advancement of that nature which he took into union with himself, to the right-hand of the Majesty on high.

(2.) Consider him as a *Mediator*, as one who partook of both the natures for which he was concerned,

SERM. 40. cerned, and his glory comes under another view. Thus Angels, principalities and powers, are made subject to him.

(3.) He has a glory antecedent and superior to each of these; what he calls a glory *with the Fa-* John xvii. *ther*, the same that he had *before the world was.* 5. This is underived and independent, what he has in himself, and in a transcendent communion with the other two persons of the Divine Nature.

The Scripture has given us all these in a plain distinction; for, as there are many places that make it evident the glory of the Son is inferior to that of the Father, that there is between them the distance of a creature from a God; so there are others that we cannot understand but of an equal glory between the Father and Son, without changing the sense of the words, and making them signify *that* in divinity, which they never did, and never could do in any thing else.

(1.) I begin with that glory of our blessed Saviour, which he was received into as *man.* Indeed I ought to make an apology for this, because as the character of Deity is conveyed through all the branches of the mystery of godliness; as he is *God* who was manifest in the flesh, and is now received up into glory; so it is plain he speaks of *that* which is infinitely superior to the account we have of him as man. The words belonging to him as God, should be considered so as to keep *that* always in view.

I take the objection to be pertinent enough, but I humbly hope it may be over-ruled by this answer: That though it is very true the Holy Spirit in my text speaks all along of a *God,* yet it is of him as appearing *in our nature,* and managing the greatest concern *with it.* The first branch of this mystery led us to consider him not only as a God, but as *manifest in the flesh.* And though the glory that I am now going to enlarge upon, which is given to the human nature, is no proof of a Divinity, yet he received it into fellowship with that which *was*.

He who is a God, as he had a *body prepared for him* in which he died; so *that* he has taken with him, and by an unspeakable union has derived unto it a glory. This glory of the human nature, which our blessed Saviour is pleased to mention, will comprehend the following particulars, and may be considered as opposed to the humiliation that he suffered by. You know, 1*st*, That his body was weak and frail, subject to the same infirmities with ourselves, but now it is *perfect*. 2*dly*, He here bare our burdens, and sunk under his own, but now he is fully at *rest* and quiet. 3*dly*, He was upon earth rejected and exposed to shame, but now this Nature is admired with the greatest *reputation*. 4*thly*, His soul was subject to the *fears* and sorrows of life, but now he is above all those impressions. 5*thly*, He wanted as we do the supplies of food and rest, but now he is independent on every thing of that nature. 6*thly*, He was earthy, being made of a woman, but now his body is said to be *glorious*. 7*thly*, He here submitted to death, but now he *lives* for ever. 8*thly*, He was moving to and again, and had not where to lay his head, but now he is *fixed*. 9*thly*, He was in this world as a servant, he sits in the same nature in the other as a *judge*. 10*thly*, His union with the Deity was but little seen upon earth, to what it will be in heaven. You observe that all these particulars, except the two last, may be considered in him not only as our head and friend, but our original and pattern, that it will be with us as it is with him.

1. One article of glory that Christ is received into as man, or rather that into which He as God took our nature, was the perfection of that nature.

SERM. 40.
Acts iv.
27. 30.

He is *the holy Child Jesus*, he is made better than ever Adam was, both in soul and body; and that is more than can be said of him here upon earth. For though he had no sin, nor was he tainted with the least impurity, yet there was a great deal of difference between him and our first parents, when they came fresh out of the hand of God. Christ was as holy as they, but not so strong and lively. His human nature had the Divine Image in all the spiritual characters that belong to it; but there was a greatness, a health in Adam's body, and an happiness in his soul, which our Saviour had not; and the reason is plain.

The first Adam was created by God to have a heaven upon earth; his paradise was to be a state of glory below; and therefore he was framed and wrought up in such a way as to be capable of receiving all the delights of the place; and that could not be without a full strength of body, and the utmost perfection of mind. But the second Adam was sent down from a heaven above, not to find one below. This earth was rather a *hell* to him, because there he endured what they do, the wrath of God, the curse of the law, *the wages of sin*. It is said by way of dignity, that man was

Heb. ii. 7.
ver. 9.

made *a little lower than the Angels*, as a creature *crowned with glory and honour;* but when *Jesus was made a little lower than the Angels*, it was *for the suffering of death.*

— 17.

Upon this account *it behoved him in all things to be made like unto his brethren.* Without that, he could never have been a *faithful High-priest* to God, or *a merciful* one *to us.* He was to feel our infirmities, that he might be able to *deliver those that are tempted.* And as the *children were partakers of flesh and blood, he likewise himself took part of the same, i. e.* in the way that they had it; a weak body, a contracted soul; the one liable to hunger, pain, and death, the other to sorrow, mistake,

mistake, and fear, any farther than it was guided SERM. 40.
by a nature that is light, and in which there is no
darkness at all; for we read of him, that he *grew* Luke ii. 52.
in *wisdom* as well as *stature: he was found in* Phil. ii. 8.
fashion as a man, he came in the likeness of sinful Rom. viii.
flesh. 3.

But now he has this nature in perfection, as good as it was when God made it *after his own image, and in his own likeness.* There was something in the human nature in Adam, that bore a resemblance of the Divine. He was made *in the similitude of God.* Whatever this was, our Saviour, who was pleased to be without it upon earth, possesses it all in heaven. There is a glory both in his soul and body, which Paradise never knew. All the spiritual faculties, all the outward members are filled and fashioned, so as to make him *the first-* Col. i. 15.
born of every creature. He is fairer than the sons Pf. xlv. 2.
of men. That was not true upon earth; for *his visage was marred more than any man, and his form more than the sons of men;* but now *grace is poured* ver. 7.
into his lips, and God, even his God, has anointed him with the oil of gladness above every creature.

The human nature of Christ may be called *the beginning of the creation of God:* not that it was made *first,* but as it is made the *best* of any thing. Our first parents were crowned with glory and honour, and made a little lower than the Angels. Their constitution was agreeable to their station; as they were set over the lower world, they were framed but a little worse than the higher. But this nature in its first edition, is not equal to what heaven discovers in the second: *There is a natural* 1 Cor. xv.
body, and there is a spiritual body: the first Adam 44, 45,
was a living soul, the last Adam was made a quick- 46, 47.
ening spirit. The first man is of the earth, earthy; the second man is the Lord from heaven.

There were but three bodies that the hand of God is said to form; all the rest he leaves to the

course

course of nature. The first was Adam's, wrought out of the earth; the second Eve's, which was taken out of man; and these being the Divine workmanship were perfect in their kind, and carried in them the full glory of the nature. Angels might see what sort of creatures they were; but there is a *third* that exceeds in both, and that is our blessed Lord's. He speaks of it to the Father with joy, *A body hast thou prepared me.* Though he was made of a woman, yet God himself had the working of the materials, the preparation was all divine. It was by the *overshadowing of the Holy Ghost,* by the coming down of *the power of the Highest;* and therefore upon this account, that holy thing which was born of the Virgin, should be *called the Son of God.*

This was the masterpiece of the creation, the noblest work of God's hand. It is said of Adam, *Out of the ground thou wast taken, dust thou art;* and it will be true of us all, that *the dust shall return to the earth, as it was;* but there was *a holy One* who should *never see corruption.* It is true, this glory was much hid during the time of his life: He was far from being seen to an advantage here. When his face did once shine as the sun, it was a *transfiguration:* and therefore he is taken up, where he appears to be made so *much better than the Angels,* as a man; as he has by *the inheritance* that belonged to him as a God, *obtained a more excellent name than they.*

In this he is our pattern. When he *fashions our vile bodies,* it is unto his *glorious Body.* We can make no judgment of it here. The beloved disciple was astonished at what he saw; though it is plain the vision was adapted to his capacity, and confined on purpose to make it familiar; but he tells us, that *his head and his hairs were white like wool, as white as snow, and his eyes were as a flame of fire, and his feet like unto fine brass, as if they burned*

burned in a furnace, and his voice as the sound of many waters: and he had in his hand seven stars, and out of his mouth went a sharp two-edged sword, and his countenance was as the sun shining in his strength: and when I saw him, I fell at his feet as dead; [This is said by one who had so often leaned on his bosom, and spoken into his ear.] *and he laid his right hand upon me, saying,* **Fear not, I am the first and the last.** Saul, as he went to Damascus, *at mid-day, saw a light from heaven, above the brightness of the sun;* that is, he saw *Christ Jesus the Lord.* In Him we have the original of our happiness; for thus, in our degree, it shall be with us. When we come *to the measure of a perfect man,* it is into *the fulness of the stature of Christ Jesus.*

2. The glory of the human nature in our Redeemer takes into it a full rest and quietness. Here he bare our burdens, and carried our sorrows: nay, there were several things that shewed the imperfection of this nature. He was far from having the strength of Samson. Though he is said to have *the government upon his shoulder,* yet this cannot be understood of him as a man; for when they only laid upon him his cross, he was not able to bear it. He fainted in the day of adversity, which shewed his strength to be small. He submitted in his private capacity to a toilsome business, as we read of his father's being a carpenter; so the Scripture has told us he was *subject to him.* When he went about after his baptism, though his being anointed with the Holy Ghost gave him *power* in a spiritual sense, yet he complained of *weariness* when he sat down at the well of Samaria. It is observed that the multitude thronged him; that he was tired with long exhortations and fastings; and he crossed the sea of Tiberias, on purpose that he might have leisure to eat. He once taught them out of a ship, the multitude being on shore, left he should suffer

SERM. 40. suffer any inconvenience by the croud; and a great deal more we read of, to shew us that he had both the quality and the afflictions of human nature:
Job xiv. 1. that as he was man *born of a woman*, so, like all others, he was but *of few days, and full of trouble.*

We have his own sentiments of the load that was appointed to him, in the lamentations of the
Psal. xxii. 14, 15. Psalmist: *I am poured out like water, all my bones are out of joint; my heart is like wax, it is melted in the midst of my bowels; my strength is dried up like a potsherd; my tongue cleaves to my jaws; and thou hast brought me to the dust of death.* This is
Jam. i. 13. not the language of the Divine Nature; that *cannot be tempted with evil;* but these things prove that he was the man Christ Jesus; and therefore in the story of his life, the title that seems to be the most beloved, is that of *the Son of man;* as if he was determined to rivet this doctrine into the minds of his people, that as being near of kin to us, he had the right of redemption in him. He made himself *of no reputation,* and took upon him *the form of a servant,* and was made *in the likeness of men.*

But now, all these incumbrances to the human
Isa. lvii. 2. nature are over. It is said of his people, *They rest in their beds, they enter into peace, each one walking*
Rev. xiv. 13. *in his uprightness. Blessed are the dead who die in*
Job iii. 17, 18. *the Lord, for they rest from their labours.* There *the prisoners hear not the voice of the oppressor, there the wicked cease from troubling, and there the weary*
Heb. iv. 9. *are at rest.* There is *a rest that remains for the people of God;* and into this Christ has led us the way. For though many thousands got to heaven before his resurrection, yet *his* was the first *body*
Heb. xi. 5. that went thither out of the grave. *Enoch was*
1 Cor. xv. 20. *translated that he should not see* death; but *Christ is risen from the dead, and become the first-fruits of*
Acts ii. 34. *them that slept.* For *David*, as the Apostle observes, *is not yet ascended into heaven.* You will

see

see of what part this must be understood by the argument that he brings for it, *That he is both dead and buried, and his sepulchre is with us unto this day. But Christ is entered into his rest, and has ceased from his own works, as God did from his.*

The great God speaks oftentimes after the manner of men, and he was pleased to give us this account of the creation, that when he appointed the Sabbath day, *he rested and was refreshed.* With allusion to this, our Saviour's mediation upon earth was compared to a creation, *He that sat upon the throne, said, Behold, I make all things new*; and it is represented as a work of toil, but heaven is to him a Sabbath. When he bowed down his head upon the cross, *he said, It is finished.* He has gone through the work that was given him to do, as a faithful servant to Him that appointed him. God speaks otherwise both to Moses and Joshua, than he did to Christ. He saith to the former, *Thou shalt not bring this people over Jordan,* he was to leave the design incomplete. And he speaks with such a limitation to Joshua, *The days draw near that thou must die, and yet there remains very much land to be possessed.* But this could never be said of our blessed Lord, who *glorified God on earth, and finished the work that was given him to do.*

The Apostle observes, that there was a certain plan by which his enemies proceeded with him. This was laid in God's decree, and revealed in his book; but as they could not enter into the one, so they were strangers to the true sense of the other. And yet it is said, that *when he fulfilled all things that were written of him, they took him down from the tree, and laid him in a sepulchre.* There is now an end of those *strong cryings and tears that he offered in the days of his flesh.* There is no more *obedience by the things that he suffered.* He is said now to be *made perfect,* not only in the constitution, but in the situation of his nature. He is placed

SERM. 4e.

1 Pet. iv. 1.

Gen. ii. 3.

Joh. xvii. 4.

Acts xiii. 29.

Heb. v. 7, 8, 9.

ced above all his fears and troubles, and has no burden but *that*, which his people shall enjoy with him, *a far more exceeding and eternal weight of glory*. He saith to the Father, *I am no more in the world, but I come unto thee*.

<small>Joh. xvii. 11.</small>

3. The glory of Christ's human nature is distinguished from, and opposed unto that shame and reproach which he suffered by: *He was despised and rejected of men; they hid their faces from him, and esteemed him not.* Sometimes this was owing to the meanness of his person, *They saw no form or comeliness in him, that they should desire him;* and sometimes to the vileness of his character, *We did esteem him stricken, smitten of God, and afflicted.* As he saith, *They that see me laugh me to scorn; they shoot out the lip, they shake the head, saying, He trusted in the Lord, that he would deliver him; let him deliver him, seeing he delighted in him.* And again, he cries out, *Many bulls have compassed me, strong bulls of Bashan have beset me round about, they gaped upon me with their mouths like a ravening and a roaring lion.* Every title of greatness that he took upon him became their jest. They bantered him with a *purple robe*, put a *reed* into his hand, a *crown of thorns* upon his head, *bowed the knee* before him, saying, *Hail King of the Jews! He gave his cheeks to them that plucked off the hair, he hid not his face from shame and spitting.* But he knew this would not be always: he submitted to it, like one that waits for the morning, and in the words of the Prophet, saith, He should *not be confounded*, because the great God was *near to justify him*, and therefore he *set his face like a flint, and should not be ashamed*.

<small>Isa. liii. 2, 3.</small>

<small>ver. 4.</small>

<small>Psal. xxii. 7, 8.</small>

<small>ver. 12, 13.</small>

<small>Ifa. l. 6, 7.</small>

Now, it is plain, that when he looked upon this change of condition, he expected it in another world. He died under all the scandal that a person could have upon him; accursed by the ceremonial law, for it is written, *Cursed is every one that*

<small>Gal. iii. 13</small>

that is hanged on a tree: loaded with reproach and darkness by the very people that had once owned his miracles, He saved others, himself he cannot save; blasphemed by the priests, insulted by the rabble, neglected by his followers, who stood afar off, grieved and confounded with the sight of what they did not understand.

SERM. 40.

But out of all these clouds he rose into glory; and though his name was then covered with darkness, yet now he has *a name above every name.* The title of *Jesus of Nazareth, King of the Jews,* was writ upon his cross in letters of Hebrew, Greek, and Latin, to distribute his infamy all over the world; but *in this name of Jesus every knee shall bow, and every tongue confess that Jesus is Lord, to the glory of God the Father.* However scandalous and filthy the high-priest's garments might appear when they were stained with the blood of sacrifices, yet this was no blemish to him, when he went into the holiest of all. And thus is our great High-Priest *glorious in his apparel; he has trod the wine-press* of the wrath of Almighty God: *Having by himself purged away our sins, he* FOR EVER *sat down at the right hand of the Majesty on high.*

Phil. ii. 9, 10, 11.

Isa. lxiii. 1, 3.

Heb. i. 3.

****

SERMON XLI.

Nov. 22. 1719.

4. THERE is another glory that our dear Lord, as the Son of man, is now possessed of, by which he is distinguished from what he was upon earth; and that is, the *pleasure* and satisfaction that will fill *his soul* for ever. Even this part of his human

SERM. 41.   human nature came under the weight of humilia-
Heb. iv. 15. tion. He was liable to sorrows and fears, being *in
             all points tempted as we are*, sin only excepted. He
— v. 2.   was touched with *the feeling of our infirmities, and
             compassed about with infirmity*, as if he determined
             in making good the blessing of Abraham, to revive
             the experience of Abraham; for it is observed of
             the old patriarch, when he entered into covenant
Gen. xv. 12. with God, that *a horror of great darkness fell upon
             him:* and so it was with Him who is called *the son
             of Abraham*.

In the transaction between the Father and him, though it was upon a council of peace that had been agreed on before, yet he recoils, he flinches, and cries out, *If it be possible, let this cup pass from me.* In that agony there was not only a pressure and force upon his body, to make his sweat like drops of blood; but he complains that the main
Mark xiv.   weight lay more within, for *his soul was exceeding
34.   sorrowful unto death*. At the entrance upon the
Mat. xxvi.   solemnity, it is said, that *he began to be sorrowful,
37, 38.   and very heavy;* not in the same sense that the word is used of the disciples, that *they were heavy with sleep*, but his mind and affections were borne down, *The arrows of the Almighty stuck within him, the poison whereof drunk up his spirits;* and no wonder that he complained of a load, when
Isa. liii. 6. *God laid upon him the iniquity of us all.* This was all along designed to be the chief part of his sufferings; and therefore we read not only that it *pleased the Father to bruise him,* but *to put him to grief.* And, as if it was not enough that he should be a sacrifice *in the body of his flesh through death*, he also *made his soul an offering for sin*.

It was from an adversity that fell upon this part,
Ps. xxii. 1. that he bewailed his case upon the cross, *My God, my God, why hast thou forsaken me?* That cannot be understood of a nature which, as he says, was still in heaven. There is no conceiving of an an-

ger

ger or a distance between the Father and Son as they are one; nor does the affliction he there complains of relate merely to his body; for the violence of his death was no argument that God forsook him. We know that he did not forsake the Martyrs; they were not left of God; and so Christ might be hung upon the cross, torn with nails, and pushed with spears, hated, derided, and killed, and yet all this while God be with *him* as he was with *them*.

But the Father's forsaking him is to be understood of a cloud upon his soul, not unlike that which the damned feel; for he is said to be *made a curse to redeem them that were under the curse*. When he saith, *Thou wilt not leave my soul in hell*, it intimates the nature of his torments, that he *trod the wine-press of the fierceness of the wrath of Almighty God*. This signifies a great deal more than his body was capable of enduring; but as he was partaker of our flesh and blood, he likewise received such a soul as we have: *His soul was an offering for sin; he shall see the travail of his soul; he poured out his soul unto death*.

SERM. 41.

Gal. iii. 13.

Isa. liii. 10, 11, 12.

This, by the way, shews us what wretched work the new scheme makes of our religion, and of Him that established it. Their notion is, that λόγος the Word was a created spirit, but far above the Angels; and that this spirit was made to animate the human body; and as we are compounded of soul and flesh, so the man Christ Jesus has nothing of ours about him but the external part; that the soul which moved his body was not like ours, but a supernatural spirit that had so glorious a being before; so that, you see, having denied his proper *Deity*, and supposed him no more than a spirit, inferior to the great God, they will do the same by his *humanity*, not allowing him to be a proper man. He shall have nothing of God but the name, and nothing of man but the flesh.

Are

SERM. 41.   Are these the discoveries of our polite age? Is it by such talk as this, that we are to trample upon the names and works of those who have served their several generations according to the will of God, and whose praises, till now, were in all the churches of Christ? Is it thus that we improve upon *the hoary heads that have been found in the way of righteousness?* Are people resolved to make clear work with our religion, and come among the doctrines that belong to it as *roaring lions, seeking what they may devour?*—Shall we have a Saviour that is neither God nor man? Can they deny the reality of the two natures at once? We were told long

2 Joh. 7, 8. ago, *that many deceivers are entered into the world, who confess not that Jesus Christ is come in the flesh. This is a deceiver and an antichrist; but look ye to yourselves, that we lose not those things that we have wrought.* It is apparent from all the language of Scripture, that he had a soul inferior to what they will allow, capable of sorrow from what it felt, and of fears from what it dreaded; to which the Almighty was a terror, and which became an offering for sin. Now,

The glory that this soul was received into, is that of eternal quietness. There is no pain to make it grieve, no danger to make it uneasy. *He entered*

Heb. xii. 2. *into his rest,* in the view of which, *he endured the cross, and despised the shame;* for I would observe to you, that Christ Jesus as a man was the greatest believer that ever lived. We have a noble instance

1 Pet. ii. 23. of his faith, that he *committed himself to Him who judges righteously.* The Apostle Peter, who brings over the words of the Psalmist to him, gives us

Acts ii. 25, this eminent example: *David speaks concerning him,*
26, 27, *I foresaw the Lord always before my face, for he is*
28. *on my right hand, that I should not be moved.* David's speaking concerning him may be understood two ways: *First,* Of David's own experience, that his support under all troubles was *having this Lord be-*
                                                                  fore

fore him; or, *secondly,* That David speaks in his name, and so it must be applied to Christ, that the Lord was before *his face;* ' *And therefore,*' saith he, ' *did my heart rejoice, and my tongue was glad; my* ' *flesh shall rest in hope, because,* though my soul ' must be thrown into something like a *hell,* yet ' thou wilt *not leave* it there, no more than my ' body is to be left in the grave, for *thou wilt not* ' *suffer thy holy One to see corruption: Thou hast* ' *made known to me the ways of life, thou shalt make* ' *me full of joy with thy countenance.*'

This varies a little from the passage as we have it in the Psalms. The Apostle does not keep to what some call plain words of Scripture, for there it is, *Thou wilt shew me the path of life, in thy presence is fulness of joy, and at thy right hand are pleasures for evermore.* But the meaning is this, that the soul of Christ, which had so much bitterness appointed to it, was to be refreshed as those of his people will be. He rejoiced, as believers do, *in hope of the glory of God.* This was *the joy set before him,* προκειμένη χαρὰ, lying over against him. The ways of life were made known to him. It was to this nature that *the Angel appeared* in the garden *to strengthen him.* How can that passage be reconciled to the beloved notions of our day? In what sense could an Angel strengthen him? Not in his body, for giving strength to that would be easing it of its load; but instead of any abatement, immediately after the Angel had done this, *his sweat was as great drops of blood falling to the ground.* And if he had no other soul than that spirit which was so much above the Angels, how would an Angel strengthen that, for *without controversy the less is blessed of the better.* As to his body he *received* no strength, and as to his soul he *needed* none. But if you consider him possessed, as he really was, of a spirit liable to be overwhelmed with grief, and tortured with fear, *made a little lower than the Angels,*

one

SERM. 41. one of them might come down and do a friendly part to an inferior creature, as his human nature certainly was.

5. The glory that he was received into as man comprehends an independence upon all those supplies that are needful here below. He wanted, as we do, the recruits of rest and food. *Meats are for the belly, and the belly for meats.* Our heavenly Father knows that we have need of these things. The Angels who appeared in the Old Testament, and put on a human form, seemed to eat and drink. Abraham made a dinner for those that came to him in the plain of Mamre. *Lot entertained Angels unawares.* It is easy to conceive, that they could have several ways of conveying food out of the sight of men, and making a shew of doing what they really did not. For we are not to suppose that they, who in *that world neither eat nor drink,* would come down into this upon any such errand. Only they appeared to do thus to establish and comfort the faith of those they conversed with.

But our Lord's body was of another kind, and could not subsist without the common ways that we are forced to take. It is reckoned in Moses an extraordinary thing, that he should be in the mount with God *forty days and forty nights, and neither eat nor drink.* It is the same in Elias, who fasted so long, *till he came to Horeb, the mount of God.* These things are indeed miraculous, that the human nature should be so supported by unusual favours. And thus we are to conceive of our Lord's being in the wilderness, and yet it is said, that *he afterwards hungred.* His desires for meat, (as we read *he would have eat*), were so strong, that upon this Satan raises a temptation, *If thou be the Son of God, command this stone that it be made bread.* He sat down for mere weariness

Deut. ix. 18.

Mat. iv. 3.
John iv. 6.

ness at the well of Samaria, and begged a cup of cold water from the woman who came thither to draw. But

Now this body is received into glory. As he is God, and has a power of subduing all things to himself, so he is the author of that change that shall pass upon us; as man he is the pattern or example of it. You have both these in one verse: *He shall change our vile bodies and fashion them like unto his glorious body, according to the power whereby he is able to subdue even all things to himself.* Our translation flattens the sense and fulness of the original. It is said, we look for a Saviour Christ Jesus the Lord, ὃς μετασχηματίσει, who shall transform, give a new appearance to our bodies; and what we render vile body, is σῶμα τῆς ταπεινώσεως ἡμῶν, the body of that frailty that now belongs to us. Our vanity, meanness and disorders are seen in the bodies that we carry about with us. But these shall be σύμμορφα, conformed to, cast into the same mould with, σῶμα τῆς δόξης αὐτῶ, the body of his glory, that which he wears in the state of his reward and perfection.

Phil. ii. 21.

It is indeed the same that he had below, but it moves and appears in quite another manner; no longer wanting either food or rest. We are now maintained with the bread that perishes. It does so in our using it, to put us in mind of what I observed before, *That meats are for the belly and the belly for meats, and God shall destroy both it and them.* These are bodies of our vanity; but the body that our Lord has received into his glory is the sample of what we shall be at the resurrection.

I do not know that ever men of polite notions and generous principles have yet considered the subsistence that the body of Christ has at present, or those that his people shall have when they rise again; but is easy to guess what they will say. About the year 1655, one Mr Biddle published a

Catechism,

SERM. 41. Catechism, wherein the answers were all plain words of Scripture, and in the preface to which he makes a terrible outcry about laying aside *the form of sound words*, those that the Holy Ghost teaches, and bringing in terms of man's devising; but by his questions, he leads on the sense of the answer: and accordingly, when he puts the case, whether the great God has not a bodily shape as we have; whether he is not confined to a place, and liable to the turbulent passions of grief and anger; his answers are out of these texts, where we read of *the eyes, the ears, the hands and feet, of the Lord;* that his throne is in the heavens, that he grieves at his heart and repents, his wrath kindles, and his spirit is disquieted.

If they will do thus by him, *whose dwelling is not with flesh*, it is no wonder if they make gross work with their expositions of those scriptures that relate to the bodies of Christ and his people, that were once really maintained with food; and the probability lies but too open, how they would understand our *sitting with him at his table, drinking the new wine in our Father's kingdom*, eating of the tree of life in the midst of the paradise of God: Nay, I may add that gracious promise that Rev. iii. 20. relates to this world, *Behold, I stand at the door, and knock; if any man hear my voice, I will come and sup with him, and he with me.* These are all of them words that the Holy Ghost teaches, no other than Scripture-language; and the Holy Ghost teaches how to understand them; for *to the pure, all things are pure;* we compare spiritual things with spiritual, not spiritual things with Tit. i. 15. carnal: *But to the unbelieving, nothing is pure. Their minds* that should receive what God teaches, and *their conscience* that should obey what he commands, *are both defiled.* There is a carnality and filthiness in all their conceptions; but we know that

the

the departed saints *hunger no more, nor thirst any more, neither shall the sun smite them, nor any heat.* SERM. 41. Rev. vii. 16.

6. Our Lord is said to have *a glorious body.* He once bore the image of the first Adam, who was *of the earth earthy;* he was *made of a woman;* he came *in the likeness of sinful flesh,* though not in the pollution of it. But now we are expressly told, that he has *a glorious body;* what the *words* mean we shall not be able to tell, till we see what the *thing* is. We must *see him as he is;* that at present we cannot do; for as it does not appear what *we shall be,* it as little appears what *he is.* He tells Moses, *His face shall not be seen; no man can see him, and live.* There is a glory even in his body, that our eyes are not able to bear. When he was transfigured before his disciples, *his face did shine as the sun, and his raiment was white as the light.* His raiment then was doubtless the same poor cloathing that he took into the mountain with him. He had none of those soft and sumptuous garments that are fit for kings houses, and yet even then he was *glorious in his apparel.* What could this be owing to, and especially the brightness that his body appeared with? Gal. iv. 4. Rom. viii. 3. Phil. iii. 21. 1 John iii. 2. Exo xxxiii. 20. Mat. xvii. 2. Isa. lxiii. 1.

Methinks he came to this world as Moses did out of the mount, putting a veil upon his face that his enemies should see no comeliness, that his friends might behold *a visage marred more than any man's;* but now he was out of their company who could bear none of his true countenance. In the mountain he will be more unlimited, and for a little time look like himself, to suit his acquaintance who met him from heaven, and to astonish those whom he took up with him from the earth. Moses and Elias *appeared in glory, and talked with him.* They made a thousand times a greater figure than he did among men; but upon the occasion of meeting with them, he will take off the veil, that Peter, James and John, who were his companions Luke ix. 31.

from

SERM. 41. from below, might have a little sketch of what he shall be above. It is said, *The fashion of his countenance was altered.* Though they knew him to be the same person, yet the lustre of his face was new to them, and *his raiment white and glittering,* as if it had been full of an inward glory, and prepared to send out the rays of what it contained. Human nature could not bear this; it so wasted the spirits of Peter and his company, that they were *heavy with sleep.* It was living too fast. The attraction, the drain of such a vision was too great for these houses of clay; and they just awake again to *see his glory, and the two men that were with him.* And yet,

This was nothing comparable to the body that he has in heaven. It is now rewarded for all the meanness that it submitted to, *the shame and spitting* that it suffered by. The Martyr Stephen, when he saw the heavens opened, and Jesus standing at the right-hand of God, is said to *look stedfastly thither.* He valued no noise of people, no rattling of stones. He might be joyfully untouched with all the thunder of death and the roar of devils, when he looked stedfastly to heaven, as if his soul was to go out through those eyes at which this glory came in, and immediately pass from seeing to taking, feeding, and possessing for ever. Such a vision would have killed him without the execution of stoning; human nature might die away in that happy gaze, as if his soul was not driven out by the wrath of this world, but licked up by the strength of another; exhaled, allured, and sucked away by the throne of the Lamb.

Acts vii. 55.

What a body was this! what a glory is it received into! it outshines the sun in all its brightness. Saul's eyes were scorched with what he saw, a sort of scales grew upon them, which held three days and three nights. *He could not see for the glory of the light.*—When our Lord comes to sit

— ix. 7.

on

on a great white throne, from his face the heaven and the earth will flee away; and there shall be found no place for them. [SERM. 4t. Rev. xx. 11.]

Well may it be said, that it does not appear what we shall be, when we are told that like unto this glorious body ours are to be fashioned in all things. Hence we read of *a spiritual body*. Philosophy would call this a contradiction, but it is opposed to *a natural body*, that which he had by nature, and that with which he lived in it. All the other descriptions of the resurrection are to help us a little, though they still leave us short of knowing what a spiritual body means; but we are told that it is raised *in power*, capable of doing all the work of heaven; *in glory*, filled and adorned with all the delights of heaven: it is raised *in incorruption*; as it was put into the grave to moulder and return back again to dust, so it raised to die no more, but to be a pillar in the temple of God. That leads me to the next head. [1 Cor. xv. 44.]

7. The man Christ Jesus is received into the glory of an immortal life. He came down hither to die. *It is appointed for all men once to die*, and so it was appointed for him; death had passed upon him, as it has done upon all that have sinned; for though he knew no sin, yet being made sin for us, *he became obedient to death, even the death of the cross*. He looks upon this as a trust committed to him: *I have power to lay down my life, and I have power to take it again; this commandment have I received of my Father.* And indeed by this he submitted to all the meanness of our nature. It is by dying that God *stains the pride of all glory, and brings into contempt all the honourable of the earth*. When tyrants and mighty men have flourished long enough, *he looks on every one that is proud, and brings him low, and treads down the wicked in their places; he hides them in the dust together, and* [Heb. ix. 27. John x. 18.]

binds

SERM. 41. *binds their faces in secret.* This our Lord submitted to, but

His resurrection did two things: *first,* It closed up all the design of one death; and, *secondly,* It was a security against the return of another. *Christ being raised from the dead, dies no more; death hath no more dominion over him: For in that he died, he died unto sin once; but in that he lives, he lives unto God.* There are two things that may be considered in our blessed Lord, his person and his office; as a man he could but *die once,* but as a priest he must have done it *often,* if he had not been more than a man; and upon this the Apostle gives us a great argument, *That he should not offer himself often, as the high-priest enters into the holy place once every year; for then he must often have suffered since the foundation of the world.* Well, why does he not? Not merely because he died, for that the creatures which were typical of him did in vast multitudes, and a continual succession.

Rom. vi 9, 10.

Heb. ix. 25.

Had he been only a man, his sacrifice could have had no more than a yearly virtue. But now *once in the end of the world he has appeared to put away sin,* to send it all a-going *by the sacrifice of himself. He was once offered to bear the sin of many,* and that once was enough; so that now *to them that look for him, he shall appear the second time without sin unto salvation.* He observes again in the following chapter, that *we are sanctified through the offering of the body of Jesus once for all: Every priest stands daily ministring and offering oftentimes the same sacrifices, which can never take away sin; but this man after he had offered one sacrifice for sin, for ever sat down at the right-hand of God; from henceforth expecting that his enemies should be made his footstool: for by one offering he has for ever perfected them that are sanctified.*

ver. 28.

Heb. x. 10, 11, 12.

Thus does Christ tell the beloved Apostle, *I was dead, but I am alive, and I live for evermore.* He

Rev. i. 18.

is

is to come down here again. His body is to live where it was before. He shall *come and every eye shall see him, and they that pierced him, and all kindreds and nations shall wail because of him. This same Jesus,* say the two Angels that stood in white, *shall in like manner come down from heaven, as you have seen him go into heaven.* He is to be revealed *from heaven with his mighty Angels in flaming fire.* But it is not to live here again. This earth that was the place of his suffering shall feel his power; for when he sends out his voice, *the earth shall give up his dead.* There is a *second death* that comes after the second resurrection, that is, when soul and body shall be thrown together *into the lake that burns with fire and brimstone;* as there is a first resurrection that comes before the first death. This is what God's people have, and the other is what they shall be delivered from. *Blessed and holy is he who has part in the first resurrection, over them the second death shall have no power.*

SERM. 41.
Rev. i. 7.
Acts i. 11.
2 Theff. i. 7, 8.
Rev. xx. 15.

Now in this we are conformed to Christ Jesus. In our first resurrection, we are *risen together with him,* that *like as Christ was raised by the glory of the Father, so we should walk in newness of life.* This is called a *being planted together in the likeness of his resurrection.* Well, they that are so, over them the second death shall have no power. The first indeed shall, as it had over him, but the great danger is from the second. There is but a small account made of *them that kill the body,* because after that, *there is no more that they can do:* But there is a great deal more, infinitely more that we may suffer. Now it is the happiness of believers that death comes but once to them, as it did to him.

Rom. vi. 4. 5.

8. The glory of the human nature in Christ Jesus signifies the eternal settlement that he entered into. Here he had no continuing city, he was

<small>SERM. 41.</small> a stranger and pilgrim upon earth. *The Son of*
<small>Luke ix. 58.</small> *man had not where to lay his head,* but went about
doing good in Jerusalem, in Galilee, and Samaria,
wandering to and again. Thus he expresses his
<small>—— xiii. 33.</small> own life, *I must walk to-day, and to-morrow, and*
<small>Heb. i. 3.</small> *the day following.* But now he *has sat down for
ever at the right-hand of the Majesty on high,* no
more to toil and travel.

This was the reward that the Father appointed
<small>Psal. cx. 1.</small> to him : *The Lord said unto my Lord, Sit thou at my
right-hand, till I make thine enemies thy footstool.*
Sit thou there, not only as a dignity that he should
be possessed of, but what he shall never be driven
from. He is *for ever* sat down there; it is an
eternal dignity. He had before prepared his throne
<small>Rev. vii. 15.</small> in the heaven, and thither he takes his body. *His
people are before the throne day and night.* He that
sits upon the throne, and the Lamb, are objects of
their praise and adoration for ever and ever.

And this was a proper reward for the hurry that
he submitted to here; in his duty he was going
about from place to place, for which he sometimes
<small>Luke iv. 43, 44.</small> gives this reason, *I must preach the kingdom of God
to other cities also, for therefore I am sent; and he
preached in the synagogues of Galilee.* Thus it was
<small>Isa. liii. 8.</small> in his sufferings; he is led *from prison and judgment;*
first to the high-priest, and then to Pilate, then to
Herod, and then back to Pilate again; then out to
the people, and at last to the cross; driven, hauled,
<small>Psal. cix. 22, 23.</small> and compelled with force. As he saith, *I am poor
and needy, and my heart is wounded within me. I
am gone like the shadow that declines, I am tossed
to and fro as the locust.* But

Now it is fixed: He is among things above;
<small>Col. iii. 1.</small> there *Jesus sits at the right-hand of God.* It is
from heaven that we wait for a Saviour, Christ Je-
<small>Acts iii. 21.</small> sus the Lord. *The heavens have received him till
the time of the restitution of all things.* The ap-
pearance he made to Stephen and to Saul was

not

not by coming down, but by looking down; and in this he is a pattern to us. *Him that overcomes, will I make a pillar in the temple of my God, and he shall go no more out.* This is the portion of our souls, and there is the same provision for our bodies. When the dead in Christ are risen, then *they that are alive and remain, shall be caught up together with them in the clouds, to meet the Lord in the air; and so shall we be ever with the Lord.*

SERMON XLII.

Dec. 25. 1719.

9. THE glory that the **human nature of** Christ is now received into, comprehends in it the greatness and the office of a Judge. This was all along designed for him as the reward of his humiliation. *The Father judges no man, but has committed all judgment to the Son. He has given him authority to execute judgment, because he is the Son of man.* When he had told them this, he opened the way of his entrance upon the charge: *Marvel not at this, for the hour is coming in which all that are in the graves shall hear his voice and come forth; they that have done good, to the resurrection of life, and they that have done evil, to the resurrection of damnation.* This he speaks as a person deputed to the work; for which reason he adds, *I of myself can do nothing; as I hear, I judge; because I seek not my own will, but the will of the Father who has sent me.* These and several other scriptures make it plain, that he is to appear upon the throne in our nature, and therefore must be

considered

considered in that transaction as a servant. For *when all things are put under his feet, then shall the Son himself also be subject to Him that put all things under him, that God may be all in all.* He must give back *the kingdom to God even the Father.*

But though his coming to judgment shall be with honour to him as a *man*, yet it supposes that he has a nature infinitely above it; for we are expresly told, that *God is judge of all*, in which account he is distinguished from *Jesus the Mediator of the new covenant:* And in the 50th Psalm, when the Lord speaks and *calls the earth, from the rising of the sun to the going down thereof*, it is to proclaim this as an incommunicable glory, *that God is judge himself;* and indeed the characters of him who *sits on the throne judging right*, are too great for our nature.

It is not as man that Christ can *search the hearts, and try the reins;* it is not as man, that he *makes the dead hear his voice*, and causes those that hear to live; it is not from any excellency in this lower nature, that he *opens the books*, and tries all mankind by what is written there, bringing iniquity to remembrance. This is the prerogative of Deity: *I am God, and there is none besides me, declaring the end from the beginning, and from ancient times the things that are not yet done.* And as this perfection is necessary to a judge, so the office that our Lord appears in, supposes him to be more than man, nay, more than a creature, in order to his discharge of it. When he told the high-priest that he was Christ the Son of God, he speaks of his *sitting at the right hand of power, and coming in the clouds of heaven*, which they accounted no less than *blasphemy*. This in another place he calls *coming in the glory of his Father, with the Angels, to reward every man according to his works.* Upon his saying, *Ye shall see the Son of man sit on the right hand of the power of God*, they ask, *Art thou then the Son of God?* concluding, that this could never be the dignity of a creature.

But then it may be said, that he shews himself in the very nature that he took upon him: *When he comes, every eye shall see him, and they that pierced him.* He is to come with the marks of their injury, and *all nations* and *kindreds of the earth shall wail because of him.*

How different is this from the station allotted to him on earth! He came not hither to judge the world; he was far from pretending to any such character during his life among us. He professes himself not to be made *a judge and divider over us.* Instead of that, he took upon him *the form of a servant,* both to God and man. He was a *servant of rulers.* His enemies used him at their pleasure, as *one whom man despises, and nations abhor;* carried as a lamb to the slaughter, and as a sheep before the shearers is dumb, so he opened not his mouth. He was subject to his parents; nay, when he became master of a family, though they that called him by that name said well, yet he was *among them as one that serves.* You find him *washing their feet,* which was the greatest and lowest act of respect in those countries; not only as a pattern of humility, but as an instance of humiliation. It is part of the obedience that he was sent into the world for. Thus the Evangelist puts it: *Jesus knowing that the Father had given all things into his hands, and that he was come from God, and went to God;* knowing this, he conforms himself to it; and how is that? *He rises up from supper, and laid aside his garments, and took a towel and girded himself.* There was a mystery in this action which the Spirit of grace and truth would afterwards explain to them: *What I do,* saith he to Peter, *thou knowest not now, but thou shalt know afterwards.* He was to be convinced with all other believers, that the design of Christ, in taking upon him our nature,

nature, was to sink him as low as that nature could fall, not only for the suffering of death at last, but to be a sort of *universal servant*. We ought therefore not to please ourselves, for even *Christ pleased not himself, as it is written, The reproaches of them that reproached thee, fell on me.* Under this contempt did he go through the life that was appointed for him. But,

He has the full reverse to all this meanness in being received up into glory. He is now no longer the servant of rulers, of disciples, or of enemies. *Every tongue must confess that Jesus is Lord, to the glory of God the Father.* The very nature that appeared as *a plant out of a dry ground,* shriveled, withered, and defiled, is now to be placed on a throne. He does not lay aside his humanity till the work of judgment is over, and put on state by hiding it; no, but in the very flesh and blood with which he lived so meanly shall we *behold the glory that the Father has given him.* He is as much found in fashion as a man upon the judgment-seat as he was upon the cross. *All nations* are to be collected and crouded *before him;* and he is so far from being ashamed of his conversation among us, that the trial of that day all along supposes it. *I was hungry, and ye gave me no meat; I was thirsty, and ye gave me no drink.* The meaning, as he himself explains it, is, that his people were so used in a wicked world; but however, his putting it into these terms is a memorial that he was among us, and liable to the same usage.

Nay, in this quality shall he judge the very devils; they are to stand and tremble before a nature lower than their own: as in that nature he subdued them, and took from them *the power of death,* so in that nature he will condemn and lay upon them the punishment of death. Herod and Pontius Pilate tossed him from one to another. His name and his people since that time have been the jest

jeſt of *kings;* but when his wrath is kindled, they above all others are to *periſh from the way.* Whatever his title was formerly, it is now *the bleſſed and only Potentate, the King of kings, and Lord of lords.* It is part of his royalty. As a Prophet he is the *faithful witneſs*, as a Prieſt *the firſt-begotten from the dead*, and as a King *the prince of the kings of the earth.* Thus he was revealed to Ezekiel: *Above the firmament there was the likeneſs of a throne, and upon the likeneſs of the throne was the likeneſs as the appearance of a man above upon it.*

SERM. 41.
Pſal. ii. 12.
1 Tim. vi. 15.
Rev i. 5, 6.

Ezek. i. 26.

10. The union with the Divine Nature, which is the greateſt glory that the human could have, is better known, revealed, and admired above. His name *Immanuel,* ſignifies, *God with us,* and that not merely in a gracious preſence; for in that ſenſe God was always with his people, *known in their palaces for a refuge:* But the words are to be underſtood of an union between two natures, that he ſhould be with us as one of ourſelves, like unto his brethren, and yet be God, truly, eſſentially, and eternally ſo. The people who knew him here had the diſcovery of this: *They ſaw his glory as the glory of the only begotten of the Father.* They did not merely take him for an extraordinary perſon, for that the very Jews did.

Mat. i. 23.

Joh. i. 14.

There was no conteſt between them and their enemies, whether he was not the beſt teacher, and the moſt accompliſhed prophet that ever aroſe in Iſrael; inſomuch, that they who denied his being the Son of God could not but aſk the queſtion, *When Chriſt comes, will he do more miracles than this man has done?* Nay, their wild and roving way of talking about him, though it was very wrong, yet ſhewed the prodigious opinion they had of him. Saith he to Peter, *Whom do men ſay that I the Son of man am?* By that they underſtood his queſtion to be, not whom do the Phariſees, the perverſe and hardened enemies of his kingdom, ſay he was; for

then

SERM. 42. then they would have anfwered, Some fay, thou art a deceiver, others that thou haft a devil, and art mad, and feveral that thou doft by *Beelzebub, the prince of the devils,* caft out devils. But it is plain they take his queftion in another view, and therefore give fuch an account of his reputation in the world, as we may be amazed at: *Some fay thou art John the Baptift,* who but about half a year ago was beheaded; others thou art *Efaias,* others *Jeremias, or as one of the prophets.*

This extravagant way of guefling fhewed their wonder as well as their ignorance. If they had not difcovered in him fomething which they thought no mortal ever had, they would not have imagined a thing which the Scripture never fpoke of, but was indeed the dream of Platonic philofophy, that after a man died, he was to live again. It was a foolifh imagination; but they could not any other way account for the wifdom and authority with which he taught. And yet, though they fuppofed him more than a man, they fell fhort of what he really was. Therefore he puts the queftion again: *But whom fay ye that I am?* Peter anfwers, *Thou art the Chrift, the Son of the living God.*

This good confeffion does not only regard his *office,* but his NATURE. So that if holinefs, wifdom, and all his other capacities for the work he comes about, could have given him the title of *the Son of God,* I do not fee but the Jews might have been brought to it. If they had thought, as fome do now, that the name fignified no more than a derivative deity, they that fuppofed that he was a perfon raifed from the dead, wanted but a very little of the truth. But it is apparent what Peter means by *the Son of God,* was fomething which they had not the leaft apprehenfion of; as he faith, *Bleffed art thou Simon Barjona, flefh and blood has not revealed this unto thee, but my Father which is in heaven.* Flefh and blood had revealed it to the

Jews

Jews that he was an extraordinary person: *They* SERM. 42.
knew that Jesus of Nazareth was a man approved Acts ii. 22.
of God among them by signs, and miracles, and won-
ders, which God did by him in the midst of them.
His being approved of God, and God's working
by him, which is all that some would have to be
the doctrine of Christianity, you see was the doctrine of Judaism. But his being united to God,
that he and the Father were one, was always the
great offence.

We are told by some interpreters now, that the
oneness he claims to have with the Father was no
other than that of consent. If that is all he meant
by it, the Jews would have allowed it. A little of
this critical learning among them then, would have
prevented their taking up stones to throw at him:
so that the persons who deny the *Divine* Nature
might have come in seasonably to have saved the
human. But this doctrine was *that rock upon which*
he would build his church: And though the gates
of hell have opened against it in every age, they
have never been able to prevail.

Now, this union between the two natures was
so glorious, that even as man he is called *the Son*
of God. Several things relating to this lower nature are brought in as reasons of the title. Thus
his miraculous conception is dignified: *The Holy* Luke i. 35.
Ghost shall come upon thee, and the power of the
Highest shall overshadow thee, and therefore that
holy Thing that shall be born of thee, shall be called
the Son of God. The commission which he received at his baptism is another ground of the title:
Say ye of him whom the Father has sanctified, and Joh. x. 36.
sent into the world, Thou blasphemest, because I said
unto you, I am the Son of God? His resurrection
declared him to be the Son of God *with power;* and Rom. i. 4.
with respect to this, as the Apostle observes, the
Father saith, *Thou art my Son, this day have I be-* Acts xiii.
gotten thee. 33.

This

SERM. 42. This was all along the confession of his people:
Joh. vi. 68, *To whom shall we go but to thee, for thou hast the*
69. *words of eternal life.* It cannot only mean that he
proclaimed it, and directed to it; for every preacher in that sense has the words of eternal life; but
he has them in a way suitable to a God: *We believe and are sure, that thou art that Christ, the Son
of the living God.* This faith increased by the
light with which he fed it. Thus at the close of
—xvi. 27. his life, he tells them, *The Father loves you, because
29, 30. ye have loved me, and believe that I came out from
God. His disciples say unto him, Lo, now thou
speakest plainly, and speakest no proverb. By this
we are sure that thou knowest all things, and needest
not that any man should ask thee. By this we believe
that thou camest forth from God.*

To this faith of theirs does Christ himself give
—xvii. 7. a testimony in his last prayer: *They have known*
8. *that all things whatsoever thou hast given me are of
thee, for I have given unto them the words that thou
gavest me, and they have received them, and have
known surely that I came out from thee, and they
have believed that thou didst send me.* And this he
mentions as the grand distinction between them
and others: *O righteous Father, the world has not
known thee, but I have known thee, and these have
known that thou didst send me.* There is no believing without this. This hypostatical union between God and man, this mystical union between
Christ and his people, are the great heads both of
truth and wonder: *I in them, and thou in me.*

And yet it is but little, even of this, that we are
let into now, in comparison of what we shall come
ver. 51. to see hereafter: *In that day,* saith Christ, *ye shall
know that I am in the Father, and the Father in me,
and I in you.* Though they knew it then, and witnessed a good confession to it, yet there was more
of this *light sown for the righteous.* It was not yet
come up, as it shall do in the time of harvest, with
perfect

perfect evidence and full pleasure. When the men that blaspheme this union shall dread the wrath of the Lamb, then shall grace and nature in God's people be equal to one another. There will be no grace but what is become nature, and no nature that is any thing else but grace. There is to be no knowing in part, but entire day-light shall reveal the mystery, and bless the faculty. There we shall see what we now subscribe, that a Child born is the *mighty God*, and a Son given is *the everlasting Father*.

Thus have I gone through these glories that belong to the human nature of our dear Lord, what are given to him as a man; but you may remember I told you the Scripture informs us of other glories, those that he enjoys as Mediator between God and man, and such as he had with the Father *before the world was*. These are to have a distinct meditation, as he said to Nathaniel, *You shall see greater things than these, the heavens opened, and Angels of God ascending and descending upon the Son of man*. All that I have spoken of, thus far, relates to *the man Christ Jesus;* in which he has put a dignity upon our nature, and is equally the friend and the sample of our happiness, *the first-born among many brethren*. But the others are peculiar to himself; they are glories that he will not give to another. In these we are to regard him not as an example, but as a head. I shall proceed to consider them in their order.

Joh. i. 51.

Rom. viii. 29.

(2.) Christ as MEDIATOR manages the great concern that lay between God and man. Our notion of a Mediator is, that he transacts for two parties, and that he may be capable of doing it with the greatest equality, he must have his character one of these ways, either by negation, or by participation.

First, There may be a mediator, or middle person in a way of *negation, i. e.* he has no share in either of the natures. Such a one we might have had in any of the Angels, who is neither God nor man. This is reckoned a good character in any umpire or referee upon earth. We think it a qualification that the judge, or person who determines between us, hath no interest in either party, but is purely indifferent, equally unswayed, and undetermined on both sides. Now this would have done, if the mediator was to be at no expence. An Angel might have transacted between God and us, if there was no more than carrying messages; but it cannot be expected that a creature, who has nothing to do with either party, should die by the *command* of the one, and for the *guilt* of the other. As an Angel had not a greatness to deal with God, so it would never be thought that he should have the tenderness to die for man; though he might be impartial, yet he was insufficient. The divine nature required more than he could *do*, and the human nature wanted more than he could *give*. Therefore,

Secondly, A mediator may be as well fitted for his work by participation, *i. e.* by having a share in *both natures*. This does as much qualify him for an equity in his proceedings, as if he had a concern in *neither*. If he is both God and man, he is as likely to move with an evenness between the two parties, as if he was neither. Had he been only God, our nature would have wanted a representative; had he been only man, the divine nature had wanted an equal, and therefore these two are united: from whence we may conclude, 1*st*, That the whole transaction will be steady, fair and uniform; and, 2*dly*, That the whole management will be zealous, hearty, and continued. Christ has a double interest in the mediation; he has that of a God; he is to see to it, that his own eternal nature is not injured, obscured, or neglected; and then the nature he took upon him is also his own, and

and he muſt ſecure that from being loſt, condemned, and ruined.

Now the glory belonging to him as Mediator you may conceive of in theſe particulars: the ſtupendous union of the two natures, a ſeparation to the work that is all his own, a diſcharge of the duty, an acquittance given him by the Father, the confirmation of this union for us, the wonder of the Angels and ſaints as it is in heaven, and the continuance of the mediation there.

1. One glory of our dear Lord as Mediator, is the ſtupendous union of the two natures, by which he was capable of it. This is a ſubject that I have but newly parted with under the former head, where I conſidered the evidence that would be given to it as a great branch of that glory that is put upon the human nature. Nothing higher, better, or more comprehenſive can be ſaid of the body and ſoul that were prepared for him, than that they are united to a God.

Father, Son, and Holy Ghoſt, are all repreſented as carrying on the work of ſalvation, bringing many ſons and daughters to glory; and the honour that riſes out of this deſign, the ſongs and praiſes that are filled with it, do equally regard them all. It may be ſaid of each perſon, that *he is the only wiſe God our Saviour*. Our happineſs is ſometimes aſcribed to one, and ſometimes to another, as if each one of the three had been the ſole agent. Thus it is *the God and Father of our Lord Jeſus Chriſt, who has bleſſed us with ſpiritual bleſſings in heavenly things in Chriſt Jeſus*: Eph. i. 3. And yet our praiſes are directed *to him who has loved us, and waſhed us from our ſins in his own blood*: Rev. i. 5, 6. And again it may be ſaid without any diminution, that *we are ſaved by the waſhing of regeneration, and renewing of the Holy Ghoſt*. Tit. iii. 5. We have them all mentioned together, *the foreknowledge of God the Father, the ſanctification* 1 Pet. i. 2.

SERM. 42 *of the Spirit unto obedience, and the sprinkling of the blood of Jesus Christ.*

However, there is something in the character of Christ Jesus as Mediator peculiar to himself. We say that he was God and man, both Creator and creature. He is the only person in the divine nature who was united to the human, and he is the only part of the creation that was united to God.

The doctrine of three Persons in the Deity is so plainly revealed in Scripture, that because people could not flatly deny it, they have tugged in vain at an explication, and professing themselves to be wise, have become fools. The Sabellians imagined there was no other way to secure the unity of the Godhead, and yet keep up a Trinity but this, that we are to conceive of no more than one person under three sorts of names. When we look upon God as a Creator, we call him Father; as a Redeemer, he is the Son, and as a Sanctifier, the Holy Ghost. This delusion made the ancients call them Patripassians, because they asserted that the Father suffered as truly as the Son. Thus do men lose their hold when they get out of their depth. Sabellius was convinced there could be but one God, and yet he knew that the divine attributes were plainly ascribed to him who came in the flesh, so that his error consisted in denying the distinction of persons. But it is plain from the whole language of the Bible, that Christ sustained those characters which the Father and the Holy Ghost did not; neither of these appeared in our nature, was *made of a woman, or made under the law.* So that

Isa. ix. 6. Here is the first glory that belongs to him, who was born as a *Son*, and given as a *Child*, that his name should be called *Wonderful:* Wonderful indeed! His human nature is *the beginning of the creation of God,* not because it was made first, but as it is distinguished from the whole universe.

Though

Though it is a creature, yet there is something **SERM. 42.** said of it, that can be true of no other; and so; though our praises are directed to the Divine Nature, and not to the man Christ Jesus, we regard the Father and the Holy Spirit as much as him in all our devotions. Yet there is something stupendous in his person, besides the greatness of a God. We are to contemplate that union in him which there is in no one else; *for in him dwells all the* **Col. ii. 9.** *fulness of the Godhead bodily.*

2. The consequence to this, is his separation to the work that he came about. Though saving the elect was a general concern, and *the Three in heaven bear record to it,* yet there was a part that he took in this design peculiar to himself: *In ordaining him before the world unto our glory, the counsel of peace was between them both.* We are redeemed by the Father and the Spirit, as well as the Son. *Our God is the God of salvation, and to God the Lord,* to each Person, *belong the issues from death.* But it cannot be said of any besides the Son, that he took part of our flesh and blood, that he died for us. *He trode the wine-press alone.* Thus was he set apart to a work that none in the creation could do, and that none but himself in the Deity had done.

The virtue, the merit, the success of his death, were all derived from that nature which he has equally with the Father and the Holy Ghost; but the torment, the suffering, the actual expence was all personal. It is the *precious blood of Christ* by **1 Pet. i. 19, 20.** which we are redeemed, who was made *manifest in these last times.* We may not say that the Father was born, or that the Spirit was crucified.

I am sensible a thousand questions may be asked upon this subject, which the wisdom of men and Angels will be unable to manage; but are we therefore to be driven out of it? Does it cease to be a *truth,* because it is a *wonder?* No, whatever
controversy

SERM. 42. controversy there has been and will be in the manner of talking about it, yet *without controversy great is the mystery of godliness, that God was manifest in the flesh.* God above us is to be understood of a nature, but *God with us* is the description given of a person. This is the mystery that

Col. ii. 2, 3. we are called to the acknowledgment of: *The mystery of God, and of the Father, and of Christ, in whom are hid all the treasures of wisdom and knowledge.*

Jan. 3. 1719-20.

SERMON XLIII.

3. ANOTHER glory belonging to Christ as the Mediator between God and man, arises from his discharge of the duty devolved upon him. He received our nature into an union with his own, for the sake of doing that which was left with him alone. There is none in heaven but he that undertook it, and none upon earth was

1 Tim. ii. 5, 6. able to succeed him in it. For there *is one God, and one Mediator between God and men, the man Christ Jesus, who gave himself a ransom for all, to be testified in due time.*

This was no less important in itself, than expensive to him. He came upon earth to transact with God the things that appertained to the reconciliation of his people. This world having been the stage of rebellion must be the place of an atonement. He came to bear our sins, to carry our burdens: *The Lord laid on him the iniquity of us all;* such a weight as no creature could be able

to

to manage. Every believer sinks under the pressure of his own guilt; when iniquities go over his head, they are a burden too heavy for him to bear. How then would he be capable to answer for all the sins of all the elect, in all the places and ages of the world? Thousands of thousands are got to glory, and vast numbers are yet to follow. Every one of these could say with David, *Innumerable evils have compassed me about, so that I am not able to lift up my head.*

Now, there must be a full compensation made to the justice of God for the whole number of their abominations. And who was able to pay such a debt? What merit could be equal to this heap of collected guilt? If the justice of God is to be satisfied, not only for every person, but for every particular crime, we must all be *concluded under sin. When we were without strength in due time Christ died for the ungodly; when we were yet sinners Christ died for us.*

Whatever was the meaning of John's vision, when he *saw in the right-hand of him that sits on the throne a book written within and on the back side, sealed with seven seals,* it gave him an inward concern; whether this was the book of the decrees, called in some places the book of life, which was to be of no avail till it was opened and unsealed; or whether it was the book of trial by which the world is to be judged, and taking off the seals was to answer the charge recorded there, I cannot pretend to determine the sense of this awful emblem: But it is plain, the happiness of good people was a thing in the nearest connection to the opening of that book; that if the book was always shut, there could be no access for them, no security of the covenant, no entrance into the joys of the kingdom; and yet here seems to be a bar in the way of that design; for a *strong Angel* proclaimed

SERM. 43. *claimed with a loud voice, saying, Who is worthy to open the book, and to loose the seals thereof?*

You may argue from this, *first*, That the design of love was at a stand; that the seals upon this book hindered the mercy of God from taking its compass; till these were loosed, nothing could be done: *Secondly*, You farther see, that it was an universal concern, what the whole creation must be attentive to; *a strong Angel with a loud voice* delivers out the proclamation: And, *thirdly*, It is also evident from the nature of his cry, that whoever undertook this great affair, he must go through it in a way of merit. The question is, Who is worthy to do it? This includes both a dignity of person, Who is *great* enough to attempt it? and a value of obedience, Who can do actions *good* enough to deserve it?

Some people make but a small matter of redemption, as if it was no more than what a creature might perform; but the Apostle tells us, that

Rev. v. 3. *ἴδης, no man,* no person *in heaven, or on earth, or under the earth, was able to open the book, neither to look thereon.* This shews that the design was too glorious and dazzling for them; for if they could not behold it, much less were they able to

ver. 4. unseal it. Upon this, faith the good man, *I wept much.* He thought it was heavy tidings; it rendered the whole creation insignificant to him, *because no man was found worthy to open and read the book, neither to look thereon.* Those in heaven, Abraham, Isaac, and Jacob, Moses, David, Samuel, and the prophets, *the spirits of just men made perfect*, had as much holiness and capacity as their natures could hold, and yet the book confounded them as well as their brethren who were still in houses of clay. Think of this, if any of you run into the vanity of praying to the saints; there is something needful to your salvation, which all the

saints

faints in heaven dare not so much as attempt. But

Whilst the Apostle was all in tears, *one of the elders faith to him, Weep not; for behold the Lion of the tribe of Judah, the root of David, has prevailed to open the book, and to loose the seven seals thereof.* These titles, the Lion of the tribe of Judah, and the root of David, plainly refer to his incarnation. He was of the seed of David, according to the flesh, he came of the fruit of his loins; but if that was all, why should not any of the Angels have done it as well as he? For it is certain, when he took upon him our nature, he was made *lower than the Angels.* He no farther belonged to the tribe of Judah than as a man, and nothing that he received from any relations could make him equal to that affair. Supposing, as some tell us, that as the son of David he had a claim to the throne, yet what is that to the opening of a book in heaven, and the great negotiations there? Therefore you will find there is something in the wording of these titles that shews him to be above the tribe of Judah, and the family of David.

Our translation indeed tells us he is the Lion of the tribe of Judah, but that is flat and falls below the majesty of the Greek, for there it is ὁ λίων ὁ ὢν ἐκ τῆς φυλῆς Ἰούδα, the Lion who is of the tribe of Juda. And then again, when he is called the root of David, it expresses a great deal more than the relation; for if that was all, we may rather say that David was the root of him; but this name shews us that he communicated to David as well as received from him. Though David lived so many ages ago, he derived from a person who came after him. Hence he has both those titles together, which seem to contradict one another, he is *the root and offspring of David;* but they are to be understood in the way that our Lord's question

SERM. 43 to the Pharisees was to be answered: *That if David in the spirit called him Lord, how is he then his son?* Well,

It is said of him here, *that he has prevailed to open the book, and to loose the seals thereof.* Compare these two accounts together; the enquiry was about one who should be *worthy* to do it, the report is of one that has *prevailed* to do it: which shews, as I said before, that there must be a dignity of person in him that undertook it. You see, it is reckoned a great victory, a mighty success, that he has gone through with it: It supposes that an opposition would be made, against which he has prevailed. This twisting and joining of the characters tells us, that in so awful an affair Christ is considered both in his majesty and in his merit; as one that *prevails* to do a thing that was very hard and difficult, he is called a *Lion*; and yet the next view that the Apostle takes of him is as a *Lamb*. As a Lion he would be in all the po-

Rev. v. 6. stures of triumph, but as *a Lamb in the midst of the throne*, he is like *one that has been slain*. The sacrifice of a Lamb supposes death, misery, and the lowest condition that can be; the victory of a Lion supposes quite the contrary; and therefore what is said of him in one character looks as if it came to raze out all the other; but here they are consistent, to be an eternal monument in heaven, that the success of our Redeemer was owing both to the greatness of his arm and the misery of his life. As he sustained a character that none other did either in heaven or in earth, so he went through the design for which he was consecrated. He was made a *High-priest* for the atonement of his people, he was a *Captain* of salvation for their dependence; and he has done what was expected from him in both relations, though the one was an extreme to the other. Nothing could be viler and meaner than what he submitted to as a Priest,

and

and nothing nobler and greater than what he tranf- SERM. 43.
acted as a King.

4. He is farther glorified as a Mediator, in that the Father has given him an acquittance, and declared that he did all that was appointed to him. This he was affured of beforehand, and therefore at the long diftance of a prophecy he faith of him, *Behold my fervant whom I uphold, mine elect in* Ifa. xlii. 1. *whom my foul delighteth.* And again, he faith, *Thou art my fervant, O Ifrael, in whom I will be* ———xlix. 3. *glorified.* He gives him the name of *Ifrael,* which he had given to Jacob, on account of his having *power with God and man, and prevailing.* So he faith in another place, *By his knowledge fhall my* ———liii. 11. *righteous fervant juftify many, for he fhall bear their iniquities.* And with the fame confidence of being accepted does Chrift himfelf fpeak, *I fhall be glorious in the eyes of the Lord, and my God fhall be my ftrength.*

His rewards are put upon his integrity and obedience: *Thou lovest righteoufnefs, and hateft wicked-* Pfal. xlv. 7, *nefs; therefore God, even thy God, has anointed thee* 8. *with the oil of gladnefs above thy fellows.* This refers to the reputation that he was received up into: *All thy garments fmell of myrrh, and aloes, and caffia, out of the ivory palaces whereby they have made thee glad.* It was upon this that he depended in his whole courfe of duty. *As the Fa-* John x. 15. *ther knows me, fo I know the Father,—I lay down my life for the fheep;* as if he had faid, ' This
' furrender of my life does not only proceed from
' a love to the fheep, but it is the effect of a bar-
' gain with the Father; we know one another;
' I know what he has commanded, and he will
' know what I have deferved.'

This was *the joy fet before him,* when he endured Heb. xii. 2. the crofs. It is faid, that he then *defpifed the fhame.* The fhame of the crofs was very great, not only as a fcandalous fort of death, *Curfed is*

VOL. II.   X   *every*

SERM. 43. *every one who is hanged on a tree;* but as by that means his enemies insulted him, and seemed to do it with reason, *He trusted in God that he would deliver him, let him deliver him, seeing he delighted in him!* Then did they *esteem him stricken, smitten of God, and afflicted.* But all that reproach he did not value, as he saith in the prophecy, *The Lord God will help me, therefore shall I not be confounded, therefore have I set my face like a flint, and I know that I shall not be ashamed: He is near that justifies me; who will contend with me? who is mine adversary? let him come near unto me: Behold, the Lord will help me; who is he that shall condemn me?*

Isa. l. 7, 8, 9.

What expressions are here! He seems to challenge his enemies, and dare them to come near, though they crouded about his cross; he talks of God's being near, though he complained of his forsaking him: But all this was true, for he despised the shame of the cross, because of a joy set before him; that is, as it stands in the prophecy, God would *justify* him, he would plead his reproach. They insinuated that God had forsaken him, but that would soon appear to be false. He used to say, *He that sent me is with me, the Father has not left me alone, because I always do the things that please him.* But now when he came to die, he seems to want that Divine presence; for how shall we know that what he did was pleasing to the Father? Well, *that* he had an evidence of two ways:

John viii. 29.

First, In the agony of his dying; he found, he felt a Divine approbation then; though the human nature was to suffer under a thicker darkness than that which covered the earth, I mean a suspence of the light of God's countenance, yet still as Mediator he had a testimony given him then; and all that whole period of his suffering was filled with the Father's witness to him. When Judas went out to open the tragedy, *Now,* saith Jesus, *is the*

—xiii. 31.

the Son of man glorified, and God is glorified in him. SERM. 43. The former of these expressions shews what he *had*, the latter what he *did*, that in the same moment he received his approbation and discharged his duty. This he said as soon as ever that wretch had left them; and as the time of his death approached, so the joys of his soul increased. When he is upon the brink of the pit, he cries out, *Father, the hour is come, glorify thy Son, that thy* John xvii. 1. *Son also may glorify thee.* There never was any moment of his life in which the Father had not glorified the Son: He had all along *the glory of the only begotten of the Father;* and so constantly did the Son glorify the Father, that *In him,* saith the Father, *I am always well pleased.* But now the hour was come for these mutual glorifications, these exchanges of love and duty to be more abundant. In the hour of his death, as the Son went farther in his obedience to the Father, so he received a greater testimony upon his soul from him.

It is true, this is what sinners did not see. The spear could not reach these inward joys, they lay deeper than the place where that went. But it is what the devils felt; though men were unbelievers, *they* believed and trembled. For in his cross he *triumphed over principalities and powers, he made a* Col. ii. 15. *shew of them openly in the air.* And though mankind saw nothing in his case but a gross and wretched death, yet by that he *subdued him that had the power of death, that is, the devil.* Thus the acquittance that the Father had given him, the divine approbation that he received in his sufferings were plainly seen to the powers of darkness. They cried out, before the Centurion said it, *Truly this was the Son of God.* But besides this, the acquittance must be legible even to us. There is a way for men to know, that what he did and suffered was approved of; and that is plain from another testimony

SERM. 43. testimony that God gave him, and every way prepared for our conviction, and that is,

Secondly, His resurrection. This discharged him from all farther atonements, and opened the way to his throne. Hence he is said not only to be *de* Rom. iv. *livered for our offences,* but to *rise again for our* 25. *justification.* Our justification is in the death of Christ; we are pardoned on the account of what he suffered; it is *his blood* that cleanses from all sin, and yet here it is put upon his *resurrection*, not as the price of our acceptance, but as a public evidence to it. And therefore, as the Apostle —— viii. saith, *Who shall lay any thing to the charge of God's* 33, 34. *elect? It is God that justifies: Who is he that condemns? It is Christ that died, or rather is risen again.*

There were to be two glories succeeding his trouble and death; one was, that as a High-priest he should go into the holiest of all, to plead the virtue of his blood; and the other, that as a Judge he was to render a reward to his enemies, and a recompence to those that hate him. Now his resurrection is an argument of both these; for when Heb. ix. 24. he rose again, it was to *enter into heaven itself, there to appear in the presence of God for us,* be admitted nearer the mercy-seat than any creature can pretend to. When the high-priest went into the holy of holies, he did that which no person upon the face of the earth besides himself was appointed to do. He went thither *alone,* and that but *once a-year.* Christ is alone in this honour, but in this he differs from the man who was typical of him, that he does not return back again: —— vii. *He ever lives to make intercession for us.* Whilst he 25. lay in the grave this honour was deferred; nay, whilst he conversed with his disciples those forty John xx. days after his passion, he *had not ascended to his* 17. *Father;* but he informed his brethren, that *he would ascend to his Father and their Father, to his*

God

God and their God. Thus the Father owned him as a *Priest* by his refurrection.

The other honour defigned for him, and to be difcovered this way, was that of a *Judge*. The Apoftle tells the Athenians, *God has appointed a day in which he will judge the world in righteoufnefs, by that Man whom he has ordained, whereof he has given affurance to all men, in that he has raifed him from the dead.* His refurrection proclaims the character; by that it appears that he has the power of life and death; the power of the death that he fuffered, and the life that he refumed: *I am he who was dead, and is alive, and I live for evermore, and I have the keys of eternity and of death.* [As I have gone through this paffage, I now controul it.] Thus you confider the great Mediator as one approved of God. It was this that he himfelf valued above his chiefeft joy; and this he had not only to the fatisfaction of his own foul, but to the confufion of devils, and the conviction of men.

5. Another glory of a Mediator is, that the union between the two natures is now confirmed for ever. He was not a partaker of our flefh and blood merely to ferve a turn, to live with it, and die in it, and then lay it afide as a garment that is moth-eaten; no, but though from eternity he was not man, yet to eternity he fhall be fo. I believe a more comprehenfive defcription was never given of him fince the foundation of the world, than you have in the Affembly's Shorter Catechifm, in anfwer to the twenty-firft queftion, ' Who is
' the Redeemer of God's elect?—The only Re-
' deemer of God's elect is the Lord Jefus Chrift,
' who being the eternal Son of God, became man,
' and fo was and continues to be God and man, in
' two diftinct natures, and one perfon, for ever.'
I am apt to think, a plainer and more copious fentence is not eafily to be met with: every word is

both

both open and full; there is not an expression that is either difficult or superfluous. And therefore I will venture to say, that the men who call this a polite age, perhaps in compliment to their own dear selves, may sooner reproach this work than equal it. Here you are told,

1st, What this Redeemer of God's elect *was* antecedent to his design, no less than *the eternal Son of God.* 2dly, You read that he *became man;* the Scripture has given us abundant evidence of both these. 3dly, That he *was so* quite through his life: nay, 4thly, That he *continues to be God and man,* as much in heaven as upon earth, and yet this without any confusion: for, 5thly, It is *in two distinct natures;* the Divine never mingles with the human, nor does the human rise into the Divine: and, 6thly, He is but *one Person* in both these natures; the natures are distinct, but not divided: and, 7thly, Thus he will continue *for ever.* That as *by* this union he did his work, and suffered his pains, so *in that* he will possess his glory. We read oftentimes of Angels appearing to them under the Old Testament. Whatever those bodies were, perhaps only a little thickened air, yet it is probable they were laid aside when the expedition was over. But as the body of Christ was more solid and penetrable than theirs, so he will always preserve it. Hence we read of the fulness of the Godhead dwelling in him *bodily;* and that *because he continues for ever, he has an unchangeable priesthood.*

6. In this union he receives the praises and wonders of the saints and Angels. They are *to behold his glory,* not only that of his reward, but that of his person. There is not any of these mysteries that the world do laugh at, which the believer does not wonder at. The Christian and infidel are both amazed that the Son of God should become man: that as God he is a Son without beginning, and as man he is a Son without begetting; in neither

ther of thefe can any one *declare his generation.* Here is the difference between him that believes and an infidel. The defpifers they *behold and wonder;* but it is to *perifh.* This is foolifhnefs to them, they hate the light, they ridicule it, and cry out, not with humility, but with fcorn, *How can thefe things be?* The fame queftion may be put by better people, and fo it is, but with a better fpirit.

Thefe are *unfearchable riches of Chrift:* in them we find *the manifold wifdom of God,* πολυποίκιλ σοφία, a wifdom that is rolled up, and has laid its defign in folds, which muft be hid till they come to be opened. This is among the reafons why a believer *groans earneftly, defiring to be unclothed,* becaufe when he is fo, then this wifdom which he pries into will be unfolded. This, which is the contempt of finners, will be the entertainment of faints. The myftery of God, and of the Father, and of Chrift, is now acknowledged; but then as it will be more feen, fo it will be better loved. Unbelievers are then to gnafh their teeth in pain as now they do it in fcorn. Their indignation at the truth will grow upon them, and become their torment as it is here their crime. They all hated to *hear* that Chrift was God, and then they muft hate to *feel* it. Whilft they who have kept his name fhall fee his face, and as through faith they have believed the promifes, fo at the end of that faith they fhall go to inherit them.

Angels themfelves, who at the time of his birth called him *a Saviour, Chrift Jefus the Lord,* behold him in both natures. They loved him whilft he lay in the manger; there was *a multitude of the heavenly hoft to fing his praifes then:* And yet at that time the human nature was imperfect, and the Divine obfcure. But now he has the complete glory that can be given to a man, and the full manifeftation that will be the delight of a God The man Chrift Jefus is the higheft creature above all things:

Eph. iii. 8. 10.

SERM. 43. things: the God Christ Jesus is before all things, and *by him do all things consist;* and in his whole Person he is *in all things to have the pre-eminence.* Here is in him a nature that cannot be adored without idolatry, and yet there is another, upon the account of which, we read of the same praises given to *him that sits upon the throne, and to the Lamb for ever.*

7. Another glory belonging to Christ as Mediator, is the continuance of the mediation; that he, having reconciled us to God, should ever live to introduce us. Our approach to the Divine Nature must be through *him* who took upon him the human. This indeed being the experience of heaven, it is but little that we know of it. But from the Scripture I observe these two things,

First, That this must be in a more familiar way than it is at present. The mediation is not with that distance and compass: *In that day*, saith Christ, *ye shall ask me nothing; Verily, verily, I say unto you, whatever ye ask the Father in my name, he will give it you. And I say not unto you, that I will pray the Father for you, for the Father himself loveth you, because ye have loved me, and have believed that I came forth from God.* And yet,

John xvi. 23. 26, 27.

Secondly, That there is to be an eternal mediation seems to be the plain language of the Bible. Whatever nearness we have to the Divine Majesty, though it will be unspeakably more than we can pretend to now, yet it all comes this way. Thus we read of the Martyrs that came out of great tribulation, that *they washed their robes, and made them white in the blood of the Lamb. Therefore,* upon the account of that purification, *they are before the throne of God day and night, and serve him in his temple, and he that sits upon the throne shall dwell among them.* But yet it is added, that *the Lamb in the midst of the throne shall feed them, and lead them to living fountains of waters; and God shall*

Rev. vii. 14, 15. 17.

shall wipe away all tears from their eyes. As he does upon our first arrival present us *unblameable and unreproveable in his sight,* so all our acceptance is still *in the Beloved.* We may well therefore desire to be *found in his righteousness* here, for we shall be found in no other to eternity. Thus when we read of a happiness that is to be had in the Divine presence, the care of a Redeemer is joined with it. There is no temple above, for *the Lord God Almighty, and the Lamb, are the temple of it. The city has no need of the sun, neither of the moon, to shine in it; for the glory of the Lord does lighten it, and the Lamb is the light thereof.*

Rev. xxi. 22, 23.

SERMON XLIV.

Jan. 17. 1719-20.

(3.) THERE is another glory which by the Scriptures we are taught to contemplate in our great Redeemer; and that is, what he had independent on his mediation, and antecedent to it: *The Lord possessed him in the beginning of his way, before his works of old: he was set up from everlasting, from the beginning, or ever the earth was.* This, I conceive, is what he speaks of in that moving prayer, *Father, glorify me with thy ownself, with the glory that I had with thee before the world was.* There are three things which may be observed in the language he there uses:

Prov. viii. 22, 23.

Joh. xvii. 5.

First, That he is a distinct person from the Father. The Evangelist tells us, *The word was with God,* and here he himself speaks of his being glorified *with* the Father, and refers to a glory that he had

had *with him* before the world was. This remark is destructive of Sabellianism. Thus he saith in another place, It is written in your law, that *the testimony of two men is true: I am one that bear witness of myself, and the Father that sent me bears witness of me.*

Secondly, You may also take notice, that he had a pre-existence, not only before his coming into the world, but before the very creation of the world. Though he prays to be received into the rewards of a service done in the fulness of time, yet he plainly affirms, that he had not only a being, but a *glory before the world was.* This lays flat the whole fabrick of Socinianism. And,

Thirdly, It is also evident from these words, that he had a glory independent on any concern about the redemption of his people. He enjoyed it *before the world was,* and desires to have it again.

I do not find that this will be disputed by those who are enemies to *the present truth.* They will allow Christ Jesus every thing but his Deity; and therefore, as if they would make a more honourable composition than the Socinians did, they tell us, that he was *before* all worlds, that he had a glory *above* them; nay, that he was appointed by the Father to *make* them, that he is the great deputed agent in the creation, and the chief minister of state in providence. Now this glory that he had with the Father before the world was, must be considered in one of these three explications. Either,

1st, It relates to him as the Supreme Creature, the first and best work of Omnipotence; and this he prays to be restored to, as what he had been kept out of for some time; so that his petition is no more than to go back again, to sit at the head of Angels and saints, being made so much better than they; that his seat had been empty at the King's table; he had obscured the pre-eminence

that

that was given him by creation; he wanted to be gone out of a world, where he lived below the sons of men, and into another, where his throne was set *above the stars of God.* Or,

2dly, This glory that he had with the Father must be understood of the relative character which he there assumed. He considered himself as *ordained before the world* to the happiness of his people. He then *rejoiced in the habitable parts of the earth, and his delights were amongst the sons of men.* Thus he is called *the Lamb slain from the foundation of the world.* And upon the credit of that obligation which he put himself under, a provision was made for the elect as soon as they sinned, and a happiness was ready for them as soon as they died. And therefore in this sense desiring the glory that he had with the Father, is a petition for the brightning up of his title; that being always known to be a Mediator between God and man, he might now be received as having answered his trust. This to me is a more plausible exposition than the other, and stands fairer to be the sense of the words. But yet,

3dly, I am of opinion that *the glory* which he speaks of, must be that which he had IN HIMSELF *with the Father*, and which is to be considered apart from all relations to his people. He applies to the Father, not as the *giver* of it, but as a *partner* in it. It is true, every one of the saints above have a glory with the Father; but methinks there is something in the words impatient of being drawn down to a low and common sense. We are said to be glorified *in God*, Christ was glorified WITH *him;* and that argues no more dependence in the Son, than it does in the Father. He here speaks of that which went before any service or duty. Though he pleads for it, after he had finished the work that was given him to do, yet he esteems it above all the characters of a reward.

SERM. 44.

If he had been only a creature, and from the higheſt dignity had come down into the form of a ſervant, he muſt have demanded *more* than he once enjoyed. For ſuppoſing an Angel had gone through the toil and ſorrow that *he* took upon him, it had been no reward to that Angel, that he went back again into his place. There would be no proportion between his ſuffering of death, and making him what he was before; for the rule of recompence was, *He ſhall drink of the brook in the way, and therefore ſhall he lift up the head.* Indeed as a man, Chriſt Jeſus is highly exalted, *crowned with glory and honour for the ſuffering of death.*

Pſ. cx. ult.

Heb. ii. 9.

But this is not the glory that he begged for; this glory he *had not* before the world was; it was all new to him. It begun upon his return to heaven; his body was never there till after the reſurrection. When he is ſaid to come down from heaven, it is not to be underſtood of the human nature. And therefore, though he begs that this may be glorified, yet it is not the thing that he deſigns in that part of the prayer that is now under our meditation. This had no *glory*, becauſe it had no being *before the world was: It was not till the fulneſs of time came, that God ſent forth his Son, made of a woman, made under the law.*

Gal. iv. 4.

And, if he only pleads to go back into that preeminence that he, as the beſt creature, had above all the reſt, I do not ſee where the reward lies; he could be no higher than he was. Every thing was put under his feet after the reſurrection, as man, and ſo was every thing before, as a ſuperangelical Spirit. So that here is a moſt grateful obedience to the Father, that has no retribution made to it. But, If you will underſtand this glory that he has *with the Father*, of ſomething that declares him *equal to the Father*, the petition is unincumbered, and ſtands clear of all the force and danger that other interpretations have thrown it under.

Indeed

Indeed there is one objection against it, and that is this, that if he begs for a glory that belongs to the Divine nature, he begs for that which he had already. And to this the answer is easy enough, that he does so. And there will be no absurdity in that, if you do but consider that he delivers this prayer in the hearing of his disciples, and therefore only speaks in a supplication, what he had before told them in a doctrine. The great instruction he had given them was, that *he is in the Father, and the Father in him:* and the main revelation of another world is, *In that day ye shall know that I am in the Father, and the Father in me.* This was a bold assertion, and what ought to be supported with equal proof. Now, to convince them that it was all true, he demands *that* from the Father, which he had proclaimed to his disciples.

SERM. 44.

Joh. xiv. 20.

He speaks of a glory that he had with Him; and this was indeed uninterrupted; he had it at the time that he desired it; but he uses that petition for the establishment of their faith. It was the same that he did at Lazarus's grave: *I thank thee, that thou hast heard me, and I know that thou hearest me always; but because of these that stand by I said it, that they may believe that thou hast sent me.* And so he says here, *I come unto thee, and these things I speak in the world, that they may have my joy fulfilled in themselves.* If the glory that he had with the Father was only the rank that he possessed in the creation, this was no reward. It cannot be said, that by restoring him to *that*, God did highly exalt him, and *give* him a name above every name; because *that* he might demand, not from his service, but from his nature. But here he speaks of a glory that he had *with the Father*, as that which could never be exceeded, amended, or enlarged.

— xi. 42.

— xvii. 13.

This is what I am now called to lay before you. His glory as a man is the *sample* of your happiness;

his

his glory as a Mediator is the *means* of it; but his glory as a God is the *fountain* out of which it is supplied. *I give to them,* faith he, *eternal life, and they shall never perish, neither shall any man pluck them out of my hand.* This is infinitely above the other two. They were very dazzling, and threw an aſtoniſhment into all our pleaſures; but in *this* we are ſwallowed up. We cannot by ſearching find out God, we cannot find out the Almighty unto perfection. When we follow a Redeemer, as he appears in *the faſhion of a man, and the form of a ſervant,* there is a limitation upon his character, it is finite and bounded. But when we read that *the Word was with God,* and *the Word was God,* we are loſt in a nature that has all depth and glory. And yet, thus we are to conſider *him,* who was made of a woman, and made under the law. There are *unſearchable riches in Chriſt.* He is not only *the elect of God, and precious,* but one exalted above all bleſſing and praiſe.

We do not worſhip him as a man; in that nature he is only the head of the family, *the firſt-born among many brethren.* Nay, we do not worſhip him as Mediator; for though that ſuppoſes him to be God, yet under that notion, it is *by him that we approach to the Father.* He was *fore-ordained before the foundation of the world, but was manifeſt in theſe laſt times for you, who* BY HIM *do believe in God, that raiſed him from the dead, and gave him glory, that your faith and hope may be in God.* But yet,

A worſhip, without any rule of abatement, is given to him, and appointed for him. He is the object, as well as the pattern and the medium, of our faith, and love, and reverence: *Let all the Angels of God worſhip him,* ſaith the Apoſtle; *Worſhip him all ye gods,* ſaith the Pſalmiſt. We do not aſſert this upon the foundation of ſynods and councils, but in the plain light of revelation. God himſelf

himself has told us so; and that, not by obscure and uncertain consequences, but in palpable declarations. He that runs may read them. And *if this Gospel is hid, it is hid to them that are lost, in which the god of this world has blinded the eyes of them that believe not, lest the light of the glorious Gospel of Christ, who is the image of God, should shine into them.*

SERM. 44.

2 Cor. iv. 3, 4.

I will shew you, that the glory of Christ is spoken of in the Bible as the glory of the GREAT GOD; in the same terms, with the same force and fulness. The Father speaks of the Son, just as he does of himself; and though some vain men will pretend to bound the sense of the words, yet we have no such distinction between a supreme and subordinate God in all the Scriptures. I will shew you some things that the Divine Nature has always claimed as its own glory, and under every one of these heads you shall see, that it is *thus* we are to conceive of the great Redeemer; not as a Redeemer, but in his antecedent Being. And before I enter into the particulars, I would only give you this note upon the glory of God, that it is taken in a twofold sense:

First, For that perfection which he has in himself, and which he had eternally before there were any to own it. God had a glory, when there were no Angels nor saints to give it. His happiness lay in the contemplations of his wisdom: The full object to an infinite mind was an infinite nature. It is a raw and impious notion that some people have published of late, that the name of God is a relative word, and he is only called so with respect to what he has made. A vile undigested fancy, and abominable both to all revelation, and all the light of nature. Before the mountains were brought forth, or ever thou hadst formed the earth or the world, *from everlasting to everlasting Thou art God.* Psal. xc. 2.
But it is no wonder, that people are given up to a reprobate

reprobate mind, that they who deny the Godhead of Christ should be left to debase the Godhead in general. So true is the observation, *He that honours not the Son, honours not the Father who sent him.* Therefore what the Scripture calls the glory of God, is not always to be understood of the tribute and praises that his creatures give him, but the felicity and fulness of his own nature. That which he had before there were any to tell him so, and that which he will have, if the whole creation were expunged and reduced to nothing. By the glory of God, therefore, I understand his perfection: *O Lord, our Lord, how excellent is thy name in all the earth! who hast set thy glory above the heavens!* And yet,

Secondly, Sometimes this glory of God that we find in Scripture is to be expounded of those acknowledgments that are made from the works of his hands, or those discoveries that arise from what he has done: *The glory of the Lord shall endure for ever, the Lord shall rejoice in all his works.* Thus we read that *the heavens declare his glory,* and the saints in his temple *behold his glory.* This is done very different ways: the one is the argument, the provocation, and ground of his praises; the other are the people who look upon what he has wrought, and pay him the tribute of it. They *consider his heavens the work of his fingers, the moon and the stars that he has ordained.*

Now, this glory that he has, either from his works or his people, gives nothing to him. It is only their admiring or shewing what *he is* in himself, by what he has declared to them. So that, shewing his glory is but sounding forth the glory that was in him before. And here,

When we speak of the glory of the Lord, it is to be understood of that which is peculiar to himself. We are told of *a glory that he will not give to another.* The naming of *that* which none but a God can have, is properly aſcribing him glory. This is talking of his wondrous works, and making mention that his name is exalted.

There are ſeveral things which by the Scripture we are taught to believe no creature can ſhare in; God has claimed them as ſo many prerogatives; that he is a *Spirit*, that he is infinite in *knowledge*, that his *power* is almighty, that his *truth* endures for ever, that he is *holy* and *good*, **that he is *eternal*,** that he is the ſupreme *Agent* in nature and grace, and that he has a right to the *homage* of all his creatures. Theſe are ſo many royalties of the Divine Nature, which I ſhall conſider in this order; and there are three things that I would affirm of them all.

1ſt, It is very true, the characters I have now mentioned are beſtowed on creatures: they may be ſpirits, may have great knowledge, power, truth, and ſome of them will be eternal: they are employed in the works of nature and grace, and a tribute of worſhip is given to them. This agrees to the language of Scripture; but that ought by no means to take off the force of an argument, becauſe, though theſe words in a lower ſenſe may be underſtood ſo as to imply nothing of Deity, yet,

2dly, It is by theſe very terms that God has given us an account of himſelf. And when he ſpeaks of his own as a glory diſtinct from the whole creation, it is upon the head of ſpirituality, knowledge, power, truth, holineſs, and eternity. And therefore, if there is not a meaning that theſe words have which is incommunicable to a creature, the accounts given us of a God are ſtruck out of the Bible. But certainly there muſt be ſomething true of him, which is true of no other. Now,

3dly, I will ſhew you, under every one of theſe particulars, that what the great God claims to himſelf is given to Chriſt Jeſus: not as man, for ſo he would have refuſed it, but as One who is *over all*,

God *blessed for ever.* And in doing this my business is more adoration than argument; not so much to convince you of a truth, as to lead you into a temper of duty.

1. One glory of the Divine Nature is its spirituality: *Thou canst not see my face,* saith God to Moses; *for there is no man shall see me, and live.* And yet we are told of this good man, that *with him God spake mouth to mouth, even apparently, and not in dark speeches, and the similitude of the Lord did he behold.* This our Saviour tells the poor woman of Samaria, *God is a Spirit, and they that worship him must worship him in spirit and in truth.* Of this indeed we have very narrow conceptions, not being able to explain the spirit that is within ourselves; but, however, we must remove from it all that is gross and corporeal. And though God has told us of his eyes, and ears, and hands, and feet, yet we are by no means to conceive so heavily of him, as if he was *altogether such a one as ourselves;* for *he has not eyes of flesh, nor does he see as man sees.*

I think there is a fatality upon all those who deny the Divinity of our blessed Lord, that they are *changing the glory of the incorruptible God* into something that is beneath him. In the last age the most notorious enemy to the Deity of Christ represented the spirituality of the Divine Nature as a metaphysical notion; and in opposition to it, very crudely tells us, that you read of God's remembering, and forgetting, and repenting, and coming down from heaven; a plain instance that *to them who are unbelieving nothing is pure, but their mind and conscience are defiled.*

And now in our days, one that pursues the same argument, with a vehemence as if he thought himself born to do his utmost against the Godhead of Christ, tells us, that we are not to trouble our heads with God's omnipresence, immensity,

and

and invisibility. But, does he call those acts of faith that regard the Divine perfections, a *troubling of our heads?* It is indeed receiving a notion that is above us, but it is far from being any trouble upon the heart of a good man to think that he approaches to One who is everywhere present. *Blessed be his glorious name, which is exalted above all blessing and praise.* They may boast of the Protestant principle as long as they will, but such talk as this prepares us to be thrown into the sink of Popery, and the vilest of all their abominations, which is making to themselves *the likeness of the great God.*

When he speaks of himself it is thus: *Do not I fill heaven and earth? saith the Lord. Am I a God afar off, and not a God near at hand? Can any hide himself from my presence?* David was so sensible of it, that he cries out, *Whither shall I go from thy presence, or flee from thy Spirit? These are invisible things of him, even his eternal power and Godhead.* Christ is the *image of the invisible God.* The very heathen could say, *He is not far from any one of us.* And though the Apostle blames the rough idolatry they had run into, yet he mentions a principle agreeable to the voice of nature, *That we ought not to esteem the Godhead like unto gold or silver graven by art or man's device.* Thus faith the Apostle James, *God is not tempted with evil;* so that though we read of *tempting the holy One of Israel,* and his being *grieved with our iniquities,* yet you must not understand these passages in a way inconsistent with his eternal happiness. And though there are threatenings and rewards in which he shews his resentment and his pleasure, yet we are taught thus to speak of God: *That a man cannot be profitable to him; it is no pleasure to the Almighty that thou art righteous, and no gain to him if thou makest thy ways perfect.* Thus are we then to conceive of the great God, as a Spirit

SERM. 44.

Neh. ix. 5.

Jer. xxiii. 23, 24.

Psalm cxxxix. 7. Rom. i. 20.

Col. i. 15.

Acts xvii. 29.

Jam. i. 13.

eternally

SERM. 44. eternally above all the paſſions and confuſions that come into our nature. Such a Being, that the ſpirits of juſt men made perfect, and the very Angels themſelves cover their faces in his preſence. *The heavens are not clean in his ſight.*

Now enquire whether this does not agree to what is ſaid of Chriſt Jeſus in the Holy Scriptures. That as a man theſe characters do not belong to him is plain enough: He bids them *handle and ſee him, becauſe a ſpirit had not fleſh and bones as they ſaw him to have.* So that it would be in vain to ſearch out any of theſe glories for the human nature. He could not be truly a man, if he was only a ſpirit. But had he not a being that was inviſible? Does not the Scripture ſpeak of him under theſe adorations? The Redeemer is one whom Job calls by the name of God. I think there are two paſſages that muſt be underſtood of him, unleſs we violate all the laws of connection.

Job xix. 25, 26.

The one is, 2 Tim. i. 16. *For this cauſe I obtained mercy, that in me firſt Chriſt Jeſus might ſhew forth all long-ſuffering, for a pattern to them that ſhould believe on him to life everlaſting.* Here Chriſt Jeſus is conſidered, *firſt*, As the Author of his regeneration; and, *ſecondly*, As ſhewing all long-ſuffering. It is the name of the Lord that he proclaimed, *long-ſuffering and gracious. Thirdly*, He is repreſented as the object of faith, people in all ages are to believe *on him;* and, *fourthly*, The fountain of happineſs, for they believe on him *to everlaſting life.* Now when he had declared Chriſt Jeſus ſo much his friend for what is paſt, and what is to come, it is the faireſt way of expounding, to ſuppoſe that the next words purſue the ſame ſubject, and that he does not ſtart from one perſon to another. *Now*, faith he, *to the King eternal, immortal, inviſible, the only wiſe God, be glory for ever and ever. Amen.* That Chriſt as Mediator was not eternal, and that he will not in that character be immortal, is plain enough, for he he muſt give up the kingdom to the Father, and it is equally true, that he is not inviſible; but as the adverſaries of his Divinity do now grant that he had a nature above that which might be ſeen, which was born and did die, ſo theſe words may be underſtood of that. Theſe paſſages can belong to none but the perſon whom he had ſpoken of before; and is it too much to have it ſaid of one, who ſhewed all long-ſuffering, and who is believed on to eternal life, that he is *the King eternal?* Are not the titles proportioned to the account? What is ſaid of him is but equal to what is done by him: It is He whom Moſes *ſaw*, as **the** glorious inviſible.

Heb. xi. 27.

The other paſſage is in the ſame epiſtle, chap. vi. 15, 16. He had charged Timothy to *keep the commandment to the coming of Jeſus Chriſt, which* (*i. e.* which coming) *in his own times He ſhall ſhew, who is the bleſſed and only Potentate, the King of kings, and Lord of lords, who only has immortality, and dwells in that light which no man can approach unto, whom no man has ſeen nor can ſee, to whom be glory and power everlaſting. Amen.* Theſe are ſaid to be ἴδιοι καιροί, his own times, though we know that the Father has put the times and ſeaſons in his own power. The thing that is to be ſhewn at the appearing of Chriſt is ſomething that the world would not believe; therefore he tells us, there are times of ſhewing it. And what is that he diſcovers? A perſon who is **the bleſſed and only** Potentate, the King of kings, and Lord of lords. This is plainly affirmed of Chriſt, as his public and diſplayed character: *He has on his veſture and his thigh a name written, The King of kings, and Lord of lords.* Why ſhould we think a title too much for him in one place, which can be underſtood of no one elſe in another? That the Father is the King of kings, and Lord of lords, was an unconteſted doctrine, there was no need of

Rev. xix. 16.

making

making that appear; but that which in his own time he would shew, was the very thing that men denied him.

If it should be said, he might have this as a man, it is true enough, for he is to rule in the very nature that suffered: But then from that account he passes on to another, that must be understood of a Divine Nature, that *he only has immortality, and dwells in that light to which none can approach, whom no man has seen nor can see.* This is still affirmed, without any transition to another person, of Him who is the blessed and only Potentate, who elsewhere is called *the Prince of the kings of the earth.*

<small>Rev. i. 5.</small>

That he was seen upon earth is not to be denied, but you find here is an invisible part; and thus he speaks of himself, even in the days of his flesh, as alone equal to a mutual contemplation with the Father: *Not that any man has seen the Father, save he that is of God, he has seen the Father.* He speaks here of a privilege that no creature ever had, he was alone in it. Now what but an infinite nature could behold an infinite nature? The eye must be equal to the object. The seeing of God is too much for any but Christ; and, which completes the argument, the seeing of Christ was too much for any but God. *No man,* saith he, *knows who the Son is, but the Father, and who the Father is, but the Son, and he to whom the Son will reveal him.* It is plain, these words are to be taken in an eminent sense, for several knew the Son, and it is here supposed that many knew the Father, to whom the Son revealed him; but *that* cannot be the meaning; there was something in his wonderful person, which required an infinite mind to comprehend. None knew him but the Father.

<small>J.h. vi. 46.</small>

<small>Mat. xi. 27.</small>

To this glory of the Divine Nature does he give a testimony to Philip, whose desire was delivered

livered in these words: *Shew us the Father, and it* SERM. 44. *suffices us.* Jesus answers, *If ye had known me,* John xiv. 7. *ye should have known my Father, and henceforth ye have known him and seen him.* He does not in this contradict what he had said before, that *no man has seen God at any time,* but he declares himself so united to the Father, that *he who had seen him had seen the Father.* Not merely in the effects of his grace and power: *Believest thou not,* faith he, *that I am in the Father, and the Father in me; the words that I speak, I speak not of myself, but the Father that is in me, he does the works.*

SERMON XLV.

Jan. 31.
1719-20.

2. ANOTHER character that the great God has taken to himself, which yet the Scripture numbers among the glories of Jesus Christ is, that he is infinite in knowledge: *O the depth of* Rom. xi. *the riches both of the wisdom and knowledge of God!* 33, 34, *how unsearchable are his judgments, and his ways* 35, 36. *past finding out! For who has known the mind of the Lord, or who has been his counsellor? Or who has first given to him, and it shall be recompensed to him again? For of him, and to him, and through him are all things, to whom be glory for ever. Amen.*

This observation the Holy Spirit has carried quite through *the lively oracles;* and it became him to fill his own book with these accounts of a Divine wisdom that will distinguish him from every other author. For he speaks of an infinite nature

as

as no one elfe can do, becaufe he *fearches all things, yea the deep things of God. Who has directed the Spirit of the Lord, or who has taught him?* Thus we read that *he made the earth by his wifdom, and ftretched out the heavens by his underftanding.* He is admired in the works of his hands, becaufe *in wifdom he made them all.* We are taught to conceive of this attribute with the loweft veneration and wonder. *Great is our Lord, and of great power, yea his underftanding is infinite.* Thus we read of him as a Creator; and in the work of redemption we are to fay, *To God only wife, be glory for ever.*

SERM. 44.
1 Cor. ii. 10.
Ifa. xl. 13.

Pf. cxlvii. 5.

Rom. xvi. 27.

With this reverence and godly fear do his people approach to him. Job had gone fo far in giving his opinion about the wonders of nature and providence, that the Almighty tells him out of the whirlwind, *he was darkening counfel by words without wifdom.* This laid him under the rebuke of his own confcience, and made him cry out, *I know that thou canft do every thing, and no counfel can be withholden from thee. I have uttered things that I underftood not, things too wonderful for me, that I knew not.* Here is a confeffion both of his own emptinefs and the divine knowledge. And to this agrees the language of all good people ever fince men began to call upon the *name of the Lord.* For as there never was any religion without the duty of prayer, fo it is always fuppofed that we go to one who is able to hear us. This perfection of the Divine Nature is what we can neither deny nor multiply. It muft be owned in the great God, and cannot be given to any creature. For *he that fearches the hearts, knows what is the mind of the fpirit, when he makes interceffion for the faints according to the will of God.* We frequently meet with one example of Omnifcience, that it is *he who fearches the heart, and tries the reins of the children of men.* Peter fpeaks of this as a divine title:

Job xxxviii. 2.
—xlii. 2, 3.

Rom. viii. 27.

Jer. xvii. 10.

title: *God who knows the hearts, bare them witness.* [SERM. 45. Acts xv. 8.]

Now the question is, Whether we do not read of this very perfection in our great Redeemer without any abatement of language? Are not the same things, with an equal fulness of words, ascribed to *him*, that are spread through the Bible as the glory of the Father? We read of a Lord who *will bring to light the hidden things of darkness, and make manifest the counsels of all hearts:* And in another place, that *we must all appear before the judgment-seat of Christ.* [1 Cor. iv. 5.] [2 Cor. v. 10.] Let us only compare spiritual things with spiritual; set the distant parts of Scripture in the same light; look at them together, and observe if either the Spirit of God has made any difference, or left it to the humour and pride of men to make any. If there is room for a distinction between a supreme and subordinate God, an original and a derivative Omniscience, in the Bible, we will own, receive, and adore it; but if there is not, if the characters of the Father and Son are laid down with equal forms of speech, how bold must it be for persons of a finite nature to employ their fancies in setting bounds to what is infinite!

The objections that are brought against our Lord's complete knowledge may be allowed without any damage to his glory as God. It is very true, that *he grew in wisdom,* which supposes an imperfection, and that he confesses, there was *an hour which neither men, nor Angels, nor the Son himself could tell, but only the Father.* [Luke ii. 52.] This agrees to the weakness and limitation of the nature that he took upon him, and shews that he was *in all points made like to his brethren.* [Heb. ii. 17.] He himself was *encompassed with infirmities.* But [— v. 2.]

That is the wildest way of arguing in the world, to bring in the characters of one nature as an objection against the prerogatives of another, to prove that he is not God, because he is man; and to confront what is said in some places about his infinite perfections, by those accounts that we have in others of his infirmity and trouble. If this must pass for reasoning, we may go and dash the several parts of the Bible against one another. As, for example, suppose we meet with this argument, as it is well known we often do,—He that grew in knowledge, he that knew not the hour or the day of judgment, could not be omniscient; but the Redeemer of the world confessed this, and therefore he is not omniscient,—it is an unfair insinuation. The people that run on with such talk are throwing a veil over that distinction of natures which was always affirmed: and therefore the question is not, Whether we may not, and must not consider this High-priest of our profession in a state of weakness and limitation? *that* is never denied; but the whole debate hinges upon this, Whether the Scripture has given us any foundation to think and speak of *him* as we do of the Most High God?

Are there any passages that ascribe to him an unbounded wisdom? Is he ever called *the searcher of hearts?* And, in particular, is he ever represented as knowing that day and hour which he tells us, *as the Son of man* he did not know? Let us fairly enquire into this, and just speak as we find. Now,

The former of them is what the Scripture abounds in: *In him are hid all the treasures of wisdom and knowledge.* Very early in his ministry *he did not commit himself to man, because he knew what was in man.* He tells the disciples, *I have chosen twelve, and one of you is a devil:* For, saith the historian, *Jesus knew from the beginning who they were that believed not, and who should betray him.* Certainly these things are not spoken of that nature concerning which we read, that he came to the fig-tree if haply he might find fruit, and was

was so disappointed that he cursed it presently, and it withered away. We must not be so far imposed on as to believe, that He who could not tell the growth of a tree, should be able to see the workings of mens hearts at the distance of several years. There is nothing in human nature that could make him capable of knowing the thoughts of their hearts when they reasoned within themselves, much less of foreseeing an apostacy so far off, and calling a man a devil for what he was to do some years after, at a time that he made the full profession of a saint.

The Prophets had things revealed to them on particular occasions, but never did any of them pretend to give accounts of mankind beforehand at their own pleasure. They were often deceived as well as others. And the Apostles, who had the discerning of spirits, could not by that be secure from false brethren who crept in unawares. No person ever used such language as Christ did upon these occasions.

Peter speaks to him as a God, though he spake to Peter as a man. *Simon, son of Jonas, lovest thou me more than these?* The good man does not answer to inform him, but makes a profession of the contrary, *Yea Lord, thou knowest that I love thee.* Had he gone no farther than this, we might have supposed that he meant no more than that he had given evidence enough in his whole life of an affection to Christ and his cause. But you see he puts it upon something else: *Thou Lord, that knowest all things, knowest that I love thee.* What could he have said more of a God? What is the difference between Job's confession, *I know that no counsel can be withholden from thee,* and this of Peter? Our Lord's enemies owned him to be a teacher come from God, and saw God was with him, but they could not go this length. They took him for a wonderful person, but ascribing to him

John xxi. 15. 17.

him *the knowledge of all things* muſt have been condemned for blaſphemy.

How vain is it to confront ſuch a paſſage as this with the compliment of the woman of Tekoah to David, *My Lord is wiſe as an Angel of God, to know all things that are done in the earth!* Is there any compariſon between the flattery of a deceitful perſon, who was hired to be the tool of a hungry courtier, and that of an Apoſtle in his converſation with one who had been dead and was then alive? I ſhall not entertain a ſuſpicion ſo rude, as to think you need to be told the difference between theſe two caſes;, and only mention it to ſhew you, how low that cauſe muſt run, that can ſerve itſelf by theſe profane and vain babblings.

2 Sam. xiv. 20.

Solomon in his dedication of the temple had as awful thoughts of the Divine perfection as a man could be filled with, and in the warmth of his devotion uſes theſe words, *Thou, even thou* ONLY, *knoweſt the hearts of all the children of men.* From whence it appeared to be his opinion, that as God looked into the heart, ſo *none but* HE *could do it.* This was an incommunicable glory: how then are we to conceive of what the great Redeemer faith, *All the churches ſhall know that I am* HE *that ſearches the hearts and tries the reins, and I will render to every man according to his works?* Are all the churches to know, that omniſcience is a perfection transferred, a glory that God gives to another? that what Solomon thought He had alone, is now an attribute poſſeſſed in partnerſhip?

2 Chron. vi. 30.

Rev. ii. 23.

The religion of the Old Teſtament, we ſee, took a great deal of care to ſpeak of God with language that was uſed of no creature either in heaven or earth; and has the Goſpel thrown down this incloſure, and put the Maker of all things upon a level with the work of his hands? It is ſaid, that *hell and deſtruction are before the Lord;* and of Chriſt, that *there is not any creature that*

Pro. xv. 11.
Heb. iv. 13.

that is not manifest in his sight, for all things are naked and open to the eyes of HIM with whom we have to do.

But to come to the other instance, our Lord's *not knowing the day of judgment*. That he confessed this, is true enough; we understand it of his human nature, that he there spake as a man. Now, the question is, Whether there be any other places of Scripture upon which we may say, that he was possessed of this secret? He tells the disciples, that those *times and seasons* are *what the Father kept in his own power*; he would have them conceive of it as the grand reserve of the Throne; and yet are we not to think and say the same of Him who will, ἰδίοις καιροῖς, in *his own times, shew who is the blessed and only Potentate?*

Is not this frequently called *the day of Christ?* We read of *the day of the Lord*, in which he is to be revealed: And the Scripture has in a promiscuous way used the words, calling it either the day of *the Lord*, or the day of *Christ*, both of which are to be understood of that day and hour that the Angels know not; so that really if we are not to look upon Christ as this Lord, and the proprietor of this great day, we could have wished that the Holy Spirit had been more distinct. Compare but a few passages together.

2 Thess. ii. 1, 2.—He had told them in the former chapter, that Christ Jesus was to be *revealed from heaven with* HIS *mighty Angels*. He uses this as a compellation, beseeching them *by the coming of our Lord Jesus Christ, and our gathering together unto him;* and yet that he understands one of these sentences of His last coming, is plain; for he bids them *not be shaken in mind, nor troubled, as that the day of Christ is at hand*. Had he meant a spiritual day, those greater affections of grace, and light, and love, that we are waiting for, this could be no matter of trouble to them. But *the day of Christ*

Chrift here is the fame which Peter calls *the day of the Lord*, and which fhall come *as a thief in the night*. This is the fame comparifon that our Saviour ufes to one of the churches in Afia, *Behold I come as a thief*.

> SERM. 45.
> 2 Pet. iii. 10.
> Rev. iii. 3.

Now, is it not evident, that what one Apoftle calls the day of Chrift, and another the day of the Lord, is not to be underftood of two days? and a man muft be a great mafter of his own refolution, and grown to be evidence-proof, if he fays they are fpeaking of two Lords. I am fenfible fome will indulge themfelves in a fecret boaft, that this does not come up to an argument, that none denies Chrift to be this Lord; but if you look down two verfes farther, you will find that it is called *the day of* God; and the defcription is the very fame, almoft in a literal repetition, as if the Holy Ghoft had done it on purpofe to confound the gainfayers of our day.

In the 10th verfe we have this account of the day of Chrift, that *the heavens fhall pafs away with a great noife, and the elements melt with fervent heat:* and no lower down than the 12th, we are faid to be *looking for, and hafting to the coming of the day of God, wherein the heavens being on fire fhall be diffolved, and the elements fhall melt with fervent heat*. Thefe paffages are very near together, but we muft not call them a vain repetition; it is not in vain to fhew that the day of *Chrift* is the day of *God*, and to let us fee, that though this day is what none knew, no not the Son himfelf as man, though it is the time that the Father has referved in his own power, yet we are to have fuch a confideration of Chrift, as to call it *his day*. And furely the confequence is not very far fetched, that a day within his government muft be a day within his notice. It is *He in whom we have believed, and are perfuaded that he is able to keep*

> 2 Pet. iii.

> 2 Tim. i. 12.

keep what we have committed to him against THAT DAY.

It would have been robbery for him to be equal with God in this glory, if he was not so in nature. To invade the Father's great reserve, is against all our notions of his being a righteous servant, and his not coming to do his own will,—if there was not another character that belonged to him. We are sure that *he knows all things, and needs not that any man should ask him.* John xvi. 30.

3. I pass on to another attribute of the Divine Nature, and that is omnipotence. There is nothing but what he does know, there is nothing but what he can do. *He has a mighty arm; strong is his hand, and high is his right-hand.* Making the whole creation so well, doing it by his word, and upholding it by his providence, are public arguments of an infinite Majesty. When he told Job out of the whirlwind the great things he had done in distributing heaven, earth, and sea, to their several bounds, *Lord,* saith that good man, *I know that thou canst do every thing.* Ps. lxxxix. 13.

It is thus that he argues against the unbelief of his servants, *Is there any thing too hard for God?* He calls that sin by a name that shews it to be scandalous; it is a limiting the Holy One of Israel. Our faith is *strong in the Lord, and in the power of his might.* Abraham, who is the great example of it upon record, reasons thus: *He accounted that what God had promised he was able to perform,* because he believed *before that God, who raises the dead, and calls the things that are not as though they were.* I will go no farther into the vast field that the Scripture has given us, as a proof that God will be known by his Almighty power, but shall at once enter into the argument, that Rom. iv. 21.

These very things are said of Christ. *When I came,* saith he, *there was no man. Is my hand shortened at all, that it cannot redeem? or have I* Isa. l. 2, 3, 4, 5.

SERM. 45. *no power to deliver? Behold, at my rebuke I dry up the sea, I make the rivers a wilderness; their fish stinks, because there is no water, and dies for thirst. I clothe the heavens with blackness, and make sackcloth their covering.* That it is Christ who speaks, you will be convinced by the next words. *The Lord God has given me the tongue of the learned, that I should know how to speak a word in season to him that is weary: he wakens morning by morning, he wakens mine ear to hear as the learned: The Lord God has opened mine ear, and I was not rebellious, neither turned away back. I gave my back to the smiters, and my cheeks to them that plucked off the hair; I hid not my face from shame and spitting.*

Thus he delivers himself in language suitable to both his natures. The whole glory of omnipotence is ascribed to him. That we here read of him in a state of weakness, as feeble and sore broken by the disquietness of his heart, cannot be denied. There was no room to call *him* Almighty, who was grieved, and tired, and fainting, and crucified. He was executed in weakness as *to the body of his flesh*. But let us enquire fairly, whether He who came of the seed of David is not over all God blessed for ever. Though we have the *book of the generations of Jesus Christ*, who was the son of David and the son of Abraham; yet let us examine if the Scripture has not set him in such a light, as that *none can declare his generation*.

You will see a chain of argument and adoration in the 40th chapter of Isaiah. He begins with these words, *Comfort ye, comfort ye my people, saith your God.* Here he speaks, either of the Jews, or of believers, in every kindred, and tongue, and nation, as his people, and he is *their God*. The comfort they have is by his direction. *I create the fruit of the lips; Peace, peace to him that is nigh,*

Isa. lvii. 19.

and

and to him that is far off, faith the Lord, and I will heal him. Will they ever own themselves to be the people of one that is not God? or can they bear the thoughts of giving this name to one who is only subordinate? No; they had *none in heaven but him,* and none upon earth that they could defire besides him. And yet,

From this proclamation he passes into the great historical article of a believer's comfort, and that is the arrival of the Messiah. He describes the ministry of John the Baptist, as *the voice of one crying in the wilderness;* and what does he cry? does he use deceitful words that are not to be understood without a distinction, several hundred years after the prophet was dead? The thing itself that he delivers is this, *Prepare ye the way of the* LORD, *make strait in the desart a high way for our* GOD. Is not He, whom he calls *our God* in this verse, the same whom he had mentioned under the title of *your God* in the first? Thus did Zechariah apprehend the birth of his son. The Angel told him, that *many of the children of Israel shall he turn to the* LORD THEIR GOD, *and he shall go before Him,* i. e. before the Lord their God, *in the spirit and power of Elias.* When John was born, the Spirit came upon his father; he was *filled with the Holy Ghost,* and prophesied, *Thou child shalt be called The Prophet of the* HIGHEST, *for thou shalt go before the face of the* LORD *to prepare* HIS *ways.* Who is this that is called *the Highest?* We have the word in another part of the same chapter, the Angel said to the Virgin Mary, *The power of the Highest shall come upon thee.* Now the question is, Whether the word, in one of these places, signifies a person that is not the highest? Will it not be as grofs a contradiction as any you ever heard, to talk of a subordinate supreme,—of one that is the highest, and yet has another infinitely above him?

SERM. 45.

Luke i. 16, 17.

—ver. 35.

SERM. 45. Could the Holy Spirit find no words when he was speaking of a creature, but such as so confound our imaginations both of him and of the great God, that we cannot distinguish one from another? The sense of the word *Most High*, in the Old Testament, is so very plain, that we are in no temptation to fix it upon any but One: and it is the way to make us think the Gospel is *the snare that shall come upon all the earth*, if it has not set the same bounds to the Divine nature that the law did to the ark. But, to return to the 40th of Isaiah.

The passage I have already given you refers to the coming of Christ, the entrance upon his own ministry. From that the Prophet goes on to the work of the Apostles, and those that should succeed them in the preaching of the Gospel: *O Zion, that bringest good tidings, get thee up into the high mountain: O Jerusalem, that bringest good tidings, lift up thy voice with strength; lift it up, be not afraid.* What is it they are to tell with so much courage and diffusion? *Say to the cities of Judah, Behold your* GOD! This is the third time we have the expression: He that comforted Jerusalem is *your God*, he whom John the Baptist prepared the way for, is *our God*, and he is mentioned to the cities of Judah as *their God*. To them first, *God having raised up his Son Jesus, sent him to bless them: They were the children of the Prophets, and of the covenant made with Abraham;* and he is called *their God*.

Isaiah xl. ver. 9.

From them this word sounded abroad to the ends of the earth, that this *Lord God will come with a strong hand, his arm shall rule for him: behold, his reward is with him, and his work before him.* And lest any one should think that the Prophet had got his thoughts above a Redeemer, when he uses these expressions, he does, without any pause, descend into his more familiar character, that *he shall feed his flock like a shepherd, and ga-*
ther

ver. 10.

ver. 11.

ther the lambs with his arm, and carry them in his bosom, and gently lead those that are with young.

Shall we lose a Saviour out of this verse, rather than admit him into the other? Will any deny him to be our Shepherd, that he may not be owned as our God? Is it not more desirable to keep what God has joined together? Are we offended that He who gathers the lambs with his arm, should have an arm to rule for him? Shall we take pains to contract his majesty for the sake of his love, and argue, that because he is a Shepherd, he cannot be a God?—What a wilful thing is unbelief!

It is the same Person whom the Prophet goes on to speak of, that *he has measured the waters in the hollow of his hand, and meted out the heaven with a span, comprehended the dust of the earth in a measure, weighed the mountains in scales, and the hills in a balance. It is He who sits upon the circle of the earth, and the inhabitants thereof are as grashoppers; that stretches out the heavens as a curtain, and spreads them out as a tent to dwell in.* Can these words, *It is* HE, be understood of any but Him whom he had spoken of before? Nay, let me add what the Prophet does in the next words, and which you may refer to the enemies of his doctrine and Divinity, *They shall not be planted, they shall not be sown, yea, their stock shall not take root in the earth, and* HE *shall blow upon them.* And,

Lest any should rush in upon the argument with the foolish talk, That he is a God by the donation and grant of One that was above him, he confounds the vain thought with this question, *To whom will ye liken me, or shall I be equal, saith the Holy One?* When he had spoken of him as a preacher of righteousness, as coming into the deserts of Judah, and there called him the Lord *our God;* when he had considered him as declared in the ministry of the Apostles, as one presented to the cities of Judah,

under

under the title of *their God;* when he proclaimed him as the Lord of Providence, coming with his strong hand,—he speaks of him as the great Creator: *Lift up your eyes on high, and behold who has created these things, and brings out their host by number;* HE *calls them all by names, by the greatness of his might, for that* HE *is strong in power; not one fails.* This is the very thing that the Psalmist enters among the perfections of God, that *he tells the number of the stars, and calls them all by their names.* And upon the whole, the Prophet makes this application, *Why sayest thou, O Jacob, and speakest O Israel, My way is hid from the Lord, and my judgment passed over from my God?*

Can this be called a transition to any other than he had been speaking of quite through the chapter? No, surely. With what does he encourage their faith in a Redeemer, but with the same argument that the Apostle uses many ages after, *viz.* that our faith is *strong in the Lord, and in the power of his might?*—*Hast thou not known, hast thou not heard, that the everlasting God, the Lord, the Creator of the ends of the earth, fainteth not, neither is weary? there is no searching of his understanding.* Now, lay all these things together; see whether the exposition is forced; and judge upon the whole, with what truth we are told, that Christ is called God only by a grant and participation from another; that we must not look upon him as the Supreme: that is, in one word, we are no better than heathens, who do service to them that *by nature are no gods.* They may be called gods, as he is, and that is all. It will be said, that they have no preeminence conferred upon them; but, consider their crime is not mistaking the deputed deity, but supposing there is any at all: for, if he whom either we or they do worship is not a God by nature, the religion that is paid to him is idolatry.

From

From this scripture that gives you an account of our Lord's omnipotence in the Old Testament, I will lead you to another in the New: *I am Alpha and Omega, the beginning and the ending, faith the Lord, which is, and which was, and which is to come, the Almighty.* The argument why the title of Almighty should not be understood of the Son in this verse, is because it is joined to those characters that plainly belong to the Father in the fourth: *Grace be to you, and peace, from Him who was, and who is, and who is to come, and from Jesus who is the faithful witness.* But I cannot think this a fair conclusion, because the same title is undeniably given to the Son in the eleventh verse, which has a nearer situation to the fifth than the fourth has.

The Apostle saith, *He heard behind him a great noise as of a trumpet, saying, I am Alpha and Omega, the first and the last.* Can we think he speaks of the Father as the Most High God, under such a description as would afterwards be claimed by a creature? If one, who is not God, saith of himself, *I am Alpha and Omega, the first and the last, the beginning and the ending,* then these words which are supposed to be the distinction of the Deity do not answer the end.

Christ is usually spoken of throughout the whole book; it is *his Revelation* that he gave to his servant John. The Father is never brought in as speaking; our Lord claims it to himself, *He that testifies these things, saith, Behold I come quickly.* And who was this? you will find, first, by what he saith of himself, ver. 17. *I am Alpha and Omega, the beginning and the ending, the first and the last.* And then, by the reply the church makes to him, *Amen, even so come Lord Jesus.* This book represents his government in the world, and therefore we must not dare to exclude him from those praises: *We give thee thanks, O Lord God Almighty, which art, and wast, and art to come, because thou hast*

SERM. 45. *haft taken to thee thy great power, and reigned.* Nor are these titles to be separated, *Great and marvellous are thy works, Lord God Almighty, just and true are all thy ways, thou King of saints.* The voices of the multitude in the heaven, and the mighty thunderings are directed to him under this name, *The Lord God omnipotent reigneth.*

Feb. 14.
1719-20.

SERMON XLVI.

Num. xxiii.
19.

1 Sam. xv.
29.

4. WE all along read of the great God, that his *truth* endures for ever: *He is not a man that he should lie, nor the son of man that he should repent. The Strength of Israel will not lie or repent, for he is not a man that he should repent.* I need not lead you into a great number of Scriptures that give a testimony to this perfection in the Supreme Nature. Both the Old and New Testament are crowded with them; he that runs may read. What I shall fix upon, under this head, you will have in these two particulars: 1st, That eternal truth conveys to us the notion that we ought to entertain of God; it is thus we are to think of him: and, 2dly, That this attribute, with equal fulness of words, with the same undistinguished phrase, comes in among the characters of Christ

Pf. xlv. 4.
7.

Prov. viii.
7, 8.

Jesus: *In his majesty he rides prosperously, because of truth; he loves righteousness, and hates wickedness. His mouth shall speak truth; wickedness is an abomination to his lips; all the words of his mouth are in righteousness.*

The

The former of these is what the enemies of our Lord do rather choose to stick at than the latter; and give their argument this turn, That it is possible a person may have all that is affirmed of Christ as to his truth and integrity, and yet be no more than a creature. They that are with him in heaven, are *true and faithful*, and this title ought to comprehend all the churches upon earth. It is the imperfection and scandal of our societies, that men *speak lies in hypocrisy;* and it will be a happy, though a very severe reformation, when *the remnant of Israel shall not do iniquity, nor tell lies, nor suffer a deceitful tongue to be found in their mouths.* Whether such a purifying of the sons of Levi happens in our day or no, yet we hope our next look, and our next remove, will be to a place where *nothing enters that defiles or works abomination, or loves and makes a lie.* All the armies that follow the Lamb, *are called, and faithful, and chosen.* The hundred forty and four thousand that attend him upon Mount Sion, are not only distinguished by his Father's name in their foreheads, but by something that lies more within, *They are without guile before the throne of God.*

Rev. xxi. 27.

——xiv. 5.

Thus much then we must own, that the mere character of truth is so far from being peculiar to God, that it ought to belong to every creature, and will be found in the general assembly and church of the First-born, whose names are written in heaven. But I do not see how that is any defence against the argument I am upon; for though truth is one of the communicable perfections, and what God imparts among the works of his own hands, yet it is plain, with an evidence above that of the sun at noon-day, that under this head he speaks of himself. And therefore if the word can signify no more than what may be affirmed of a creature, it is wrong placed among the names of the Deity.

To

SERM. 46. To what purpose does Moses leave the Jews a song for their anniversary devotion, in which he introduces the titles of his God with great solemnity? *Give ear, O heavens, and I will speak, and hear, O earth, the words of my mouth; because I will publish the name of the Lord; ascribe ye greatness to our God.* Would not any one expect, after such an alarm to heaven and earth, that what he calls *the name of the Lord* is to be understood of something above all the shares that man can have in it? and yet he saith no more than what may be affirmed of every saint in heaven, according to the methods of interpretation that are used when any thing is said of Christ: *He is the Rock, and his work is perfect, for all his ways are judgment; a God of truth, and without iniquity, just and right is he.* It is evident that the character of truth, in which he ascribes greatness to the Lord, must be numbered among the perfections of the Divine Nature.

Deut. xxxii. 1. 3.

——ver. 4.

Jer. x. 10. We read of him elsewhere, that he is *the true God, and the everlasting King.* Nebuchadnezzar, when he issued his proclamation, that all nations should honour the King of heaven, gives this reason for it, because *all his works are truth, and his ways judgment.* Thus was he adored in the faith of his people. Abraham therefore believed, but it was *before Him who quickens the dead, and calls the things that are not, as though they were;* and *against hope, he believed in hope,* judging Him *faithful who had promised.* This was *giving glory to God,* which is a name that the action could never bear, if it did not signify a dependence upon him for that which no other has, and a confidence in him that we dare not place upon the best and highest of all creatures.

Dan. iv. 37.

Rom. iv. 17, 18, 19, 20.

Now it is thus that the Scripture has spoken of Christ Jesus, and left us no directions to read his character with a drawback. I need not be afraid to say the same things of him that I do of the Father,

ther, when the Holy Spirit has done so before me. SERM. 46.
If I find the names given with an equality, I must endeavour to preserve it, however inconceivable it may be to a corrupt and a contracted mind. Thus,

When Christ tells us, he is *the way, the truth,* Joh. xiv. 6. *and the life,* I cannot but imagine, though in those words he declares himself to be a Mediator, yet there is something in them that carries our thoughts a great deal farther. He is the way, because *no man comes to the* Father *but by him;* that name plainly signifies his office. But how is he the *truth?* Not merely as *grace and truth came by him;* not because he published it to the world, for then all faithful ministers may be called the truth. Certainly, as calling ourselves the truth and the life, because we make a declaration of both, would be too much for us; so such an interpretation of the words is too little for him.

If he is not equal to the Father, would it not have been better, more modest in him, and more secure for his people, had he not used a word with so much freedom, by which the great God has so often revealed himself? Is it not an unhappy snare to his disciples, and all the ages of his people, to tell them, that as *they believe in God,* he would Joh. xiv. 1. have them also *believe in him;* and immediately after such an exhortation, speak of himself as the Scripture has always spoken of God? As he had claimed an equal faith, he lays hold on an equal title. The distinction that we make in the sense of these expressions can never be safe, unless we had an easy direction to it in the words themselves.

How well did he keep his distance in that prayer, *Father, let this cup pass from me, yet not as I will, but as thou wilt.* Any one may see that he is there to be considered as an inferior to the Father; and what a small matter in other places would have prevented any person's saying that they are equal! Could he not have hinted to his disciples, that he

VOL. II. C c called

called for no more than a subordinate faith to a subordinate God? that though he bid them believe in him as they believed in God, yet he meant it only in a lower way? and though he is *the truth and the life*, yet he is not the fountain of life?

Did not he know how mankind are apt to worship and glorify the creature as they do the Creator? and is it likely he would have given the directions so loose and unguarded as he has done, and instead of opening the difference between himself and the Most High, leave the matter more entangled and obscure? *If ye had known me*, saith he, *ye should have known my Father also, and henceforth ye have both known him and seen him. He that has seen me has seen the Father; I am in the Father, and the Father in me.* Who could imagine that the Scripture had the least design to encourage the thoughts of a distinction in nature between the Father and the Son, when every divine title is given to them in common?

What! have we never a peculiar name for our God in all his Book? Has he no words that belong to himself? Is there an infinite difference between Him and the Mediator with respect to his being and perfection, and has the Holy Spirit found out no expressions to shew it? It is his work to *glorify Christ*, and how does he do it, but in the way that our Lord has informed us of? *He shall take of mine and shew it unto you.* What is that? *All that the Father has are mine*, therefore, with reference to that fulness of the Deity, *I said, He shall take of mine and shew it unto you.*

I can easily accommodate that title to Christ in his lower nature, that he is *the faithful witness;* but methinks it sounds a great deal more in other places. *These things saith he that is holy, and he that is true, he that has the key of David, who opens and none can shut, and shuts when none can open.* So again, *These things saith the Amen, the faithful and*

and true Witness. Can we go any higher in speaking of Him whose *mercy is above the heavens and whose truth reaches to the clouds?*   SERM. 46. Ps. xxxvi. 5.

When we say, *Who is a strong Lord like unto thee,— or to thy faithfulness round about thee?* would not any one think it was an adoration; that it could not be given to a creature without falsehood and blasphemy? And yet this is the song of the Lamb, *Just and true are all thy ways, thou King of saints.* He that sits upon the white horse is called *Faithful and True; in righteousness does he judge and make war.* Who is this? *He is clothed with a vesture dipped in blood, and his name is called The Word of God.* We read of a salvation *in Christ Jesus,* and then it is added, *If we deny him, he will also deny us; he abides faithful, he cannot deny himself.* It is just the same that is said of God, that *he cannot lie.*   lxxxix 8. Rev. xv. 3. —xix. 11. 13. 2 Tim. ii. 13. Tit. i. 2.

The religion of the Heathen taught the doctrine of a supreme and subordinate God better than ours does. The titles they gave, the devotions they offered, were plainly distinguished. They spake one way of Him whom they reckoned to be *Pater hominumque deûmque,* Father of men and of gods, and with more diminution of their inferior deities. But our Bible is a mere heap of confusion according to the Arian argument. We have an account of the supreme God, who, they say, is no other than the person of the Father: We are also led to consider the Son as infinitely below him, and yet there is not one title, attribute, or glory, mentioned of the former, but what is equally given to the latter. Were ever people so unhappy as Christians are? we must make a distinction, and yet the book we go by has not taught us how to express it. Thus, *The Son of God has come, and has given us an understanding that we may know Him that is true:* Yet he saith the same of himself that he does of the Father; for *we are in him that is true,*   1 Joh. v. 20.

even

even in his Son *Jesus Christ ;—this is the true God, and this is eternal life.*

5. Holiness and goodness are other attributes of the Divine Nature, and proper characters under which we are to conceive of a God. The objection that this is liable to, is the same with what we have cleared off under the former head; the same answer will do, That though these are qualifications found among creatures, yet there is a sense that limits them to the Divine Nature.

The great God is so holy and good as no other being ever was, or ever will be. *There is none holy as the Lord, for there is none besides thee.* He delighted in that name, *The Holy One of Israel. Thou art holy,* saith Christ himself, *O thou that inhabitest the praises of Israel.* In the days of his flesh he renounced this title as a man, *Why callest thou me good? there is none good but one, that is God.* Certainly there was no harm in calling him *good master;* it is a name that we may use lawfully to any serious person, especially one who teaches the way of God in truth: but our Lord would tell the young man, that goodness was a divine attribute, and is among the titles that belong to God.

Now examine whether the Scripture has set any bounds to this in the account that we have of Christ Jesus. It is a doctrine that the devils owned: *I know thee who thou art, the Holy One of God.* This is above the scorn of a prophane wit; for as the Apostle says, *If thou believest there is one God, thou dost well; the devils also believe and tremble.* But besides, it is what the Angel said, *That holy thing that shall be born of thee shall be called the Son of God.* This is more than could be said of John the Baptist, though he was to be *filled with the Holy Ghost from his mother's womb.* But antecedent to Christ's sanctification as a man, he is called the *holy thing,* because the Holy Ghost would overshadow his mother, and the power of the highest

est come upon her, which are words that confound us; they strike our minds with an awe, for they are all the description we shall ever have of a thing we shall never know. Thus do they speak of him: *Against thy holy child Jesus have they taken counsel*, and, *Let signs and wonders be done in the name of thy holy child Jesus.* [SERM. 46.] [Acts iv. 27. 30.]

Certainly this account signifies a great deal more than the purity of the human nature; for it was not *that* that the people of Israel appeared against, but his pretensions to the Divine. It was not *that* in the name of which he desired signs and wonders to be wrought. Ananias tells Saul, *The God of our fathers has chosen thee, that thou shouldest know his will, and see that Just One, and hear the voice of his mouth.* It is the same title that Peter had used before to the Jews: *Ye denied the Holy One, and the Just, and desired a murderer to be granted to you.* You may indeed pull down these majestic names, and make them signify no more than they would have done, had they been given to a creature: But will not a common reader be amazed when you tell him, that the Holy Spirit who *speaks* here as he used to do of a God, does not *mean* one? [xxii. 14.] [ch. iii. 14.]

Let us enquire into the adorations of heaven: *Behold, there was a throne set in heaven, and one sat on the throne; he that sat was to look upon like a jasper, and a sardine stone.* Let any one now tell me, whether it is most proper to understand this of a God manifest in the flesh, or of *the Father, whom no man has seen or can see?* You read afterwards of *four beasts*, which might have been translated more decently, as it is in the prophecy of Ezekiel, *four living creatures.* It is said of them, that *they rest not day nor night, saying, Holy, holy, holy, Lord God Almighty, which was, and is, and is to come; and they give thanks to Him who sits on the throne, and lives for ever and ever, saying, Thou art* [Rev. iv. 2, 3.] [ver. 8, 9, 10, 11.]

art worthy, O Lord, to receive glory, and honour, and power; for thou haft created all things, and for thy pleafure they are and were created.

Is there any thing in this, which the Scripture has not in other places given to Jefus Chrift? We often read of him, that *he was, he is, and he is to come;* and though fome will tell us, that it is too much to call him Lord God Almighty, yet Thomas could fay, *My Lord, and my God.* And we know, that *he fits upon the throne, and makes all things new.* And he has created all things: *By him were all things created, that are in heaven, and that are in earth, vifible and invifible, whether they be thrones, dominions, principalities or powers; all things are created by him, and for him; and he is before all things, and by him all things confift.* And,

Whether we have any ground to fay, that the Angels give him the repeated adorations of *Holy, holy, holy,* let us enquire into the Scriptures. The moft remarkable place where we meet with that abounding manner of praife, cannot be underftood of any other befides him. It is, Ifa. vi. 1. *The Lord fat upon a throne high and lifted up, and his train filled the temple: Above it ftood the Seraphims, and one cried unto another, faying, Holy, holy, holy, is the Lord of Hofts, the whole earth is full of his glory.* His train filling the temple, and the whole earth being full of his glory, are plain intimations to whom thefe titles belong. When the Prophet faw *the King, the Lord of Hofts,* we think it moft likely that he meant that King who fhould be born to David; nor was the retinue and pomp with which he appeared too much for the Meffiah, for he had Angels always to attend him, both out of heaven and into it; both at his birth, when he took our nature on, and at his afcenfion, when he took it up.

But we are not left to guefs and fuppofe, and beg our way into an interpretation. The Holy Ghoft

Ghost himself is our expositor; the Evangelist John tells us, *These things said Esaias when he saw his glory and spake of him.* Saw whose glory? His whom the Pharisees would not confess though they did believe him, *left they should be put out of the synagogue.* Excommunication was to them more dreadful than infidelity. Was it the Father whom they were thus afraid of owning? No certainly, every one knows who it is they would not confess, and this is the very Person whom Esaias spake of; and at the time he did it, he *saw his glory;* the Angels appeared to be employed in such a manner as they never used to any but the great God, crying, *Holy, holy, holy.*

Cannot they worship a God either in earth or in heaven with titles that are incommunicable? It was a crime in Lucifer to set his throne as the throne of God, and to be *like the Most High:* and will our blessed Saviour suffer his people to approach him as if he thought it no robbery to be equal with God, when it certainly must be the vilest of all robberies? Are we by the direction of the Scripture to speak to him in such a manner, that we cannot possibly outdo it or go beyond it in our applications to the Father? Has he not only the same titles, but the same repetitions of them? How proper would it have been for him to check the Angels as he did the young man in the Gospel, 'Why call ye me holy, there is none 'holy as the Lord, for there is none besides him? 'Do not confound your respect to me with the 'language of that religion that is only owing to 'him.' Had any such caution as this been revealed, it might have instructed two worlds at once. But let Angels and men go on in their old way, *honouring the Son even as they honour the Father;* and though some among us call it idolatry, as indeed it is, if he is a creature, yet we see it

obtains

SERM. 46. obtains in the temple above, which has *no fellow-ship with idols.*

Some vain men give us diſtinctions that ſhew the authors to be *puffed up in their fleſhly minds, and intruding into things which they have not ſeen.* We know no more of heaven than what is told us in the Bible, and that has made no difference between the praiſes, the bleſſing, the power and glory that are given to Him that ſits upon the throne, and to the Lamb for ever. And *who is this that darkens counſel by words without knowledge?* from whence are people inſtructed to tell us, that theſe adorations are *chiefly* given to Him that ſits on the throne, and only in *a lower degree* to the Lamb? Thoſe perſons know nothing what worſhip means, who ſuppoſe it is to be directed in different degrees to different objects.

We are to worſhip none but God, nor is any part of our homage to be withheld from him, as a ſort of ſecond ſervice to another. You muſt *love the Lord your God with all your hearts, with all your minds, with all your ſtrength, and with all your ſoul,* not merely with the chief of theſe powers and affections; *and him only ſhould you ſerve.* The love we have for men and Angels, and the worſhip we are ſaid to pay them, is not of the ſame kind with that we give to God, nor has it the leaſt degree of religious adoration in it. Our worſhip, taking it for an act of devotion, is not given to the higheſt Angel, nay, not to the Son himſelf in our nature, but merely as he is God; and therefore this diſtinction teaches to talk about worſhip in the way that the Scripture abominates.

I have again exceeded my own deſign by an enlargement that ſwells and grows upon me. I had thought to have gone through the other characters that belong to the Divine Nature, but that I could not without ſliding faſter over theſe things than is agreeable to the importance of the ſubject. And

I hope none will think discourses of Christ Jesus too long. This doctrine being the riches of heaven, what Angels desire to look into, may justly be the perfume of our assemblies on earth, for *his name is as ointment poured forth.*

SERM. 46.

SERMON XLVII.

Feb. 28. 1719-20.

6. ANOTHER glory of the Divine Nature, and under which we are taught to conceive of God, is the *eternity* of his being. *He is the King eternal, immortal, invisible; he only has immortality.* It is in vain for any to shun the argument, by telling us, that the terms of everlasting, and being for ever, and several others of the like sound, are often to be taken in a limited sense. Thus the covenant of God with the Jews is said to be *for ever;* their possession of Canaan, their ceremonial worship, are mentioned under these majestic words; and yet we know that the former is dissolved by the wrath of Providence, and the latter by the light of the Gospel. This is all true, but not to the purpose of those that urge it; for the question is not, whether some things that are called eternal were not at last to perish, but whether or no there is not such a meaning in those titles as can be applied to none but the Most High God.

1 Tim. i. 17.
— vi. 16.

You know we always distinguish between a twofold eternity; by one we mean that which had no beginning, by the other that which has no end. The title in the latter sense is given to a vast multitude

titude of persons and things. Angels and the souls of men are created for an unchangeable duration. We also read of an *everlasting righteousness*, because it shall be ever pleaded in heaven, and *an everlasting covenant* which shall maintain its character and virtue when the visible creation is all gone. Under this head we may bring in the *eternal life*, that contains and supplies the happiness of God's people; and that house not made with hands is *eternal in the heavens*, where they are to enjoy it, and shall be *ever with the Lord.* Nay it is as true, that the torment of those who shall be condemned is *for ever and ever,* the wicked are to go into *everlasting punishment ;* as they dwell with devouring fire, so it is with *everlasting burnings.* These and several other particulars are distinguished in the Scriptures from the visible world, for *the things that are seen are temporal, but the things that are not seen are eternal.*

But none of these are comprehended in the full and proper sense of the word eternity; that is, though they are to have no end, yet every one of them had a beginning: Once they were not, and it is by the appointment of another that they both are and shall be.

This complete eternity, as we may call it, is peculiar to God, and we speak both *of* him and *to* him in those terms that can be used of no creature, when we say, *From everlasting to everlasting thou art God.* That which always had an existence can be no other than the Supreme Being. Both the light of nature, and the revelation of Scripture, gives us this as an uncontestible truth: *That ye may know and believe me, and understand that I am He ; before me there was no God formed, neither shall there be after me ; I, even I am the Lord, and besides me there is no Saviour.* So again, upon this head he exposes the folly of idolaters: *Remember the former things of old, for I am God, and there is none*

none else; I am God, and there is none like me, declaring the end from the beginning, and from ancient times the things that are not yet done, saying, My counsel shall stand, and I will do all my pleasure. Here he proclaims an existence which was alone with himself, and he mentions that as the foundation of his independent counsels.

It would be a fraudulent usage of this, and the like places, to assault them in the way that is taken with several others, and tell us, that these words *in the beginning* do not signify any thing that had no beginning; for either the Holy Ghost has in such phrases given us the eternity of God, or he has not mentioned it at all, and so has left us nothing about that which is the first principle in nature. When we read of an *eternal purpose*, that he had in' himself before the world was, it is not to be debased and plundered; we are to look upon it as a resolution taken, not only before our world was made, but laid in the mind of Him who had all being within himself.

Here let us enquire whether this is not a glory that the Holy Scripture has given to Christ Jesus in language that is easy enough to be understood. We read of Melchisedec, as a type of him, that he had *neither beginning of days nor end of life; but made like the Son of God, abides a priest continually.* What the Bible tells us of the Son's eternity is liable to no other objection than may as well be brought against the Father's. Does not the Psalmist write of the Most High God? does he not declare the name of the Lord, of JEHOVAH, *when the people are gathered together, and the kingdoms, to serve the Lord?* He says, *O my God, thy years are throughout all generations; of old thou hast laid the foundations of the earth, and the heavens are the work of thine hands: they shall perish, but thou shalt endure; yea all of them shall wax old as a garment; as a vesture shalt thou change them, and they shall be changed; but thou art the same, 'and thy*

SERM. 47.

Heb. vii. 3.

Psal. cii. 22.—27.

thy years have no end. This is with very little alteration of the words applied to Chrift: *Thou, Lord, in the beginning haſt laid the foundations of the earth, and the heavens are the work of thine hands; they ſhall periſh, but thou remaineſt; and they ſhall all wax old as does a garment, and as a veſture ſhalt thou fold them up, and they ſhall be changed; but thou art the ſame, and thy years ſhall not fail.*

We read that *in the beginning was the Word, and the Word was with God, and the Word was God: The ſame was in the beginning with God.* The Socinian interpretation of that paſſage was this, that in the beginning of the Goſpel Jeſus Chriſt was, he was then with God, *i. e.* employed by him; and he was God by donation and appointment to the office of Mediator. They believed no more of him than the perſons did who crucified him, that *he was a man approved of God by miracles, wonders, and ſigns, which God did by him in the midſt of the Jews, as they themſelves alſo knew.*

But though the word of the Lord is for ever, yet errors grow old, and the opinions of men who have riſen up againſt divine revelation change and vary with the humours of ages. This expoſition is now as much decried by thoſe who will not allow the Divinity of Chriſt, as it is by thoſe that maintain it; and ſo it will fare with *their* opinion; as much as it is now in vogue, with a few years, gray hairs will appear here and there upon it. It will be no longer admired than whilſt it is a *new ſcheme;* and as time itſelf ſhall eat out that character, ſo *that which decays and grows old is ready to vaniſh away.* Whilſt the truth of God is ſtill the ſame; like a rock in the ſea, though it is daſhed with waves of all ſorts, and bruſhed with winds from all quarters, yet it remains unmoved. The oppoſition that is made to it varies juſt as

Satan

Satan finds it needful to change hands, but the doctrine itself is still the same that it ever was, and ever will be.

We have no other term of communion or ground of Christian concord than every generation of God's people had before us. This was the only *unity of the Spirit,* and the only *bond of peace* seventeen hundred years ago: ***That which was from the beginning, which we have heard, which we have seen with our eyes, which we have looked upon, and our hands have handled of the Word of life; for the Life was manifest, and we have seen it and bear witness, and shew unto you that eternal Life, which was with the Father, and was manifested to us.*** What he calls eternal Life, is to be understood of a Person, and not of a thing; of one who was *manifest*, whom they saw with their eyes, whom they looked upon, and their hands handled; which cannot without a violence upon language be applied to the future glory; because that is not seen, for it *does not appear what we shall be.* He here speaks of one who was born in time. *The Life*, as he saith, was manifest, and we have seen it, and bear witness; but then antecedent to such a discovery, this eternal Life was *with the Father*. As in his Gospel he called him *the Word*, so here he calls him *the Life;* and upon the preaching of this doctrine were all their societies founded; as he goes on to tell them, ***that which we have seen and heard, declare we unto you, that ye also may have fellowship with us.*** A fellowship without such a declaration is what the beloved disciple knew nothing of; and the reason is plain, because it was ***a fellowship with the Father and with his Son Jesus Christ.*** And it is only *if we walk in the light as he is in the light, that we can have fellowship with one another.*

The objection that is brought against this testimony is like a sword in a madman's hand, that

cuts

cuts his own flesh; it strikes as much at the error they maintain, as it does at the truth they oppose. We are told that these words, *In the beginning was the Word*, do not prove the eternity of a person any more than the first verse in Genesis proves the eternity of the creation, when it is said, *In the beginning God created the heaven and the earth*, and that the expression in both places must take its sense and force from the things that are spoken of. In the one Moses gives us an account of the world, in the other the Evangelist writes of the Gospel.

This may be pleaded by a Socinian, but it comes ill from the mouth of an Arian; for these do own that the Son of God had an existence before all worlds, and they bring this very scripture to prove it. Now if the words do refer to a being that he had before his incarnation, they may with as much propriety signify the same that they do when applied to a God; and if his being with God may be understood of a Person that is limited and derived, I cannot see why an Atheist may not take the same liberty with the phrase when it is spoken of the Father, that others do when it gives us an account of the Son; for we are expressly told, that *all things were made by him, and without him was not any thing made that was made; in him was life, and the life was the light of men.*

Consider what the Apostle tells us, *Jesus Christ is the same yesterday, to-day, and for ever*. Compare this with what we are told of *the Father of lights, that with him there is no variableness, nor shadow of turning*. We are directed to be as clear and fixed as possible in this article by the following words: *Be not carried about with divers and strange doctrines*. It is the same expression that another writer uses, when he describes those who are departed from the faith, they are *clouds without water, carried about of winds*. These doctrines that are *divers* from one another, and *strange* to the

the people of God, we are to keep our ground against; and you will judge what they are by their opposition to that great truth he had laid down before. *Jesus Christ is the same yesterday, to-day, and for ever.* If this is applied to the human nature the proposition is false, for that submitted to great variations, he was dead and is alive; and if you refer it to his mediation, that also is not unchangeable; for there is a time when the Son himself shall be subject, *i. e.* declared in a most public manner to be so, and shall then *give up the kingdom to the Father, that God may be all, and in all.*

The kingdom that the Apostle there speaks of cannot be the same with what the Angel mentions to the Virgin Mary, *He shall rule over the house of Jacob for ever and ever, and of his kingdom there shall be no end.* In one place the kingdom is to be given up, and in the other, there is to be no end of the kingdom; with respect to the former, Jesus is *not* the same yesterday, to-day, and for ever; and therefore if we are not to conceive of him in a character higher than his mediation, these scriptures cannot be owned with truth; for to say that his being the same for ever, may signify that he continues for ever some way or other, is trifling both with words and things; or to say, that *for ever* signifies a long time, to the end of the visible creation, is such an insult both upon language and the mystery it belongs to, as proclaims a man to be void of fear:—such foolish and unlearned questions only gender strifes. Suppose I should say of the Father of lights, who is without any variableness or shadow of turning, that he is the same yesterday, to-day, and for ever, would not all mankind take the terms to be equivalent? or can any exceptions be made to the latter, that would not have the same force against the former?

Luke i. 33.

When

SERM. 47. When an author tells us, as he that writes against M. Troffé's arguments does, that Chrift cannot be unchangeable, becaufe he was born, he died, he rofe again, and went to heaven, does not fuch a one virtually fay, this fcripture is to be razed out. May we not plead as much againft his being the fame for ever, as againft his being without any variablenefs? Indeed if there was any pretence for ufing this text as they do *that* 1 John v. 7. it would have diverted the difpute, and then we muft not have argued about the *meaning*, but the *authority* of a fingle verfe; not what it faid, but whence it came; juft as a man who cannot anfwer the charge of an indictment, demurs to the jurifdiction of the court. This confronting of copies is much eafier work than anfwering of reafons; but here is a text in full force, we find it in a chapter that is ungarbled, and what fhall we do with that?

Prov. viii. 22, 23, 24.

Nay, to this I may add a multitude of other places. Thus Chrift tells us himfelf under the title of Wifdom, that *the Lord poffeffed him in the beginning of his ways, before his works of old; he was fet up from everlafting, or ever the earth was; when there was no depth, he was brought forth.* I am fenfible that thefe expreffions of *being fet up*, and *brought forth*, will be catched at as an abatement to the truth that I am contending for; but I will leave you to confider what the criticifm would end in, if it was applied to another text that I have already given you, which certainly ftands for a declaration of God's eternity. That, Ifa. xliii. *Before me there was no God formed, neither fhall there be after me.* Suppofe we fhould ufe this phrafe, *the forming of a God*, as they do the other, I believe you would tremble at the grofs produce of fuch an argument.

Mic. v. 2.

Again you read, *Out of Bethlehem Ephratah He fhall come forth to me, that is to be a ruler in Ifrael.*
This

This is easily to be understood of a natural birth, and a spiritual kingdom. But then it is said of Him who is thus to be born, that *his goings forth have been of old from everlasting.* Some late authors are impatient when we distinguish between two natures in the Person of Christ Jesus, though you often read of him thus, in one and the same verse. His *coming* out of Bethlehem cannot be that *going forth* that is mentioned afterwards; nor would a King that was then future, be said to be *of old*, and from everlasting.

If it is objected that the word *from everlasting* does not always signify a proper eternity, I believe it may be sooner said than proved: And till I meet with a passage in Scripture, where that which had a beginning is said to be *from everlasting*, I must take that opinion to be no more than the storm of a terrible one, which, for all its sound, is only a blast against a wall. I durst no more set bounds to that expression, *His goings forth have been from everlasting*, than to the other, *From everlasting to everlasting thou art God.* I am not one of those that pretend to *declare his generation.* The Spirit who *searches the deep things of God* has given us the titles of Father and Son in the same language; and I am sure, that the spirits who tell us of a distinction between them, and will adjust the value of words, have made no such searches as these are. Let us therefore speak as those who have received, *not the spirit of this world, but the Spirit which is of God, that we may know the things that are freely given to us of God.* 1 Cor. ii. 12.

7. The Great God takes pleasure to be known as the chief Agent in all the works of nature and grace: *Of him, and through him, and to him, are all things; to whom be glory for ever, Amen.* Thus the harmonious inhabitants of heaven are singing to him, *Thou hast created all things, and for thy pleasure they are and were created:* And believers up- Rom. xi. 36. Rev. iv. 11.

SERM. 47.
Pf. lxviii. 10.
— xcv. 4, 5, 6, 7.

on earth can say, *Our God is the God of salvation: In his hand are the deep places of the earth, the strength of the hills is his also: the sea is his, and he made it, and his hands have formed the dry land. O come, let us worship and bow down, and kneel before the Lord our Maker; for he is our God, and we are the people of his pasture, and the sheep of his hand.*

To suppose that the Most High made the Son to be an agent in the creation, and the Spirit to have the management of our redemption, and that the Divine Nature was not *immediately* employed in either, is a scheme that I shall take in pieces in the next discourse, and let you see that it is dishonourable to the Father, as well as to the Son and Spirit, and brings in the old Heathen notion of an inactive God, only frothed up with the nonsense of two omnipotent creatures. Such folly as this must never be charged upon the Holy Scriptures: it is indeed talking without book; I am sure, without *that Book*. At present I will confine myself to the point that I gave you in laying down the head, that it is the character of the Deity to be *chief Agent* both in nature and grace. God has always mentioned this as His peculiar: *The heavens are the work of his hands, the moon and the stars he has ordained.* We can go no higher in our no-

Heb. ii. 10. tions of him, than that it is He *for whom are all things, and by whom are all things.* They are *for him* as the great end, and *by him* as the chief cause. Now,

Col. i. 16. It is said of the Son, that *all things are created by him and for him.* What is the difference between these two texts? Why must *by him* in one place signify only an instrument, and in the other a Supreme Agent? and why must *for him* in one scripture declare a subordinate, and in the other an ultimate end? If God had designed this distinction for the use of his churches, he could easily have

given

given it. I am sure, they that talk against the use of human words in Divine things, are forced to contradict themselves; for without the barbarous terms of a *subordinate Deity*, a derived, dependent, and *originated Godhead*, it is impossible to drive in their notion. There must be a great noise of axes and hammers in the building of their temple, much *lifting up* of those *tools* that pollute God's altar. If these are not words that man's wisdom teaches, I know not what is confounding us with *philosophy and vain deceit, after the tradition of men, after the rudiments of the world, and not after Christ.*   Col. ii. 8.

* Supposing we were to have a catechism in Scripture-language, which that party have so long demanded, what would they get by it? Is it not easy to drive them out of these beloved measures? As, for example, if the first question is this, What is your opinion of the Great God? you cannot answer better, than that it is *He for whom are all things, and by whom are all things:* or, that *He has created all things, and for his pleasure they are and were created.* If the next question be, Who is that Jesus *in whom we have redemption through his blood, the forgiveness of our sins?* the Scripture has taught us to say, that *it is He by whom all things are created that are in heaven, and that are in earth, visible and invisible, whether they be thrones, or dominions, or principalities, or powers; all things are created by him and for him; and He is before all things, and by him all things consist.*   i. 16, 17. And does not such a text teach us to answer the question we find in another, *Hast thou not known, hast thou not heard, that the everlasting God, the Creator of the ends of the earth, fainteth not, neither is weary? there is no searching of his understanding.*—If you should ask again, Who is our God? we cannot answer in better words, than that *our God is the God of salvation:* And if you follow this with another question,   Isa. xl. 28.

question, Who is that Jesus whom we look to? we may say, *the author and finisher of our faith,* or, *the author of eternal salvation to as many as obey him; neither is there salvation in any other.*

Is it by any human decision, or remote and uncertain consequences,—do we depart from express words of Scripture, when we say, that Christ is equal with God in the works of nature and grace? Say we these things as men, or saith the Gospel the same also? What! shall a God be known to be the God of salvation, and shall a creature be the author of that salvation? shall they in heaven adore the great God for his having created all things, and shall the things they admire him for be the work of another? When will vain words have an end, or how long will they darken the counsels of God by words without knowledge!

If they tell us that God created these things, both in nature and in grace, *by Christ* as his instrument, why should that instrument take to himself the glory of a chief Agent, and speak of his own performance in royal language, in the same words that are used by the Supreme Efficient? *Shall the ax boast itself against him that hews therewith, or shall the saw magnify itself against him that shakes it?* Must there be any room for such a complaint in the laying of our salvation? What care did our blessed Saviour take to talk like one who came down into a lower nature! When he speaks as man, he tells us plainly, that *the Son can do nothing of himself, but what he sees the Father do.*

And why should not all the account we have of him be thus guarded? for, when he saith, *My Father works hitherto, and I work:* that *he gives eternal life,* though we know that eternal life is the gift of God: that he is *the Author of faith,* though faith is *the operation of God:* that he is *the Finisher of it,* though he *that has wrought us for the self-same thing is God:* that he *gives life, and*

and gives it more abundantly, though it is God who works in us both to will and to do:—how is it possible that these scriptures should be matched to one another, without supposing an equality between the Father and the Son? *There is one God* Eph. iv. 6. *and Father of all, who is above all, and through all, and in us all:* And yet Christ is *over all, God blessed for ever*, and *Christ lives in us.* Christ is in Gal. ii. 20. us as *our hope of glory*.

We must deny these things to be peculiar to the Deity, though they are always represented so, if One, who by nature is no God, can be capable of doing them. There is no need to say with David, *Among the gods there is none like unto thee, O Lord,* Pf. lxxxvi. *neither are there any works like unto thy works.* 8. For here is one like to him, with a nature infinitely below him, and there are works like his works. The very greatest and best works that ever God has done, Creation, Providence, and Redemption, are ascribed to one who is not his equal. So that, though *God* does not give his glory to another, yet, according to the new scheme, *we* must give that glory to another. We are told of *the* 1 Pet v. 10. *God of all grace, who has called us to his eternal glory by Christ Jesus*, that he will *make us perfect, stablish, strengthen, and settle us.* Now, this is no more than that *the grace of our Lord Jesus Christ* Rom. xvi. *should be with us, for he is of power to stablish us.* 24, 25.

8. The last thing that I shall observe in the character of a God is, that he has a right to the homage of all his creatures. All things are made *for him* that were made by him; and especially in that business that is called *Religion*, it is all directed to Him. *Thou shalt worship the Lord thy* Mat. iv. 10 *God, and him only shalt thou serve.* The laws of devotion he has distributed among Angels and Saints. When these come into the same place, they shall with the greatest perfection of their natures be employed in the same work. And though

we do not act as we shall do in heaven, yet we have but one object of our reverence and godly fear. There is none in heaven whom we have but him, and none upon earth whom we desire besides him. *Hear, O Israel,* saith he in the opening of his law, *the Lord our God is one Lord.* He puts this in the front of his commandments, *Thou shalt have no other gods before me: thou shalt not bow down thyself unto them, nor serve them; for I the Lord thy God am a jealous God.* Now,

The greater *that* deity is that we make to ourselves, the more it engages his jealousy. We cannot better account for it, to worship an Angel than an ox that eateth grass; but the former will be more resented by a jealous God, than the latter. And if the Son and Spirit are but creatures, our adoration of them is still more provoking to the Divine jealousy. The greater the rival is, the worse must our error be that makes him so.

But has the Most High God expressed himself with any fear, that we should exceed in our homage to the Son and Spirit? Are we so guarded, contracted, and held in, upon our devotions to them, as we are to the Angels? Have either of these Persons in the eternal Trinity said to any of us, *See thou do it not, but worship thou God?* No; we find that our blessed Saviour, who blamed the young man that knew not his Divinity for falling down before him, takes all the connected praises that are given him both in heaven and earth. He sits in the temple of God, and gives out himself to be God. And this would be as bad in him, if he was only a representative Deity, as it is in the man of sin, who calls himself a representative Saviour. He has set his throne as the Most High.

Sometimes you have Him that sits on the throne distinguished from the Lamb in title only, but not in praises: And lest you should think this argues two different natures, how often do you read in the

the same book, that there is *a Lamb in the [midst] of the throne*, and that *he sits down with the [Fa]ther upon his throne?* Surely those people [who] will illustrate the mediation of our Lord, by Joseph's ministry in Egypt, have forgot that though Pharaoh made a prodigious grant, yet he gave this closure to the whole, *In the throne I will be greater than thou*. But we have no such saving as this in what is said of Christ; so far from it, that *to the Son* the Father (not the Psalmist, but the Father) saith, *Thy throne, O God, is for ever and ever*. Heb. i. 8.

His establishment in the office of Messiah would never entitle him to any more than a subordinate glory. He is not to be worshipped upon that account, if he had not a prior claim. But this is the mind of infinite wisdom; such things are done, that all men may honour the Son *as* they honour the Father. Nor could it be said upon any other foundation than that of an equality, *He that honours not the Son, honours not the Father who has sent him*. John v. 23

❁❁❁❁❁❁❁❁❁❁❁❁❁❁❁❁❁❁❁

SERMON XLVIII.

March 13. 1719-20.

[2.] HAVING in these particulars given you some account what the glory of our Redeemer is, I am in the next place to consider the manner of his coming by it: And the words of my text tell us, that this is what he was RECEIVED into. You will soon apprehend that this expression is to be opened with the same variety that we

have

have observed in the other. Our Saviour's being *received*, is as different as the *glory* that belongs to him. For if the word be applied to what he carries his human nature into, it must be understood of that which by no means can be said of him either as Mediator, or as God over all blessed for ever. And yet as the text led us to consider all his glory in the several parts of his character, so his being *received* into it may be distributed under the same heads; that is,

1. We shall enquire what this receiving into the glory conferred upon him as he is *man*, was.

2. How it belongs to him as *Mediator*.

3. In what sense it may be said of him, as he is *the mighty God, and the everlasting Father*. As different as these names and titles are, the Scripture has concentred them all in Him. Nor can we lose any of them without a waste of that doctrine that has hitherto nourished us up, and in which we ought to *abound with thanksgiving*. For though our great concern lies with him as Mediator, yet denying either of his natures is destroying the offices that he sustains in them both.

1. When it is said he is received into glory, if this is to be understood of the *human nature*, there are several things that may have their interpretation that way. 1st, We read that a cloud received him out of the Apostles sight. 2dly, That Angels attended him all along, from his resurrection to the place of his reward. 3dly, That he is fixed in Heaven, never to remove out of it, till he comes to judge the world, and fetch up the bodies of those that sleep in the dust. 4thly, That the Father has pronounced the great sentence of honour, and given him a name above every name. These things relate to the manner of his being *received* in our nature, and therefore fall short of that upon which he claims the adoration of his people; and in going over them, we may observe the hope that

is

is set before us; for in these respects he is *the first-* SERM. 48. *fruits of them that sleep,* and a pattern to all his followers. The man Christ Jesus is thus exalted as *the first-born among many brethren:* they that Rom. viii. serve him as God, are to follow him as he is man; 29. and *where he is, there shall his servants be. He* 2 Cor. iv. *that raised up the Lord Jesus, shall raise up us also* 14. *by Jesus.*

(1.) I begin with that which the Scripture has taken notice of, that a *cloud received him out* of the Acts i. 9. sight of those that were gazing after him. This being no more than a very general circumstance, I enter first upon that, before we come to the other things that were of greater importance to his glory.—Thus you read the grand event that closed up all his conversation with the disciples, *That it came* Luke xxiv. *to pass whilst he blessed them, he was parted from* 1. *them, and carried up into heaven.* As in that blessing he opened heaven to *them,* so the same moment it was opened to *him.*

The historian in another book speaks of *the day* Acts i. 2. 9, *in which he was taken up,* and afterwards he de- 10. scribes the manner of it, that *when he had spoken these things, whilst they beheld, he was taken up, and a cloud received him out of their sight. They looked,* as it is added, *stedfastly towards heaven, as* he went up; partly to see him as long as they could, to follow the moving glory; and partly to give the world an account in what way he will come again, which, as the Angels who stood by them in shining garments reported, would be *in like manner as they had seen him go into heaven;* that is, in a visible way; *shall he come in clouds, and every eye shall see* Rev. i. 7. *him.*

And though this intimates his lower nature as a man, yet it is among those things that in other places give out the majesty of a God. Thus we read of him that he is *exceeding glorious;* and it Psal. civ. 2, appears in this, that *he makes the clouds his chariot,* 3.

and rides upon the wings of the wind. And again, the church prays, *O that thou wouldst rend the heavens and come down!* Though these expressions signify the greatness of God, yet neither of them relate to a matter so important, as *that* upon which our Saviour was to be revealed; I mean, to judge the world: *Clouds and darkness are round about him, righteousness and judgment are the habitation of his throne.*

The martyr Stephen had a sample of this, when he saw the heavens opened. The way how that was done is no more to be explained than the vision that he had within it, *Jesus standing at the right hand of God.* The opening of the heavens, the unfolding of those *everlasting doors*, is what we never saw; nor do I suppose that any of the croud about Stephen could be witnesses to it. His eye was strengthened to see that, because afterwards it was to see no more in this world. However, this agrees to the accounts that we have of a Redeemer. Thus we read of his accession to the reward: *I saw in the night-vision one like the Son of man come with the clouds of heaven; and he came to the Ancient of days, and there was given him dominion and glory, and a kingdom, that all-people, and nations, and languages, should serve him.* This coming in the clouds of heaven answers to what David saith, *He made darkness his secret place; his pavilion round about him were dark waters, and thick clouds of the skies.*

Thus will Christ be revealed as a judge; and when he so comes, it is *in the glory of his Father. The powers of heaven shall be shaken, and then shall they see the Son of man coming with power and great glory.* The gates of that palace are to fly open, and *the Lord to descend with a shout.* He shall issue out of the cloud, just as he entered into it, with a joyful noise. In the creation God set the firmament in the midst of the waters, and it *divided the waters*

waters that were above it from those that were below it. This is represented as a body of prodigious firmness, as Elihu faith, *Hast thou with him spread the sky, which is strong, and as a molten looking glass? i. e.* as a piece of shining glass, able to let the light through, and to keep the water in. Now *this* gave way in a manner that we cannot account for, when our Saviour went back to heaven. —There are two improvements we should make of this noble circumstance in his being received up to glory.

First, That we will stick close to his doctrine, not give up any part of the honour that belongs to him: *He that abides not in the doctrine of Christ, has not God; he that abides in the doctrine of Christ, has both the Father and the Son.* The Apostle himself has led us into this inference, *Seeing we have a great High-Priest that is passed into the heavens,* through one heaven into another, *Jesus the Son of God, let us hold fast our profession.* An indolence about the truth, or a cowardice in maintaining it, are a virtual reproach upon One that is gone away with so much pomp. His piercing the clouds, his entering the heavens, is an argument for us to hold fast our profession, and not be either wheedled or bullied out of it. For

Though this is said of him as a man, yet according to his own reasoning, it supposes another nature; for *no man has ascended up into heaven, but He that came down from heaven, even the Son of man who is in heaven.* As a man, he had not ascended into heaven at the time that he said it, and as the Son of man, he was not in heaven, nor in that character did he come down from heaven: But he speaks of his going thither, and being there, even whilst he was upon earth; which no one could say but He who had declared before, *Do not I fill heaven and earth? faith the Lord.*

2 John 9.

Heb. iv. 14.

Joh. iii. 13.

If

SERM. 48. If we *hold faſt* our profeſſion in this article, we ſhall ſcarce be perſuaded to let it go at the pull of a whiffling criticiſm upon thoſe words, The Son of man who *is* in heaven: That becauſe the expreſſion ſignifies he *was* there, in another place, therefore it muſt do ſo in this. He muſt have a looſe hold of his faith indeed, who parts with it ſo eaſily; and to carry on a force upon a word ſhall make nonſenſe of the whole verſe. For if the phraſe *who is in heaven* ſignifies *who was in heaven*, it tells us no more than we had in the former ſentence, that he *came down from heaven*. Is there any neceſſity when I ſay I came from a place, to tell you that I have been there? does not my coming thence ſuppoſe all that? But it is plain, our Saviour was to convince Nicodemus of his Divine perfections, and therefore he talks to him of his aſcending into heaven, which cannot be underſtood of his reſurrection. But to take off his ſurpriſe, he affirms again, that even at that time he *was in heaven:* As it had been obſerved before,

Joh. i. 18. that *the only begotten Son is in the boſom of the Father*, whilſt he declared him upon earth. He was
— xiv. 10. *in the Father, and the Father in him. Thou, Father,*
— xvii. 21. *art in me, and I in thee.* And though this Jeſus is now ſet at nought, and the profeſſion we make of him ſlurred by ſome, and lampooned by others, yet let us hold it faſt, from the conſideration that we do it in the cauſe of One who has *paſſed into the heavens*. And,

Secondly, This takes off all the objection of unbelief againſt our following him, We are ready to ſay, How can he judge through the *dark cloud?* And it is a more difficult queſtion, How ſhall we paſs through it, when we are taken out of the graves? Indeed *how* it will be we know not; but he that opened the heavens for himſelf, can find a way thither for our bodies as well as his own. They

1 Theſ. iv.
17, 18. who are *alive at the coming of the Lord*, and they
who

who sleep in Jesus, shall be *caught up together in the* *clouds to meet the Lord in the air,* when they go to be *ever with the Lord; wherefore comfort one another with these words.*

(2.) Another thing included in his being received up into glory is the attendance of the Angels. This reaches from his grave to his throne. One of them came with *great power, and rolled away the stone from the door of the sepulchre.* Two of them staid behind, the one at the head, and the other at the feet, *where the body of Jesus had lain,* to tell his disciples what had happened. As they had made the keepers like dead men, they struck a new life into his followers, bidding them not fear, because *the Lord was risen indeed.* And though we do not read much of them during his forty days converse with the disciples, yet when he was to go away, the same *multitude of the heavenly host* went with him up, who came with him down.

How mean soever his abode in the world might be, yet his coming into it, and going out of it, had the magnificence of heaven. This was all along foretold, not only as a reward to the human nature, but as a testimony to the Divine. For we read that *the chariots of God are twenty thousand, even thousands of Angels.* As the title of *God* shews us to whom these Angels paid their homage, so when they are called *his chariots,* it refers to some particular season in which they gave their attendance: And you read in the next words when that was, *Thou hast ascended up on high, thou hast led captivity captive.* It is in vain to wrest this last expression from an application to our Saviour, and to that very period that I am now speaking of. The Apostle by repeating the whole passage has fixed this sense upon it. And they must be hard put to it who will say, that the *chariots* belong to one, and *ascending up on high* is the act of another. He who

SERM. 48.

Mat xxviii. 2. 7.

Psal. lxviii. 17, 18.

ascended

SERM. 48. afcended is our **Saviour**, and He who was the owner of thefe chariots is the Moſt High God.

The Angels loved his human nature as the beſt ſervant to the Divine; but yet it was to a God appearing and manifeſting himſelf in that nature that they paid this eminent duty. As a man, the Angels had a charge concerning him, that in their hands they might bear him up; but as a God, he was not worſhipped as though he needed any thing; for Angels, principalities, and powers, being created by him, were created for him. In all things, and over all perſons, *he has the pre-eminence.*

This ſhews us what good hands we are put into. As all the Angels of God, upon his reſurrection, are called to worſhip him, ſo they are ſent forth as *miniſtring ſpirits* to thoſe who are the heirs of ſalvation. Upon the road they help them on, and at the end they help them up. It is ſaid of Luke xvi. 22. Lazarus, that *he was carried by the Angels into Abraham's boſom.* And they who have done ſo much for our ſouls, will wait for the day of fetching up our bodies. For *the Son of man comes with his Angels to ſever the wicked from among the juſt, to gather out of his kingdom thoſe that offend and commit iniquity,* to fetch out of the graves thoſe that are ſleeping there, and rebuild the duſt into bodies. This we are aſſured of from what they did to our bleſſed Lord. As they received him, ſo they are to receive us; for their love is under the ſame rule with ours: *Every one that loves him that begot, loves him alſo who is begotten of him.*

(3.) His being received into heaven muſt be underſtood of an abode there. The Lord ſaid unto Pſal. cx. 1. this *our Lord, Sit thou at my right-hand.* That expreſſion ſignifies both the greatneſs and the duration of the dignity: therefore we read, that *having* Heb. i. 3. *by himſelf purged away our ſins, he for ever ſat down at the right-hand of the Majeſty on high.*

The

The doctrine of transubstantiation is folly to our senses, and blasphemy to our faith; it is impossible, both in nature and religion, that the body of Jesus should be any where but in heaven. He is to come no more upon earth, till he comes to judge it. All the stories of his appearing in cloisters, and upon mountains, to some favourite saints, make the Christian religion as ridiculous as the fables of Jupiter and Mercury did that of the Heathen. When he carried his body up to heaven, it was to stay there, not to be wanting one moment from the throne. We have no more occasion for it upon earth, till the time of the restitution of all things. The believer, who knows what he talks of, does not desire to see *Jesus in the flesh* upon a visit to us here below. He is not in heaven as the Angels are, the messengers between two worlds, always going and coming; no, but *the heavens have received him: He ever appears in the presence of God for us.* The disciples saw him no more. The Apostle Paul, who saw Christ Jesus the Lord, did not see him come down upon earth, but only looking down from heaven. His descending to live here a thousand years in Person, is a scheme so little revealed in the Scriptures, that the admirers of it are forced to seek out many inventions.

I know of no season in which he will come upon earth, but when he comes to burn up that earth, and suffer it to be no more. When the earth has given up her dead, there is an end of it. It is first to be opened, and then to be consumed by the glory of the Lord. For when He sits upon the great white throne, *from his face both the earth and the heaven will flee away, and there shall be no more place for them.* When he went to Him that sent him, he had finished the work that was given him to do; and therefore saith, *I am no more in the world.*

SERM. 48.

Heb. ix. 24.

Rev. xx. 11.

SERM. 48. Thofe many declarations that he makes of a continual prefence with his people, cannot be underftood of his human nature, without a violence both to Scripture and reafon. Though we know him no more after the flefh, yet *he manifefts himfelf to us.* Though he is far above all heavens in place as well as dignity, yet he is *in the midft of two or three* who are met together in his name. Though he has left us and is gone away, neverthelefs he is *with us to the end of the world.* As to his body, it is no where elfe but before the throne of God; but there is *no fleeing from his prefence, or going from his Spirit.*

Here is a twofold comfort for his faithful fervants. *Firft,* That they truft in One who is every where: they may in all places call upon the name of the Lord Jefus. Let any perfons try how they can manage the notion of an omniprefent creature, that is both limited and infinite. And, *fecondly,* Notwithftanding this, it is our joy that we have a Saviour who is confined to one place: In that nature which he took *from* us, and took *for* us, he is a perpetual inhabitant in heaven.

In this he is our example; thus it is to be with us: *Him that overcomes,* faith he, *will I make a pillar in the temple of my God, and he fhall no more go out, or come in.* Indeed we do not go thither with our full nature all at once, as he did. We are carried off by parts. But, *firft,* The foul is taken up to *ftand before the throne of God day and night, and ferve him in his temple; and He that fits upon the throne will dwell among us.* And, *fecondly,* When the time of the dead comes, then fhall our bodies be raifed up once for all; not to ftay out another life upon earth, or look back to the places where once they lived, as Lot's wife did, but to be caught up at once; ἁρπαγησόμεθα, we fhall be fnatched away, and move with fpeed as well as glory, to be *ever with the Lord.*

Rev. iii. 12.

——vii. 15.

(4.) Chrift's

(4.) Christ's being received into glory, as a man, signifies the Father's pronouncing the sentence of reward upon him. He was a *righteous servant*, he *glorified the Father upon earth, and finished the work that was given him to do.* For this they could appeal to the Jews: *Ye men of Israel, hear these words; Jesus of Nazareth was a man approved of God among you, by signs, and miracles, and wonders, which God did by him in the midst of you, as ye yourselves also know.* He became *obedient to death, even the death of the cross; and therefore God has highly exalted him, and given him a name above every name; that in the name of Jesus every knee should bow, both of things that are upon earth, and things that are in the heavens; and that every tongue should confess that Jesus is Lord, to the glory of God the Father.*

[marginal refs: Joh. xvii. 4. Acts ii. 22. Phil. ii. 8, 9, 10, 11.]

Here are two things plainly to be observed in that scripture. *First*, A dignity conferred upon a suffering nature. This is exalted with a happiness that it had not before. But, *secondly*, This is all along considered as united to one who is really God; because here is a mention of those glories that are understood to be the peculiar of a Divine nature: as, in particular, that *in his name* every knee should bow, both in heaven and in earth, and every tongue confess that Jesus is Lord, or that Jesus is JEHOVAH, as the words would have run had they been expressed in the Hebrew language. It is true, the bowing of the knee, and confessing of a delegated empire, might have been given to a creature, if God had not reserved it to himself; yet it is now too late to suppose that it ever shall or can be so, when he has said, *I have sworn by myself, and the word is gone out of my mouth in righteousness, and shall not return, that to me every knee shall bow, and every tongue shall swear, and in the Lord, in* JEHOVAH, *shall one say, I have righteousness and strength.*

[marginal ref: Isa. xlv. 23, 24.]

SERM. 48. What! shall the Great God with all that solemnity challenge this bowing of the knee to himself in the Old Testament, and does he give up his glory to another in the New? To say, that this is *to the glory of God the Father*, does not abate, but confirm the argument; for *that* either denotes an equality of nature, or otherwise it is a consideration of no force. It is not to the glory of God the Father, that what he always called his own, should by a transfer be given to one who is infinitely below him. And therefore,

Rom. xiv. 10, 11, 12.
We have both these expressions united in another place: *We must all stand before the judgment-seat of Christ*; FOR *it is written, As I live, saith the Lord, to me every knee shall bow, and every tongue shall confess to God*. Its being written that every knee shall bow, and every tongue confess to God, is no argument at all that Christ has the judgment-seat, if he himself is not *that God*. But the Apostle, who reasons thus, concludes upon the whole, SO THEN *every one of us shall give an account of himself to God*. Standing before the judgment-seat is the same with giving an account:—*that* judgment-seat is *Christ's*,—*that* account is to be given to *God*.

And though he will come to judgment in the human nature, yet his capacity for it supposes a divine. As a man he must have the highest place, and be above the Angels; but it is only as a God that he *searches the hearts, and renders to every one according to his works; for God is judge of all*. It is only as God that he bestows eternal life, for *eternal life is the gift of God*. As God he calls us out of our graves, for it is *God who quickens the dead*. It is only as God that he can answer the dependence of all his people, for *our faith and hope must be in God*.

Thus have I considered his being received into glory, as that was a reward to the human nature; and

and I hope it is not in vain, that I have endeavoured to keep in your view the belief of a Divine Nature: For as it was *that* which made the human always pleasing to the Father, as it was *that* which made the death of the human an acceptable sacrifice, so this is the greatest article of glory to it, that *the fulness of the Godhead dwells in him bodily.*

2. I have formerly shewn you, that he has a glory as *Mediator.* Now, his being received into that, gives us quite another manner of thinking. For though this does suppose him to be the man Christ Jesus, yet in every notion of his mediatorial character, we must of necessity look upon him as God; there is no leaving out either of the natures. We can think and speak of him distinctly as a man, we can also tell what is peculiar to him as God, but as Mediator we must take in both. Now, he is received into *this glory,* 1. As the Father owns him in an union of both natures; 2. As the Angels recognize him in this comprehensive character; 3. As he himself declares his resolution to continue both God and man for ever; 4. As all his proceedings in nature, grace and providence are with this mysterious union.

(1.) He was received by the Father into the glory of the *Mediator,* as he is owned in this union of both natures. As he was the Father's delight, brought up with him, and rejoicing always before him, so he could be considered only as a God. *The glory that he had with the Father before the world was,* is no other than the glory of the Divine Nature; but now upon his ascending into heaven, here is a new state of the case.

The question is, Whether he must not lay down the nature he so lately took up, in order to continue this fellowship that he had with the Father before the foundation of the world? This is so far from being a condition, that the Lord said unto to our Lord, *Sit thou at my right-hand:* By which he proclaims, that the perfon of the Son is the fame fince he became a man that it ever was before. The Father acts in communion with him as he always had done: *The Lord fhall fend the rod of thy ftrength out of Zion.* It is the rod of THY ftrength, and yet the Lord fhall fend it out: *Rule* THOU *in the midft of* THINE *enemies. Thy people fhall be willing in the day of thy power.* It is fometimes called *his*, and fometimes *thine*; for the appellation feems to change in thefe words, *The Lord at thy right-hand fhall ftrike through kings in the day of his wrath:* Here one would think the Son fpeaks to the Father, as before the Father plainly does to the Son.

Now the Apoftle argues from this very inftance, that he can be no creature : *To which of the Angels faid he at any time, Sit thou at my right-hand, till I have made thine enemies thy footftool?* If this fitting at the right-hand does not denote an equality, he might have faid it to any of the Angels a thoufand times, and made it to fignify no more in their cafe than it does in ours, a place of happinefs; for the godly are to be at his right-hand. But it is plain the Apoftle means by it fomething that never was given to them, nor ever could be ; and if he never faid *that* at any time to one of the Angels, much lefs would he ever fay it of a man. Can it be expected, that he fhould at any time call one made of a woman, to come and take a place at his right-hand? And yet this he has done, not by advancing the human nature to an adoration, for it can never ceafe to be a creature, but by owning Him who took it, in the Deity that he had before ; that his being a Child born, and a Son given, did not hinder him from continuing *the mighty God, the everlafting Father.*

SERMON XLIX.

Mar. 27 1720.

(2.) HE is received by the Angels and Saints into the glory of a Mediator, as they recognize him in this comprehensive character: *Let all the Angels of God worship him.* The union of two natures in one person, makes his name *Wonderful* to them. By *that* they are satisfied, pleased, and secured of their own happiness. They are admitted to a greater insight into the scheme of our redemption; and as there is nothing more surprising in it than the composition of a Saviour, so this lies more open to them than it used to do. They see how He that was *made of the seed of David, according to the flesh, is declared to be the Son of God with power, and is over all, God blessed for ever.* Heb. i. 6.
Isa. ix. 6.
Rom. i. 3, 4.
— ix. 5.

I believe that at the resurrection of Jesus Christ, or rather at his ascension to the right-hand of God, as he carried the two natures along with him, so the union between them became more visible and entertaining than it had been. *That* was not only a period of greater revelations to our world, but to theirs above. The Apostle acquaints us with both these particulars: *Unto me, who am less than the least of all saints, is this grace given, that I should preach among the Gentiles the unsearchable riches of Christ.* The subject of his ministry was the *riches of Christ,* not only what he brought to his people, but what he contained in his person, and therefore they are called *unsearchable.* Eph. iii. 8.

This

SERM. 49.

This description that he gives of his work throws us full upon the objection that some make against the Gospel, That if it is a mystery, it cannot be preached, because a mystery is what people cannot know, and preaching is upon a subject they do know, or otherwise they are supposed to talk in the dark. This sort of reasoning is admired, as if it was invincible; but apply it to the text I have now given you, and try the force of it then. Paul tells us, that he was in an extraordinary way sent to preach the riches of Christ, and yet in the same breath he saith these are *unsearchable* riches. He was to preach what he could not find. The thing that he made known to others was a depth that he never came to the bottom of himself; and if people will laugh at that as a contradiction, it is no matter. It just happens to our Saviour's doctrine as it did to his person: *It is a stumbling-stone and rock of offence to some,* but *to those that believe it is precious.* They find a pleasure in rolling and swimming where they cannot reach the ground.

Eph. iii. 9.

This Apostle knew he was called to *make all men see what is the fellowship of the mystery that from the beginning of the world was hid in God, who created all things by Jesus Christ:* And, as if from this time of revelation some light was to spring upwards as well as come downwards; as if the other world was to be a receiver as well as a giver, he adds, *To the intent that now unto the principalities and powers in heavenly places might be made known by the church the manifold wisdom of God, according to the eternal purpose which he purposed in Christ Jesus our Lord.* These principalities and powers that have their dignity in heavenly places need not to be told by us, that God is wise; they have seen and admired *that* attribute in the frame of nature, and the revolutions of Providence: But here is a *manifold wisdom* of God,

ver 10, 11.

God, which has a particular pofition to the good of his church upon earth: and the fcheme that is wrought here below fhall be ever wondered at above; it is a new gofpel to them, the day-fpring from on high to heaven, as well as to the habitable parts of the earth; it is indeed according to the eternal purpofe which he purpofed in Chrift Jefus our Lord: but this was a thing *hid in God*, known with a limitation even in heaven itfelf, till He that all along defigned our redemption carried up the nature in which he completed it; and now though we have it at the *firft* hand, they have it at the *beft*.

The wonderful union between God and man was eftablifhed in our world. It is here that the Child was born and the Son given; but it is moft beheld and admired in their world. They fee at large what we only fee in part. They that beheld his glory in the flefh, and they that behold it now, do it by faith; and if this is oppofed to fight, it is a fort of feeing and not feeing. All the love that proceeds from it is, a love to one *whom we have not feen*, in whom though now we fee him not we yet believe; but in heaven faith is no longer the medium of an imperfect vifion, nor the hindrance of a complete one. They own him in both his natures, as God and man. Thus their praifes to him, and for him, go together, according to that prophetic pfalm, *Prayer fhall be made for him continually, and daily fhall be be praifed.* This mixture of loving the human nature, adoring the divine, and admiring the union between both, will be more eminently the work of heaven. We find Saints and Angels employed upon thefe delights.

You have an inftance of this in the *Saints*, who plainly in their language weave together the properties and the merit of the two natures. They call him *The faithful Witnefs*, which, though it is true

SERM. 49. true of him as a man, yet may be understood of his attribute as a God. They say he is *the first-begotten from the dead;* this you know must refer to his body: That *he is the Prince of the kings of the earth;* though *that* may be considered as a reward to the nature in which he suffered, yet it is often mentioned as the glory of another, *that he is the King of kings, and Lord of lords;* and He of whom this is said *only has immortality, and dwells in unapproachable light.*

Having thus described his *person,* there is the same variety to be observed in the tribute of their Rev. i. 5, 6. devotions: *Unto him that loved us, and washed us from our sins in his own blood, and has made us kings and priests unto God and his Father; to him be glory and dominion for ever and ever.* Amen. His loving us, which always led on the purchase that he made of us, is called an everlasting love. The blood that he shed can be understood of him no otherwise than he is man; but the virtue of this, its washing us from our sins, must be derived from him under other considerations: For it is the prerogative of God to *pardon iniquity, to put away transgression;* and therefore *the finishing of sin* is not the effect of his dying as he was a creature; for all *that* he might have done without any be-
Dan. ix. 24. nefit to us; but it is grounded upon his *bringing in an everlasting righteousness.* This making us kings and priests is what he deserved, or rather attempted as a man; but it is an honour that comes from the Throne. It is only a God who can make us fit in the Divine presence as *kings,* and serve him as *priests.* It is not with the blood of a man that we come to the Lord, and bow ourselves to the Most High God. The Divine Majesty would be always inaccessible if He was not the *way,* who is
John xiv. 4. also *the truth and the life.*—Thus you see in what language their praises are formed and sung; that
they

they both admire what he suffered as man, and receive what he gives as God.

In the same strain do the Angels take notice of him. You may ask, indeed, what concern they have in a nature that is below their own, or how it should ever be a part of their praises, that *Jesus died and rose again:* and it is very true, he is not their Redeemer in that fulness of relation in which he is ours; yet it is said, *He made peace by the blood of his cross, i. e.* he restored peace where it was lost, and he established it where it was continued; for both these senses are within the comprehension of the word: *By* HIMSELF, as it ought to be translated, *to reconcile all things, whether they be things in earth or things in heaven.*

Col. i. 20.

Reconciling things in heaven, is not to be conceived of in the way we speak of that work among things on earth; to us it is a procuring, a deserving, and an opening out, a treasure of happiness; to them it is a closing them in, and giving the stamp of eternity to what they enjoy; and therefore they admire what he did upon the cross. The purchase that he made there, was a confirmation for them; so that the Apostle saith, *I beheld, and heard the voice of many Angels about the throne; and the number of them was ten thousand times ten thousand, and thousands of thousands; saying with a loud voice, Worthy is the Lamb that was slain to receive power, and riches, and wisdom, and strength, and honour, and glory, and blessing.* What they admire in him is his being slain,—the death that no other than his human nature could bow to; but the merit that arose out of this, and was equal to all the honour, and glory, and blessing, that are ascribed to him, leads up their thoughts to God. For a creature can never deserve what is peculiar to God. No obedience can make a person equal to Him that sits upon the throne, if he was not so in nature; and thus do both the Saints and Angels own Him who

Rev. v. 11 12.

is God and man, and celebrate this union in their praises, and will do so for ever.

(3.) He is received into glory as Mediator, with regard to his own act; that is, he has declared his resolution to continue both God and man for ever. As the human nature is what he took in the fulness of time, so he might lawfully lay it down again at the end of time, and when he had given up the *kingdom*, throw off the *union:* But this he will not do. Though he has our nature to very different purposes from what he once pursued, yet it is the same in substance that ever it was; a created, limited, and dependent soul; a real, a penetrable, and solid body.

There is a great dispute among those who are in the humour to maintain it, whether Christ's taking upon him the human nature was an act of humiliation. The trick of the question lies in this, That the human nature is now a part of his glory, and possessed of a full reward, and therefore *having it* could be no branch of his suffering. But, not to trifle with unedifying talk, it is very plain, that his taking upon him *the form of a servant*, and being *found in fashion as a man*, is a great instance of his obedience to the will of God. He is still in the same nature; praised in it, and admired for it. He has truly loved it: he does not come into it as a way-faring man, to tarry for a season: But to shew that the union between him and his people is everlasting, he makes that between the Divine and the human nature to be so too; and this will farther appear from the examples I shall give you under the next head; and that is,

(4.) He proceeds as God and man in all the works of nature, grace and providence: And therefore you will often observe, that those things are said of Him as a man, which can be true of none but a God; nor must they be understood of
any

any other nature than what is Divine; but it is to express the durable union between them, that the Scripture has thus difpofed of words that relate to one, as if they might be transferred to the other. SERM. 49.

Thus you are apprifed of that well known text, that there is *a church of God* which he has *purchafed with his own blood.* Now, though the *blood of God* founds with a contradiction, yet the fentence is foon underftood. It is but a tranfplanted word, and only proves that He who did fo bleed was no lefs than God. Thus he proceeds in all his remaining defigns. I have mentioned them under the heads of nature, grace, and providence. He declares the hypoftatical union in every one of them. Acts xx. 28.

1ft, In the works of nature. Thus we read of *him* who fpake to us in thefe laft days, that by *him* the Father made the worlds, and that *he upholds all things by the word of his power.* God's fpeaking to us *by him,* fignifies his being a man, *made out of the clay,* as Job had wifhed it might be: but *making the worlds by him,* is not to be comprehended in this notion of him; becaufe thefe worlds were made before he was made, *i. e.* before a body was prepared for him; and He, who as a man could not bear the weight of his own crofs, does neverthelefs *uphold all things by the word of his power.* This upholding of all things, fignifies a maintaining them in their being; and the term *all things* muft include Angels as well as men. Thus, when it is faid, *Angels, principalities and powers, are created by him, and for him,* it is added, that *he is before all things, and by him do all things confift.* Now, in that notion of him we fpeak as Job did to God, *What fhall I do to thee, O thou Preferver of men?* Or, as the Pfalmift fays, it is He who *holds our fouls in life*: Or, as Mofes had faid before him, *He is thy life, and the length of thy days.* It can never be faid of a lower nature, that it upholds a higher: Heb. i. 2, 3.
Job xxxiii. 6.
Col. i. 16, 17.
Job vii. 20.
Pf. lxvi. 9.
Deut. xxx. 20.

SERM. 49. higher: It is against all proportion to say, that the Son of man is the Lord, or the support, of Angels; and yet you see these things are mingled together.

Heb. i. 3, 4. Thus the Apostle goes on, that *having by himself purged our sins, he for ever sat down at the right-hand of the Majesty on high, being made so much better than the Angels, as he had by inheritance obtained a more excellent name than they.* That expression, *he purged away our sins,* will easily bring us down into the lowest conceptions of him; but that, *for this,* he should for ever sit at the right-hand of God, is no way to be accounted for, but from an antecedent dignity. It is true, as a man, as a creature, as a servant, he is made better than the Angels; but it is still with a view to this, that he has by inheritance a more excellent name than they. He was originally, and by right of nature, called by a name which they had not: *For to which of the Angels said the Father at any time, Thou art my Son?*

You are thus to look upon Him who is both God and man, as one that bears up the pillars of the earth. In this manner he speaks by the prophet.

Isa. l. 2, 3. *At my rebuke I dry up the sea; I make the rivers a wilderness; their fish stinks because there is no water, and dies for thirst. I clothe the heavens with blackness, and make darkness their covering.* And who is this? One who afterwards speaks of

ver. 4, 5, 6. a much lower nature: *The Lord God has given me the tongue of the learned, that I should know how to speak a word in season to him that is weary. The Lord God has opened mine ear, and I was not rebellious; I gave my back to the smiters, and my cheeks to them that plucked off the hair; I hid not my face from shame and spitting.* Would it not be strange to hear a person whose very face was covered with darkness, to talk of his covering the heavens with it! But it shews us, that as these things are to be understood of two different natures,

tures, so they are carried on by an union between them both. [SERM. 49.]

2dly, This is still more visible in the works of grace. What he does as a days-man between God and us, supposes that he is both God and man in his own person *There is but one God, and but one Mediator between God and man, the man Christ Jesus.* [1 Tim. ii. 5.] That phrase is not to be understood as exclusive of his divinity; for, as a way is made for us *through the vail, that is to say, his flesh,* so our welcome there is owing to his being *High-priest over the house of God.* [Heb. x. 20, 21.] And whence does this arise? It is indeed a constitution, but it supposes an eternity of nature. Hence, as the Lord has sworn to him, *Thou art a Priest for ever,* so the foundation of *that* is, that *this man,* or, as it ought to be rendered, this *person, because he continues for ever, has an unchangeable priesthood.* [—vii. 24.] His continuing for ever is considered as antecedent and fundamental to his unchangeable priesthood. This, as the words there tell us, is to continue for ever, both by a Divine appointment, and by his own choice: *For though the law made men high-priests that had infirmity, yet the word of the oath, that is since the law, has made the Son, who is consecrated for evermore.* [ver. 28.]

It is in this complicated way that he gives promises to his people. One time he would have them take the comfort of this thought, that *he went to the Father, and they saw him no more;* [John xvi. 10.] from this does the Spirit *convince the world of righteousness;* i. e. his going to the Father and making no return back again, is an argument that the righteousness which he brought in upon the cross, he now brings forth before the Throne. This plainly refers to his human nature, we are to *see him no more after the flesh;* and yet the same mouth has told us, that which is contradictory to the other, if it is not to be understood of another nature,

Yet

SERM. 49. *Yet a little while and the world sees me no more,*
John xiv. *but ye see me, and because I live, ye shall live also.*
19. This is more than we can either believe to be true, or expect to be made good from Christ himself as a man. It is not the human nature that we see again; it is not because *this* lives that therefore we live also. The life of *that* is an argument of our resurrection, but it is not the fountain out of which we are supplied with the graces of the Spirit.

3dly, It is thus that he proceeds in all the designs of his providence; by which I do not understand any thing distinct from nature and grace, but rather what is comprehensive of both. Under this head I will give you two particulars, which do express the union of the Divine and human natures, *viz.* his conduct of the Church, and his judgment of the world.

First, It is as God and man that he rules his Church; giving them laws and life below, and managing the whole stock of their affairs above.
Eph. i. 22, He is *Head over all things to his Church, which is*
23. *his body, the fulness of Him who fills all in all.*
Rev. xix. Hence, we read of *heaven opening, and behold a*
11, 12, *white horse; and he that sat on him was called Faith-*
13. *ful and True; and in righteousness does he judge and make war.* This you will apply to what he does for his people against all their enemies: *His eyes are as a flame of fire, and on his head are many crowns; and he has a name written that no man knows but he himself.*

You find, though some among us will allow no mysteries, no unintelligible things on earth, yet there is a great deal of them in heaven. It is added, *He was clothed with a vesture dipped in blood, and his name is called The Word of God.* Here is a plain reference to the two natures. The garment that he wears is dipped in blood. It is thus that he is *glorious in his apparel.* You cannot possibly strike off this from a relation to his humanity. And
yet

yet He who is so attired is called by a name that he had eternally before these garments: for he is the Word of God, *the Word that in the beginning was with God, the Word that was God himself, by whom were all things created, and without whom was nothing made that was made.*

SERM. 49.

John i. 1, 2, 3.

Nay, the Apostle goes on to tell us the signification both of the garment that he wears, and the name that he is known by, that *he trod the wine-press of the fierceness and wrath of Almighty God.* No wonder, then, that he is red in his apparel, and his vesture is dipped in blood. This he did, when *the Lord laid on him the iniquity of us all.* He was then bruised, his soul was put to grief, and made an offering for sin. And yet upon this vesture, which is the memorial of his sufferings, he has a name written, *The King of kings, and Lord of lords.* Thus you see, how he preserves the united character, the dependence of the human nature with the supremacy of the Divine.

Rev. xix. 15.

ver. 16.

It is from hence that we have access to the mercy-seat. Both these considerations enter into our hope: First, That *all things are naked and open to him with whom we have to do; that there is no creature that is not manifest in his sight; and that Jesus, the Son of God, as the great High-Priest, is entered into the heavens.* And, secondly, That *we have not an High-Priest which cannot be touched with the feeling of our infirmities; but was in all points tempted as we are, yet without sin.* The former is plainly to be understood of the Divine Nature, and the latter of the human; but from both of them we argue for our *coming boldly to the throne of grace, that we may obtain mercy, and find grace to help in every time of need.* As a man he can have *compassion on the ignorant, and them that are out of the way, seeing that he himself was compassed about with those infirmities:* And as God he has not only compassion but relief for us; and in that notion of him

Heb. iv. 13, 14, 15, 16.

— v. 2.

it

SERM. 49. it were blasphemy to say, that he is compassed about with any infirmity.

Secondly, You will also see that the Scripture has represented him as a judge of the world, under this union of natures. *God has appointed a day in which he will judge the world in righteousness, by the man whom he has ordained, whereof he has given assurance to all men, in that he has raised him from the dead.* As man he sits upon the throne; thus the suffering nature is to be rewarded: As God he *judges the world;* thus the obscured nature is to be declared. *The Father*, that Person of the Trinity who was not incarnate, *judges no man, but has committed all judgment to the Son. He has given him authority to execute judgment, because he is the Son of man.* And yet this is no way destructive of what the Christian religion tells us, that we *come to Jesus the Mediator of the new testament, and to God the Judge of all;* which it would not do, if He who is judge of all, was not over all God blessed for ever. *Our God shall come, and shall not keep silence; a fire shall devour before him, and it shall be very tempestuous round about him: he shall call to the heavens from above, and to the earth, (that he may judge his people), Gather my saints together unto me, those that have made a covenant with me by sacrifice. The heavens shall declare his righteousness; for God is Judge himself.* What an honour will be put upon our nature, when He who has taken it into union with him, comes to awake the dead, and close up the eternal fate of men and Angels! Thus we know that *our Redeemer lives, and that he shall stand at the latter day upon the earth; and though after our skin worms destroy this body, yet in our flesh we shall see,* Him who is really, God.

Acts xvii. 31.

Joh. v. 22.

Heb. xii. 23, 24.

Psal. l. 3—6.

Job xix. 25, 26.

SER-

SERMON L.

April 10. 1720.

3. AS you have heard at large that the glory of Christ Jesus is what belongs to him as God, and is mentioned with a fulness of language peculiar to the Divine Nature; so when we consider his being *received* into that, we must take the word in a very different sense from what it bore under the other two particulars. Receiving the human nature into glory was giving it what it never had, and carrying it where it never was: But to say that a God is *thus* received into glory, is to blaspheme *his* nature, and confound *our own*, and darken counsel by words without knowledge.

There is no place where he was not; there is no perfection that he had not. Whilst he was on earth he called himself *the Son of man, who is in heaven;* which phrase, as I have lately shewn you, can refer to nothing but his omnipresence. And if Nicodemus had not taken it so, he must have fallen into the same contempt of him that the Jews did, whenever he opened out any pretensions to Divinity: *They had a law, and by that law he ought to die, because he made himself the Son of God.* The high-priest adjured him by the living God, that he should tell them *whether he was Christ the Son of God:* And when he had owned it, the man who asked the question rent his clothes, and charged him with blasphemy; and they all *said, He is guilty of death.* Though they looked upon him as *a man approved of God among them, by signs, and miracles, and wonders,* yet it always raised an impatience

Joh. iii. 13.

—xix. 7.

Mat. xxvi. 63.—66.

a Acts ii. 22.

tience when he affirmed his Deity: *What need we any farther witness, ye have heard his blasphemy?* —You may see this in a few examples.

The first I will give you is John v. 16. where you find, that Jesus, having healed a poor lame man who had been long waiting at the pool of Bethesda, by *that* run himself into the displeasure of the Jews, *because he did it upon the Sabbath-day*. He, in vindication of this, provokes them by saying, *My Father works hitherto, and I work.* Several in our days could easily have explained these words in such a way as to clear him of blasphemy, though perhaps at the expence of running into it themselves. They would have pleaded to Jews as they now do to Christians, that calling God his Father, instead of proving that he had a Divine Nature, was a plain argument that he had not: that the very title of Father signified his subordination to Him who was called so. Now, if this is a right way of arguing, it is a pity that the discovery should be reserved to the last days, that the Jews did not know it seventeen hundred years ago, because it might have prevented his death, and their wickedness; for it is said, THEREFORE *sought they to kill him, because he had not only broken the Sabbath, but said that God was his Father, making himself* EQUAL WITH GOD.

Could not he as readily have answered for himself, as the men of our age can answer for him, that he had asserted no equality? that the word *Father* is what Angels and men are allowed to use in all their approaches to God, and that therefore the enemies had done violence to his words, that they might introduce violence against his Person? But instead of setting them right in their way of thinking, and placing himself to a better advantage in their opinion, he goes on with a vast enlargement upon those very heads that had so confounded them. That *the Father loves the Son, and shews him*

him all things that he himself does; for as the Father raises the dead, and quickens them, even so the Son quickens whom he will; that all men should honour the Son as they honour the Father: he that honours not the Son, honours not the Father that sent him.

Observe here upon this argument, that if there is any distinction between the Father and Him, it must be infinite; and as they thought he had denied all that, and had made himself equal with God; as this would have been the greatest blasphemy in him to say so; it was the greatest unkindness to them, if he should let them go away with the opinion. He was bound to undeceive them: As he came to do *God's will*, it cannot be thought he would encourage the least suspicion of running away with *his glory;* and therefore to leave the Jews ignorant of his true meaning here, was not only a cruelty to them, but a breach of trust in him, and could be no better than a neglect of the Father's honour.

Another example you will meet with, John vi. He had wrought a miracle in feeding five thousand people with five loaves; upon which many went after him: And had he contented himself with the title of a Prophet that should come into the world, they would still have followed him; but he thought it needful to assert a great deal more, and that was his coming down from heaven: at this the Jews murmured. Now, instead of striking off the sense which they put upon it, and shewing it to be false, he repeats it again: *As the living Father has sent me, and I live by the Father, so he that eats me shall live by me. This is that bread which came down from heaven; not as your fathers did eat manna and are dead; he that eats this bread shall live for ever. Many, therefore, of his disciples when they heard this, said, This is a hard saying, who can hear it?* And what method does he take with them?

Joh. vi. 57. 58. 60.

Does

SERM. 50. Does he drop the doctrine to please the men?
Joh. vi. 61, no, far from it: *When he knew in himself that the*
62. *disciples murmured at it, he said unto them, Does this offend you? what and if you see the Son of man ascend up where he was before?* It is plain the matter of their offence was his pretending to *that* which they thought too much for a creature. That though they admired his preaching, and were astonished at his miracles, yet they could have no conceptions of his Divinity. Jesus said unto them, *Moses gave you not that bread from heaven, but my Father gives you the true bread from heaven: they said, Lord, evermore gives us of this bread. Jesus said unto them, I am the bread of life; he that comes unto me shall never hunger, and he that believes on me shall never thirst; but I said unto you, That ye also have seen me and believed not.*

And no wonder, because, as he himself tells us, there is more than external evidence necessary to that: *Therefore, as I said unto you, no man can come unto me, except it were given him of my Father.* Many thousands had already come to him with abundance of zeal, as we are told all along in that very chapter. In this they acted by no higher a principle than carnal reason, which some people will not have us to speak of with any diminution. But there was a coming to him which signifies a believing in him; and this they knew nothing of, nor would they ever have known it without a supernatural revelation: For, *no man*, says he, *comes unto me, except the Father that has sent me draw him. From that time many of his disciples went back, and walked no more with him.*

This doctrine has always proved a parting-matter between him and hypocrites, between hypocrites
1 Cor. xi. and believers: *There must be heresies, that they who*
19. *are approved may be manifest among you.* When he asked Peter, *Will ye also go away?* he answers,
Joh. vi. 68. *To whom shall we go, for thou hast the words of e-*
ternal

ternal life? If he means only, thou haft preached to us the doctrine of eternal life, they that were gone knew this as well as they that ftaid. But he defigned to exprefs as much in that confeffion, as Chrift himfelf had done before in his declaration, *I am the bread of life; and the words that I fpeak to you, they are fpirit, and they are life.* They that forfook him took this for an extravagance that no creature ought to run into. At this they murmured, as a thing profane in him, and unintelligible to them: *The Jews murmured at him, becaufe he faid, I am the bread which came down from heaven. They faid, Is not this Jefus the fon of Jofeph, whofe father and mother we know; how is it then that he faith, I came down from heaven? Jefus therefore anfwered and faid unto them, Murmur not among yourfelves.* Again, *I am the living bread which came down from heaven: if any man eat of this bread, he fhall live for ever; and the bread which I will give is my flefh, which I give for the life of the world. The Jews therefore ftrove among themfelves, faying, How can this man gives us his flefh to eat?* and yet he goes on with this unintelligible doctrine, *Verily I fay unto you, Except you eat the flefh of the Son of man, and drink his blood, ye have no life in you.*

This was the declaration that he made. To this did they that continued with him give their teftimony: *We believe, and are fure, that thou art the Chrift, the Son of the living God.* If by this title, *The Son of the living God,* they did not mean one equal to the living God, they were only trifling with great words of vanity, and faid no more than what the apoftates would have faid as well as they. Every believer is the fon of the living God by creation and fanctification: and is it likely that giving him a title, which might be taken in a contracted fenfe, was *that* upon which the twelve Apoftles divided from the reft? Would not the whole

whole croud who once followed him have said as much as the remaining difciples, if the words might have been taken in the fenfe that fome would give us?

Indeed the queftion turns very fhort upon us, Can the Son of God be God? and I think the anfwer may be as fhort, Yes, as truly as the Son of man is man. Thus you read in the eighth chapter of the fame hiftory, that the Jews held an argument with him a long time; and though he ufes very provoking expreffions, that they were the *fervants of fin*, nay, that they were *of their father the devil*, and fulfilled his lufts in lies and murders, they fo far bear with him, as only to rail at him: *Say we not well, that thou art a Samaritan, and haft a devil?* but when he tells them, *Before Abraham was, I am*, they are out of all patience, and take up ftones to throw at him as a blafphemer. They would allow him any thing but Divinity. I will give you but one example more; and *that* is

In the tenth chapter, where he tells them of *laying down his life* as a good fhepherd. He would not have them think by this that he quitted his pretenfions to a Divine fovereignty. No: faith he, *No man takes it from me, I have power to lay it down, and I have power to take it again*. It is obferved *there was a divifion among the Jews for thefe fayings; for many of them faid*, (what might fit eafy enough where it is thrown as a reproach upon any minifter), *He has a devil, and is mad; why hear ye him?* Upon this the Jews come round about him, and defired that he would put them out of their uncertainty, and tell them plainly whether he was the Chrift. He, in anfwer, faith, *I have told you, and ye believe not*. What was it that they did not believe? that he had a Divine commiffion? No; this was clear enough from a Divine power: they knew no man could do the things that he did, except God was with him: but they did not believe

lieve that he could *give eternal life.* And they stuck above all at that sentence, *I and my Father are one.* ^{SERM. 50.} ^{Joh. x. 30.}

Thus they stumbled at that stumbling-stone; as it is written, *Behold I lay in Sion a stumbling-stone, and a rock of offence;* **whoever believes on him shall not be ashamed.** If he had meant that the Father and he were one in consent and in design, would not all mankind think *that* of a Christ, nay of a Prophet who came to do wonders upon earth, that the person who wrought such things was one in agreement with him who sent him? Might not Moses have said it? and did he not say what was equivalent to it? Was there any occasion, if that was all that he designed, for them to take up stones, which, as they profess in the innocency of their error, was *for blasphemy, because he being a man had made himself* God? ^{ver. 33.}

You see, from these examples, where the matter stuck. Now, what he saith, which so offended the Jews, might have given the same provocation to Nicodemus, when he tells him, that *the Son of man was then in heaven.* But *every one that had heard and learned of the Father came to him:* it had pleased God to *reveal his Son in him;* so that his being received into glory as God, cannot be understood in any sense inconsistent with eternal felicity, and unchangeable fulness. In this respect *he is the same yesterday, to-day, and forever.* I therefore take the phrase to denote such things as these: 1. He threw off the vail that was upon his Divine Nature; 2. He did this with a design of never taking it on again; 3. He afresh exposed himself to the adoration of Angels; 4. He used the language and prerogatives of God in heaven; 5. He acted as God among his people upon earth. ^{Joh. iii. 13.} ^{Gal. i. 16.} ^{Heb. xiii. 8.}

(1.) He laid aside, he threw off the vail that was upon the Divine Nature. That he obscured himself for a while is plain from all history, and the

wonderful

wonderful expressions which the Scripture has delivered it under. We read of him, that *he being in the form of God, made himself of no reputation; and how was that, but by taking on him the form of a servant? being made in the likeness of men, and found in fashion as a man, he humbled himself.* You see by this vast variety of phrases, the Apostle would have us established in two things.

First, The reality of Christ's human nature; that appears by the death of the cross, which, as it was the most shameful way of dying, so it must be the most evident and certain, the least liable to any trick or deceit. The Jews themselves, who might laugh at the miracles of his birth, were satisfied there was none at all in his death; and yet, as here was the utmost evidence given to our nature, so,

Secondly, You may also observe, that here was the hiding of another. The fashion of a man, that form of a servant, his becoming of no reputation, hindred the world from seeing any thing of an antecedent glory. He did not then appear to them as having *the form of God*, whatever is the meaning of the expression. They that passed by reviled him, wagging their heads, and saying, *If thou be the Son of God, come down from the cross:* and, *He trusted in God; let him deliver him now, if he will have him; for he said, I am the Son of God.*

That sentence is enough to confound the world, *To us a Child is born, to us a Son is given, and this is the name that he shall be called,* THE MIGHTY GOD, THE EVERLASTING FATHER. A God that is born as a child, a Father that is given as a son, do not sound so altogether void of mystery as we are told every thing in our religion ought to do: But if there are any degrees in incomprehensibles, we should think it was still more wonderful to be told, that He *who hid not his face from shame and spitting*, was always *full of joy with the light of God's countenance!*

countenance! that He who died upon the cross as a man, as a malefactor, was without any interruption, over all *God blessed for ever!*

The Scripture has told us the one as plainly as the other; and though some are angry that we talk of two natures in one Person, yet these things can never be said of one and the same Nature. It is vile to say, that a God died, or that a body was at the same time in mount Calvary, and in the mount Sion that is above, the heavenly Jerusalem; that He whose *goings forth have been from everlasting,* came in the fulness of time; that He who is the Son of the Father, is made of a woman. The Jews objected against it, he had said, *If I be lifted up, I will draw all men to me. This he said, signifying what death he should die. The people answered him, We have heard out of the law, that Christ abides for ever; and how sayest thou, The Son of man must be lifted up? who is this Son of man?* [Joh. xii. 32, 33, 34.]

Are not such characters to be distributed under their proper heads? Do not they fully contradict one another, and must do so eternally, if you would refer them to different natures? He came to a world that knew him not, though he had made it; nay, he came to his own, and they received him not, though he was the Lord whom they sought, and the Messenger of the covenant in whom they delighted: But *to them that received him he gave power to become the sons of God, even to them who believed on his name;* that is, he gave them a new nature. Their believing in him, their receiving him, was a thing given to them; for they were born not *of flesh, nor of the will of man, nor of blood, but of God; and the Word was made flesh, and dwelt among us,* as a partaker of the same flesh with ourselves. They had seen him with their eyes, they had looked upon him; as the Apostle saith in another of his writings, *their hands handled the Word of life:* not as he was the Word of life, [i. 12, 13.] [1 Joh. i. 1.]

life, but he submitted to an evidence that was thus familiar and sensible: and they beheld his glory; and what was that? *the glory of the only begotten of the Father.* They beheld it indeed, but others did not; and it was very needful they should not; for, as the Apostle argues, *had they known it, they would not have crucified the Lord of glory: through ignorance they did it, as did also their rulers.*

You remember he charged the devils that they should not make him known; nay, when he carried three disciples with him into the mount of transfiguration, and there came a voice to him from the excellent glory, he saith to them, *Tell the vision to no man* till the Son of man be risen from the dead. And even before that, he had bound them with a caution: Whom do men say that I am? and by their answer it appears, that though men knew not what he was, yet they had a wonderful opinion of him, when they took him to be one raised from the dead; an old Prophet, not only raised up by heaven, but sent down from it: *But whom do ye say that I am?* Peter saith, *Thou art the Christ, the Son of the living God.* This they must ascribe to supernatural discoveries, *Blessed art thou, Simon Barjona, for flesh and blood has not revealed this to thee, but my Father who is in heaven.* And yet, though he saith *this is the rock upon which he will build his church,* he orders them *not to tell any man* that he was Jesus the Christ. What! must they tell no man now, what they were to tell all men afterwards? shall the testimony that should be diffused among all nations, be at present concealed from their own? Yes; and the reason is this, *because the Son of man must be delivered into the hands of sinful men.* But now,

He as God is received into glory. He was *declared* to be the Son of God by the resurrection from the dead; not *made* the Son of God by that, but ὁρισθεὶς set in a proper light, brought into view.

What

What the Pſalmiſt ſpeaks of God's *ſetting his King upon the holy hill of Sion*, in ſaying to him, *Thou art my Son, this day have I begotten thee*, the Apoſtle fixes to the reſurrection; that this was the day the great God ſpoke of. He was called the only begotten of the Father long before that. It was not the firſt time that he took the name himſelf, or was known by it among his people; but from that time he ſhould be better known, not only in his mediatorial capacity, but in his infinite and eternal nature.

SERM. 50.
Pſ. ii. 6, 7.
Acts xiii. 31, 33.

(2.) This obſcuring of the Divine Nature is over for ever: he is no more to ſuffer as a man, no more to be hid as a God: *When ye have lift up the Son of man, ye ſhall know that I am.* If the Goſpel that declares him *is hid, it is hid to them that are loſt*: for where the light of the glorious Goſpel ſhines, He appears to be *the image of the inviſible God;* that is, he ſhews himſelf to us under all the notions that we have of God, or otherwiſe he is not the image, unleſs you think the image makes one diſcovery, and the original another; that is, unleſs it is a falſe image. If Chriſt is not what the Father is, he cannot be *the brightneſs of his glory, and the expreſs image of his perſon.* For, the brightneſs of the Father's glory, in that place, is not to be underſtood of an attribute, or a maniſeſtation of that attribute; for if ſo, the creation, the Goſpel, the graces of his people, are the brightneſs of his glory. But if this is a title given to a being, a perſon, a ſubſiſting agent, and if we are told theſe things of ſuch a one's nature, he cannot have the glory of that other, nor be himſelf the brightneſs of that glory, if he is inferior to him.

John viii. 28.
2 Cor. iv. 3, 4.
Heb. i. 3.

The expreſs image of any perſon denotes the ſame nature with that perſon, when we are ſpeaking of real and original characters. Thus, for example, when it is ſaid, that God made man in his image and his likeneſs, it can ſignify no more than a similitude; that there was something in that nature which had a resemblance of the divine: But when it is said, that Adam begat a son *in his own likeness, and after his image,* there the words must signify a great deal more than a mere similitude; for that son had the very nature that the father had, and the description is on purpose to tell us, that they were both creatures of the same kind. This is observed in a nature which is not at all altered by succession; there is no subordination of essence between a father and a son, *i. e.* a son is as truly and fully of the human nature as a father.

Now the question is, Whether the Apostle, in saying that Christ is the express image of his person, means only what Moses does, when he saith man was made in God's likeness? I think the words contain a great deal more; because, as soon as he had said this, he immediately adds, (that which is peculiar to God), that *he upholds all things by the word of his power.* Though he designs to speak of him in the mediatorial characters, yet he introduces them by those that are antecedent to them.

God's *speaking to us by his Son,* must be understood of the Son as he was man: His appointing him to be *the heir of all things,* that is, to receive the glory of all things, makes his inheritance relate to him as a Mediator: But his *making the worlds by him* is the sentence upon which the dispute begins. The question is, Whether these words denote a nature that is equal to the Father, or one that is subordinate to him? Whatever be the meaning of that expression, it is evident that from it the Apostle ascends to consider, not what Christ is as a creature or as a Redeemer, but what he was in himself, abstracted from all his works; and then tells us, that *he is the brightness of his Father's glory, and the express image of his person.* This does not come in among any rewards bestowed upon him. It is not the recompence of his death:

No;

No; that is mentioned in thefe words, *He fat down at the right-hand of the Majefty in high places.* Upholding all things, and doing it as a God does, *by the word of his power,* is confidered firft, before he enters into the particulars of his merit, and the glory that arofe out of it. This he did long before he took upon him our nature. And therefore,

As he has thrown off the vail under which he was for fome time obfcured, he never defigns to take it on again. The human nature fhall no more darken the divine to the fons of men. They above fhall *fee him as he is,* fee one like themfelves united to a glory that no man has feen or can fee. He is at the fame time confeffed to be *the Lamb in the midft of the throne,* and *the invifible God, who only has immortality, and dwells in the light that none can approach to.*

(3.) He may be faid to be received into the glory of the Divine Nature, as he did afrefh expofe himfelf to the adoration of Angels. There were new orders iffued out upon his refurrection, as the Apoftle obferves in a paffage that I have often addreffed to your thoughts: *When he brings the Firft-begotten into the world, he faith, And let all the Angels of God worfhip him.*

The period of his bringing the Firft-begotten into the world, will be eafily confeffed by all to be, either his birth, or his refurrection. What is here affirmed is true of both, but it feems more natural to underftand it of the latter: For the words are, ὅταν δὲ πάλιν εἰσαγάγῃ, when he brings him *again,* which he may be faid to do from the time of his rifing again, or his being revealed from heaven by the effufion of the Spirit. Here I would defire your notice of two things.

Firft, That this is a quotation out of the Pfalms, and therefore muft carry the fame fenfe here that it does there, or otherwife the Scripture is rather perverted

perverted than applied. You find it, Pf. xcvii. 7. *Worſhip him, all ye gods.* Indeed you may obſerve here is an alteration in the words, which the Apoſtle would never have made, if it was abſolutely needful to preſerve the very ſound of the letter: Nor would the Holy Spirit have thrown ſuch a reproach upon himſelf, in departing from the plain words of the Old Teſtament, by bringing them with any variation into the New. However,

Secondly, He who is called the Firſt-begotten is recommended to the worſhip of all the Angels of God; not only ſet *above* them, for that he might be as a creature, but placed *before* them as the object of their religious adoration. That the term *worſhip* very often ſignifies no more than civil reſpect, cannot be denied; but it muſt ſignify in this place what it did in the Pſalms. The Holy Spirit never runs into the impertinence of bringing out words, and leaving the ſenſe behind him, and therefore you ſhall have no human deciſion to determine the meaning of this paſſage; read it in the Old Teſtament: *The Lord reigns, let the earth rejoice, let the multitude of iſles be glad thereof: clouds and darkneſs are round about him, righteouſneſs and judgment are the habitation of his throne; a fire goes before him, and burns up his enemies round about; his lightnings enlightened the world, the earth ſaw and trembled; the hills melted like wax at the preſence of the Lord, at the preſence of the Lord of the whole earth; the heavens declare his righteouſneſs, and all the people do ſee his glory. Confounded be all they that ſerve graven images, that boaſt themſelves of idols: worſhip him all ye gods.* The queſtion upon the whole paſſage is, Whether it is to be underſtood of a ſupreme or a derived God? I need only ſay, *Conſider of it, take advice, and ſpeak your minds.*

SERMON LI.

April 24. 1720.

(4.) OUR blessed Lord is received into the glory of the Divine Nature, inasmuch as from the time of his resurrection he speaks the language and uses all the prerogatives of God. We may suppose what he saith in heaven, by what he said when he was just going thither. He began to put on majesty at the time when he was most to conceal it. He talks, in the view of all his sufferings, like a conqueror more than a captive. Having told his disciples, *that the hour was come, that they should be scattered every one to his own, and leave him alone,* by which he describes the unhappy and shameful condition that he was thrown into; he runs immediately into another view of that same period; *and lifting up his eyes to heaven, he said,—— Father, the hour is come;*—the same hour that he spake of to his disciples, when they were so faint in their zeal and he in his strength,—the hour of thick darkness that was to come upon him,—the thing itself that he had prayed against, *Father, if it be possible save me from this hour, nevertheless for this cause came I to this hour;*—it is what he tells his enemies was *their hour,* and the power of darkness:—and yet, after all these melancholy things, he now speaks of it as *his own, The hour is come; glorify thy Son, that thy Son also may glorify thee; as thou hast given him power over all flesh, that he may give eternal life to as many as thou hast given him:*

John xvi. 32.

—— xvii. 1, 2.

him:—Let him have a glory equal to his empire over the whole extent of all nature, and to his title as the Fountain and Finisher of all grace.

It is plain from this language, that he puts on the King, the Sovereign, at the time that he was going to be a sacrifice. Though he appeared in his dyed garments, he was then *glorious in his apparel, travelling in the greatness of his strength, speaking in righteousness, and mighty to save.* In that very hour when the human nature was to be laid low, he breaks through the clouds, by asserting the existence, and claiming the privileges of *another nature.* He can scarcely be said to plead in the form of a servant, though he was just a-going to give the most dreadful instance of his being so.

He was then upon the last and greatest part of his obedience, that *unto death, even the death of the cross*, and yet even then he speaks the language of a God. What could the disciples think of his prayer, when they saw him in that passive helpless way upon the cross! How would they be able to reconcile the shame and scandal of his dying, to what he said of *a glory with the Father before the world was!* When they beheld his agonies, and heard the greatest complaint that ever was uttered, *My God, my God, why hast thou forsaken me!* what harmony could there be between such words and these that had lately flowed out of his mouth, *Father, I will that they whom thou hast given me be with me where I am, that they may behold the glory that thou hast given me, for thou lovedst me before the foundation of the world!*

This was not the language of a suffering nature. He spake not these things as a man, but as he saith in that very prayer, *These things I speak in the world, that they may have my joy fulfilled in themselves.* Though they were in a little time to see him under the wrath of God and scorn of sinners, they

they muſt underſtand *that* as no more than the atonement that was made in one nature; but all this while, he had the unchangeable perfections of another.

There is ſomething in this prayer, and eſpecially in that part of it which I have lately given you, inconſiſtent with his character as a ſufferer, and his dependence as a creature. When he conſidered and expreſſed himſelf in faſhion as a man, no word ſo aſſuming came out of his mouth, as *Father I will;* no, he diſclaimed all authority as a ſubject; and *being made under the law*, never placed himſelf in that nature above it: *I came not to do my own will, but his that ſent me;* and when *in the days of his fleſh, he offered up ſtrong crying and ſupplications, with prayers and tears,* he demands nothing; *not as I will, but as thou wilt.* It is evident, that in theſe words he talks within the limits of a creature and in the form of a ſervant; that though he was the beſt of creatures, the beginning of the creation of God, the chief of ſervants in whom God would be glorified, yet ſtill he claims no authority; *he learned obedience by the things that he ſuffered.* But,

What a nature is that which changes the language, that always gave us ſo great an example of humility? Who is this, that, ſpeaking of his people's happineſs, ſaith, *Father, I will* have it ſo; though when he ſpeaks of his own, it is no higher than, *Not my will, but thine be done?* Theſe parts in his carriage would be inconſiſtent if you did not underſtand them of two different natures. No creature ought to ſay what he ſays, becauſe, whatever his merit might be, there is ſtill an infinite diſtance between him and the Moſt High God; and eſpecially conſidering the thing itſelf that he demands, *That they whom thou haſt given me be with me where I am, that they may behold my glory.* What! ſhall one that durſt not inſiſt upon his own

own preservation, be thus positive about the disposal of all his people?

When the mother of Zebedee's children came with a petition that her two sons might sit, the one on his right-hand, and the other on his left, in his kingdom, he tells her it *was not his to give*. As man he was so entirely subject, that he had no right to appoint a precedency in his Church. And this shews, that they who call themselves his vicars and representatives, go a great deal farther than ever their principal did. They that think themselves empowered to bestow the chief places in a Redeemer's kingdom, assume a greatness that he himself never pretended to; for he tells this woman, who wanted to have her two sons dignified and distinguished, that it was not his to give, but it should be given to them for whom it was prepared of his Father. And yet here he talks quite otherwise: ' A precedency in the Church
' below is not mine to give as a man, but eternal
' life is mine to give: I have a right to bestow
' all that.' And how can this be allowed in one that is not God? ' I must leave it to the Father
' to fill these two places at my right and left hand
' in my kingdom, because in this human nature
' he is greater than I. But I can tell even the
' Father himself, that *I will* have all my people
' with me in heaven.'

Certainly one that spoke after this manner, *thought it no robbery to make himself equal with God.* And what will he have them there for? *To behold the glory that thou hast given me;* and lest we should look upon this as no other than the glory of his reward as a Mediator, he adds, *For thou lovedst me before the foundation of the world.*
' The glory I speak of is that which consists in
' thy love; this love I enjoyed eternally before
' any of the duty that I have now gone through.
' Besides a glory that is given as a recompence to
' my

' my actions, I had one with thee in perfon before
' the world was; and the glory that arifes from
' this, is what I would have them behold in hea-
' ven.' So that if you invert this whole paffage,
there are three things contained in it.

Firſt, That the Father had a love to the Son
before the foundation of the world, antecedent to
the obedience that he threw himſelf into. *Secondly*, That this love is the ground, the matter,
the conveyance and perfection, of his chief glory.
Though the human nature is advanced and highly
exalted, yet the glory that he had before the world
was, is the main inheritance, and what he would
have his people behold; and this they will find is
comprehended in an eternal love. And, *thirdly*,
This glory is ſo great, that he ſets his throne as
the throne of God. He ſpeaks the language of
the Moſt High, and that not only to the world,
but to the Father himſelf. He uſes words that
conceal every thing of a ſubordination. When
the Father ſpeaks to *him*, it is in theſe terms: *To
the Son, he ſaith, Thy throne, O God, is for ever and
ever.* When he ſpeaks to the Father, he claims
the ſame equality, that the Father in ſpeaking to
him had owned: *I will*, that they whom thou haſt
given me be with me where I am.

Thus has the Scripture declared him to be a-
bove every name in Heaven. We read that *the
throne of God, and the Lamb*, is there. Glory is
aſcribed to Him that fits upon the throne, and to
the Lamb, for ever. Can we think that an inferior nature ſhall have equal praiſes? Indeed, if
the diſtinction of ſupreme and ſubordinate worſhip had come from heaven, we might have carried it thither again. But theſe are no words that
the Holy Ghoſt teaches; no worſhip at all is allowed in that ſtate but what is given to the Moſt
High, if we may judge of what they do in the
city, by the account we have from one who ſaw
the

the best representation of it; I mean the Apostle John. He would needs have fallen down at the feet of the Angel to *worship him*. No manner of doubt he meant no more than a subordinate worship; there is no room to imagine that he looked upon this Angel as a God; and yet the answer is, *See thou do it not, for I am of thy brethren, worship thou God*. The force of what he saith lies in this, ' The worship thou owest to God is so great and ' comprehensive, that *we* must not have it even in ' a lower degree. Every creature here, is thy fel- ' low-servant.'

Christ himself, as a man, is one of our brethren. If an Angel, because he is one of our brethren, is not to be worshipped at all, then He who is the first-born among many brethren has no claim to it; and it is certain he has not in that relation: but yet it is equally evident, that the praises given up to the Father are, in the same language, offered to him, which makes it needful for us to conceive of him as infinitely more than a Mediator, and that is, *over all, God blessed for ever*.

(5.) He may be said to be received into the glory of the Divine Nature in the Church upon earth, because he reveals himself to his people in this world as the Most High God. This is a doctrine that I hope you have already heard in the evidence of it through several discourses, and therefore I have no need to enlarge upon it again.

I have shewn that he could not be *justified in the Spirit* if he was not God. It is beneath the eternal Spirit to come down from heaven, and lay out all his testimony to the honour of a creature. No; when he glorifies Christ, he does it by taking the things of Christ, and shewing them to us, *i. e.* letting us know what he is: and what are the things that he thus discovers? no less than the whole treasure of the Divine Nature: *All that the Father has*

has is mine, and therefore I said, He shall take of mine and shew it unto you.

He could not be *preached unto the Gentiles* if he was not God. The great subject of our ministry is more than a creature. We durst not call people from their dumb idols to trust in a Saviour, if he were not *the living God*.—Nor is he *believed on in the world* under any other notion; believing that he was an extraordinary prophet, is no more than believing that he had a miraculous birth; neither of these is believing in him, or resting our souls upon him for salvation.

If an Angel were to come down into our nature, he might be produced in a glorious manner, and would be furnished with great qualifications, and I could believe all that was said of him; but this falls vastly short of believing *in him*. I can commit the keeping of my soul to none but *a faithful Creator*. Any of the inhabitants above may be *the messenger of glad tidings*, but it requires a nature greater than was ever created to be *the author of eternal salvation*. David thought so, when he said, *Into thy hand I commit my spirit, for thou hast redeemed me, O Lord God of truth:* And Stephen meant no less in the last cry of his faith, *Lord Jesus receive my spirit.*

Thus is he revealed *unto us*, but how is he revealed *in us?* for that is the expression that the Apostle uses when he speaks of practical religion, *it pleased God to reveal his Son in me.* As this is a word which man's wisdom never taught, so it belongs to a thing that man's wisdom never felt, and what no hypocrite has been acquainted with.

Our Lord told the disciples, *I am with you always to the end of the world;* that relates to their work in general: in particular he says, *Where two or three are met together in my name, there am I in the midst of them;* not in a bodily presence, or visible representation, but in such a manner as shews

his

SERM. 51.
Rev. xxi.
2, 3.

his Divine glory. *The New Jerusalem, the Gospel Church, comes down from God out of heaven, prepared as a bride adorned for her husband:* Upon which ther was *a great voice out of heaven, Behold the tabernacle of God is with men, and he will dwell with them, and they shall be his people, and God himself shall be with them, and be their God.* Who is this God? He that spoke afterwards, and *said, It is done: I am Alpha and Omega, the beginning and the end: I will give to him that is athirst of the fountain of the water of life freely: He that overcomes shall inherit all things, and I will be his* God, *and he shall be my son.* It is He who has his tabernacle with men.

—— 6, 7.

Thus converted sinners have found it. If a man that is unlearned, or ignorant, comes into your assemblies, and *the secrets of his heart are made manifest, he is convinced of all, he is judged of all.* Christ Jesus, whom he once despised, has laid him open to himself; and what is the consequence of this change? *He falls on his face and worships God, and confesses that* God *is among you of a truth.* What he saith gives no testimony to Christ's being among them, or the truth of that religion which he did not understand before, unless you will make his saying, *God is among you,* to tally with our Saviour's promise, *When two or three are met in my name, I am* in the midst of them.

1 Cor. xiv.
24, 25.

We read of *God's raising him from the dead,* which must be understood of his human nature. The Divinity could not die, and was not buried. *Setting him at his own right-hand, far above all principalities and powers,* you must refer to his office as Mediator. *He is made Head over all things to the Church, the fulness of him that fills all in all.* A head of *authority* he may be by constitution, but his being a head *of influence* supposes a nature agreeable to what shall be done by him, and that is to *quicken those who are dead in trespasses and sins.*

Eph. i. 20,
21, 22.

—— ii. 1.

It

It is all one to the argument, whether thefe laſt words are to be underſtood of the Son or of the Father. If we may apply them to the Son, that it is he who converts the foul, then the proof is made at once; and if this is mentioned as an act of the Father, it is that we may conceive of it as the greateſt work of God. Now, it is no more than we read of our Saviour in other places, that *as the Father quickens the dead, and raiſes them, even ſo the Son quickens whom he will:* It is *He who fanctifies;* He is the *Author,* and will be the *Finiſher,* of our *faith.*

Thus have I conſidered the manner of our Lord's coming by this glory, or how we are to apprehend his being RECEIVED into it, in his lower nature as *man,* in his office as *Mediator,* and, laſtly, as he is in the form of *God.* I will give you an application of this part of my ſubject, before I paſs on to another.

(1.) If he was thus received into glory, then you may be very well aſſured, he will never loſe that glory: *He ſits at God's right-hand, till all his enemies are made his footſtool.* And this is a perpetual honour, as the Apoſtle obſerves in his quotation of that paſſage, *After he had offered one ſacrifice for ſin, be* FOR EVER *ſat down at the right-hand of God; from henceforth expecting till his enemies be made his footſtool.*

You muſt not conclude from theſe things, that there will be no oppoſition made to him; for as *the god of this world* is his great antagoniſt, ſo his way of puſhing on the war is by *blinding the eyes of them that believe not, leſt the light of the glorious Goſpel of Chriſt, who is the image of the inviſible God, ſhould ſhine into their hearts.* Satan's own eyes are open enough, he knows Him who he is, (as he has often confeſſed), *The Holy One of God;* and therefore as he can never ſucceed upon himſelf in contradicting the Divinity of a Saviour, he throws

the

the rebellion into another form, and has his tools in an unbelieving world. His influence upon them, they may apprehend, does only lead them into the acts of *free thinking*, but it is indeed *blinding* their eyes. It is no matter what splendid names they may give to this temper, when the Father of lights himself has called it a blindness. Jesus himself has said, *For judgment am I come into this world, that they that see not might see, and that they which see might be made blind.* Thus Esaias had said before, *He has blinded their eyes, and hardened their heart, that they should not see with their eyes, nor understand with their heart, and be converted.*

We read of great men that are engaged against him; but all this while *the heathen rage, and the people imagine a vain thing, when the kings of the earth set themselves, and the rulers take counsel together, against the Lord, and against his Anointed.* The Apostles gave a twofold interpretation of this passage. *First*, It was true personally, referring it all to the malice of men against our blessed Lord himself. *The heathen raged,* and the people, (that is, the Jews), imagined a vain thing : *For of a truth, against thy holy child Jesus, whom thou hast anointed, both Herod and Pontius Pilate, with the Gentiles, and the people of Israel, have joined together, to do those things which thou hast determined should be done.*

Secondly, They take the sense of the prophecy to be extended farther, and believed themselves included in the design of these words : *Now, Lord, behold their threatnings, and grant unto thy servants that with all boldness they may preach thy word;* and they did not only pray for this mercy, but were confirmed in their belief of it : for this they could rest themselves upon the words of David, that *He who sits in the heavens shall laugh, the Lord shall have them in derision; yet have I set my King upon my holy hill of Zion.* He laughs at their rage, he he sees it is a vain thing that they imagine, and notwithstanding all their opposition, the Father will maintain his own appointment in these two particulars with respect to a Saviour:

1. In his sole authority over his Church.
2. In the full and proper Divinity of his Person.

These are things that He has established. Christ is not only exalted in heaven above all the injury that their unbelief and malice would do him, but they shall not be able to carry their point upon earth.

1. One thing which He that sits in the Heavens will secure, is the authority of a Redeemer over his Churches. *I have set my King upon my holy hill of Zion.* And this is not only true in fact, but he has raised up witnesses to own it. Though these are oftentimes *clothed in sackcloth,* nay, more than that, have their vestures, like his, *dipped in blood, yet they overcome by the blood of the Lamb, and the word of their testimony, and they love not their lives unto the death.* Rev. xii. 11. If cruelty and fraud could have rooted this principle out of the earth, it had swum away in the rivers of innocent blood that have been shed in the defence of it. We should have lost it with our martyrs, seen it killed at their executions, and buried in their graves: But it is still alive; upon *that* our *God has founded Zion, and the poor of his people shall trust in it.* Isa. xiv. ult.

No manner of doubt, when persecution brings us under a scrutiny, many thousands will rather give up the truth than give up themselves, and will scarce be Protestants at the stake, though they are well paid for being so in the church. But I make no question, that when all the greatness and the establishments of this world turn against the doctrines of religion, the God of grace will raise up some to assert the Gospel without a human law, which they have honestly professed with one. With such a spirit was the Protestant religion spread over the nations. They tore the name of Christ out of the hands of the man of sin, who pretends to represent him. The Lord *consumed him with the breath of his mouth, and destroyed him with the brightness of his coming.*

2. Another thing that the Great God will not give up, is the doctrine of our Lord's Divinity. Who is this King upon the holy hill of Zion? Or rather, let us first enquire what is meant by *Zion* itself? Certainly not the hill which is now ploughed as a field, and made as the high places of the forest, but the Church of the New Testament, the *mount Sion which is the city of the living God:* and who is the *King* exalted there, but He that suffered in view of the former Zion? Now, it is said, that *the Lord shall reign for ever, even thy God, O Zion, to all generations.* He that is exalted upon this hill is *Jehovah, whose kingdom is an everlasting kingdom,* and who is also the God of his people. Thus, Zion that published glad tidings about the Messiah, speaks of him in this language, *saying to the cities of Judah, Behold your God!*

And indeed the Psalmist having introduced the Father as giving out that resolution, *I have set my King upon my holy hill,* brings in the Son as replying to it, or rather enlarging upon it, *I will declare the decree, the Lord has said unto me, Thou art my Son, this day have I begotten thee.* The season that this refers to, the time of Christ's making the declaration, the Apostle tells us was his resurrection. The decree itself is, that the Lord saith to him, *Thou art my Son,* not that the relation began then, but the meaning is, that from this time it shall be owned; he would shew him afresh to the world; and as the resurrection itself is an evidence by which he was *declared to be the Son of God with power,* so the sending down of the Spirit afterwards was to carry the testimony into the hearts

hearts of men; and therefore all our owning him to be King upon his holy hill of Zion, amounts to little without a confession of this, as the most important doctrine, that he is *the Son of God*.

We are not merely contesting with the Jews, whether Moses or Jesus shall be head of the Church, *i. e.* whether this person or that shall give us laws; but the question is, whether He who is the head of the Church, is a creature or a God: Now, the decree which He declares, and which they that are faithful will never shun to declare, relates to his Divine Nature.

That he is called the Son of God because of his miraculous birth, his great qualifications and purity, is true enough; but this falls short of the *decree*. If that was all that he meant by it, the name might have been given to the Angels, and the Apostle could not have bore up with this challenge, *To which of the Angels said he at any time, Thou art my Son, this day have I begotten thee?* They are called the sons of God; and though it is true, they are not raised from the dead, yet if the day of resurrection would have been the day of his declaring them begotten, it is what all the saints shall have.

But it is plain, that the title of *Son* here, is to be taken, as it is every where else when we use it properly, to express a sameness of nature with the Father. Angels and men are only called the sons of God by a figure; and though it is said, *Of his own will has he begotten us by the word of truth*, it is to be understood with a limitation: But when the highest name that God gives to our blessed Saviour is calling him *his Son*, the generation he speaks of is not to denote any period when it was done, but an equality of existence; or otherwise the words Father and Son must be made to signify in the Divine Nature what they never do in the human, two different sorts of being.

(2.) If

SERM. 51. (2.) If he is thus received into glory, let it be an argument for receiving him into your own souls. Admire the condescension that shines through those Rev. iii. 20. words, *Behold I stand at the door and knock, if any man hear my voice and open unto me, I will come in and sup with him, and he with me.* O sinners! will you reject Him who delivers his importunity from a throne? He begs admittance into your hearts ever since he has laid aside the form of a servant.—Cry out as Thomas did, *My Lord, and my God!*

(3.) Consider the happiness of as many as re-
Joh. i. 12. ceived him: *To them gave he power to become the sons of God, even to them that believe on his name.* I will mention but two things in a way of exhortation and comfort.

First, Take care that you do not let him go, ei-
Heb. xiii. ther in doctrine or practice. *Jesus Christ is the*
8, 9. *same yesterday, to-day, and for ever; and therefore, be not carried about with divers and strange doctrines.* You have heard of his perfections; it is not enough that you admire those of his human nature; the princes of this world owned all that, and it was pure ignorance of other things that *made them crucify the Lord of glory.* If you give up his Divinity, you will be but empty professors of him, and he but an empty Saviour to you. As it is a God whom you are contending for, so he can be no less whom you depend upon. He that is able
Jude 24, to keep what you have committed to him, *able to*
25. *keep you from falling, and to present you faultless before his own glory with exceeding joy, is the only wise God our Saviour.* Know the truth, and the truth shall make you free. This is your crown, and take heed lest any man run away with it. He that saves your souls, he that will raise your bodies,
Phil. iii. 21. must have a power by which he is *able to subdue all things to himself.*

Secondly,

Secondly, Support yourselves with the hope of being received where he is. Then you will behold the glory that some deny with rage and confidence, foaming out their own shame; and which is always owned to be unspeakable. It s the matter of our testimony upon earth. We believe, and are sure, that he had a glory with the Father before the world was; but what this is, is a question that overwhelms us all at once; however, the day is coming, when we shall know, *That he is in the Father, and the Father in him, and he in us.* John xiv. 11. & 20.

SERMON LII.

May 8, 1720.

THE second general head which I have always given you under every branch of this great subject, was to open what we have been insisting on, as an argument of our Lord's Divinity: and therefore by the rules of method that I have all along observed, I must now have shewn you, that as God was manifest in the flesh, justified in the Spirit, seen of Angels, preached unto the Gentiles, and believed on in the world; so it is no other than the same living and true God who is *received up into glory.* But a small return of thought upon what you have heard, will shew you, that this design is already answered; for I have in several particulars fairly proved, that the glory which Jesus Christ is now possessed of, is the peculiar of the Divine Nature, and that many things which

the

the Scripture faith of him, could not be laid down, with either modefty or juftice, if he was not the Moft High God.

This argument I have drawn through the particular attributes of fpirituality, omnifcience, almightinefs, omniprefence, and eternity; the creation that he has wrought, and the worfhip that he receives. You have heard at large, that thefe things are never faid of a creature; that God has always claimed them as his own, and has frequently told us, that they fhall not be given to another; that if fuch characters do not belong to him alone, we have no notion left under which to conceive of a God; all diftinctions are thrown down and laid open, that he has eftablifhed between himfelf and his creatures. If another being has a power that is almighty, and an underftanding that is infinite; if he can fill the heaven and the earth; if he is unchangeable in his nature, and receives the higheft expreffions of homage; I fay, if any one can have thefe things affirmed of him, and yet not be God, we are at a lofs to know what God is, and have not one character left for him which may not be given to another.

And yet in the fulleft manner, with terms unlimited and undifguifed, are thefe divine perfections revealed as belonging to the great Redeemer. Thus the Holy Spirit has declared him; thus his people in every age have received him. Thomas calls him *his Lord and his God*, and fo muft we, if we are of thofe bleffed ones that have not feen, and yet have believed. *Thefe things are written, that we might believe that Jefus is the Chrift the Son of God, and that believing we might have life through his name.* This is the truth they have witneffed to, this is the food they lived upon, and the good doctrine they were nourifhed with.

I have given you the arguments juft as I have found them, propofing this great article in no other light

John xx. 28, 29. 31.

light than that of plain Scripture, comparing spiritual things with spiritual. Had the arguments been charged with insufficiency, I should gladly have attended to any thing that might prove it. But when, instead of fair answers, the whole work is called *enthusiasm*, you may be sure the victory is gained; for that is always the last refuge of a baffled enemy, who goes off the field, running and railing, and rather than not be insolent grows profane; *turning aside to vain jangling, understanding neither what they say, nor whereof they affirm. They speak evil of the things they understand not, and shall utterly perish in their own corruption, counting it pleasure to riot in the day time, spots and blemishes, sporting themselves with their own deceivings.* On these accounts I am prevented of considering this branch of our religion in the way that I have taken with all the rest; for, having in the first part of my work, proved that the glory of Christ is a glory that he had in communion with the Father and in full equality to him, I would not enter upon that argument again.

I shall therefore pursue this proof another way, by considering what is offered against it. By the faithful word *we are to exhort and convince the gainsayers, the unruly and vain talkers and deceivers, whose mouths must be stopped, because they subvert whole houses, teaching things which they ought not.* That an opposition is made to this glorious doctrine, can hardly be denied by any of us. *Do they not blaspheme that worthy name by which you are called?* If you have not heard the arguments, yet you have *heard the slander of many.*

The defamation that flies at large, *the trial of cruel mockings*, cannot be for our subscribing what we believe, but for believing what we subscribe: Could we have been content to stab the doctrine with the very pen that signed it, we might have gone untouched in our reputation. If they could once

SERM. 52. once have made us ashamed of our glory, they had soon brought us to *glory in our shame*. But it is for the sake of Christ that men separate us from their company, and *cast out our names as evil:* And we are taught what to do in such a day; to *rejoice and be exceeding glad, for the great reward that is laid up in heaven.* However, let us *stand* Phil. i. 27, *fast in one spirit, with one mind, striving together for* 28, 29. *the faith of the Gospel; in nothing terrified by our adversaries; which is to them an evident token of perdition, but to us of salvation, and that of God: For to us it is given in the behalf of Christ, not only to believe in his name, but to suffer for his sake.*—I shall do these three things:

1. Give you some account of the *opposition* that is made to this doctrine of Christ's Divinity.

2. The *reasons* that are pleaded for the opinion.

3. The *ways* that are taken to promote the cause.

1. The opposition that is made to our Lord's Divinity has been various. Truth, like the sun, has kept its place for several ages; the faith delivered to the saints is the faith that is yet admired by the saints; they are *built upon the foundation of the Apostles and Prophets, Jesus Christ himself being the chief corner-stone.* But error keeps wheeling round, carrying on the same design through all forms and shapes. The corruptions in doctrine are usually called after the people that spread them in the world; and all these names have been taken up, as God foretold, *for a curse among his chosen.* The men that perverted the truth, made a little rumbling in the Church for a while; but as *their root was rottenness,* so *their blossom went up as dust.*

Samosatenus was one of this wretched number a long while ago; a man of a most vicious life, who having denied the Lord that bought him in practice, as a bubble to his conscience, did it afterwards in doctrine. His notions were very little different

different from those that the two *Socinus's* the uncle and the nephew, revived a great many ages after, by which they blasted the Reformation in Poland, and with respect to the Protestant faith, *turned a fruitful land into barrenness*. These assert, that Christ is no more than a man divinely inspired, and deny that he had any existence before *that* in the womb of the Virgin Mary. I do not find that their notion goes any higher than what the Apostle tells us his very enemies had of him: *Ye men of Israel, Jesus of Nazareth was a man approved of God among you by signs, and miracles, and wonders, which God did by him in the midst of you, as ye yourselves also know.* [Acts ii. 22.]

Others have carried on their quarrel with the truth in a different way. These were those called *Aetians* and *Eunomians*, who said God might be comprehended by us, (as if they were resolved to set out with impudence enough), and that the Son was altogether unlike the Father in being, power, and will, and that the Spirit was created by the Son; that Christ did not take to him a human soul, but only a body.

These were also the opinions of the *Arians*, though they spake with a greater veneration for the dignity of the Son than the other had learned to do, calling him the best and most glorious creature. The *Ebionites* were much earlier than these that I have mentioned, but held almost the same opinions with those that make up the Socinian system.

The *Macedonians* seem to be only the dregs of the Arians about the year three hundred and twelve. Their boasted opinion was, that the Son is not of the same essence with the Father, but only like him. Besides these, we read of the *Noetians*, the *Praxeans*, and the *Sabellians*, who made the names of Father, Son, and Holy Ghost, to be no more than three different characters and representations

presentations of God; so that when we consider him as a Creator, he is to be called the Father,—as a Redeemer, the Son,—and as a Comforter, the Holy Ghost. These denied the *Persons* as the other did the *Nature*: Hence they asserted, that the Father was born, suffered upon the cross, and rose again from the dead; for which they were called *Patripassians*.

As these persons were very confused in their opinions, they could be no less in their practice. The *Arians* spake of Christ with more respect than those that went before them, but denied him to be the proper object of worship. The *Samosatenians* would not baptize in his name. The *Socinians*, though they conceived of him in the same manner, nevertheless declared that divine adoration should be paid to him. This very difference was the thing that split the antitrinitarian interest in Poland, and you may be sure it will have the same fate in England, when the hot humour that now breaks out against the truth is struck inwards, as it seldom fails to do in a little time.

At present we have a scheme advanced that would seem to be different from all those that I have mentioned; but if you enquire into it, you will find it distinguished from *Arianism* by nothing else but cowardice and confusion: That is, if it is not Arianism, it is nonsense. Thus a certain author in our days has delivered his thoughts in these propositions.

That ' with the Father, who is the first and su-
' preme cause, there has existed from the begin-
' ning a second person, who is his Word and Son;
' and with the Father and Son there has existed
' from the beginning a third divine person, who is
' the Spirit of the Father and the Son. That
' the Father alone is self-existent, underived, un-
' originated, and independent. That the Father
' is the sole original of all power and authority,
' and

' and is the author and principle of whatever is
' done by the Son or by the Spirit; and that the
' Scripture, when it mentions the one God, or
' the only God, always means the Supreme Person
' of the Father. That the Son, or second Per-
' son, is not self-existent, but derives his being, or
' essence, and all his attributes, from the Father,
' as from the supreme cause.'

In the next proposition he distinguishes himself both from the Arians and from those that I hope we may be yet allowed to call *orthodox*. ' They,' saith he, ' are worthy of censure, who either, on
' the one hand, presume to affirm that the Son was
' made ἐξ ἐκ ὄντων out of nothing, or, on the other
' hand, that he is a self-existent being.' And the ground of this critical peculiar he lays down thus:
' That the Scripture in declaring the Son's deri-
' vation from the Father, never makes mention of
' any limitation of time, but always supposes and
' affirms him to have existed with the Father
' from the beginning, and before all worlds. They
' are also justly to be censured, who, presuming to
' be *wise above what is written*, and intrude into
' things which they have not seen, presume to
' affirm, that there was a time when the Son was
' not.'

Thus have I laid before you what is usually called *the new scheme*, in the very words of the man that has drawn it. I hope you have heard so much of the Deity of our blessed Lord, in a long train of discourses, as will convince you it is not a thing to be distinguished away into some uncertain medium between a God and a creature.—I would observe two things upon all these propositions.

First, That they are far from being delivered in Scripture words. I believe there never was a creed or catechism in the universe that did more positively determine the sense of the Bible with less use of the *language;* and therefore it is cutting

ting us both ways, that this is admired as *Scripture-doctrine* by the very people that talk so much against *Scripture-consequences*. Though perhaps one may find an excuse for that management; for indeed I cannot take these propositions to be *Scripture-consequences*, as has been abundantly shewn by severals, whose praises are in all the churches of Christ, and will, I doubt not, farther appear from different quarters, as we come to be daily taken off from our lower debates, and driven to secure the foundation.

Secondly, I may farther observe, from this man, and his communication, that it is a hard thing to escape his censures. His charity has pitched itself in a point, and we lose it, if we take one step beyond the narrowest notion that ever was advanced in the world. *They are to be censured* who say the Son is a creature, and they are to be censured who say he is a God; and what then must become of all the world, who till now never imagined there was any medium between these two? We must not be allowed to say he had a beginning, or that *there was a time when he was not,* nor must we call him eternal. Reason and Scripture, philosophy and revelation, the light of nature itself, have always taught us to say, that there was one supreme cause, and every being is either that first Being, or made by him. If he was made, there must be some moment of time when he was not made. Every thing, but that individual first cause, had a beginning; no existence could be eternal but what was necessary.

Did ever any learning talk against these maxims? Well may that be called a New Scheme that destroys all the principles that are as old as human nature! And how bold is it to *censure men* for not coming into an opinion that is flat folly to universal reason! that a Being may be neither made nor unmade, neither have a beginning,

ning, nor be without beginning! neither be a God nor a creature! derive from another, and yet be coeternal with that other!

No wonder that we read so much against a *certainty* in matters of *faith*; for this is the way to lose it in matters of *reason*. Was there ever any mystery so inconceivable as this heap of thoughts? Cannot I as soon believe that three are one, as that any thing can *be* and *not be*? Can there be in any doctrine of the Christian religion a more horrible jar, than to talk of a derived God, an originated eternal essence?

You see what a wilderness we are thrown into, a wide and howling wilderness, when we leave the right ways of the Lord. I believe verily that the Arian scheme is never the more agreeable to Scripture than this; but I am sure it is more agreeable to sense. These people are fairer adversaries than such as send out their opinions in masquerade. The *Arians* are *censured* by their younger brethren for speaking out, and acting in open day-light. And though *they* made a terrible slaughter in the peace of the churches, yet nothing is so frightful to an honest man, as *a pestilence that walks in darkness*, that we suck in without seeing it.

Others have lighted their candles at this author's; but as they do not write with his caution, it will be very hard for them to keep clear of his censure. We are told by one, ' that the Word, ' or the λόγος, was an intelligent Agent or Being ' distinct from the one God the Father; and ' that to assert that he was the same Being with ' the Father, is to assert that he was the Father.' And again, ' That Christ is not represented in the ' Scripture as equal to God, and that the same ab- ' solute perfections are not ascribed to Christ which ' are to the Father.'

I hope the contrary to this has appeared from such a collection of scriptures as all the adversaries in the world will not be able to gainsay or resist. And yet this person in another of his propositions tells us, 'Christ is to be worshipped.' The very thing which another of them exclaims against, and storms in a question, 'What shall we 'say in the great day of account, when we are 'accused under pretence of honouring the Son, of 'giving him the honour that is only due to the 'Father?' That which the one makes dutiful, the other makes tremendous! The one faith, we are not Christians without it in this world; the other faith, we shall be condemned for it in another.

What a strait is a serious person drawn into by the clashing of two authors who both write for the same cause! There is not such a venture for a poor soul in this case, as there was for the lepers at the gate of Samaria. They knew if they went into the city they should die with famine, if they staid on the outside they must die with waiting; but they had a *third way* for it. Now, here faith is hung in suspense in the greatest doctrine, whether Christ is God or creature; and it must be so in a continual practice, whether he is to be worshipped or no. Having first determined that we worship we know not what, they at last leave us undetermined whether there should be any worship or no.

He that is against the worship of Christ *calls* it idolatry, and he that is for it *proves* it so; for his next proposition is this, 'That Jesus Christ in 'both natures, and not in one only, is to be con-'sidered as the object of that worship which Chri-'stians are to pay him.'

This is destroying natural and revealed religion together. The human nature of Christ never received any worship. Christianity has not advanced any thing so monstrous as an opposition to the first principle of all religion: *Thou shalt worship*

worship the Lord thy God, and him only shalt thou serve. This is one of our best arguments against the superstition of the *Papists*, the splutter they make with crucifixes and transubstantiation; for if the body of Christ were really there, they ought not to adore it. But these *new schemes* will bring us into our old abominations; and by breaking the bonds of a divine authority asunder, they prepare us for a return under that yoke, that *neither we nor our fathers were able to bear.*

Another proposition of this author's, which he gives as the ground of what I have now considered, is but a broken reed to it. He saith, that 'the grand reason the Scripture gives why we are to worship the Son, is because the Father has appointed us so to do, and has given him a right to our worship.'

But did the Father ever appoint us to worship a creature? Has he not, both in the Old and New Testament, challenged all religious worship to himself, always professing that *he will not give his glory to another?* Has he changed his mind after so many oaths? for *he has sworn by himself, and the word is come out of his mouth in righteousness.* But besides, has he made the human nature of Christ capable of our worship? Worship is an inward act of the soul, the employment of our faith, fear and hope, upon certain objects; and this is often expressed in the duty of prayer, calling upon such a one, drawing nigh to him, and depending there, with an adoring esteem of his perfections; knowing that he is able and willing to help me. Now, this can never be said of any person, or any nature, that is not omnipresent; and therefore if the human nature of Christ is not so present with me on earth, as I believe the divine is, I worship it in vain.

The Scripture has given me no room for such filthy folly as this is. I know that *it* is in heaven, and

SERM. 52. and we cannot part with it from thence: *it* is always *before* the throne, as the *divine* is always *upon* it; and therefore to worship this nature, is to call upon that which is not omniscient, and so cannot hear me; nor omnipotent, and so cannot help me.

Thus do men talk at random about the greatest things that ever the world had a concern in; what they are to *think*, and what they are to *do*. The Heathen are charged with serving those who by nature are no Gods; and we have our dependence upon One who by nature is not so, but only by office. Or, if he is called a God, we are told that he has not what agrees with every man's notion of the supreme God, that he is *not self-existent*.

I am sorry to find so dangerous an expression in a book called, *Self-dedication personal and sacramental*, where we are exhorted to 'trust the Lord 'Jesus Christ with our souls, and to pray to him 'as the object of worship, and fountain of good.' But I fear what follows will rather shock the faith of a Christian than direct it. 'It is true,' saith the author, as if he was afraid his readers should overdo it in their duty to Christ, 'he is the be- 'gotten of the Father, and sent of the Father, 'and the Father is greater than he, and the head 'of Christ is God. The Son derives of the Fa- 'ther, and is not properly self-existent.' And it makes the matter still worse, for those passages out of the Athanasian and Nicene creeds that have always been understood for an opposition to this notion, to be thrown into the margin as a defence of it.

To talk of one that is eternal God *deriving* from another, is to throw out a vile contradiction. If it is to be understood of his mediation, or his office as a servant, those places of Scripture are easy enough, that *the Father is greater than he, and the head of Christ is God*. But a deriving Deity, or that

He

He who gives existence to all other things, should not be *self-existent;* that He by whom all the creation consists, should himself be dependent; what a confusion is this to reason, what a crush to faith?

I shall only mention one person more who has openly told us, that 'the commonly received opinion about the Trinity has its best advocates among the Jesuits.' In a book, which, according to his notorious modesty, he called, *The western Inquisition*, he has given us this confession of his faith: 'I am not of the opinion of Sabellius, Arius, Socinus, or Sherlock; I believe there is but one God, and can be no more; I believe the Son and Holy Ghost to be Divine Persons, but subordinate to the Father; and the Unity of the Godhead I think to be resolved into the Father's being the fountain of the Divinity of the Son and Spirit.'

I shall in the next discourse lay before you the *arguments* they give for their opinions, and some account of the *methods* they take to promote them. And as I think the former will never convince a man that is *serious*, I am sure the latter will never be endured by one that is *honest*.—I will dismiss you at present with one reflection upon what is offered against that good confession, 'that there are three Persons in the Godhead, the Father, the Son, and the Holy Ghost; and these three are one God, the same in substance, equal in power and glory:'

That this has been always received wherever the *Christian* religion hath broken out in its full light, and wherever the *Protestant* cause hath revived it. In the truth of this faith our fathers lived, in the joys of it they died; and therefore what Jesus and Holy Spirit are we now called to? *Gods whom ye knew not, new gods newly come up, whom your fathers feared not. Of the Rock that begat us* we are growing unmindful, and have *forgot the God that formed us*. And is our religion so trifling,

SERM. 52. fling, that we shall lose it in our sleep, or change it for a dream? No; *let us continue in the things that we have known and been assured of, knowing of whom we have learned them.*

2 Tim. iii. 14.

May 22. 1720.

SERMON LIII.

I HAVE given you, without any fraud, the opinions that have broken the peace of our churches, to the defilement of the Christian faith, and the confusion of brotherly love; an argument, that *wisdom* must first be *pure* before it can be *peaceable, gentle, or easy to be entreated.* I have not acted in the way that these men use with others, but in their own words, and in full quotations. The sum of what they say you may take in these four particulars.

Jam. iii. 17.

1. They are agreed that the name *God* is given to Christ in the Holy Scriptures; but it is a poor and scandalous hypocrisy which they come into upon this head. One while declaring that they are as much for the Divinity of Christ as others, and yet upon some occasions speaking of his title with all the diminution that can be. Such an uncertain declaration is that, when persons say ' they 'are for *the proper Divinity* of our Saviour, though 'they knew that by proper Divinity, one side 'means the same with what is ascribed to the Fa-'ther, and the other no more than may be affirm-'ed of a creature.' *We have renounced these hidden things of dishonesty, and dare not walk in craftiness,*

2 Cor. iv. 2.

ness, or handle the **word** *of the Lord deceitfully, but by a manifestation* **of** *the truth would commend ourselves* **to** *every man's conscience in the sight of God.*

2. They say, notwithstanding their calling him God, that he is *not self-existent,* that he *derives* from the Father, and that they have no other way to secure the Unity of the Divine Nature, but by affirming there is no more than One Person, who is truly and eternally God. It is here that the ways part; upon this question we are divided, whether the Scripture in calling Christ *God,* means any less than it does in calling the Father *so.*

We have no controversy whether *He* has the name or no, or whether a *creature* may not have it. They yield the former to us, and we the latter to them; and therefore it would be the shortest, as well as the fairest way, to examine, whether the Holy Spirit has taught us to make any abatement in calling our Saviour God, which it would be blasphemy to suppose when we speak of the Father.

In that view I have all along proceeded quite through this copious argument. You have heard what the Scripture has said about his Divinity under those several heads: and I have shewn you, that the Arian has no more reason to diminish the sense of those passages that relate to the Son, than an Atheist has to curtail and darken those that speak of the Father: that it is as easy to argue from the Bible that there is no God at all, as to deny the testimony that is given to our Saviour's Deity.

We think that none can be called God, in the true and proper sense of the word, but One who is supreme, self-existent, underived, unoriginated, as some love to speak in their *great swelling words of vanity.* That there is a God whom we read of under these characters is plain; and therefore we should be guilty of robbery, to lessen or contract the sense of those scriptures that are brought to

prove

SERM. 53. prove it. What an injurious way of expounding would that be, for me to say, Though I read *of the mighty God Jehovah, the Creator of the ends of the earth, the Father of lights, without any variableness or shadow of turning*, it is possible these words may not signify a supreme Being, and an original perfection!

And yet thus unfairly must we act with the same expressions concerning Christ Jesus, if we dispose of his character into their scheme. That is, when he is called *the mighty God*, it must be only a derivative Deity, though if the word was not used of *him*, it would signify what it sounds. Thus the Father of lights, in whom their is no variableness nor shadow of turning, must be an independent, unchangeable, and eternal Being, and they say right: but if *Jesus is the same yesterday, to-day, and for ever*, though the titles are equal, they do not signify so much. Those scriptures are exactly upon a level: *From everlasting to everlasting thou art God*, and *he is the mighty God, the everlasting Father*, and *his goings forth have been of old from everlasting*. We read of God, that *he is blessed for ever*, and of Christ, in the same epistle, that he *is over all God blessed for ever*.

Psal. xc. 2.
Isa. ix. 6.
Mic. v. 2.
Rom. i. 25.
—ix. 5.

3. They are divided, as I have shewn you, about the worship that is paid to him. The Bible stares them so full in the face, that it is declaring their sin as Sodom to deny him that devotion which his people have hitherto given him. The disciples *worshipped him* after he was parted from them, and the saints do *in every place call on the name of the Lord Jesus*. On the other hand, this practice is so unwieldy to their scheme, that some of them quite disown it, and others are forced to soften it with a distinction that the Scripture has taught us to abhor, of a supreme and subordinate worship. So that,

Luke xxiv. 5'
1 Cor. i. 2.

4. That

4. That which they glory in as their peculiar and purgation from Arianism, is nothing but a little dust thrown into the eyes of the world. They will not say as the Arians, there was a time when the Son was not; but they tell us, that he was derived, and that whatever is derived, began to be; and I am sure, whatever had a beginning, once was not. This is plunging into contradictions merely to avoid a name. It is to no purpose that they tell us, there was not the least moment of time when the Son and the Spirit were not; for what is the consequence of that, from those that deny him to be self-existent, but a principle that overthrows the very first maxim of our doctrine against the Atheists.

We plead, that there must have been a principal cause of all things, and that he must have existed when nothing else did; that his existence proves him to be the original of all things: but now we find there are two other persons who have existed equally with him, though they are infinitely unequal to him; that is, they are as much eternal as he. There never was a moment when the Son and the Spirit were not, which is as much as can be said of the Father; and yet an essence from everlasting, which *proves him* to be the first and independent cause, does not prove *them* so; what is the consequence of that, but that it proves nothing at all? As, for example,

When I argue for the being of a God, and the glorious perfections of his nature, I put it thus: He that is before all things, and by whom all things consist, is the supreme original essence; but the great God is before all things, and by him all things consist. I should have thought the first of these propositions would have stood unmoved through all the ages and parts of the world, but our new scheme has given it up: for *Christ is before all things, and by him all things consist,* and yet nevertheless he is God only, as we are beings, by derivation,

SERM. 53.
Rom. xi.
36.

rivation, though *of him, and to him, and through him are all things.*

I know not what these people will leave us; the doctrines of revealed religion are not, and will they take away the principles of nature too? *all these things are against us.* Do we not only lose our Saviour from the throne of God, but are we to quit the very notion itself under which we have conceived of a God? Shall we, in complaisance to a blasphemous whim, say, that a person may be *the Creator of the ends of the earth, the mighty God, the Alpha and Omega, the first and the last, the beginning and the ending,* that he may be *over all blessed for ever,* that he is *before all,*—and yet not self-existent? Are these perfections separable from the Divine Nature? Can one be all this, and not be a God? or if he is called a God upon these accounts, must the word signify less in him than it does in another?

Shall the Scripture, which we reckon to be the best book in the world, leave us no distinction either in our language or our practice between the first cause, and the chief of second causes, between him that is derived, and him that is not? the *Mahometans* have none of this difficulty in their *Alcoran;* they do not pretend to call their prophet by the name of God. And has the only Divine Book that is given to men, left them confused, where above all things they ought to be most determined?

John iv. 22.
Acts xvii. 23.

Are we, like *the Samaritans, worshipping we know not what?* or, with the *Athenians,* setting up an altar to *an unknown God?*

The question whether Christ is God or no, enters into the very life of our devotion; it is impossible we should take one right step till this is cleared; because if he be, we may neglect to honour him as God, and if he is not, we may worship more than the true God. We think the Scripture has made it evident enough; but if the

noblest

noblest expressions are distinguished away, and that calling him God is not to be understood of his being so, let us never talk of a veil upon the hearts of the Jews and the Mahometans. No; Christianity, according to this scheme, is the most clouded religion in the world, where we are *ever learning, and never able to come to the knowledge of the truth*. But I must remember my promise; and that is,

2. To lay before you the reasons they give for their opinion, that Christ is *not self-existent*. And the plea lies in less room than perhaps you imagine. For,

1. They mightily insist upon what is never denied, that he is inferior to the Father; and to that end bring in swarms of scriptures that are nothing at all to the purpose, but must every one of them be understood either of his human nature or his mediatorial office. This is no part of the question, nor ever was, whether or no in some sense or other the Son is not subordinate to the Father. It is universally owned, that he was *made of a woman, and made under the law*. In this respect he is a creature; a body has God prepared for him. And to this head you may place a vast number of sentences: that *the Father is greater than he*, that *the head of Christ is God*, that He is *the God and Father of our Lord Jesus Christ*, that *the Son himself is made subject*. Gal. iv. 4. John xiv. 28. 1 Cor. xi. 3. Eph. i. 3. 1 Cor. xv. 28.

If they bring in these to confront what is said of his Divinity, it is trifling with the argument. They may as well plead against the immortality of the soul, that man was made of the dust of the earth. This is a sorry shuffle, to contradict what is said of one part by what we read about the other. Christ, as *in the form of a servant*, is not so much as a subordinate God; in that respect he is no God at all, but as Mediator between God and man, he is *the man Christ Jesus*. So that, here you

SERM. 53. may keep your stand, and tell them, that the question is not whether the Son is a creature, and inferior to the Father, as he appeared in our nature, and as he undertook our cause. To prove that the Scripture has said this of him, is only a laborious impertinence.

It is an unhandsome insinuation to say, that for one text that speaks of him as God, there are an hundred that declare him to be subordinate. The reason of that is plain, because the chief revelation we have of him is as Mediator. We read very little of his original and absolute perfections; but the question is, Whether there is not one passage in all the Bible that represents him as equal to the Father? If there is but a single text to this purpose, the doctrine must be true. We can easily understand such a scripture harmoniously to those
John x. 30. of a different sound. These words, *I and my Father are one*, must refer to another nature than what he speaks of, when he saith, *My Father is greater than I.*

The *Jews* would never have charged him with making himself *equal with God*, had he talked of nothing higher than his human soul and body. When he speaks of his dying, he could not be supposed to give that as an evidence of any more than a created nature; that was not *making himself God*. But it is plain, besides this, he uses other language which they thought too much for a creature.

And therefore keep the adversary to this point; let him not wander into the proofs of what you do not deny. Remember the question is, Whether the Holy Spirit has not spoken of him in the same language that he does of the Father? and this Spirit that bears witness of him is *truth*. If they tell you that the words do not signify so much when applied to the Son, examine whether the Bible itself has given you any foundation for making

king the difference: *Hold faſt that you have, and let no man take away your crown.*

2. Another argument uſed for this opinion is, that to ſuppoſe the Son is God in the true ſenſe of the word, is to make him the ſame Perſon with the Father. Thus we may behold them pleading in full career. One author tells us, that it is abſurd to ſuppoſe that Chriſt made ſatisfaction to himſelf, that he was both the giver and the receiver of the price. And what does all this amount to? Has it any other force than from our unacquaintedneſs with the myſteries of the Divine Nature? Does it prove any more than that *we cannot by ſearching find out God, that we cannot find out the Almighty to perfection?* [Job xi. 7.]

(1.) Muſt that be laid down as a maxim, that nothing can be true of the Deity, but what appears likely to human reaſon? *Who is this that darkens counſel by words without knowledge?* Are we not *uttering things we know not, things too wonderful for us, that we underſtand not?* It is no part of the queſtion, whether the doctrines we have concerning God are ſuch as we ſhould have thought moſt *probable;* but whether they are *revealed* or no. If he has told us ſome things of himſelf which appear very inconceivable, it is no offence to my faith, that the Divine Nature is not to be comprehended by the human; that he is not ſuch a one as I am; that ſomething may conſiſt with the unity of *his* eſſence, that would not do ſo with *mine*. [Job xxxviii. 2. ―xlii. 3.]

Indeed I ought not to receive any thing concerning God which appears unlikely, upon the teſtimony of man, becauſe ſuch a one intrudes into what he has not ſeen; he is *wiſe above what is written*. But the record that God himſelf has given us, is about things that *He* has ſeen: And therefore, I have no other enquiry than this, whether he has *ſaid* it or no? If he has, my faith

Vol. II. P p does

does not assent to it, upon the rational objective evidence that I have of the thing itself, but upon the veracity and wisdom of Him who has revealed it.

I could make a thousand objections against the resurrection of the dead; and such difficulties go along with it, as perhaps we shall never answer till we come to the thing itself: but no doctrine is the less true for its being incomprehensible. Suppose I ask, With what body shall I arise? what becomes of that which gave this flesh and bones a consistence, when they are both reduced to dust, or, it may be, converted to another form? If I am to have this body again, what is it for? What will be its proper food? it was made for the supports of meat and drink, before the defilements of sin: hunger and thirst are not owing to the fall: how then is it to be the same body I now have, and yet have none of the subsistence that it now enjoys?

Such questions as these would multiply, a new swarm would rise out of every one of them. But what then? Is there to be no resurrection because I cannot explain it? Does my reason stand centinel to my faith, that what the one will not admit, the other dare not receive? No; this is quite destroying the nature of faith, which is an assent to a proposition upon the testimony of another. I believe the resurrection, not because it is a thing likely, but purely because it is told me in plain and easy words: it is not a thing incredible with me, that God *can* raise the dead, but it would have been very incredible that he *will* do so, if he himself had not said it.

Acts xxvi. 8.

And just so it is here: there is nothing that I have in nature fit to illustrate, and much less to *prove*, that three are no more than one, and one no less than three. And I wish that the fancies of men had been more sparing and modest upon this head. Explaining a mystery is nonsense; proving it

it is dutiful. I have no more to do with a myste- SERM. 53.
ry, than to shew that it is so; but it ceases to be
mysterious, if I can shew *how* it is. I am very
sensible that to say that Abraham, Isaac and Jacob,
were one in nature, makes them three men;
and I must own that no testimony but that of
Scripture could have taught us to say, that the Father,
Son, and Holy Ghost are but one God.

If he has not told us this, it is not true; but
never let us go that way to work, to suppose that
he has not said it, merely because *we* cannot understand
it. If the question had been to Nicodemus,
whether Jesus Christ really spoke of the new
birth, he would have owned he did. His difficulty
was not upon that head, whether Jesus spake
so or no, but upon the truth of the doctrine itself,
How can these things be? Can a man enter a se- John iii. 4.
cond time into his mother's womb and be born? Now
if he had believed both the wisdom and the truth
of this person that told him so, that he could not
be deceived himself, and would not deceive another,
he must have been satisfied about the matter,
though he knew not *how* to conceive of it.

(2.) You may farther observe, that in this argument
they will not attend to the distinction of two
natures in the Mediator, and of three Persons in
the Deity, which we always assert: *There is one* 1 Tim. ii. 5.
God, and one Mediator between God and man. It
is an unhappiness that we are forced to repeat a
thousand times what these people are resolved to
take no notice of. It looks as if they were sworn
to deaden us with noise, like those at Ephesus, who
cried out for two hours together, *Great is Diana of
the Ephesians.*

What signifies it to urge, that making the Son
God, is supposing him to be the person who both
gives and receives the satisfaction, and that is making
him the Father? as if they were resolved to
bully us out of the doctrine we contend for, and

thought

thought that a mere noise of words would persuade us we had actually given up what they themselves are angry with us for holding fast. Do not we al-, ways observe the distinction of persons, when we speak of the work of redemption? Is not that one of the things in question, whether the Father and the Son are really distinct? And must we be charged with denying this, at the same time that we take all the pains we can to affirm it? Are they resolved that we shall say there is but one person, merely because we say there is but one Divine Nature, though they hear so often from us that there are *three?* But,

(3.) It shews that men are unpersuadable, when they will admit no medium between *Sabellianism* and *Tritheism, i. e.* if we will not deny three Persons, they say we must assert three Gods. This is the hardest usage that people can meet with, when no confessions, protestations, or subscriptions, can avail us against the noise of impudence. The declaration that all the Protestant churches came into at the time that God began to stir the world with a concern about religion, is equally against both these errors. And though the phrases are a little different, yet the sense of them all strikes upon this single point, that

‘ There is one only the living and true God,
‘ and that there are three persons in the Godhead,
‘ the Father, the Son, and the Holy Ghost; and
‘ these three are one God, the same in substance
‘ or essence, and equal in power and glory.’ If notwithstanding all this, they resolve that we shall be either against three persons, or for three Gods, they only give the greater evidence of being *wicked and unreasonable men;* which the Apostle affirms of the *men that have not faith.* They are like the person whom Solomon tells us of, that he is *not to be corrected with words; for though he understands he will not answer.* False witnesses

2 Thess. iii. 2.

Prov. xxix. 19.
Ps. xxxv. 11.

rise

rife up, and lay to our charge things that we know not. And yet,

(4.) If we do fay, that Chrift gave fatisfaction to himfelf, I do not fee it is fuch a grofs way of fpeaking as thefe polite men would perfuade us; for we muft ftill take the Scripture to be *a form of found words,* and *that* tells us, that He *prefents the Church unto himfelf,* and that he will *prefent us fault- lefs before the prefence of his own glory.* I cannot imagine there is any contradiction in fuch a phrafe as this, though it lies as open to the petulancy of their remark as that at which they are fo angry. [Eph. v. 27. Jude 14.]

3. Another of their pleadings is, that their fcheme is moft agreeable to the light of nature, and the language of the old philofophers. I fhall anfwer this in two particulars.

(1.) I partly believe it; for there is fomething in their way that comes nearer to *an excellency of fpeech and wifdom* than the Apoftle had a mind to do. Theirs are not words that the Holy Ghoft teaches; and indeed the account I have met with of ancient writers, does abundantly convince me, that what they are contending for, is but fo much foreign foam brought into the Chriftian faith. [1 Cor. ii. 1.]

I will lay before you fome opinions of the learn- ed men among the Egyptians and Perfians, and leave you to compare them with what we hear of a fupreme and a derived God, and the one being the inftrument of the other in the work of crea- tion. *Mercurius Trifmegiftus* faith with *Zoroafter,* that 'the Father of all things produced not the
'world by his own hands, like a workman, but by
'*the word;* and that this word, which proceeds
'from him, communicating its fecundity to nature,
'has given the water a power of generation and
'production.' They tell us of 'a fupreme Being,
'or the only God who exifted before the Creator
'of the world, remaining in the folitude of his
'unity: that it was not the Father who produced
'the

'the universe, for he was superior to the Creator.' Again, we are told, that ' the Egyptians acknow-
' ledged the second person inferior to the first, who,
' though he never was separate from him, yet he
' received his ideas of him. He was no produc-
' tion, but the *emanation* of the first God. He was
' the Agent of the universe, and therefore called
' Δημιυργὸς, the master of the world.' This is the
very name that the ancient heretics gave him.

And because a certain author, who out of the
abundance of his heart has set his tongue a speaking, and his pen a rambling, has laid his charge
against me, of writing as vile things of the Christian religion as *Porphyry*, the known enemy of
that doctrine, ever did; I will give you an account
what Porphyry's sentiment was, and you shall
judge who comes nearest him. He is quoted by
Cyrill of Alexandria, as saying, that ' the first
' power has produced the intellect, or word, un-
' speakable to man, by whom are all things, who
' came out of the Deity, who shone forth before
' all ages, who is eternally before all time, for
' there was no time when he first appeared. It
' was not by any command, or even by an act of
' the will that the Deity brought him forth, but
' by a necessary emanation.'

Thus wrote the great enemy of Christianity then, thus write the perverters of Christianity now. But, are we to be turned from the truth to Jewish fa-
bles, and Egyptian darkness? Are we to learn our religion from those that knew not God, but *became vain in their imaginations*, and had their foolish hearts all over darkened? We are bid to *beware left any man beguile us by philosophy and vain deceit, after the rudiments of the world, after the commandments of men, and not after Christ.* Have they got the Egyptian follies with their mummies? Are they resolved to seek the living among the dead? Was there any need of Christ as a teacher, and the Spi-
rit

rit to lead us into the way of all truth, if instead of hearkening to them we must seek to wizards that *peep and mutter?* But, when men *turn away their ears from the truth, they are turned to fables;* not only to a falsehood in the matter of their doctrine, but to a fabulous silly way of telling it. With a contempt, and a very just one, does the Apostle call them *old wives fables*, that are equally opposite to sense and godliness. For,

(2.) Is this scheme of theirs so very agreeable to reason?· Do not they tell us of a God who did not create the world in person, but only by proxy? Must we not hence conclude, that creation is not the work of an almighty, but a derived power? and that it ceases to be, what all ages have hitherto made it, the argument of a Deity? *We worship and bow down before the Lord our Maker. Know that the Lord he is God; it is he that has made us, and not we ourselves. The invisible things of him from the creation of the world are clearly seen, being understood by the things that are made, even his eternal power and Godhead.* Is it not very strange, that God himself should give us a book, that we might have eternal life in the knowledge of him, and of Jesus Christ, whom he has sent; and that we should read of Jesus Christ in the same fulness and glory of language that is used for himself; and yet be obliged to take the same words in different senses? that we must neither know whether he is God or a creature? whether he is to be worshipped or no? have no bounds set to our veneration of him, and to keep it from rising into idolatry?

SER-

SERMON LIV.

June 19. 1720.

WE will now take a little more compass in examining whether this new scheme is so very agreeable to human reason, and whether the dignity of our nature will be most secured by faith or by unbelief. The doctrine they contend for is this, ' That the Father produced the Son, the ' Arians say, by creation; and these younger bre- ' thren say it is by emanation. The Father and ' Son made the Spirit, and the Father left it to ' the Son to create the world, and to the Spirit to ' sanctify the Church.'

This is the notion which they set out with all the pomp that their learning is able to give it, as more scriptural and rational than a Trinity of Persons, who are the same in substance, and equal in power and glory. But does not every one see that,

1. This is running into the old Egyptian folly, which represented the supreme God as altogether unactive, a lumpish Deity, who did nothing himself, but committed all the affairs of nature and worship to deputies and vicegerents? Our Lord tells us, *My Father works hitherto, and I work.* And, *By faith we understand that the worlds were made by the word of God: He spake, and it was done; he commanded, and it stood fast.* His people, who had their instructions from himself, were always taught to approach him as *the Lord their Maker*. They looked upon themselves as *the work of his hand, and the sheep of his pasture.* We are to

Joh. v. 17.
Heb. xi. 3.
Pf. xxxiii. 9.
— xcv. 6, 7.

conceive of creation as the produce of an infinite agent. It is the Lord who *stretches forth the heavens, and lays the foundation of the earth, and forms the spirit of man within him.* His providential kingdom rules over all; he gives out the word indeed, and great is the company of those that publish it; but he himself is *the former of all things, the Lord of hosts is his name.* He made the earth by his wisdom, and stretched out the heavens by his understanding. We must *fear God, and give glory to him, and worship him who made heaven and earth, the sea and the fountains of waters.* His *hands have made and fashioned us round about.* He is said to *make the morning darkness, and tread upon the high places of the earth, and to declare unto man what is his thought. None of the vanities of the heathen can give rain, neither can the heavens of themselves give showers. Art not thou He, O Lord our God? therefore we will wait upon thee, for thou hast made all these things.*

The revelation of the Bible never taught us to consider the world as any thing else but the effect of the great God: *He set it in his heart,* contrived the model, and afterwards looked on all things that *he had made, and behold they were very good.* And is not this a more useful notion, that creation was the immediate agency of the supreme cause, than to dream, as the heathen did according to the vanity of their mind, that he was obliged to employ servants? They thought of the Divine nature just as they did of the human; that activity was an expence and fatigue. But this is owing to the impurity of their imaginations; for we know that *the Creator of the ends of the earth fainteth not, neither is weary, and there is no searching out of his understanding.* It was no difficulty to him; he did it all by his word, and by the breath of his mouth.

SERM. 54.
Zech. xii. 1.
Rev. xiv. 7.
Job x. 8.
Amos iv. 13.
Jer xiv. 22.
Gen. i. 31.
Isa. xl. 28.

Vol. II.   Qq   Creation

SERM. 54.
Rom. i. 20

Creation is to us a visible argument of the *invisible things of Him* that wrought it, *even his eternal power and Godhead.*

But if we suppose that he built the world, as Solomon did the Temple, only by appointing others, there is nothing in the argument. Creation ceases to be the evidence of an almighty power, and proves no more than a commission issued out to an inferior. It is not the work of a Deity, but of a delegate. Whereas, we find a Person in the Divine nature distinct from **Christ**, and speaking to him, representing himself as the author of the universe:

Isa. xlii. 5, 6.

Thus saith God the Lord, he that created the heavens, and stretched them out; he that spread forth the earth, and that which comes out of it; he that gives breath to the people upon it, and spirit to them that walk therein. That this is to be understood of the Father, you will see by the next words, *I the Lord have called thee in righteousness, and will hold thine hand, and will keep thee, and give thee for a covenant of the people, for a light of the Gentiles.*

How vain must the Apostle's discourse have been at Athens, if he had carried any disciples of this new scheme in his train? His doctrine was, *Him*

Acts xvii. 23, 24.

whom ye ignorantly worship, declare I unto you. And who was that? *the God that had made the world, and all things therein, the Lord of heaven and earth.* Might not a Grecian have pulled him back from that assertion, and said, It is true, God *appointed* the world to be made; and *that* Jesus, whom your doctrine speaks of, was the trustee of the whole affair. But the Apostle was a stranger to these profane babblings; he looked upon heaven and earth as the immediate work of the great God, who had made *of one blood all nations of men; in whom we live, and move, and have our being, and who is therefore not far from any of us.*

Indeed, both the Son and the Spirit, in different places of Scripture, are spoken of as the efficients of

the

the creation, but without any subordination to the Father: for, as it is sometimes said, that *God created all things by Christ Jesus*, so it is as plain that Christ himself was the supreme Creator, as you have heard at large. Creation itself is God's own making all things out of nothing by the word of his power. And which is the most reasonable to say, with the Scripture, that he who made all things out of nothing was the supreme cause, or, with these men, that he was only an officer appointed by him?

2. This scheme has made a clumsy distribution of the works committed to the Son and Spirit. They suppose that the former is charged with the creation of the world, and the latter with the religion of it, and yet they speak of the Son as the maker of the Spirit. Now, lay all these together, and you will conclude, that the lower the agent, the greater the work. What the Son does, in their range of notions, is no way comparable to what the Spirit does, so that we are quite struck off from saying with David, *Among the gods there is none like unto thee, O Lord, neither are there any works like unto thy works.* Pf. lxxxvi. 8.

What is that notion that we feel within ourselves, or see displayed before our eyes? what are these visible heavens, and this earth, that is so full of God's glory, if you match them with the more important work that is produced in every believer? It is more to make a saint, than it is to make a world. When *God caused light to shine out of darkness at first*, he did less than causing *the light of the glorious Gospel of Christ to shine into our hearts.* It is a greater *day of his power* to make us *willing*, than to make us living souls.

And is it not strange that He to whom they deny the name of a God, should be charged with the most wonderful things that are ever to be done? The Son rejoices in the creation that he has wrought;

SERM. 54. wrought; but this is all to vanish. These heavens that are so bright a volume, and which he has filled with so many glories, are to be rolled up as a scroll, to pass away and be no more: And yet one whom they suppose to be a lower agent does nothing but what is for eternity. So that according to this, which they will needs pass upon us for *rational religion*, at the consummation of all things, the nobler efficient shall have nothing to shew, and one that is inferior will have his whole performance about him.

The great God takes care of the world, 'he satisfies the earth with his works; he gave the horse 'his strength, he clothed his neck with thunder; 'he gave the goodly wings to the peacock, and fea-'thers to the ostrich; the rain calls him Father, he 'alone has begotten the drops of dew.' Either he did all these things immediately, or he committed them to the Son. Well, of this there will be no remains in that eternity of fulness and glory that his people are going into.

The Spirit is beneath the Son; he must have a lower nature, and therefore, one would think, a lower charge. Now, what does *he* do? I answer, from him we have the Scriptures: *Holy men of God spake as they were moved by the Holy Ghost*. This is more than the visible heavens; for the heaven and earth shall pass away, but not one tittle or ἰῶτα of what he has inspired shall be lost for ever. And again, all that the Spirit does in us, as well as for us, shall be immortal.

2 Pet. i. 21.

'The Son is now surrounded with a vast creation: *There is not any number of his armies, and upon whom does not his light arise?* But when all these are sunk, every one that is born of the Spirit is to be an everlasting attendant upon his throne. *God gives to every seed his own body*, saith the Apostle, and these all come from him; but

such

such as the Spirit has formed are *born of the in-* [SERM. 54.] *corruptible seed that lives and endures for ever.* [1 Pet. i. 23.]

So that, upon the whole, this is their scheme: He that is truly, absolutely and properly **God**, does nothing at all in us and for us immediately by himself: He that is next him, and has the name of God, gives us all the benefits that are of a lower sort, many of which shall perish with the life we are now in: But here is a third, that has neither the nature nor the title of God, and no claim to divine worship, and yet He is the author of our best and all our immortal benefits.

Indeed I cannot think their scheme has made a fair partition, unless they believe, as I am afraid they do, it is a greater thing to be a man than to be a saint, and will deny that the works of the Spirit are superior to those of nature and providence. But we are taught to say, that *he who has* [2 Cor. v. 5.] *wrought us for the self-same thing is God. It is* [Phil. ii. 13.] *God who worketh in us both to will and to do of his own good pleasure. It is God who causes us to* [2 Cor. ii. 14.] *triumph in Christ Jesus. We are the epistle of Christ,* [iii. 3.] *written by the Spirit of the living God.*

3. These fancies are chiefly owing to philosophy and vain deceit. Whereas God sent not his Apostles to preach *with wisdom of words; for it is* [1 Cor. i. 17. 19.] *written, I will destroy the wisdom of the wise, and bring to nothing the understanding of the prudent: where is the wise? where is the scribe? where is* [20.] *the disputer of this world? has not God made foolish the wisdom of this world? For after that in* [21.] *the wisdom of God, the world by wisdom knew not God, it pleased God by the foolishness of preaching to save them that believe. The wisdom of this world is* [iii. 19, 20.] *foolishness with God; for it is written, He takes the wise in their own craftiness; and again, The Lord knows the thoughts of the wise that they are vain.*

Many of the ancient writers for the Christian religion had a great mind to bring their *Platonical*

notions

SERM. 54. notions into the myſteries of our faith. They had
1 Tim. vi. *a knowledge falſely ſo called, which ſome having pro-*
20, 21. *feſſed, concerning the faith have erred.* They had
read more than the unlearned part of the church
could do, and had not come with the Apoſtle to
Phil. iii. 8. *count all things but droſs and dung for the excellency
of the knowledge of Chriſt Jeſus the Lord.* Be-
ſides, they thought that was the way to bring in
the heathen, and make our doctrines paſs the better upon them, when they ſaw how little they dif-
fered from their own.

But how deſirable ſoever the affluence of numbers to the Chriſtian church might be, yet it is
pity to ſpoil the faith for their ſakes. They muſt
be brought to the rule, and not the rule to them.
We have reaſon enough to fear, that this *wiſdom
of words* which they admitted into their preaching
made the croſs of Chriſt of none effect. The doctrine of Chriſt forced its way with the demonſtra-
tion of the Spirit and with power, whilſt it was
not attended with the enticing words of man's
wiſdom; and if ever the purity and ſimplicity of
this truth are to be confounded with the notions
which man's wiſdom teaches, philoſophy cannot
countervail the King's damage, or reſtore what it
1 Cor. ii. 5. has taken away. For *our faith is not to ſtand in
the wiſdom of men, but in the power of God.*

4. Another grand objection is taken from that
myſterious word that the Holy Spirit is pleaſed to
make uſe of, in calling Chriſt *the begotten of the
Father.* The liberty that is uſed with that phraſe
has ſo much in it of *filthineſs and fooliſh talking*,
that we ought not without the ſevereſt caution to
take it into our lips. Upon this they found their
notion of his being *derived.*

A certain author by telling the ſtory ſo often in
his pamphlets, ſhews how full he is of his own
rapartee: When he was aſked if Chriſt was underived, he ſtaved it off, by putting the other queſtion,

stion, whether he was *unbegotten;* and how easily might an Atheist put a third, which I shall not mention? May I not say of these men, *Spots they are and blemishes, sporting themselves with their own deceivings whilst they feast with you?* What scandalous things Servetus fetched out of this word, perhaps some of you may know, and the rest of you need not. I had rather leave such objections in their own shame than pretend to answer them. But,

(1.) You are very sensible this measuring an infinite nature by a finite, is the way to plunge at once into confusion and blasphemy. *These filthy dreamers defile the flesh.* The great God has been pleased to make use of that language that obtains among ourselves, but it is impossible to understand him in such a sense as the words must have in the human nature, without becoming *vain in our imaginations.* We must give up every perfection of the Deity, if we do not throw out of these phrases all those things that signify the weakness of a creature.

Thus, his having hands and eyes and feet, may be pleaded against his being a spirit, as they are by some Socinian writers. The words of anger, grief, revenge, pity and love, would hurry us to believe, that He is of like passions with ourselves, if we did not controul the sound of them with this thought, that He is God and not man.

With these guards and distinctions ought you to consider that awful term that the Holy Spirit has adopted into his own Book. For though we read of Christ as *the only begotten of the Father,* yet *who shall declare his generation?* 'As the word itself cannot possibly signify *that* in the Divine Nature that it does in the human; methinks it is revealed on purpose to stun the imagination of men, and shew them that it means something which they know not. Agur, perhaps, had given too

much

ARGUMENTS *against the*

SERM. 54.
Prov. xxx.
2, 3.

much way to these enquiries, for which he saith, *I am more brutish than any man, and have not the understanding of a man; I neither learned wisdom, nor have the knowledge of the holy.* We may suppose of what nature these things are that he was ignorant of, by the next words, *Who has ascended up into heaven, or descended? who has gathered the wind in his fists? who has bound the waters in a garment? who has established all the ends of the earth? What is his name, and what is his Son's name, if thou canst tell?*

———— 4.

(2.) That it does not signify a derivation of nature in the way that it must do when we use it of one another, is plain from all those scriptures that speak of Christ as they do of the Father. He would never have been called Alpha and Omega, *The first and the last, The beginning and the ending,* or said to be *from everlasting,* and *before all things,* if his being was received from another. It destroys indeed the Sabellian fancy, and proves him to be distinct from the Father, for the word Son carries in it the name of another person; and though in us it would signify a beginning, yet we cannot admit it in him, without a spunge upon those passages in the Bible that tell us quite the contrary. He cannot be the *everlasting Father,* if he is a derived Son, nor is he *before all things,* if any thing was before him.

Isa. ix. 6.
Col. i. 17.

(3.) The most apparent design of the word, I think, is to express an identity or sameness of nature between the Father and the Son; that we are to conceive of the one as we do of the other. To be sure, this was never designed to explain the *manner* of his derivation, and therefore I see no necessity to understand it of any derivation at all. For whenever it is used among creatures, it is to tell us that the being is exactly the same in the parent and the offspring. The time of existence is only a circumstance. The last child that was born in-

to

to the world has the same human nature with Adam himself; and the characters of priority and subjection, of coming sooner or later, being stronger or weaker, make no difference in the nature itself. The son is as much a man as the father; and it would be an odd way of arguing, when I say that a man and his son are equal in nature, by which I mean they are equally rational, spiritual and immortal, and whatever is essential to the human nature, for any to cut me short, and say, that the father was before the son; *that* does not enter into the question; human nature is the same in a child as in a parent, in a subject as in a king. All these individuals have no other distinction among them but what is circumstantial; as to the nature itself they are equal, the same in essence.

Now, though priority and succession are neither essential nor contradictory to the human nature, yet they are so to the Divine. It is necessary in God that He be the first, *before all things;* and therefore though one who has a beginning may be very glorious, yet he cannot be God, because he must want that which is the grand essential of Deity. So that the question is not, whether Christ has a glorious capacity above every other being, whether he has not an existence before them, and inconceivably above them. This still does not denominate him a God.

If he is begotten of the Father, and yet have not the same nature with the Father, the word must be taken in a sense that it never would bear any where else. If it is designed to express a derivation, it expresses what the Father has not, nay what is opposite to his nature,—a downright contradiction to every notion of Deity; and I cannot apprehend, that in making the Son an inferior, I shall ever answer the title of his being the only begotten Son of God. Upon the whole, the word is to signify something; the *manner* of derivation it cannot, the *time* it does not; and if it signifies the *derivation* itself, it argues a different nature, for a communicated divinity is a jar upon what we always mean by divinity.

(4.) It is certain, that this word is applied to some *periods* that cannot refer to the Son's derivation of an existence from the Father. His miraculous conception in the Virgin Mary is brought as one ground of the title: *Therefore the holy thing that shall be born of thee shall be called the Son of God.* The stand that the Socinians make here, we all of us know; they tell you, that at this time he began to be; but that is an error out of fashion at present; another is uppermost in the wheel, though I believe it will not continue long so.

Will any one, now, say from this scripture, that the only reason of his being called the Son of God was such a conception? Had he not the title antecedent to it and independent on it?

Another period is his resurrection. Then he was *declared to be the Son of God with power;* but the phrase itself plainly signifies not his entering into the name, but giving it a new discovery and manifestation. The Apostle applies what David had said so long ago to that period, *Thou art my Son, this day have I begotten thee;* but will they say that the word signifies a derivation in this place? Was that indeed *the day* of his birth? Had he no existence till *then?* Every one gives up this meaning of the phrase; it is too gross to be contended for in *that scripture,* though they make it necessary in others; and therefore you need do no more upon their boasted argument, than change the situation of it: As, for example, they plead, He that was begotten was derived,—the word can signify nothing but a communication of being; try whether it does or no upon the passage I have now given you, *God spake of a certain time, This day have I begotten thee: i. e.* according to them,

This

This day thou haft received thine exiftence; and therefore if the word can bear no other fenfe but a derivation of being, it muft fignify that Chrift began to be at his refurrection.

It is plain, that in this fcripture it cannot refer to a communication of nature, for he was the Son of God in every fenfe of the word before; and therefore *that* interpretation of the phrafe is not *neceffary* in all places which is *impoffible* in one. If it *muft not* fignify derivation in this text, it *may not* do fo in another. And perhaps the Holy Spirit has ufed it thus on purpofe to fhew us, that He never meant by it, what one that is *carnally minded* tells us he does. It is effential to God that He be underived; and fo it muft be to Him who is the only begotten of the Father: If they have the Divine Nature equally, it is in all its perfections.

3. The methods they take to oppofe the truth are fuch as no integrity will allow of. I omit their *walking in flanders*, faying the moft they can againft an author, when they can fay nothing againft his arguments; throwing dirt at the man in hopes of blafting the caufe. Thefe are arts that may take in the hurry of a difpute, but they will either be matter of repentance *with* the grace of God, or of reproach *without* it. Such methods are always the fcandal of a good intereft, and a dead weight to a bad one: *No lie can be of the truth*, or capable of doing it any good. The ways they are put to are fuch as thefe.

Firft, They take all the pains they can to difguife the queftion; they love to ufe ambiguous phrafes, and keep the fenfe of them undetermined; that if they cannot *convince* you, they may have it in their power to retreat, and fay they do not *contradict* you. This unmanly fraud is the whole fpirit of their books, lurking and fhuffling under deceitful words; which method I will fhew you

they

they are guilty of, and expose it with the contempt it deserves.

Secondly, Another of their arts, that the lovers of a righteous cause will despise, is this, to pretend all along that the doctrine we are striving for has no foundation in Scripture, but has its whole authority from councils and creeds and catechisms. The falsehood of this charge we can easily shew to any ingenuous person, though the people that make it are hardened against all conviction.

Thirdly, The mysteries of our religion are reproached as so many breaches *of free-thinking;* that they are only a set of thoughts that have slid into us by education; what we have never examined, but take for granted at a venture.

Fourthly, In pursuit of their cause, they go searching into books, and bring out passages directly opposite to the design of the authors. The disingenuity of this practice is too gross for any but the advocates of a corrupted cause to admit of.

Fifthly, Their desiring the doctrines may be delivered in the express words of Scripture, is another stale artifice to *deceive the simple.* As this was never their own practice, it can be no more than a vain delusion.

Sixthly, Their intimations that a love of charity and more enlarged notions of liberty are the credit of their scheme, is what I will examine.

Seventhly, The contempt with which they speak of mysteries, and their ways to dull the regard of men to the worship of God, is the most powerful of all their arts: *They allure through the lusts of the flesh those that are clean escaped from them that live in error.*

Eighthly, The poor shuffle of denying themselves to be Arians, and reconciling their schemes to the creeds they abhor, is such an avowed dissimulation, that we may wonder that the very name of *sincerity* should ever come out of their mouths.—I shall

not

not open the charge at prefent. Thofe of you that have looked into their books will, at the firſt found of thefe particulars, know that they are eafily proved. But I will take up no more of your time now, than to give you this one reflection upon what you have heard: That

If there is a defign to affault the firſt article of your religion, if thefe are the *arguments*, and thefe the *methods* of thofe that are in it, what need have you to be eſtabliſhed! The war has fpread itſelf far and near; he muſt be a ſtranger in Iſrael that knows not theſe things. Do, therefore, as they would do, who live in an infected place; get a prefervative, by letting *the word of God dwell richly in you;* and above all, defire the protection of that Spirit who can *lead you into the way of all truth.* Let thoſe that fear the Lord fpeak often one to another: *Build up one another in your moſt holy faith, that I may be comforted together with you, by the mutual faith both of you and me.*

SERMON LV.

July 17. 1723.

THAT thefe are the ways they take to ſhew their charity and *free-thinking*, is notorious to every one who reads what they have written. It would be as ufelefs as voluminous, to give you all the examples that their books pour in upon us, of fuch an unfairnefs in argument, and hypocrify in conduct. I ſhall briefly take notice of their practice, and ſhew you the difcord there is between
the

the methods of this party, and those that the God of truth has directed us to, in proclaiming his Gospel. *The Apostles gave no offence, lest the ministry should be blamed, but in all things approved themselves as the ministers of God, by pureness, by knowledge, by the Holy Ghost, by love unfeigned, by the word of truth, by the power of God.* Where they had been *shamefully entreated, they were still bold in God to speak the Gospel of God with much contention. Their exhortation was not of deceit, nor of uncleanness, nor in guile; but as they were allowed of God to be put in trust with the Gospel, so they preached, not as pleasing men, but God, who searches the hearts; neither at any time used they flattering words, nor a cloke of covetousness.*

1. I begin with the first of these accusations that you have heard, and that is, their continual endeavours to disguise the question, that we may never know what it is we dispute about. *Every one that does evil hates the light, neither comes he to the light, lest his deeds should be reproved; but he that does truth comes to the light, that his deeds may be made manifest that they are wrought in God.* Christ himself *ever spake openly. These things were not done in a corner.*

The opposite way argues such a diffidence of their cause as they would be unwilling to own; and therefore the proposal made to them by Dr Waterland is what would soon bring the controversy to an end: ' Dispute fair, drop ambiguous
' terms, or else define them, put not gross things
' upon us, contemn every thing but truth, search
' after truth, and keep close to the question, and
' then it will soon be seen, whether Arianism or
' Catholicism be the Scripture-doctrine of the Tri-
' nity.'

1st, It is a breach of this honest rule for them to trifle with the several meanings of the word GOD in Scripture; and, when we have proved that the title

title is given to Christ as it is to the Father, to sham us off with an arbitrary distinction between a supreme and a subordinate God. They know this is out of the question; we have no need to demonstrate that he is called God in some sense or other. They allow *that,* and *we* grant that the name is given to angels, to men, nay, to Satan himself.

But what is this to the purpose? Is it not in many places a divine peculiar, and so given to the supreme Being, as it would be blasphemy to say it of any other? *Thou art great and dost wondrous things; thou art God alone. I am the Lord,* saith he, *that is my name, and my glory will I not give to another. His name alone is Jehovah.* We have *no other gods before him; the Lord our God is one Lord:* and therefore when we bring examples of Christ's being the great *Jehovah,* they must, in answer, do one of these two things:

Either, *first,* they are to shew that we have mistaken the Scripture, and that he has not the name; or, *secondly,* they must remove the evidence which arises from other places, that this *name* is peculiar to the Most High. Their way lies fair before them, and if what they pretend to was so easy, they would never turn out of it. Let them shew that there is no one name belongs to God in all the Bible, but what may be granted to *him* who by nature is no God. For we can make it evident, that there is not any title under which the Father is mentioned, but somewhere else it is applied with an undistinguished fulness to the Son.

To say that it must be understood with the qualification of *their note,* that the one is a supreme, and the other a subordinate God, is to take for granted the thing that ought to be proved: Either the foundation for such a remark is clear in the Scripture itself, or it is not. If it is, let them shew it; if it is not, let us never pretend to make the scheme

scheme more intelligible than the Holy Ghost has left it.

The Christian religion has subsisted seventeen hundred years without their distinction, and so it can do still. He who has brought it from the womb will secure it to old age. *There are indeed that are called gods, as we have gods many, and lords many; but to us there is but one God, the Father, and one Lord Jesus Christ.* He is so *called* God as no creature can be; and therefore, if Jesus Christ in other places has the title of God given him without any variation of language, we must either suppose him equal to the Father, or that the Scripture leaves us confused in a matter where above all other things it ought to be clear: Which would look like a breach of his promise, that *we shall all know him from the least to the greatest;* and Thomas did know him when he said, *My Lord, and my God.*

2dly, It is another evidence of this fraud, when they will teaze us with the distinction of a supreme and a subordinate worship. That the duty we owe to parents, to magistrates, or any superiors, is called *worship,* cannot be denied. But certainly *this* also is a word which the Holy Ghost has appropriated to the homage that we pay only to God, and cannot without the foulest guilt and danger give to any other. It must in some places describe an action that can be directed lawfully to none but him that made us.

That Christ is the Mediator of the correspondence between God and us, and the medium of our approach to him, is true enough. But we are not said to worship him when only *by him* we come to the Father. Now the question is, whether he is not frequently held forth as the ultimate object of our faith, our adoration, our inward delight and full dependence? If they say he is not, and that our worship is directed beyond him to a greater than he, let that be tried by matching the Scriptures with one another, comparing spiritual things with spiritual.

If I were asked whether or no I could prove from the Bible that our religious worship should be given to none but God, and whether the Father is the proper object of it, it is easily answered. Upon that head we argue very justly, that the words, *Thou shalt worship the Lord thy God, and him only shalt thou serve,* are as full as any can be. And if they do not command such a temper of mind towards God as we must not have to any one else, they signify nothing at all. Well, the words are as plain, the expressions as full, the command as peremptory, with respect to Christ, as they can be to the Father.

Thus, when it is said, *Men began to call upon the name of the Lord;* and, *Whoever calls upon the name of the Lord shall be saved;* and, *Call upon me in the day of trouble, and I will hear thee;* I see no more in these strong precepts than I do in others that relate to a Saviour. We read of those who *in every place call on the name of the Lord Jesus,* both theirs and ours. *All the Angels of God worship him. Into thy hands do I commit my spirit, for thou hast redeemed it, Lord God of truth,* faith David, who thus *died in faith. Lord Jesus receive my spirit,* faith Stephen, who would have given it to none but one that redeemed it. *I have redeemed thee, and thou art mine,* faith God to Israel. *Ye are not your own, but bought with a price,* faith God by the Apostle; and we know *the Lord that bought us,* this God *who has purchased the church with his own blood. Ye believe in God,* faith Christ, *believe also in me.* If he meant only a subordinate faith, it is no more than any Prophet or Apostle might have said as well as he. *He that has begun a good work in you, will perform it to the day of Christ Jesus; he that has wrought us for the self same thing is God;*

Gen. iv. 26.
Joel ii. 32.
Psal. l. 15.

1 Cor. i. 2.

Heb. i. 6.
Ps. xxxi. 5.

Acts vii. 59.

1 Cor. vi. 19, 20.
Deut. xxxii. 6.
2 Pet. ii. 1.
Joh. xiv. 1.

Phil. i. 6.

SERM. 55. *God; and yet Jesus is the author and finisher of our*
Heb. xii. 2. *faith.*

3dly, It is another instance of this fraud, when they disguise the question, and tell you, our only controversy is about uncertain speculations, which lead a man out of his depth, and make him no better. This was the temper of Ephraim, *God wrote to him the great things of his law, but they were counted a strange thing.*

Thus, how roundly is the story told, that ' we ' are contending whether the Trinity shall be un- ' derstood of three infinite minds, and whether ' they are distinguished by a self-consciousness, and ' that these being only metaphysical niceties, people ' have no concern about them:' Though themselves will keep talking of the Son's being originated, not self-existent, begotten not by necessity of nature, but by the will of the Father. They say, that Christ has left his religion plain and unclouded with such hard words.

You in this assembly have now for above two years been entertained with discourses on our Lord's divinity, and are my witnesses, whether the charge against us is true or no. Has it been our endeavour to darken the doctrine with barbarous phrases? Have we not laid it down before you, both in the evidence and the language of Scripture? Have you heard one sermon that entered into an explication, *how* three are one, and one is three? And therefore you know, that such an insinuation is not arguing, but railing.

That there is a distinction between Father, Son, and Holy Spirit, is plain, and that it amounts to what we mean by the *word* person among men; the Father is not the Son, nor the Son the Spirit. And yet, that as much is said of the Son's divinity

1 Cor. xv. as of the Father's, I hope has been apparent, *If ye keep in memory what I preached unto you, unless you have believed in vain.* That there is but one God,

is

is as true a propofition as any of the reft. That they *feem* to contradict one another, is not denied; but, if they are revealed, if God has indeed given us this account of his own nature, we are to acquiefce in the report, and adore what we cannot explain.

So that the queftion is not, whether they are infinite minds, but, as a learned author has openly told them, ' *Firft*, They are to prove, either that
' the Son is not Creator, or that there are two
' Creators, and one of them a creature. *Secondly*,
' They are to fhew, either that the Son is not to
' be worfhipped at all, or that there are two objects of worfhip, and one of them a creature.
' *Thirdly*, They are to prove, either that the Son
' is not God, or that there are two Gods, and one
' of them a creature. *Fourthly*, They are to fhew,
' that this hypothefis is high enough to take in all
' the high titles and attributes afcribed to the Son
' in Scripture, and at the fame time low enough to
' account for his increafing in wifdom, not knowing the day of judgment, and the like.'

The controverfy lies in this and nothing elfe. And though it is indeed a needlefs difpute to determine what was never revealed, the manner of the diftinction among the perfons, and the union of the nature; yet it is no vain fpeculation for a Chriftian to know, in what fenfe his Saviour is a God, and with what worfhip he is to be regarded: Becaufe, until this point is fettled, we cannot fteer fafe between impiety on the one hand, in withholding worfhip from the true God, and idolatry on the other, in giving it to a creature. Believing, which is the great act of the foul, will be the moft uncertain thing in the world; in it the Chriftian is doing he knows not what, his faith wanders about for an object, and, like the unclean fpirit, is feeking reft and finding none. He knows that Chrift in his office is no more than a Mediator, an

appointed

SERM. 55. appointed person, a delegate, a deriving and subordinate agent; but if he is any more than this, it is needful we should know it, that we may either be strong in faith, giving glory to him as a God, or not dare on the other hand to trust in one who cannot save.

And can it ever be the business of ministers to keep people in the dark about this matter? When we talk of your *believing in the name of the Lord Jesus*, and bid you *call upon him*, must we not tell you who this Lord Jesus is? If you say, he is the Messiah, is it not as needful a question, *what* is the Messiah, as *who* he is.

He is never the more the object of my faith and dependence for the *name*, but for having the perfections that are included in the title. Has the Holy Spirit made us ministers of the New Testament, where all is clear, and *with open face we behold the glory of the Lord*, to throw a vail upon our faces when we speak to you? Must we talk of a God, and have it undetermined whether he is the author of all things, or an inferior agent? Shall we press the duty of worship, and never let you know what it is, how far it may regard a Saviour, and where it should stop.

No, no, my friends, the Christian religion is no such babble as this conduct would make it. *Wizards may peep and mutter*, but ministers of the Gospel are to speak out. *If the trumpet give an uncertain sound, who shall prepare himself to the battle? so you, except ye utter by the tongue words easy to be understood, how shall it be known what is spoken? ye speak into the air. No voice is without signification; but if I know not the meaning of the voice, I shall be a barbarian to him that speaks, and he that speaks will be a barbarian to me.* If I did think that Jesus Christ and the Holy Spirit were not the supreme God, equal with the Father, I should not dare to be silent; but would take all

the

1 Cor. xiv.
8, 9, 10,
11.

the reproach that might follow a change of opi-
nion. In this open carriage I have Christ himself
for an example, as well as an object: *He preached
righteousness, he refrained not his lips.* I should
think it shameful to any discourses of mine, if man-
kind had a handle to charge me that I left them
in the dark: *We use great plainness of speech.* I
am very sure all truth of this nature, on which side
soever of the question it lies, is by no means to be
smothered. I must either be treacherous to the
Father, or to the Son, in suffering you to continue
in a false worship.

I know it is said, that the cause will lose by
being too open, and so I believe it will; but that
is no argument that it is of God. His doctrine
may be ventured out into broad daylight; it shines
upon the mind from the evidence of the Bible;
it strikes the conscience from the importance of
the matter. I have no call to dissemble my con-
cern for the Father's glory, if I think the Son is
made equal to him in our carriage, who is not so
in his own nature; and I am sure I need not be
afraid to own the dignity of the Son, in all the
smoke and fire that is raised against it, if I believe
him to be the Most High God.

Whether we are mistaken or no, we have not
dissembled with you; but *being manifest unto God,
I trust are manifest also to your consciences.* We
may walk in error, which the Arians say is an in-
nocent thing, (though they have no mercy on an
error *for* our Lord's Divinity), but ye are our wit-
nesses that we *have not walked in craftiness.* We
handle the word of the Lord imperfectly; as we
know but in part, so we prophesy in part; but we
have not *handled it deceitfully. We are not as many
who corrupt the word of God; but as of sincerity, as
of God, in the sight of God, speak we in Christ.*

2. Another of their arts is this, to pretend all
along that the doctrine we strive for has no foun-
dation

SERM. 55.

1 Cor iii. 12.

2 Cor. ii. 17.

dation in Scripture; but that in pleading for the Deity of Chriſt, we only ſet up the authority of councils, and are ſupported by the evidence of creeds and catechiſms and confeſſions. Nay, we are told this is departing from *the Proteſtant principles.*

What a noiſe have we had of reducing our religion to the Bible! as if thus far it had been taken out of ſomething elſe? What outcries againſt theſe ſeveral ways that the churches have uſed to declare the truth as it is in Jeſus: *From whom has ſounded out the word of the Lord, ſo that their faith to God-ward is ſpread abroad.* I know it is urged by ſome who are but of yeſterday, and have not prepared themſelves *to the ſearch of their fathers,* that the ancient councils were only aſſemblies of treacherous men, who to ſerve the tricks and deceits of a court had in a fraudulent way been brought together; and that their creeds were nothing elſe but ſo many monuments of their own preſumption, and engines of the emperor's tyranny; that what they have delivered as the ſenſe of Scripture is a doctrine that others cannot find there.

This indeed is very freely ſpoken; and I think, though your faith has no concern with the authority of any aſſembly, ſynod, convocation, or council in the world, yet unleſs hiſtory has made them infamous, their names ſhould not be *taken up as a curſe among us.* Let them be never ſo great, I may ſay *they have in conference added nothing to me.* I have called in no help from them, *that your faith might not ſtand in the wiſdom of men, but in the power of God.* There were two periods of the church, which lie nearer our day; and what happened then deſerves our greater attention.

Firſt, One was that happy time, when God brought about the *Reformation* in ſo many countries at once; when he put it into the heart of the nations

nations with a common heave to throw off the yoke of *Rome.—England, Scotland, France, Germany, Denmark, Poland, Sweden, Holland, Saxony,* and several more, within a little time of one another, had kings, great men, common people, and vast numbers of all sorts but the priests, combining in a national way to profess the truth of God, and claim the liberty of men.

You know what a spirit of holiness this work was carried on with: *Many running to* **and fro**, *and knowledge increasing.* If ever men **were in** earnest for the Protestant religion, it was when they loved it with their souls, and sealed it with their blood. Now, it is certain, every one of these enlightened countries published a confession of their faith. Their princes were not hauled into it, but *willingly offered themselves among the people to subscribe with their hand to the Lord God of Israel.* They were not then of opinion that such human declarations are a departure from the Protestant principle, but rather the first public effect of that principle.

And it is **very** affecting to see, though every country **had** their phrases, and some confessions **are** much clearer, fuller, and better worded than others, yet that they all agree in these two doctrines, a Trinity of Persons in the Divine Nature, and an acceptance with God only upon the satisfaction of Christ. How well our generation has refined upon the ways these Fathers took; whether the Protestant principles which they value, are accompanied with the same principles of courage, seriousness, wisdom and perseverance, for which the names of **our** reformers are blessed; I must leave you to judge: *Do you remember to magnify this work which men behold; every man may see it; man may behold it afar off.*

Secondly, Another period, in which the men of God gave themselves to this work, was chiefly in

our

Dan. xii. 4.

Isa. xliv. 5.

Job xxxvi. 24, 25.

SERM. 55 our nation about fourscore years ago; I mean the Assembly of Divines that met at Westminster. It was in a dark day that they were called together, when the scales seemed to swing in an uncertain way, whether bondage or liberty should be our lot, Protestancy or Popery our profession. At that time there was *distress of nations with perplexity; mens hearts failing them for fear, and for looking after those things that were coming on the earth.*

There could be no temptation for men to dissemble then, when a war had begun to rage in the bowels of their nation. And it must be owned, there was in these days as great an appearance of religion as was ever known in any age or country.

1643. At this time, that learned Assembly sat. What we know of the men, either from history or their own works, makes it evident they were persons of the brightest character for knowledge and piety. And I once expected that the party, who would not suffer them to be called *rebels*, would not rise against them as a company of *creed-makers*. From them we have *a Confession of Faith*, that has been received and admired all over the world for the contexture of the work and the perspicuity of the language, *sound speech that cannot be condemned*. They also published a *Larger Catechism*, which, though an uneasy author has thought fit to revile, yet it appears to me the best summary both of doctrinal and practical divinity that is now extant in the world. And of this I would take no other way to convince *you*, than if it is false must enable you to confute *me*; and that is, to read it carefully over, which I am afraid many have not done, though I do not know, next to the Holy Scripture, a better and more needful book in the universe. Thirdly, these great men gave us also *a Shorter Catechism*, in which the principles of our religion are drawn up with a conciseness and perspicuity that I think was never yet exceeded. This indeed

deed is what we have been trained up in, as the way in which our parents thought we should go; and it is strange, that some *when they are old* are taking pains to depart from it.—Having given you this history of uncontested fact, I would observe to you these few things:

(1.) That there is not one of all these catechisms or confessions that pretends to give us any other than the Scripture-doctrine. They that compiled them profess to take their sentiments out of the Bible. Whether they have done so or no, is left to the judgment of every reader. For,

(2.) The testimonies upon which the doctrine is founded, are published along with them in most of these composures. I am sure they are so in all the works of the Assembly that met at Westminster. The scriptures are inserted at large; and to say they impose their sense of the Bible upon all mankind is a notorious falsehood. If their opinions are wrong, themselves have opened the way for you to prove them so; and though some are determined to run us down with a charge that we make the catechism the standard of truth, there is not a child that repeats it but can tell whether he has learned the PROOFS or no; and by the proofs they never mean any thing but the Scriptures.

So universal and public is the evidence, that the catechism itself is to be *proved*, and carries all the credentials it pretends to in the view of every one that reads it.

And therefore it had been fairer in the adversary, to have shewn us that the expressions there do not contain the *sense* of Scripture, than to trifle with telling us they are not the *words* of Scripture. If these propositions, 'There are three Per-
' sons in the Godhead, the Father, the Son, and
' the Holy Ghost; and these three are one God,
' the same in substance, equal in power and glory,'
are any of them false, we may justly disown them;

but every one of them is surrounded with sentences out of the Bible.

It is true, the work was composed by fallible men; they were not inspired in forming the sixth answer; and if it does not agree with the word of God, if the scriptures they bring as a proof do not suffice, let us shew the weakness of the consequence; and not make a clamour, that these were *fallible* men, that they *might be* deceived, but shew, that they were *erroneous* men, and actually *are* deceived. Every proposition is either true or false, whatever language it is put into; and whether it expresses my conceptions in the best way or no, yet as far as I understand the words, I can tell whether I think it agreeable to the book of God.

(3.) I appeal to every one of you who have been my witnesses for the space of more than two years, that no human authority has ever once been insinuated as an argument of your believing that *God was manifest in the flesh.* And therefore they that charge it upon us may well be asked, Whether or no they have heard us put your faith upon creeds and confessions? if they say they have, you know it is talking against plain fact; and they appear to be a set of people who *love and make a lie:* If they have not, they only publish a sinful impertinence, and ought to be had in the contempt that is due to those *who understand not what they say, nor whereof they affirm.* For my part, I read every confession and creed, as I do any other work, as an evidence how far the author is acquainted with the Scriptures. They are no other than methodical summaries of the truth as it is in Jesus. If they vary from the law and the testimony, *it is because there is no light in them. Therefore search the Scriptures daily, whether the things are so or no.*

Jo. viii. 20.
Acts xvii. 11.

SER-

SERMON LVI.

July 31. 1720.

3. IT is a very common vanity among those who set themselves against the Lord and his Anointed, to call their scheme by the name of *free-thinking*, and represent those that do not run astray with them, as a dull sort of people, who have slid into their opinions by education, take every thing upon trust, and have no other reason to believe as they do, but only because their fathers or their teachers have done so before them. The Apostle advises Timothy to be upon his guard against this set of men: *Keep what is committed to thy trust, avoiding profane and vain babblings, and oppositions of a falsely called science; which some professing, concerning the faith have erred.* [1 Tim. vi. 20, 21.]

Under this head I may bring in the haughty temper that has, without either thought or shame, given the brand of *enthusiasm* to the faith which has been owned by the harmonious confessions of so many churches. That they go on with this disdain of those that will not follow them, as men of no critical learning, no generous principles, no solid reason, is notorious from their books and all their conversation. Thus they *cast abroad the rage of their wrath.*—Upon which I shall give you these few remarks.

(1.) It is no great argument that the cause has much foundation, when the men have so little humility. We do not find pride and vain glory among those signs of an Apostle, by which *they approved themselves to be the ministers of Christ*. When they take the title of *free-thinkers*, it is an appropriation of a great name to themselves, and can be no evidence that God has either called them or fitted them to the edification of mankind: *Knowledge puffs up, but it is charity that edifies*; *if any man thinks that he knows any thing, he knows nothing yet as he ought to know.*

I had rather be among those whom these polite people despise for madmen, *enthusiasts*, and whatever they please to call them, than be like *Leviathan*, a *king over the children of pride.* I could have no envy at such as Job complains of: *No doubt ye are the people, and wisdom shall die with you.* Though he speaks the very thought that some persons have of themselves, yet it is not much to their advantage, when he adds, *I am as one mocked of his neighbour, who calls upon God, and he hears him; the just upright man is laughed to scorn.*

And that contempt with which they speak of the good men that are gone before us, does but fairly bring them within all the descriptions that Agur throws together: *There is a generation that curses their father, and does not bless their mother; there is a generation that are pure in their own eyes, and yet is not washed from their filthiness; there is a generation, O how lofty are their eyes! and their eye-lids are lifted up; there is a generation whose teeth are as swords, and their jaw-teeth as knives, to devour the poor from off the earth, and the needy from among men.* It was with quite another spirit that they who served God in the Gospel of his Son went abroad through the nations: not like the wicked, *whose ways are always grievous, God's judgments are far above out of his sight; as for his enemies, he puffs at them; his mouth is full of cursing, deceit, and fraud.* Such a temper would never have done with such a cause.

God fits men to his Gospel both in their knowledge and in their frame; he never makes *grapes to grow on thorns, nor figs on thistles; by their fruits ye shall know them.* The Apostles had a great deal of care upon this head, to *give no offence that the ministry be not blamed.* One of them fought at Ephesus with beasts after the manner of men, yet they knew *from the first time that he came into Asia, after what manner he had been with them at all seasons, serving the Lord with all humility of mind, and many tears, keeping back nothing that was profitable for them.* He was with the Corinthians *in weakness, fear and much trembling.* To the Thessalonians he professes the humility of his carriage, as well as the truth of his doctrine: *Neither of men sought we glory, neither of you nor of others, but we were gentle among you, even as a nurse cherishes her children; ye are witnesses, and God also, how holily, justly, and unblameably we behaved ourselves among you that believe. The wisdom that is from above is first pure, then peaceable, gentle, and easy to be entreated.* You may be sure that the wisdom is no higher than earthy, *i. e.* no better than sensual and devilish, that delivers its notions in gross language, and pursues them with a haughty spirit.

Every wise man is a freethinker; he desires to use the talents that God has given him, and would improve the light of other people, not to obscure, but to assist his own. And therefore they who deny you that title, throw a reproach upon your nature. There must be a great deal of *stupidity* in you to deserve this usage, or a great deal of *conceit* in them to give it.

(2.) As to the charge of *enthusiasm* and folly, the shame of it does not so frequently fall on those that receive it, as it retorts upon them that give it. It was not the impudence of Festus that proved Paul to be mad, though it called him so, when

SERM 56.
Acts xxvi. 25.
2 Cor. xi. 16. 19.

he *spake the words of truth and soberness.* What he writes to the Corinthians will let you into the opinion they had of him: *Let no man think me a fool; if otherwise, yet as a fool receive me, that I may boast myself a little; ye suffer fools gladly, seeing ye yourselves are wise.* Such a temper ought to be treated with a disdain.

The charge of *enthusiasm* has been lately advanced against a book written in defence of the Trinity, and which I perceive is only to be answered by *gnashing of teeth.* The party seems to be cut to the heart with it. Here is no pretence that they have mistaken the meaning of one scripture, that they have either blundered or shuffled in their arguments: But the author has given a bold fling of scandal, that will affect any other doctrine as well as that of the Trinity, viz. that certainty in matters of faith is all *enthusiasm.* And, if so, as our martyrs died for they knew not what, so they

Rev. xii. 11.

died as fools do! But we know *they overcame by the blood of the Lamb, and the word of their testimony, when they loved not their lives to the death.*

It is hard, that people should be so free of a character to those who they think are wrong, when themselves say none can be sure of their being right. However, when an author has a mind to write against something, and dare not attack what he pretends to answer, he must give battle to his own imagination. The *enthusiasm,* which he sets out to the contempt of the world, is described by ' a man's *not leaning to his own un-*
' *derstanding*, being taught of God, having the
' witness of the Spirit with his own spirit, feeling
' the evidence and power of religion upon his soul.'
And, as these are the things that he means by it, may I ever have grace enough to be an *enthusiast!* may that which is the matter of his sport, be the subject of my experience and veneration! and then all sides will be pleased; some with a satisfaction

of

of what they have, and others with a profane laughter at what they have not.

(3.) It is all a slander upon the truth, and those that own it, to say, that the reason of our faith is the wisdom of men. Whatever value we have for those that are gone before us, yet believing must be our own act, and the effect of an evidence within ourselves. There is a vast deal of difference between saying of former generations that they *may be wrong*, and giving out the sentence that they *were so*. We bring what they have done to the rule that God has given us; and this without any reproach, because it was also a rule to them. But certainly, unless they were made standards of truth, there is no occasion to stun the world with perpetual outcries against them. If their opinions were wrong, the best way is to shew it; bring them to the light that they may be reproved.

Consider who they are that these men set so much at nought; and that they may not fail to strike home at the faith, they insult the people that owned it. Perhaps indeed the ministers and professors of the last age were most of them gone off, before the men that now arraign them had appeared; yet there are several among you old enough to know, that however they may be exceeded in what is now called politeness, yet as to a thorough sense of religion, an observation of the Lord's day, an acquaintance with Scripture, a contempt of the world, and, I will add, an unselfish love of their country, they are far from being equalled by the raw fraternity that now despise them.

They owned God in their lives, and God owned them at their deaths. And though it would be an excess to set them up as standards of truth, yet there is some duty owing to that exhortation: *Re-* *member them which have the rule over you, who have spoken unto you the word of God, whose faith follow,*

Heb. xiii. 7, 8.

SERM. 56. *follow, considering the end of their conversation.* And what is that? *Jesus Christ the same yesterday, to-day, and forever.* Their rule over you did not call for any blind obedience; what they spake to you was the word of God, and therefore follow their faith with regard to that, considering the end of their conversation, the end that they aimed at, and the end that they arrived to.

What they had in view was to promote the honour of Jesus; not merely his honour as a man or Mediator, but that which gives a holiness to the one, and an importance to the other, his being the same yesterday, to-day, and for ever. Whatever lower opinions they held, yet in this they were steady; Presbyterians, Congregational, and Baptists, agreed in their confessions of faith. In the profession of this truth they moved quite through the road of life; nay, in the sweetness of it they moved into another life.

A sense of *the infinite evil of sin* kept them always humble, and preserved upon their minds a powerful esteem of the redemption that was equal to it. They would never bear a doctrine which made a little matter of that which cost the Son of God so dear. They fled with joy to Christ as the propitiation for their guilt, and to him as their God and portion for ever. With these professions they kept up their duty, and at last breathed out their souls.

Can we suppose God would suffer people, who were so afraid of displeasing him, and had run every hazard for his glory, to live and die in a dangerous delusion; to adore the Son, who is no more than a God by office; and not only so, but to worship the Spirit, who is no God at all? Shall the best of Christians be upon a level with the worst of heathen, who *worship and serve the creature more than the Creator?* Were they that confessed their need of the Spirit, and were always praying for his assistance, and who admired his testimony,
—were

—were they in an error, when they thought him to be God? And is the truth of his *being*, revealed to the men that laugh at his *operations?* is he best known among those to whom his very name is a jest? has he instructed them whom he never sanctified? is he most liberal of his gifts to those who do most despise him? are the people that profane his name **greater** favourites than those that adore it?

We should never have entered into a comparison of mens characters, if **there had not** risen up among us a set of people who talk of their pious fathers with disdain, though they ought to mention their names with blushing. It **was** by the faith which their sons set at nought, that *those elders obtained a good report*. And may I be one of them who by the same faith and patience are following those that now inherit the promises!

4. That must be a poor cause that is to be served by false quotations. Passages are brought out of books directly opposite to the design of the authors. *False witnesses rise up against them, and lay to their charge things that they know not.* Of these I have lately given several examples in a public work, which has had the most natural effect upon the guilty: For a troubled sea can send forth nothing but *mire and dirt*. False **teachers** are in the New Testament compared to *raging waves of the sea, foaming out their own shame*.

I will give **you** another instance from the same author. In one of his pamphlets he presents us with a passage from Dr Manton on the 11th of the Hebrews: 'Christians need not to puzzle them-
' selves about conceiving of three in one, and one
' in three; let them in this manner come unto
' God, and it suffices; make God the object, and
' Christ the means of access, and look for help
' from the Spirit.' This quotation he has placed on the title page of his book, that he might be sure

of catching the great numbers that will look no farther.

Those words in the valuable works from which he has taken them, come in as an answer to the scruples of good men. They know not how to conceive of three persons, and cannot order their speech by reason of darkness. This difficulty becomes a temptation: now, the Doctor tells them, that they need not puzzle themselves about that MANNER of the union and distinction in the Divine Nature which was never fully revealed. Any one may see he was then speaking to the distress of a wounded conscience, and not to the caprice of a wanton Arian.

Now, if this passage does the author any service who has impaled it in his own little book, it must signify, either that Dr Manton did not believe the doctrine to be true, or that he did not take it to be of any importance. But the author knew both these insinuations to be false. For in his sermons on the same text, *(He that comes unto God must believe that he is)*, that honest uncorrupted writer is express enough of his own opinion, p. 211. ‘ He
‘ that comes unto God must believe that he is, that
‘ is, so as he has revealed himself, one in three
‘ persons; for otherwise we worship an idol, and
‘ that which is not God: We form an idol when
‘ we think of God out of the Trinity.’ And, p. 214. he bids us ‘ prize orthodoxy, and above all see ye
‘ be right in the point of belief; there are a sort
‘ of libertines risen up, that think our debates with
‘ Socinians and Arians are but vain and frivolous,
‘ and that a loose belief of God and Christ is e-
‘ nough. But if this general faith be enough, why
‘ has God revealed so many things that we might
‘ have been ignorant of?

And when he gives rules about fellowship, he is so positive as to say, ‘ We cannot be saved except
‘ we hold one God in three persons, and Jesus as
‘ Mediator.

'Mediator. These are supreme truths that are
'clearly revealed and propounded to our faith.'
And, p. 272. 'To frame fit notions concerning the
'Trinity, that there are three persons in one God-
'head, this is a mystery to be believed, not dispu-
'ted and committed to the anxious traversty of
'our own reasons.' Upon this case I will observe
a few things.

1st, It is of no great weight to any opinion who
they are that received it. That is not our rule, we
go upon a higher authority than what is human.
The learning, the piety, the numbers of those who
have espoused any doctrine, are but lower reasons
for us to embrace it. But,

2dly, It is unfair to give out men as advocates
for a notion, when we ourselves know they were
enemies to it. It is a reproach upon their names,
and *God will arise to make inquisition* for scandal as
well as for blood. It is using them like the two
witnesses, whose *dead bodies* will be exposed by a
barbarous world. That is a great inhumanity; but
methinks it is a viler insult upon their memories to
make them say what they never thought of. Certainly these writers do not remember that *the saints
shall judge the world*, who take a liberty to abuse
them by whole generations, as if it was not enough
to bring *a lying accusation* against the living, unless
they did it also against the dead. But as these
great men died in the Lord, and rest from their labours, so their works shall follow them, not to reproach, but *to praise them in the gates*.

3dly, That pretence, that the truth is *extorted*
from these people; that though they have written
for the commonly received faith, yet they are forced to own, that the evidence lies against them;
this accusation proves a notorious want of modesty
in him that brings it. The supposition is, that Dr
Owen and Dr Manton, who were persons of the
first rank, the one for a scholar, and the other for

SERM. 56. a preacher, that thefe could not write for a doctrine without dropping fomething againſt it. Now that turns upon one of thefe two things:

Either they knew that the opinion they maintained was falſe, or they did not; if they *did*, it was a breach of their integrity; if they *did not*, it is a public evidence of their folly, that a writer in the next generation ſhall underſtand them better than they did themſelves. Neither of theſe things ſhall I eaſily allow, upon the names of thoſe eminent ſervants of Chriſt; and, therefore, there is a third inference, which I will leave any one to make who hears the caſe.

4thly, It is uſing mankind very ill to put ſuch things upon us. It may be all one to me, what ſuch a *Doctor* faith about the divinity of Chriſt. His opinion is neither the argument nor the hindrance of my faith; but however let me not be impoſed on in matter of fact. Let us not have deceitful reports; *no lie is of the truth*. If the doctrine I am contending for be right, it will be ſo without fathers or doctors; but why ſhould I make a falſe muſter, both to wrong the dead and abuſe

Pſ. ci. 4, 5. the living? *Let ſuch froward hearts depart from you, do not know thoſe wicked perſons; whoſo privily ſlanders his neighbour*, cut off from your acquaintance.

And ſince I am upon this head, a certain author has obliged me by his demand, both to do him and myſelf juſtice in a quotation I gave you out of his book. I was indeed offended at the phraſe of a derived and a dependent God, and having laid before you ſome looſe expreſſions upon that head from others, I was troubled to find him among theſe unguarded writers. The paſſage I mentioned was this: after he had directed us to pray to Chriſt, he adds, ' It is true he is the begotten of the Fa-
' ther, and ſent of the Father, and the Father is
' greater than he, and the head of Chriſt is God;
' the

'the Son of God derives from the Father, and is
'not properly self-exifting.' Thus far I went,
and did not imagine there was any occafion of going farther.

But as he is pleafed to think we are unfaithful in ftopping there, I will give you the reft of the fentence. His next words are thefe: 'But then
'if it be allowed a neceffary derivation, though
'infinitely free as the rays of the light from the
'fun, and not merely arbitrary and at pleafure,
'which might never have been, it is fufficient to
'juftify the great things faid of him, and fecure
'all that we intend, namely, that he is *above the
'level of the moft exalted creature.*' This I am afraid is far from mending the matter. For,

First, He comprehends both the parts of the queftion, that ufed to be always oppofite; whether the generation of the Son is *voluntary* or of *neceffity?* He fuppofes both, which, as the terms are ufed in that difpute, I think makes a contradiction; becaufe what is *neceffary* in that fenfe, cannot be *free.* By neceffary, we mean that which *muft have been*; by free, that which *might not have been.*

Secondly, It is a very rafh way of talking, to fuppofe any neceffity upon the divine will; becaufe it makes it ceafe to be an act of the will, it leaves God himfelf at no liberty; here is one faid to be derived from another, and yet was neceffary to him. This is bold ungodly language.

Thirdly, If raifing him *above the level* of the moft exalted creature is all he intends, I can affure him it is not all that we intend. It is a *true* account, but a very *low* one, of the Great God, that he is above any creature; and, though it ufed to be always faid, that He who is not a creature is God, yet as fome have run into a wild imagination, and as wild a conduct, that will neither fay the Son is a God nor a creature, minifters that would not keep

people

people in the dark, are obliged to speak out. For, according to that position, which may be called the *nostrum* of our polite age, a being may be above the level of the most exalted creature, and yet not be the Supreme God! I see *contradictions* will pass, though *mysteries* cannot.

5thly, Though I never did, and never dare recommend any holy men to you as having dominion over your faith, yet do not suffer them to be treated injuriously, both as fools and knaves; they have deserved better of their generation, whom they served according to the will of God: and when you compare what is said of them with what they say of themselves, their enemies will be found liars.

The design of Satan in running down the faith of such great men, is to give the world a distaste of their holiness. Throwing off their opinions is an introduction to the dropping of their practice. The Lord's day goes away with the Catechism. Men that are called enthusiasts in their doctrine, are no better in their devotion: and if *thinking* as *they* did not, is called coming back to the Bible, *acting* as *they* did not, may pass for a politer sort of religion. But——may my soul be found with those whom these men despise, for I doubt not they are *among the living in Jerusalem!*

5. Their desiring that the doctrines of Christianity may be delivered in no other words but those of Scripture, is what I call a stale artifice, and has been exploded as a mere fraud in all ages. It is a pretence as old as the Arians, and it is pity that they who revived it have not thought it worth their while to clear themselves of having the same design with those that used it only as a shuffle. For,

1st, It was never their own practice. They continually run into *metaphysical* phrases, or *cabalistical* notions, that is, either the vain janglings of the heathen, or the filthy dreams of the Jews. A

learned

learned historian tells us, when they swelled in councils and swarmed in nations, they had no less than four or five creeds in the space of a few years. They were unstable in all their ways, *ever learning and never coming to the knowledge of the truth. Clouds without water* must be carried about with wind.

And are these in our day any better? Will any of them allow me to be of the same opinion with the author of the Scripture-doctrine of the Trinity, or less mistaken, because I am willing to subscribe all the scriptures that he brings, and leave his propositions to himself? No, I know this will never do; and therefore they expect, either that I do not call Christ God, or that I talk of an originated deity that is not self-existent. My orthodoxy with them is not determined by adhering to the phrases of the Bible, but controlling them with a set of impious distinctions.

One of them, who declared against the equality of the Son to the Father, was willing in a public assembly to confess, that *he is over all God blessed for evermore.* What a trifling is this with sacred words! How evident is it, that to *the unbelieving there is nothing pure!* The *unstable*, as well as the unlearned, *wrest the Scriptures to their own destruction.* Every one knows that the text I have now mentioned is usually pleaded for our Lord's supreme Divinity; and is it not defrauding and going beyond my neighbour, when I give him those words as an expression of my own opinion, which I am sure he takes in a different sense from what I do? What is that but *sporting myself with his deceivings?* But *the Lord is the avenger of all such.* The righteous Lord loves righteousness. Ministers of the Gospel are *not to walk in craftiness, nor handle the word of the Lord deceitfully, but by a manifestation* (not a concealment) *of the truth,* recommend

2 Pet. iii. 16.

2 Cor. iv. 2.

SERM. 56. *commend themselves to every man's conscience in the sight of God.*

2dly, This is no more than Papists may do in the great fundamental of their idolatry. I mean *transubstantiation*. Against this, all the Protestant Churches at the time of the Reformation declared with one voice. Now, according to the pretence of this new scheme, there is not any assembly but what may have a Jesuit for their pastor. If I desire he will satisfy me about his faith, he confidently tells me, that is an *inquisition*, and giving up the liberty that he has in Christ Jesus. If I insist upon it to know what his sentiments are about the great dividing point between us and those of Rome, he saith it is a *mystery*, and ought to be delivered in no other than Scripture-language; and he will affirm neither more nor less than that Christ has said, *This is my body*. If I ask him in what sense he takes that expression, whether proper or figurative, he runs out into declamations against words which man's wisdom teaches, and charges me with taking him away from his Bible, and setting up human decisions as standards in matters of faith.

I have carefully thought over that argument, and with all the turning I can give it, it appears to me as well calculated for a Jesuit as an Arian, and perhaps a little time may shew, it is designed for them both. This trick produced rank Popery in Poland, and it plainly gives the enemy the same advantage in England.

3dly, You know, and so do they too, though they will not own it, that the Scripture is the only plea we use for the doctrine we maintain, and I hope our sermons are not much inferior to theirs in Scripture-language and Bible-phrases. This pretence is what every enemy of the Christian Church has made in all ages. It leaves the door open for the great invaders of our liberty, to come in upon

us

us as a flood. They that have most advanced it SERM. 56.
in our day have made depredations upon the Bible;
and therefore we look upon it as the work of spies,
who *come to see the liberty that we have in Christ,* Gal. ii. 4.
and bring us into bondage.

SERMON LVII.

Aug. 14. 1720.

6. **WE** shall now consider the pretence wherein they glory, that their scheme is to promote a Christian *charity* and mutual forbearance. In this, like those of old, they have seduced the people, crying, *Peace, peace, where there* Ezek. xlii. *was no peace; one built up a slight wall, and, lo,* 10. *others daubed it with untempered mortar.* We have heard speeches delivered with a great deal of flat formality, in praise of that which every man professes to admire, and every believer has the seeds of in himself. The Holy Spirit implants it in the hearts of his own people, and therefore it is a public evidence of our interest in Christ, by which all men will know that we are his disciples, when we *have love one to another.*

But *when shall vain words have an end?* Has the Scripture said so many things of brotherly love, only to express the rancour of those that want it? Is talking over a precept, to pass for obedience to it? Are those glorious things that we read of charity, to furnish the language of reproach, and help us to rail in the name of the Lord? How

VOL. II. X x vile

vile and foolish is it on this occasion, to cool our zeal for the truth by crying up the happiness of union or the necessity of peace?

Who would imagine that when we plead for the faith that was once delivered to the saints, any preachers of the Gospel should tell us, that an agreement with them that deny it is of more importance than a contending for it, and support their opinion by these words of the Apostle, *Though I understand all mysteries, and have all knowledge, and though I have all faith, so that I could remove mountains, and have not charity, it profits me nothing;* and as he saith afterwards, *Now abides faith, hope, charity; but the greatest of these three is charity.*

Because these are some of the *feigned words* with which they make merchandise of you, and those *fair speeches* that deceive the hearts of the simple, I will lead you into the vanity of the argument by a few considerations. You will see that the scriptures they bring in to advance charity above faith, are nothing at all to the purpose; that there is no other charity but what is founded upon an agreement in the faith, and all the exhortations to it in the Bible suppose that we equally hold the head; that we are sufficiently directed with what tenderness to use those who wander from the truth, without giving up one article of religion; and that there are not perhaps in the world more notorious breaches of charity than among the very party that make such a noise about it. From them that consent not to wholesome words, and the doctrine which is according to godliness, we have examples of men who *know nothing, but are proud, doting about questions and strifes of words;* and they have shewn themselves in *envy, strife, railings, evil surmisings, and perverse disputings,* as if they supposed that *gain was godliness.* From them have come these *foolish and unlearned questions that do gender strifes.*

(1.) The

(1.) The scripture which they would reproach us with will leave them short of their design. Why should we be told with vain repetitions that the Apostle has said, *Though I understand all mysteries, and have all faith, and have not charity, it profits me nothing?* Can any one get leave of his own reason to imagine, that he designs to make an opposition between the mysteries of the Gospel and the precepts of the law, between the faith, *without which it is impossible to please God,* and the charity that governs our carriage to his people?

No, no; he is not here speaking of the great mystery of godliness, or with any lessening to that which was the continual subject of his own ministry. To talk of *understanding these* mysteries is a contradiction, they belong to those *deep things* that will never be fully comprehended. But the mysteries that are inferior to charity are of a different nature, because it is here supposed that a hypocrite may have them. Such a knowledge and skill as God gave to Daniel and his companions, in learning and wisdom, understanding visions and dreams.

And so, when he supposes a man to have *all faith* and not have charity, it cannot without violence to the words be expounded of saving faith; but as he himself declares it, a faith to *remove mountains,* that is, a power of working miracles. This, people may have; as our Lord assures us, many shall say in the last day, *Have we not wrought wonders in thy name,* and yet he professes, *I never knew you.*

But it would be impious to suppose, that a person may have the faith of God's elect, and yet want charity. For if faith is right, it will *work by love.* He *that believes with the heart and confesses with the mouth that Jesus died and that he is raised from the dead, he is born of God; and they that have purified their souls in obeying the truth*

through

SERM. 57.
1 Pet. i. 22.
1 John ii. 11.

through the Spirit, have done it *to an unfeigned love of the brethren. If any man hates his brother, he abides in darkness;* he is no believer; the truth has never shone into his soul.

Charity indeed is greater than a notional faith, or what we call the faith of miracles; but to say it is greater than a belief of the truth, is only preferring the branches to the root. Our love to him

1 Joh. v. 1. that begat, is the principle and guide *of our love to those who are begotten of him*, and there is no other love to Him but what arises from our believing in him; and there is no other believing in him but what takes into it the consent and acquiescence of the soul in the report that is given of him.

(2.) There can be no charity but what is founded upon an agreement in the faith. I own that the name of charity is not always used under the same extent in Scripture. Sometimes it signifies the benevolence that we have to all the world; and this seems to be the meaning of the word, when it is distinguished from *brotherly kindness*. I do not take it in that sense here, for it is certain, an agreement in the faith is no condition of that temper; we must do good to all men, whether they are believers or no; we consider them, not as having obtained like precious faith, but as partaking of the same common nature. Religion will teach a person to look upon himself as a brother to the whole world, and sets before his eyes the example of our heavenly Father, who causes his rain to fall, and his sun to shine upon the good and the evil, the just and the unjust; and it is so far from making an union to Christ the foundation of our good will to men, that we are to *bless those that curse us*, though in *that* they are guilty of cursing

Mat. v. 44. HIM, *to love them that hate us, and pray for such as despitefully use us and persecute us.* This is certainly one sense of the word charity, and it holds

1 Cor. x. 31. out our duty to mankind in general; we must *give*

no

no offence to the Jew or the Gentile, or the Church of **SERM. 57.**
God, but be harmless and blameless, as the sons of Phil. ii. 15.
God without rebuke, in the midst of a crooked and perverse nation, among whom we are as lights in the world. I hope none will thus underſtand the head I am now upon.

But, ſecondly, when we ſpeak of charity in a narrower way, as that which is the glory of our religion, it is not diſtinguiſhed from brotherly kindneſs, but only another name for it. It ſignifies a due temper of mind to the people of God: making the ſaints in the earth to *be the excellent* Pſal. xvi. 3.
in whom is all our delight; that we are *companions* ─── cxix.
of all them that fear God, and of them that keep his 63.
precepts. We love one another as Christ has loved John xiii.
us and them. As touching this brotherly love be- 34.
lievers have no need that any write to them, for 1 Theſſ iv. 9, 10.
themselves are taught of God to love one another, and indeed they do it towards all the brethren.

Now this, I ſay, ſuppoſes our agreement in the faith, and without that, it is not the duty that God has commanded, nor an effect of that grace that his Spirit has quickened. But then by this agreement I do not mean our having the ſame thoughts about every doctrine of religion; no, that is not only impoſſible, but the variety that is among us gives a beauty to the Chriſtian life.

There are many expreſſions of charity which ſuppoſe our opinions are not taken from one mould, ſuch as *forbearing one another,* overlooking a little difference, ſpeaking of it as God himſelf does, that *circumciſion is nothing, and uncircumciſion is nothing, but a keeping the commandments of God.*

But then what the Apoſtle calls *holding the head* is the ground of all our regard to the brethren. Without *the unity of the Spirit* there is *no bond of* Eph. iv. 3,
peace. The perſons whom we thus love are with 4. 5.
us under *one Lord, one faith, one baptiſm, one body, one Spirit, one hope of our calling.* We are *built on* ── ii. 18,
the 21.

SERM. 57. *the foundation of the Apostles and Prophets, Jesus Christ himself being the chief corner-stone; in whom all the building fitly framed together grows to a holy temple in the Lord.* In order to the course of this Col. i. 4. love, there must be a mutual profession. Our faith in the Lord Jesus Christ is joined with a *love to all the saints*. He that will not tell me what he believes, has no other demand upon my charity than a heathen man or a publican.

I am to do him good as I have opportunity, whether he is a Christian or no; but it is supposed I must know him to be a disciple, before I can love 1 Pet. iv. 8. him as one. When the Apostle says, *Above all things have fervent charity among yourselves*, does he mean no more than what I am obliged to have for all mankind? And is there any difference between a brother and a stranger, but what arises from an external profession? Have I any other rule for a mutual love besides what appears? Can I judge a person to be in the faith unless I hear it? or can I suppose him to be in a state of holiness, unless I see it? To say that I have no concern whether any one believes right or wrong about the great doctrines of Christianity, is to say I must have no charity for them. Thrusting them out of my care is excluding them from my delight; it makes me incapable of walking with them, rejoicing over them, provoking them to love, and good works, and so much the more as we see the day approaching. When the Apostle John tells 2 John 1, 2. the elect lady and her children, that he *loved them in the truth, and not only he, but all they that had known the truth, for the truth's sake which dwells in us, and shall be with us for ever*, was there no difference between his regard to such as these, and those that *did not abide* in the doctrine of Christ? and must he be charged with a breach of charity, ver. 10, 11. when he directs, that *if any come to us and bring not this doctrine, we are not to receive him into our houses,*

houses, nor bid him God speed; for he that bids him God speed is partaker of his evil deeds? Every one sees not only that he distinguished these two sorts, but the foundation of his doing so. The reason of his love to the former was their being *in the truth*, it was *for the sake* of that; and yet though Christians are to use hospitality one to another, they are ordered not to receive some into their houses, because they *bring not this doctrine.*

Was Paul advising Timothy against the rules of charity when he bid him beware of Alexander, who had *greatly withstood his words?* Was it a schismatical practice for him to *turn away from those that resisted the truth, and were reprobate concerning the faith?* or when a man consented not to wholesome words, *from such a one to withdraw himself?*

Neither charity nor faith are to be what men of corrupt minds will make them. The Scripture in giving us rules about them has made the matter visible enough. There is no cloud upon that text but what the lust of our own hearts has brought thither, *I beseech you mark them which cause divisions and offences, contrary to the doctrine that ye have heard, and avoid them.* They that plead for charity *without* faith, and especially *against* it, are only taking pains for a plant that our heavenly Father has not planted. The Apostles were limited, and so must we be: *We can do nothing against the truth, but for the truth.* How earnestly does he desire that we may *stand fast in one spirit, with one mind, striving together for the faith of the Gospel?*

(3.) We are sufficiently directed how tenderly to use those that wander from the truth, without giving up the honour of one doctrine or article to them. The servant of God must *in meekness instruct those that oppose themselves;* and what is it for? *That God may give them repentance to the acknowledgment of the truth.* Must not people be

SERM. 57.

Rom. xvi. 17.

2 Cor. xiii. 8.

Phil. i. 27.

2 Tim. ii. 25.

under

under the power of a perverse mind that will use this scripture against our zeal for the faith? It is true, the servants of God are not to strive by furious methods, by corporal punishments, or any gross severities, but be gentle to all men; what they do should be in meekness. But then,

First, He must *instruct* them; this rule does not oblige him to hold his peace. There is nothing at all in it opposite to his insisting upon sound doctrine; nay, his doing it at a time that *they will not endure* it. It is no breach of this meekness, if *he reproved them sharply, that they might be found in the faith*. He must not be silent, and neglect to instruct them, and call either his laziness or his cowardice by the name of meekness.

Secondly, This is necessary in order to a divine blessing; he does it in hopes that God will give them *repentance*. But he that is silent when the doctrine of Christianity is opposed, has no hopes that God will give them repentance; he does not use the means in order to it. God *may* give it immediately as he did to Saul; but we cannot expect a person should be reclaimed, who is not so much as admonished. *Brethren*, saith the Apostle, *if any of you err from the truth, and one convert him, let him know, that he who turns a sinner from the error of his way, shall save a soul from death, and hide a multitude of sins.* This is an honorary name put upon our endeavours. We are not able to convert an unbeliever; but God has given our zeal such a reputation, to shew the value he has for any pains we take in order to it.

Thirdly, This repentance that we pray and hope for in these that now oppose themselves is, that they *acknowledge* the truth; not only believe it, but acknowledge it. We must look upon them as impenitent till there is a public confession. And,

Fourthly, Until they do this, they remain *in the snare of the devil, and are led captive by him at his pleasure.*

pleasure. And is it any charity to leave them there? Is not our silence to them upon this head an argument that we had rather have them pleased than saved, and are watching for their favour, and not for their souls? A true *compassion* would teach us *with fear to pull them out of the fire.* <small>SERM. 57.</small>

<small>Jude 22.</small>

It is certain the rules of Christianity do not clash with one another. The way of the Lord is perfect, and therefore no command in the Bible was ever designed to raze out that, *My son, cease to hear the instruction that causes to err from the words of knowledge.* No charitable thoughts can excuse our neglect of *trying the spirits whether they be of God.* We are told of some whose *words do eat as a canker,* and though we must be courteous to all men, yet that cannot take off the plain declaration of the Apostle, *If a man purge himself from these, he shall be a vessel unto honour for the master's use.*

<small>Prov. xix. 27.</small>
<small>1 Joh. iv. 1.</small>
<small>2 Tim. ii. 17.</small>
<small>ver. 21.</small>

(4.) As when men talk of truth, so when they talk of charity, bring them to the law and to the testimony; it is not making a noise with a word that will do. There is no more in the cry of peace, than there is in that of the church. The charity that the Apostle recommends has plain and glorious characters belonging to it; and whenever they are wanting, the pretensions of men are in vain: *Charity suffers long, and is kind; it envies not, vaunts not itself, is not puffed up.* If you see a man deal in proud wrath, he may call himself as he pleases, but *proud and haughty scorner* is the name that God has given him.

<small>1 Cor. xiii. 4.</small>

Charity does not behave itself unseemly; scurrilous language is no more charity than it is decency: charity *seeks not its own, is not easily provoked, thinks no evil,* much less does it take pains to form evil: straining to torture words, setting them out to the worst light we can, has as little of charity as it has of honesty. But then, it is the glory of charity that, as it *rejoices not in iniquity,* so *it rejoices*

<small>ver. 5.</small>
<small>ver. 6.</small>

SERM. 57. *in the truth.* It is far from hating and oppoſing the truth.

God never made any grace to be a rebel againſt any doctrine; he never made a ſaint to pull revelation in pieces; practical religion is far from being an enemy to the Bible; and therefore that is an ungodly charity that works up an intrenchment to thoſe that deny the faith, and a battery againſt them that own it. But as the day is coming that *wiſdom* ſhall be juſtified of all her children, ſo ſhall

Jam. ii. 12. *charity* too; for we would *ſo ſpeak, and ſo do, as they that would be judged by the law of liberty.*

7. The moſt powerful of all their arts is the contempt with which they ſpeak of myſteries, and the worſhip of God. The underſtanding harbours either truth or error, but it is the will that fills them. Good people receive *the love of the truth that they may be ſaved.* God is pleaſed to *manifeſt the good ſavour of his knowledge by us, and we are a ſavour of God to thoſe that periſh,* as well as to thoſe that

2 Cor. ii. 16, 17. are *ſaved: to the one we are a ſavour of death unto death, to the other of life unto life.* A wicked

Joh. iii. 20. man *hates the light, and comes not to it, leſt his deeds ſhould be reproved.* And as theſe *like not to retain God in their knowledge, he gives them over to a reprobate mind.* What oppoſes holineſs oppoſes truth,

1.Tim. vi. 10 *the luſts of the fleſh, the luſt of the mind, and the pride of life. The love of money is the root of all evil, which whilſt ſome have coveted after, they have erred from the faith.*—Obſerve thoſe gradual marks of apoſtaſy.

Firſt, People begin with an indifference to the truth: they loſe a ſenſe of ſin, and the powers of a world to come. It is all one to them whether there is any ſatisfaction to divine juſtice or no. They grow careleſs about their ſouls; and a Saviour who is no God, will do as well for them, as he that is one. Then,

Secondly,

Secondly, This gives them a contempt of God's people; they despise their gifts, they hate their graces; praying, hearing, and every other action of worship is impertinent to them. The more spiritual a Christian appears to be, either in devotion or out of it, the more ridiculous they account him.

Thirdly, This will go on to an indolence about church-communion, and at last to a total neglect of it: *Remember the words that were spoken before of the Apostles of our Lord Jesus Christ, how that they told them there should come mockers in the last time, who should walk after their own ungodly lusts. These be they who separate themselves, sensual, having not the Spirit.* People shall make it more their concern to shelter those who break the peace of churches, than to fill up their places in maintaining it. They will rather be keepers of other vineyards than attend their own.

Fourthly, This shall go into a profanation of the Lord's day; the time that they once thought sacred is devoted to journies, or polluted with recreations; *saying to God, Depart from us, we desire not the knowledge of thy ways.*

Fifthly, As these practices are a plain contempt of God, so he oftentimes returns the contempt upon them: *Because they receive not the love of the truth, he therefore gives them up to strong delusions, to believe a lie.* They that declaim against a certainty in matters of faith, will soon come to certainty enough in matters of error. And thus does an awful judgment vindicate itself against those that have *no pleasure in the truth, but have pleasure in unrighteousness.*—Now here consider,

(1.) Any opposition to the truth, which appears in a hatred of practical godliness, carries its own confutation along with it. God leaves their arguments to be answered by their lives; and though people do not attend to the case till it grows notorious,

SERM. 57. rious, yet the rule that Christ has given us is sure
Mat. vii. 15. of being observed at last: *Beware of false prophets,
who come to you in sheeps clothing, but inwardly
they are ravening wolves. Ye shall know them by
their fruits; men do not gather grapes of thorns, nor*
Isa. xxxii. *figs of thistles. A vile person will utter error against
6.   the Lord;* and it will be seen sooner or later, that
Rom. xvi. they who cause divisions and offences, *serve not the
18.   Lord Jesus Christ, but their own belly.*

(2.) How unhappy is the soul that is seduced by
these means! The case is described in language
2 Pet. ii. 18, plain and dreadful: *When they speak great swell-*
19, 20, 21. *ing words of vanity, they allure through the lusts of
the flesh, through much wantonness, those that were
clean escaped from them that live in error; whilst
they promise them liberty, they themselves are the
servants of corruption; for if after they have escaped the pollution of the world, through the knowledge of our Lord and Saviour Jesus Christ, they are
again entangled therein and overcome, the latter end
is worse with them than the beginning; for it had
been better for them not to have known the way of
righteousness, than, after they have known it, to turn
from the holy commandment delivered to them.*

(3.) Let me warn you against any opinion or
conversation, that would teach you to trifle with
the Lord's day. Whenever any wicked wretches
are brought to religion, the *conviction* usually begins here; and there are very few go to the gal-
lows, but own, that the *corruption* begun here. I
know that the admired name of Mr Chillingworth
is now played against the great article of our faith,
the Divinity of the Son and Spirit, and the main
evidence of our devotion, the religious observation
of the Lord's day. If the letters pretended to be
his are not genuine, then the memory of a writer,
who has performed so well for the Protestant cause,
is loaded with injustice and calumny; and if they
are, we may say, there is a more sure word of precept

cept that we have to trust to. As he that breaks one of the least of the commandments, and teaches men so, is not fit for the kingdom of God, you had need try whether the thing be so or no.

It was in a careful regard to the Lord's day, that your ancestors passed through the world with so much pleasure in their own souls, and such a noble testimony to the conviction of others. The book of sports was the great abomination under which they groaned; and rather than promote it they fled into New England, choosing to lose their country, and keep their conscience. But the generous notions of liberty and free-thinking that some advance, make such a book either needless or irresistible. If the court should be ever so vile, here are people that will *love to have it so; and what will they do in the end thereof?*

Charles I.
1633.

(4.) It is a mean and low carriage, if people are pressed with an argument, to protect themselves against it with contempt, instead of an honest answer. Thus, when our Lord had shewn that *the children of this world are wiser in their generation than the children of light, the Pharisees, who were covetous, heard all these things, and derided him.* The cause of God needs no such baseness, but eternally abhors it.

Luke xvi.
14.

It is low and vile for people, when they meet with those that cannot dispute, to *bring in their heresies privily and unawares,* and when they are called into the battle, to turn off with a sneer. They are serious in their opinions to an inferior, and are always in jest about them before an equal. Thus, as one man mocks another, do they mock the Great God. When seducers have to do with the unskilful, they push their cause; but upon other occasions they can lurch it, and shew the world that they are in jest when we are in earnest. How different was the temper and carriage of the Apostle, who *thought it meet as long as he was in this*

<small>SERM. 57.</small>
<small>2 Pet. i. 13.</small>

this tabernacle to stir them up, by putting them in remembrance!

(5.) The laugh will quickly be turned upon them; for *surely He scorns the scorners.* The doctrine of Christ's Divinity, which is now to them a trifle, will be a solemnity, when they have no company to divert the thought, and no riot to drown it. You may have partners enough when you *deny* his perfection, but you must be alone when you come to *feel* it. *Of what punishment shall they be thought worthy who have trodden under foot the Son of God, and counted the blood of the covenant an unholy thing, and done despite to the Spirit of grace? It is a fearful thing to fall into the hands of the living God.* These free-thinkers are no friends for a death-bed, but leave a poor soul to tug and toil with that which they have taught him to defy. Like a blown deer, when he is marked by the huntsman, he is neglected and driven out by the rest of the herd; he has sported with *them,* but they will not run with *him.*

<small>Prov. iii. 34.</small>

<small>Heb. x. 29. 31.</small>

(6.) Let us be faithful to a glorious cause, that gives us an abhorrence of these methods; act worthy of the truth, *without partiality, and without hypocrisy. Follow righteousness, faith, charity, and peace, with them that call upon the Lord out of a pure heart.* The day is at hand that will *declare every man's work, of what sort it is, for it shall be revealed by fire.* Those notions bid the fairest for being right that have yielded the most comfort upon a death-bed. Enquire then how *they* have believed, who were *more than conquerors* in the last and great battle, and went off *rejoicing in hope of the glory of God; whose faith follow, considering the end of their conversation.*

<small>2 Tim. ii. 22.</small>

<small>1 Cor. iii. 13.</small>

<small>Heb. xiii. 7.</small>

SERMON LVIII.

Aug. 28. 1720.

HAVING thus considered the laſt account that is given of our *Great God and Saviour*, that he was *received into glory;* and anſwered *the perverſe diſputings of men of corrupt minds, who are deſtitute of the truth;* I now paſs on to the

III. General head, which is, to conſider this branch of our religion, as I have done all the reſt, under the notion of *a myſtery*, and what is without controverſy a *great* one. What we mean by this you have heard already:

Firſt, That it is a thing which has been kept ſecret, and to this character the whole doctrine of Chriſtanity agrees. It was ſcarcely known at all to the Gentiles, and with a mixture of confuſion and darkneſs among the Jews. Hence it is called *a myſtery which has been hid from ages and generations, but now is made manifeſt to the ſaints, to whom God would make known what is the riches of the glory of this myſtery.* Thus, the ſame Apoſtle tells us, that *God by his revelation made known to him the myſtery;* and he ſpeaks of *his knowledge in the myſtery of Chriſt, which in other ages was not made known to the ſons of men, as it is now revealed unto the holy Apoſtles and Prophets by the Spirit.* And the deſign of the Goſpel is *to make all men ſee what is the fellowſhip of the myſtery, which from the beginning of the world has been hid in God.* And again, we read of *the revelation of the myſtery which has been kept ſecret ſince the world began, but now*

SERM. 58.

Col. i. 26, 27.

Eph. iii. 3, 4, 5.

ver. 9.

Rom. xvi. 25, 26.

is

is manifest, and, by the commandment of the everlasting God, made known to all nations for the obedience of faith.

Secondly, It must be of such a nature, as to extend itself beyond the comprehension of our reasons: *O the depth of the riches both of the wisdom and knowledge of God! how unsearchable are his judgments, and his ways past finding out!* So we read of *the love of Christ that passes knowledge.*

Many people contend for this as the only notion of a mystery, that it is a secret, and therefore when it comes to be known, the title ought to be dropt. And indeed according to their way of reasoning, my text is guilty of an impropriety in language. It should by no means have been delivered in this form, that the mystery of godliness *is* great, but that it *was* so; and the Apostle referred to no more than the vail that was thrown upon it; not the substance of what we do know, but the circumstance of our *not knowing* it, makes it be called a mystery. And thus it may have its name, and be spoken of with all this wonder, not for the sake of what it contains, but merely because of those *times of ignorance* that held so long upon the whole world.

But, in vain do men depart from the words of truth and soberness. The Holy Ghost tells us what the doctrine of godliness *is*, not what it *was*; how justly it is admired by all those to whom God has revealed it; and does not call it a mystery from the stupidity of such as never heard the joyful sound. It is, saith he, a great mystery ὁμολογεμένως: we translate it, *without controversy;* but it signifies the joint profession that the people of God have ever made. They agree to be united witnesses upon this head. Whatever others may think of it, yet where divine grace has made a conquest, it never fails to give this doctrine a testimony; every one that believes it will own it. There is

not

not only *the faith of God's elect,* but *an acknow-* ⟨SERM. 58.⟩
ledging of the truth which is after godliness. So ⟨Tit. i. 1.⟩
that we have the voices of Christians in all ages
and places founding it forth, with the same confession, *Great is the mystery of godliness.*

Thirdly, By a mystery, as the word is applied
to religious matters, we understand something that
is *revealed,* and which we are sure the Great God ⟨Rom. xvi. 25.⟩
has told us. It is not for us to give out a com-
pany of *cunningly devised fables,* and pass them off
for mysteries; no, that is a profane imposture,
striking equally at the omniscience of God, and the
liberties of men. How incomprehensible soever
any doctrine may be, yet that the Holy Spirit has
declared it, is a matter that ought to be clear and
open. It is no reason that you should believe any
thing from us, because we have strong imaginations
that it is true. There are *foolish prophets who fol-* ⟨Ezek. xiii. 2.⟩
low their own spirit, and have seen nothing.

The more wonderful any doctrine is, the greater
evidence should we have of its being revealed.
And this is the way that God has taken with respect to the Christian religion. As there is something in the nature of it that exceeds all our imagination, we ought to be very sure that it comes
from heaven. To this purpose did God train up
the Jews in an unaccountable devotion, because
it was to be the emblem and figure of an unaccountable gospel. It was *a shadow of good things* ⟨Col. ii. 17.⟩
to come, but the body was Christ. They were to do
things they knew not *why,* in regard to what
should be brought about they knew not *how.* The
ark, and the mercy-seat above it, was a token of
the Divine presence among them. When David
brought these to Mount Zion, he cries out, *Arise,
O Lord, into thy rest, thou and the ark of thy
strength.*

And to what purpose did he appoint among them
such a little symbol of a great and glorious privi-

lege, but in view of this, that *the Word should be made flesh*, and take up his tabernacle among us? Why had they all their sacrifices, divers washings, and carnal ordinances, but with regard to an atonement that should be made for sin, and the great sanctification that we have from the Holy Spirit? The Jews knew by their religion that something mysterious was to come after it; and when Christ appeared, whose name was *Wonderful*, they could then see, that all the devotions they had been employed in were to fix the hope of their fathers upon Him.

So that God had abundantly testified to the truth of our religion, both in the former and latter dispensations. The language of them both was, that he would make known to the world things that could never have been invented, and which, now they are revealed, can never be explained. Such a mystery is this part of our religion, that Christ was received into glory. There is a great deal in it that leads us beyond our depth; we are lost in the delicious wonder; but then at the same time it is matter of plain revelation.—I shall here,

1. Lay before you some few of the mysteries that we find in this branch of the Christian religion.

2. Answer the objection that is made against it on the account of its being a *mystery*.

1. There are many wonders that a serious mind can observe in Christ's being received to glory. Such as these: It is strange that he who was so helpless and desolate should quickly after be possessed of all the fulness of heaven. It is farther wonderful, that he who seemed abandoned by God, the object of his wrath and justice, should be taken into so much favour; that he who was deserted by men and Angels, is now the head of influence and government to them both; and that a suffering

fering nature, which was made to die, should be united to one which is eternal and unchangeable. *SERM. 58.*

(1.) We may behold and wonder, that Christ who was so helpless and destitute should be possessed of all the fulness above. There is no similitude between his condition in the two worlds: *He was dead, but he is alive for evermore, and has the keys of hell and death.* Here below, *the Son of man had not where to lay his head,* and now he is *made higher than the heavens.* He bore upon him all the marks of an unhappy yielding nature; he suffered it to be poor and **miserable;** but *out of his fulness we are to be made rich; for he ascended up far above all heavens, that he might fill all things.* *Rev. i. 18. Luke ix. 58. Heb. vii. 26. Eph. iv. 10.*

Could any one imagine, that the characters of the same person should be so extreme, *Ye killed the Prince of life!* that one, under the notion and fate of a malefactor, should be a Prince; and not only so, but that his empire,—the gift of his power, the grant of his authority and love,—should be *life! I give to them,* saith he, *eternal life, and they shall never perish.* How strange is it to read of their crucifying the Lord of glory! that he, whom they hauled along with contempt and cruelty, should have the whole disposal of the future world! *In the days of his flesh he offered up prayers and supplications, with strong crying and tears, learning obedience by the things that he suffered;* but now *being made perfect from his sufferings, he is the author of eternal salvation to all that obey him.* *Acts iii. 15. Joh. x. 28. 1 Cor. ii. 8. Heb. v. 7, 8, 9.*

How amazed was Pilate when he put the question, *Art thou a king then? q. d.* Does captivity answer such a name as that? This he enquired upon our Lord's telling him, *My kingdom is not of this world; if it were, then would my servants fight; but now is my kingdom not from hence.* It was strange language out of the mouth of a person deserted by his friends, and pursued by his enemies to the very gates of death; and yet it is all true, *John xviii. 37.*

for

SERM. 58. for he was a King: *He whom man despised, and the*
Isa. xlix. 7. *nation abhorred, the servant of rulers,* was assured
that *kings should see and arise, princes also should worship.*

They that met him when he rode to Jerusalem,
John xii. cried, *Hosannah, blessed is the King of Israel that*
13. 15. *cometh in the name of the Lord;* as it was foretold,
*Fear not, daughter of Zion, behold thy King cometh
sitting on an ass's colt.* Though he hung upon the
cross, and heard them say, *Himself he cannot save,*
yet he was then within a few moments of an em-
Eph. i. 21. pire and dominion that should set him *above every
name that is named, both in this world and that
which is to come:* As Daniel was told in his vision,
Dan. vii. that *one like to the Son of man came in the clouds of*
13, 14. *heaven to the Ancient of days; and there was given
him dominion and glory and a kingdom, that all people, nations and languages, should serve him; his dominion is an everlasting dominion, which shall not
pass away, and his kingdom that which shall not be
destroyed.*

Indeed these extremes may well be accounted
for, because he submitted to the infelicities of this
life on purpose to *put away sin by the sacrifice of
himself;* and when that was done, the necessity of
humiliation being all over, *he for ever sat down at
the right-hand of the Majesty on high.* But who
could ever imagine that the same person, who calls
himself *a worm,* should have before him a greatness that would shew him to be a God!

His disciples themselves knew not how to conceive of this. They attended him with love and
wonder quite through his ministry, *they followed
him in the regeneration;* but when he came *to die,*
they scarcely thought it consistent with the glory
of his own person, or the redemption of Israel
that was expected from him. Had they thought
that going after him to the cross was putting
themselves into the train of a King, they would

not

not have forsaken him and fled. But though he was then *departing out of the world to the Father*, returning back to Him that sent him, throwing off mortality and all its incumbrances, yet that was more than they imagined. As Christ tells Peter, *Whither I go, thou canst not follow me now, but thou shalt follow me afterwards.* They could neither look beyond the cross nor above it. That unhappy lot was the farthest bound of their meditations, and so *they scattered every man to his own, and left him alone.* God had then hid from them what would be their joy and conviction another day; though *he was crucified in weakness, he must be raised in power.*

SERM. 58.

John xiii. 36.

2 Cor. xiii. 4.

A little distance of time brought them to reconcile these things in their thoughts, which they imagined would never come together in nature. They speak of them in the same breath: *The God of our fathers has glorified his Son Jesus, whom ye took and hanged on a tree. That same Jesus whom ye crucified has God made both Lord and Christ. Ye denied him in the presence of Pilate, when he was determined to let him go; and we are his witnesses, and so is the Holy Ghost, whom God has given to all that obey him.*

Acts v. 30, 31.
—— ii. 36.
—— iii. 13.

Is not here a mystery, that he in whom our nature was at the lowest, the greatest instance of abasement that ever lived in the world, that in him the same nature should have all its perfections! that though his body was the most abused, and his soul under the heaviest pressure of grief and wrath, yet each of these should be *full of joy with the light of God's countenance!* that a soul plunged into *hell* should *not be left* there, and a body under the empire of corruption should *see no corruption!* that under this hell, and in view of this corruption, God *shewed him the path of life!* that in going to die, he was but going to live! that he entered into hell, into all the anguish that his soul could feel,

not

not to stay there! that he made the grave his road to heaven! that the path of death was to him the path of life! and what he called an absence from God, was the means of a presence with him! These are mysteries that swarm and croud in upon us; they are too wonderful, and so high, that we cannot attain unto them: *Blessed be the Lord God, the God of Israel, who only does wondrous things; and blessed be his glorious name for ever, and let the whole earth be filled with his glory.*

Psal. lxxii. 18, 19.

(2.) It is more mysterious, if we consider this glory as an act of God's favour to a person who was lately under his wrath. The enemies of our Lord's divinity do not love to have us talk of these matters; and the reason is plain, because as bearing the indignation of the Lord is more than a mere creature could do, and therefore supposes him to be *God's fellow*, so the troubles he underwent not being on his own account, it leads us to consider the imputation of his righteousness to us, and of our sins to him.

And therefore one author who pretends to answer Mr Trofs's catechism is very premptory, that the Father was never angry with the Son; for which he gives this reason, he was always well pleased with him. It is pity that a man, who cannot himself distinguish in so plain a case, should presume that no other person is got above that stupidity. The Father was always well pleased with him as a Son, and a righteous servant; but does not the Scripture very often represent him as the object of a Divine justice? Can any words be fuller to this purpose, than that *God laid on him the iniquity of us all;* that *he made him to be sin for us who knew no sin;* that *it pleased the Father to bruise him, and put him to grief, and to make his soul an offering for sin;* that *he spared not his own Son, but gave him up for us all;* that *him he has set forth*

Isa. liii. 6, 10.
2 Cor. v. ult.
Rom. viii. 32.
— iii. 25.

forth to be a propitiation for our sins through faith in his blood.

When he prayed to be delivered from the cup that was put into his hand, and acquiesced at last in the divine disposal, those words, *Not my will, but thine be done,* shew what the will of the Lord was, that *by this will we should be sanctified through the offering of the body of Jesus once for all.* Hence we read that *to redeem us from the curse of the law, he himself became a curse for us; as it is written, Cursed is every one that is hanged on a tree.* In the place from whence we have this passage, it is said, *He that is hanged is accursed of God.*

Thus has the Holy Ghost represented him to us as bearing the wrath of the Almighty, and suffering our whole punishment. No wonder that his enemies looked upon him as *one stricken, smitten of God, and afflicted.* David as his prophet and his type speaks of this case, that the wicked would say, *Let us persecute and take him, for God has forsaken him; he trusted in God that he would deliver him; let him deliver him, seeing he delighted in him;* or as our Evangelist tells the story, *for he said, I am the Son of God.* But God was so far from owning him, that himself complains, as the Psalmist had done several ages before: *My God, my God, why hast thou forsaken me?* and as it is there added, *Why art thou so far from the words of my roarings?*

And yet this person, so forlorn, and accursed, was the favourite of heaven! What he endured was a punishment with respect to us, and a merit in himself; and therefore what he received was properly a reward. His miseries may be considered two ways; as to what is past, they are for the doing away of sin, the finishing transgression, the putting an end to iniquity; as to what is future, they are recommendation of him to the divine favour.

Here

SERM. 58.

John x. 15.

Here is the wonder; he cries to the Father for help, *If it be possible, save me from this hour.* The Father denies him this petition, and yet it is without any resentment on either side: *As the Father knows me, so I know the Father; I lay down my life for the sheep.* He has no uneasiness at the resolution that was passed for his dying; nor has the Father any contempt of him on account of the death he submitted to. Though he would not excuse him from drinking the cup that was put into his hand, yet he will give him a name above every name. He is not only received into a place of reward, but with the greatest love from the Father whom it once *pleased to bruise him and put him to grief.*

He that took delight in the sufferings of Christ, to whom his blood was a *sweet smelling savour,* rejoices in him as *a righteous servant,* and as the

ver. 17.

Son of his love, *in whom he will be glorified. Therefore does my Father love me, because I lay down my life that I might take it again.* Here then is the mind that hath wisdom; mystery and pleasure flow into us. No joy in Christ upon a throne, hindered him from being a sacrifice upon the cross; no punishment upon the cross, could hinder him from

Phil. ii. 8, 9.

being welcome back again to the throne: *Being found in fashion as a man, he humbled himself, and became obedient to death, even the death of the cross; wherefore God has highly exalted him, and given him a name above every name.*

(3.) You see, that he who was deserted by men and Angels, is now the head of influence and government to them both. He had little attendance in the former part of his life; Angels *came and ministred to him* in the wilderness, and the disciples continued with him in his temptations. He could have called in more than twelve legions of Angels to have prevented his death. He had one of them to strengthen him under his agony in the garden;

but

but we do not read that there were any of them in his last battle with the prince of this world. The disciples fled for fear, the Angels were held back by order, that he might *tread the wine-press alone*. They had no indifference to him, and no dread of the confederacy that was formed against him, but at that time he must be unassisted.

Now, this desolate person was afterwards to have his crowds; though he was hung between heaven and earth, as one that had no interest in either, yet he soon declared himself to be the Sovereign and the delight of both. When he died, nature itself groaned under a thick darkness. The sun was hid, the sky covered, the rocks rent, the graves opened, the earth shook, the temple unfolded, its vail torn at the fall of Him who was *greater than the Temple*.

But when this was over, he both gave and received a joy, both above and below; he carried a *glory to God in the highest*. We may suppose the Angels looking down, and hanging their heads over the cross whilst he suffered there. They might rejoice indeed in the great design of procuring peace on earth, and shewing so much good will towards men; but as far as we can judge of *their* nature by the softness of *our own*, when he bowed down his head and said, It is finished, they gave a shrink at the last breath of one whom they loved so well, and attended so long. And if we may imagine any such concern upon them, it was soon over, they were ready to receive a Lord that was lately sorrowful to death in the garden, and driven out by the pains of death upon the cross.

They would also guard his body in the sepulchre. They that had *disputed with the devil about the body of Moses*, would never suffer any insult upon that of Jesus. And may we not say, *Who is this that comes from Edom, with his dyed garments from Bozrah, so glorious in his apparel? Wherefore is*

SERM. 58. *be so red in his apparel? Because he has trod the wine-press alone, and of the people there was none* Psal. xlvii. *with him.* But behold him in his return, *The Lord* 5. *goes up with a shout, our God with the sound of a trumpet.*

He went to heaven *to fill all things.* Angels are the better for him. *He reconciles them in heaven*, not by bringing them from a state of enmity, but he confirms them in a state of friendship, and therefore calls himself *the Lord God of the holy Angels.* He maintains the great pomp of that world. Heaven itself is only what he makes it. Filling all things supposes in him such a perfection, that nothing greater can be said of any being, and it expresses *the fulness of him who fills all in all.* Nay, from thence he fills his Church upon earth with light and grace. *He receives gifts for men;* he conveys these gifts to them; and whilst he thus makes them grow, *they increase with the increase of God.*

(4.) It is another mystery, that a suffering nature is united with that which is eternal and unchangeable. The Scripture ofttimes speaks, under the characters of one nature, of those actions that must be attributed to another. Thus, when we read of a *God* purchasing a Church with *his own blood*, the meaning is this, that He who is God took upon him a bleeding nature, by which he was capable of making this purchase.

Now here is a wonder, that in our blessed Saviour we see a part that was liable to shame, torment and death, and yet at the same time we are to conceive of him as one eternally above all those things: not only God, but unchangeably so, blessed, and that for ever, without any interruption to his felicity. His days on the earth were a shadow, and yet he is without beginning of days and end of years. He was *tossed to and fro as a locust, his strength became as a potsherd*, and yet he is the

same

same person to-day and for ever. He never wanted a glory, and yet he is received into it. The Divine Nature is without any variableness or shadow of turning. To talk of giving *that* a happiness, or of taking any away from it, is blasphemy; and yet he had a joy set before him, which he was not then arrived to, and after he had endured the cross, and despised the shame, *he sat down at the right-hand of God.*

These are no contradictions, you will understand them of different natures; but it is very mysterious that God should be with us; that He whose dwelling is not with flesh, should take part of the same that we have; and that He who has said, *To whom will you compare me and make me equal,* should in all things be made *like unto his brethren.* That He who as a Creator is our Father, as a Redeemer should be the First-born among many brethren. Well may his name be called *Wonderful,* when a Child born is the Mighty God, and a Son given the Everlasting Father!

2. I promised to consider what men, in the vanity of their minds, have urged against this doctrine merely because it is a mystery: So that what the people of God in all ages have confessed with pleasure, they would have us ashamed of. There are two absurdities that are often used by way of insult:

First, A flat denial that there are any mysteries in religion. This indeed makes clear work with all revelation at once, and is in effect a limiting of the Holy One of Israel, a prescribing to God what he shall tell us, and making our wisdom a standard to his. It is calling His counsels to our bar, and pronouncing sentence upon what He saith, whether it is true or false, though we mean no more by it than intelligible or unintelligible.

Secondly, There is another craft by which some people think to carry their cause, and that is putting

ting us upon an explication of what we have called a myſtery; which is only a trick to make us deſtroy what we are building up. Thus does a certain author pretend to put off every argument that is brought for the Trinity, by teaſing queſtions: 'Why will they not tell us,' faith he, 'whe-
'ther by three perſons they mean three infinite minds
'or not,' which is an expreſſion of undetermined ſignification. If he that puts the queſtion will tell us whether he means by three minds three Gods, he knows, and ſo do all mankind, it would be anſwered in the negative; and yet he can allow himſelf to ruſh through all evidence, and go on, without either truth or ſhame, to aſſert that we are ſetting up the tritheiſtical doctrine, *i. e.* that we maintain three Gods. I ſhall be never the more perſuaded that theſe people give us the true meaning of God's words, who are reſolved at all hazards to pervert what they know to be the ſenſe of *ours.*—But,

(1.) Denying that there are things unintelligible in Chriſtianity, and reducing our faith to what we can explain, is giving countenance to a humour in religion that we ſhould be aſhamed of everywhere elſe. What would a mathematician or any artiſt think of me, when he has ſurpriſed me with a certain fact, if I ſhould ſay it is impoſſible, becauſe to me it is inconceivable! That the thing is done I ſee, but how it is brought about I do not know; and ſo it is here. I may be ſure that God has told me ſuch things, though I cannot by ſearching find them out.

(2.) That other way of putting us upon explications of a doctrine which we ſay is a myſtery, is an argument that theſe men *know nothing*, but love to *dote about queſtions and ſtrifes of words.* How ridiculous would this be in any other caſe! As for example, ſuppoſe the queſtion is, Whether Lazarus was raiſed from the dead or no? We affirm it, on-

1 Tim. vi. 4.

ly upon the report of a hiſtory which we know to be true; that it is there laid down in words eaſy to be underſtood. Now, there can be no anſwer to this, but to ſhew us, either that we have miſtaken the narrative, or ought not to truſt it. But how vain would it be for any one, inſtead of replying this way, to flirt upon us with ſuch queſtions as theſe authors uſe concerning the Trinity, and argue in this manner, Will they not tell us what became of Lazarus's ſoul? Was it in heaven? If ſo, it muſt be a loſer in coming back again. Or was it in hell? That opinion is as bad. Or was it in a ſeparate ſtate? That leads us into an Antichriſtian folly. Or was it not parted from his body? Then he could not be dead:—Now, what is all this to the purpoſe, when the queſtion is not, *how* it came about, but whether the thing is true in fact? Cannot I believe that Lazarus died and roſe again, without pretending to account for what was never written? And juſt ſo it is in the other caſe.

SERMON LIX.

Sept. 11. 1720.

I HAVE now only one thing more for your ſervice from this great ſubject, and that is,

IV. To conſider the Deity of Chriſt, who was thus manifeſt in the fleſh, and *received up into glory*, as it is a doctrine of godlineſs, and deſigned to promote a religion that is pure and undefiled before

SERM. 59. God and our Father. We must *obey from the heart*
Rom. vi. *that form of sound doctrine into which we are deli-*
17, 18. *vered.* We are the *servants of righteousness.* We
2 Thes. ii. are *chosen to salvation, through sanctification of the*
13. *Spirit, and belief of the truth,* and purify our souls
1 Pet. i. 22. *in obeying the truth through the Spirit.*

I have shewn you, under the several heads of Christianity that are collected in this text, that the truth contained in it is of a practical nature. By the belief of these things, men have lived in duty, and died in peace. I shall therefore in these arguments give my thoughts a new turn, and shew you how it is a mystery of godliness, under the distribution that the Apostle gives us. The three graces he mentions are all employed, enlarged, confirmed and refreshed, by our receiving this testimony, that HE who is spoken of in these words is truly GOD.

These are, as we read in that well-known place,
1 Cor. xiii. *faith, hope,* and *charity.* They are not opposed to
15. one another, as some vain men for their own ends do presume to insinuate. There is no charity but what grows out of faith, and there is no faith but
Col. i. 4. what grows into charity. We read of *faith in the*
2 Thes. i. 3. *Lord Jesus, and love to all the saints,* and that *your faith grows exceedingly, and the charity of every one of you all towards each other aboundeth.* There is no more contradiction between these two than between the root and the branches. God has joined them together, and it must be a sad confounding work for men to put them asunder.

I take these three in their more extended notion to include the whole work of the Spirit upon our souls, and the exercise of them to comprehend our whole duty to God in the world. Whatever he does in us may be reduced to some of these heads, and whatever we do for him is only bringing forth into life what he has given us in principle.

Now you will find, that there either can be no existence of faith, hope, and charity, or no use of

3   them,

them), and no benefit by them, but what has either regard to, or a deduction from the Deity of Him who was manifest in the flesh. *Whoever believes that Jesus is the Christ, is born of God; and he that loves him that begat, loves him also that is begotten of him; and whatever is born of God overcomes the world: who is he that overcomes the world, but he that believes that Jesus is the Son of God?* If he is not God, it is in vain that our faith regards his person, that our hope depends upon his promise, and our charity rejoices in his people. Every one of these graces does not only suppose that we have a revelation concerning Christ, but that this revelation tells us of his Divinity, as you will see by distributing your thoughts under the particular heads that I have now mentioned.

1. I begin, as the Apostle himself does, with your FAITH: This he makes to be the first of the three. And though some in a little spurt of wit tell us, that they know no other trinity but faith, hope, and charity; yet if their faith was right, they would know another Trinity, that is, they would receive what God has proclaimed concerning himself in the Holy Scriptures. But in the way that many of them go on, they are in great danger of knowing another trinity, *The lust of the flesh, the lust of the eyes, and the pride of life.*

I shall here take *faith* in such a view, as to keep it distinguished from hope; for we often confound them in our descriptions. What is said of one does equally belong to another. But under the head of faith, I would desire you to take these three particulars; our assent to the revelation that God has given us, our profession of this to the world, and our duty and devotion to Him in whom we believe. These things belong to faith, as it is different from the hope that is in us. Now you will find upon a just examination, that without a regard to the Deity of Christ, we may be at a loss in every one

of

of the particulars that I have mentioned. If we do not own him to be God, we neither assent to the revelation, nor can we make an honest confession of him to the world, nor is it possible we should be clear in the acts of worship and duty.

(1.) One thing contained in that faith that is the principle of every good man, and that leads him into all his practice, is, that he can rest himself upon *the record that God has given of his Son*. He reads and subscribes *to the witness of God*, the testimony that we have in Scripture. And the work of faith upon this head is to silence all the mutterings of carnal reason, and bring down every high thought to captivity and obedience.

Our minds are as unsanctified as our wills: We may as well pretend to a natural holiness as a natural wisdom. The Spirit of God is to *enlighten the eyes of our understanding*, as well as make us feel the power of his grace in our hearts, and the sweetness of it in our affections. And till he has produced upon us a glorious change, as our corruptions rise against the commands of God, so does our ignorance against his doctrines: The one we reckon bondage, the other foolishness. *The natural man receives not the things of the Spirit of God, for they are foolishness to him, neither can he know them, because they are spiritually discerned.* It is a dreadful account that we have of the *carnal mind, that it is enmity against God, and is not subject to the law of God, neither indeed can be.* Now divine grace teaches us our duty. It shews us that such a work must be done, though it be against all the temper of human nature, and such a truth must be received, though it be against all its dictates. *We receive not the spirit of the world, but the Spirit which is of God, that we may know the things that are freely given to us of God.*

Believing a mystery is a branch of self-denial, as well as complying with a precept. We have as much

much to say against taking up our cross that he has prescribed, as against any doctrine that he has revealed. The account he gave of himself was this: *As the living Father has sent me, and I live by the Father, so he that eateth me, even he shall live by me; this is the bread that came down from heaven; not as your fathers did eat manna, and are dead; he that eats of this bread shall live for ever.—Many therefore of his disciples, when they heard this, said, This is a hard saying, who can bear it? When Jesus knew that his disciples murmured at it, he said to them, Does this offend you? But there are some of you that believe not; therefore said I unto you, that no man can come unto me, except it were given him of my Father.*

It is no more unnatural for me to say, that one is three, and three are one, than to hate father and mother, and life itself, for the sake of the Gospel. There is nothing more shocking in any mystery than there is in such a command. But faith rubs through the difficulty, by saying, This is the word of a God that cannot lie, and therefore it is true; this is the will of a God who gives no account of his matters, and therefore it must be done. Reason has as full an obligation in the one case as it has in the other. How can He who appeared in the flesh be God? How is it possible there should be but one supreme eternal being, and yet the same things be said with equal fulness of the Father, Son, and Holy Ghost.

Certainly, say they, ' this can never be the
' meaning of the revelation; our religion must be
' reducible to common sense; God will never tell
' us contradictions; and what have we our reasons
' for, but to judge whether the proposition is true
' or no?'

You will see that this argument is owing to a want of faith, or an acquiescence in a doctrine purely upon a divine testimony; that if we really did believe what God saith, merely because he has said it, these objectious would be all disarmed: and *that* you will soon perceive, if you do but turn the force of this reasoning upon the practice of self-denial.

Has not a martyr, or one who for the sake of Christ suffers the loss of all things, as much to say against the troubles of life, as we can oppose to the mysteries of faith? may he not plead just as the others do? Thus,

' Has the God of nature obliged me to save my
' life, and am I taught by Christianity to think
' that it may be my duty to lose it? what! is our
' religion a heap of contradictions? Has Christ
' ever spoken of *that* with reputation in his Gospel,
' which is a breach of the sixth commandment in
' the Law? Does grace root out the very first prin-
' ciple of nature, which is self-preservation?' That three cannot be one, is no more a maxim than self-preservation is a principle with human nature; and I can as soon *believe* what God tells me contrary to the former, as I can *do* what he bids me when it is destructive of the latter.

Now, as faith saith I must do the duty that God calls me to, without asking *why;* so it equally saith, I must believe every doctrine that he has revealed, without asking *how* these things can be. The reason of this absolute surrender of the understanding and the will, is plain; because, as I know God is infinitely good, he will do nothing wrong, and therefore his ways are gracious, though I may not see them; so God that is infinitely wise, will say nothing false, though at present I cannot explain it: *What if some did not believe? shall their unbelief make the faith of God of none effect? God forbid: yea, let God be true, and every man a liar; as it is written, That thou mightest be justified in thy sayings. Every mouth must be stopped, and all the world become guilty before God.*

Abraham

Abraham in his obedience went out *not knowing whither he went*, and in his faith *believed in hope and against hope*. This is faith, to believe every thing that God faith, upon his own word, as well as to do every thing that he orders, for his own fake. Any other ground of our affent to a doctrine than a divine teftimony, is not faith, but fomething elfe; and therefore to argue, I know not how to reconcile the divinity of the Son and Spirit to the unity of God, (fuppofing thefe things to be clearly laid down in Scripture), is the rebellion of unbelief; it is the principle that *exalts itfelf againft the knowledge of God*, it is the foam of a carnal mind.

(2.) Without thinking that HE is God who was manifeft in the flefh, we cannot make a fair and undifguifed profeffion to the world. The Scripture has laid a great deal of weight upon this: *If thou believe in thy heart, and confefs with thy mouth, thou fhalt be faved; for with the heart man believes unto righteoufnefs*. Our intereft in the righteoufnefs that God has provided, our application to it, and dependence on it, is all with the heart; but *with the mouth confeffion is made to falvation*. Our falvation is concerned in what we *fay*, as well as in what we *think*. It is not enough that your hearts are filled with an efteem of Chrift, and employed in a reliance upon him, but there muft be a confeffion with the mouth.

God has called the tongue *your* glory; and he has given it on purpofe that it may be engaged for his. It was foretold that this would be the effect of Gofpel doctrine and Gofpel grace, that *one fhould fay, I am the Lord's, and another fhould call himfelf by the name of Jacob, and a third fhould fubfcribe with his hand to the Lord God of Ifrael:* that is, they would take all the ways that could be to publifh the name of the Lord, to make known his mighty acts among the fons of men, to fpeak of

the

the glory of his kingdom, and triumph in all his praise. As carnal reason would persuade us not to glorify the Christian doctrine, so carnal interest has as much to say against our confessing it. Our Lord knew all this, and therefore warns us against *denying him before men.* The Apostle, though he was very careful of Timothy's health, yet tells him, he must *not be ashamed* either *of the testimony of Christ,* or of one that was *his prisoner, but be a partaker of the afflictions of the Gospel by the power of God.*

Now, he that believes that Jesus is God has not only the ground of a good confession, but the method of a clear and distinct one; he both knows *why* and *what* to say. The Scripture has filled his mouth with arguments, that the Child born is the everlasting Father, and the Son given, the mighty God; that He who was made of *the seed of David* is over all *God blessed for ever.* In this doctrine he makes a stand; it is above the reach of his thoughts indeed, but it is what God has told him. And he can never think the Scripture would have worded these things with so little caution, that by it we should be taught to *speak* of the Son as we do of the Father, as if they were of one nature, and yet *conceive* of them as if they were of two.

Thus a Christian is at a point. This, as our Lord tells Peter, is the *rock upon which he would build his church;* and *the gates of hell* have not yet prevailed against it. Those gates have opened all ways, and poured out their forces with a prodigious variety; sometimes denying the unity of God, and sometimes the trinity of persons; and yet the Church stands, and so does the truth, just where Christ has left it. We may call this, as he

1 Pet. ii. 6.

does, a *tried foundation, and a sure corner-stone;* it has been tried above seventeen hundred years. If the batteries of impiety could have brought it down,

or

or the underminings of craft could have blown it up, we should have lost it long ago. But we are making that *good confession* now, which the Apostles and Prophets have witnessed before us.

There is nothing new *in the malice of the adversary;* they only revive exploded arguments and rotten heresies, that have no more of antiquity than the stench of it; and there is nothing new *in our cause*; we contend for no more than the faith once delivered to the saints; it is as old as our religion, it was revealed when that began, and will be glorious when that is complete.

You will see the difficulty of making any profession, when people go off from the Deity of Christ; *their ways are moveable, none can know them*, as it is said of the adulteress, and may well be applied to those who *go a whoring from their God: Now they are without, now in the street, and now in every corner;* and when they are baffled in an argument, can *wipe their mouths, and say, We have done no evil.* [Prov. vii. 12. — xxx. 20.]

Sometimes they deny that Christ had any being before his incarnation, and any existence before his human nature. This was the error of Samosatenus, which Socinus revived with a few alterations and amendments. That is now the abhorrence of our polite age; they own that he is above the Angels, and that he was before them; and because they resolve not to call their opinion by the name of Arianism, they rather choose to have it nonsense; *they* will not say he is a creature, nor allow *us* to say that he is a God; he is not produced by creation but emanation: He had a beginning, and yet there never was a time when he was not; that is, he both had a beginning and no beginning. So hard do men always find it to poise their own schemes, though they think it easy enough to see the faults of others.

What

What is it that these are witnessing a confession to who deny the Deity of Christ? what do they say of him? they answer indeed, that he cannot be God, equal to the Father and the Spirit, without making three gods; and therefore he must be distinct from the Father in nature, or otherwise you cannot secure the unity of the Godhead. Well, what is he then? a God he cannot be in the supreme sense of the word, a creature he must not be. Does he derive from the Father? they tell us, yes. Was he ever underived? they tell us, no; because the Scripture sets no time for that derivation. If we ask them, Is he self-existent? they deny it. Is he necessarily existent? they will not own it; for, as a learned person observes, Self-existence is a word with two faces, one to oblige friends, and the other to keep off enemies.

We are obliged by Christianity to make some profession of our Lord, *not to be ashamed of him and his words;* and what can we say when we throw up his Deity? we are like a tree that is loose at the root, that can stand no longer than till it is tried. A Jew asks, if he was any more than a man? we say, yes. An Atheist asks, if he is a God? we say, no. He replies, why is he called so? we tell him, he has only the name in a subordinate sense. He takes the same way to expound what is said of the Father, that we do upon those places that refer to the Son, and by our own handle of argument, he tells us flatly that the Scripture declares no supreme God at all.

No wonder that persons who go off from this doctrine are against any profession, when their scheme leaves them so unable to make one: *A double minded man is unstable in all his ways.* They may give our practice, as long as they please, the hard names of inquisition, Popery, and bondage, but the infelicity arises from within. Asking for their faith is only rummaging into their confusion.

Though

Though they seem to be so very clear in the point what *Chrift* is *not*, yet they are all in the briers when you ask them *what he is*. So that their profeffion is a fort of *negative Chriftianity*; it goes no farther than to tell us what he is not; and all this while, though it is evident what they witnefs *againft*, yet no mortal can tell what it is they witnefs *to*.

Is it to his being a creature? no, they say that is blafphemy. Is it to his being neither God nor creature? all mankind will say that is nonfenfe. If they say they cannot tell what his exiftence is, that it is between a creation and a fupremacy, that a being may be from another, and yet not made by him, this is a myftery. Thus they are driven to that as a refuge, which they object to us as a crime. They will not allow us to say that Chrift is both God and man, that there is an union between the two natures, which we cannot explain but yet believe; and now they are forced to take the fame way in maintenance of their own fcheme. A trinity in unity is no more a contradiction than a fubordinate God, or a derived eternal. I can as foon believe an union between the divine and human natures, as I can believe a medium between a fupreme and a created nature; and if I muft not pretend to account for the latter, I may be excufed in adoring the former.

(3.) I told you that there muft and will be, where there is a true faith in Chrift, a life of duty and devotion *to him*: I say, TO HIM, not only *by* him as he is Mediator, but *to* him, as he is the object of thefe applications. We *call on the name of the Lord Jefus Chrift*, as well as on the Father, through the Son and by the Spirit; and how fhall we call on his name, and fo be faved, if he is not God? *How fhall they call on him in whom they have not believed?*

Believing in any one is the great homage of our fouls to him; it is doing our all for him, it is trufting

SERM. 59. ing our souls with him; and can this faith and hope be in any less than a God? it is making him the centre and the end of all our duties: *To that end Christ both died, and rose again, and revived, that he might be the Lord both of dead and living. No man of us lives to himself, and none dies to himself:* no; but *if we live, we live unto the Lord, and if we die, we die in the Lord; so that living or dying we are the Lord's.* He means neither less nor more in this profession, than what he saith, in another place: *To me to live is Christ.* They live to Him that died for them and rose again.

Rom. xiv. 7, 8, 9.

Phil. i. 21.

If a person is doing all this to a creature, or to one who by nature is no God, what has he left for Him who is the supreme and governing cause? Is there an infinite distance between the Father and Son in themselves, and is there to be none in our devotion? There is a curse upon him who makes flesh his arm, and whose heart *departs from the Lord;* and does Christianity lead us into such a departure? has the Gospel ensnared us? is that which is life in itself made death to us? God forbid.

Thus you see how loose we shall be in our devotions, how tremulous and wavering in all our practice, when once we let go our hold of *his* Deity who was manifest in the flesh. We shall either not worship him at all, as some of these writers tell us we should not; or we must do it with confusion, if we listen to those that say we should. And what a sad way must a man be in, about a practice that conscience tells him is needful, and criticism tells him is dangerous! In worshipping the Son, he is afraid of provoking the Lord to jealousy; in not doing it, he may fear the vengeance of his wrath when it begins to burn.

And it is commanded that all men honour the Son *as* they honour the Father. Some tell him that the word AS does *not signify* an equality; but that makes him no easier in his mind, and no more settled in his proceedings, unless they can tell him

what

what it *does signify*. It certainly includes fome- SERM. 59. thing, and people do him no good who do not politively determine *how much* there is in it. For if he muft not honour the Son equally with the Father, he may be either a rebel by giving too little, or an idolater by giving too much. And can that be a doctrine of godlinefs, that does not only confound people in their thoughts, but unhinge them in their practice?

They that tell you that Chrift is God and man, leave your way clear with refpect to duty. As man you are not to worfhip him at all, but confider him as a creature, as a dependent, as an example, as a facrifice; but as God you are to love him with all your heart, and foul, and mind, and ftrength, to call upon him, to believe in him, to live by him, to derive all the exiftence and growth of your religion from him: There is no difficulty in conceiving the nature and method of your practice. But the man that will not determine what Chrift *is*, is never like to determine what you muft *do*.

2. You may obferve the fame of your HOPE, that it regards the Divinity of Chrift. This is another of thofe graces that the Holy Spirit works in us; and in doing that, he teftifies of Him. 1*ft*, We reft our fouls upon his righteoufnefs. 2*dly*, We are fatisfied in the truth of his promifes. 3*dly*, We look to him for an everlafting life. Thefe things are fometimes called our hope, and fometimes our faith; faith fuppofes them to be *invifible*, and hope to be *future*.

(1.) We reft upon His righteoufnefs; and that we could never do, if he were not the fupreme God. I have no more concern in the death of Jefus, than in that of Mofes, if no more can be faid of him than that he was made of a woman and made under the law. But when he is faid to bring in *an everlafting righteoufnefs*, that takes into it a great deal more than the extremity of his fufferings: it was *by himfelf that he purged away our fins*. and

Vol. II.   3 C   therefore

therefore this is the name whereby he shall be called, JEHOVAH *our Righteousness*.

<small>SERM. 59.
Jer. xxii. 6.</small>

I own that some who deny his Divinity, say they trust in his death; but I should think those of the party talk with the greatest unity of sentiments, who strike at both; as it is well known the champions of their scheme have usually done.

They tell us, and that in a manner which is profane enough, that God might have accepted of what he pleased as the payment of our debt. This is bold unhallowed language, to say no worse of it. I should never dare to say that God *might have done* the reverse of what it *became him to do*. The Θεοπρέπεια* that the Apostle speaks of, ought to stop the mouths of gainsayers. We are not called to determine the necessity of his nature, especially since he has told us the resolution of his will; that *it became Him, for whom are all things, and by whom are all things, in bringing many sons to glory, to make the Captain of their salvation perfect through sufferings.*

<small>Heb. ii. 10</small>

It was more decent for him to pardon sinners upon a full price; and this no creature was able to pay. He that was originally under the law, as a servant, could not be made under it, as a sacrifice; and therefore He that became responsible for our debt, must have none of his own. He that put himself under the law, on purpose to make a merit of his doing so, must have been eternally above it; and that can be true of none but God.

(2.) We trust Him for our protection. He has given us promises: *In him they are yea, and in him, Amen. We are preserved in Christ Jesus, and called.*

<small>1 Cor. i. 20.
Jude 1.</small>

---

* It is difficult to convey the exact meaning of this word in English. What comes nearest to it, perhaps, is, " The " divine honour ;" or, " The divine beauty:" and it means here, " The infinite beauty and majesty of God, in acting " for ever in a manner becoming himself, and in per-" fect consistence with his own eternal honour and excel-" lence."

ed. Now, certainly we can be kept by no lefs than the *power of God through faith to falvation.* This is the ground of our adoration: *To Him that is able to keep us from falling;* that is, to the Lord Jefus, whofe mercy we look for to eternal life; to Him who can prefent us faultlefs before his glory with exceeding joy, *to the only wife God our Saviour, be dominion and praife for ever.* See the proportion there is between what we expect from him, and what we afcribe to him; between the blefling he gives to us, and the name that we give to him. We look upon him as one that keeps us; as Paul faith, *The Lord will preferve me from every evil work, and bring me to his heavenly kingdom.* Nay, it is He that fills the place we are going to; we are prefented *before his own glory.* And He that does thefe things can be no other than the only wife God our Saviour, and muft have no lefs than glory and dominion for ever.

(3.) We give up our fouls to Him in a dying hour. As that is the laft, fo it muft be the greateft act of our faith and hope; and in this it will be hard to fuppofe, that the Chriftian who has all along been *yielding himfelf to the Lord* fhould die believing in a creature. That it is to Chrift this furrender muft be made, I have often fhewn you: *Lord Jefus receive my fpirit,* faith the Martyr Stephen: *We look to Jefus as the author and finifher of our faith,* faith another: *I come quickly, and my reward is with me,* faith Chrift himfelf: *Amen, Even fo come Lord Jefus,* faith the Spirit in the name of every believer, with which he clofes the whole Book of God. The Bible begins with laying before us the creation of a God, the heavens and the earth; and it would be a flat ending to reprefent Him who faves that earth, and fills thofe heavens, as a derived agent. But as Chrift comes to do more than ever the creation was, fo we fhall be able to fay, *This our God is the God of falvation;* and it will be faid to Zion, *Thy* GOD *reigneth.*

SER.

SERMON LX.

Sept. 25. 1720.

SERM. 60.

1 Cor. xiii. 13.

ver. 1, 2, 3.

3. THERE is no room for the question, whether charity is not another of those graces that supplies our religion as a principle, and gives a glory to our practice before all the world. The Apostle has told us plainly, that though *there abide these three, faith, hope, and charity, yet the greatest of these is charity;* that, without it, *though we had all faith and could remove mountains, though we had all knowledge and could understand mysteries,* they would each of them *profit us nothing.* *Speaking with the tongue of men and Angels,* without charity, would make us only like *a sounding brass, and a tinkling cymbal;* all noise, and no harmony. Nevertheless, let me here observe to you a few particulars upon the notion that the Holy Scripture has given us of CHRISTIAN CHARITY.

(1.) It is sometimes used for the meek and humble temper of mind that we ought to have towards the whole world. We are bid to *honour all men,*

1 Pet. ii. 17.

and be ready to *do good to all as we have opportunity; giving no offence to any, either Jew or Gen-*

1 Cor. x. 32.

tile, or the Church of God; being *blameless and*

Phil. ii. 15.

harmless in the midst of a corrupt and perverse generation, among whom we are as lights in the world. This is indeed a needful and a noble part of the conversation that becomes the Gospel of Christ; but it does not express the meaning of that charity that is greater than faith and hope.

(2.) The

(2.) The word is often made to signify the forbearance of injuries to those from whom we have received them. That, though we see in our enemies no disposition to repentance, yet we must not say, *I will recompense the man as he has done to me; but wait upon the Lord, and he shall save us.* This does indeed demonstrate religion to be the ruling principle; for Saul made it a maxim that obtains among them who know not the grace of God, *If a man find his enemy, will he let him go well away?* But as our blessed Lord gives us a greater example than David did, so He has made it a perpetual branch of the royal law, *Not to render evil for evil, or railing for railing, but contrariwise, blessing;* for even Christ, *when he was reviled, reviled not again, and when he suffered, threatened not, but committed himself to Him that judges righteously. And so is the will of God, that with well-doing we may put to silence the ignorance of foolish men. Servants must be subject to their masters with all fear, not only to the good and gentle, but also to the froward; for this is thank-worthy, if a man for conscience toward God endure grief, suffering wrongfully.*

This also, though it is a necessary character in the people of God, cannot be the charity which is so much admired by the Apostle, and is of all this importance to every believer: for, he is not here describing a temper to enemies, but that which ought to breathe through all our behaviour to the saints: *As we are the body of Christ, and members in particular,* the charity we are to follow after is that which *may edify the Church.*

(3.) Charity does sometimes denote a readiness to forgive, and receive into favour, those who have abused us. This is different from what I mentioned under the former head; for there I designed no more than a not returning upon them their own iniquities, laying aside revenge; but it is a great deal more than this, when we will use them as friends,

SERM. 60. friends, and be reconciled to them, and so pass over the transgression as if it had never been, making those who have done us harm the men of our counsel and confidence. As Achish treated David, 1 Sam. xxvii. saying, *He has made his people Israel utterly to abhor him, therefore he shall be my servant for ever;* —xxviii. 2. and afterwards, *I will make thee keeper of my head.* This is what may be our duty, and, if we have tasted that the Lord is gracious, will be our pleasure. Mat. v. 44, 45. We are bid to *love those that hate us, bless them that curse us, and pray for them that despitefully use us, that we may be the children of our heavenly Father.* Now, these phrases are certainly to be taken two ways; we are by no means to confound them, but must distinguish upon the carriage of those who have done us injuries.

First, Some of these that have hated and cursed us, continue to do so. Now, here blessing and loving them, can mean no more than negatives, not cursing them, and not hating them, doing them no harm; or, if it calls us to any more, we do it to Rom. xii. 18, 19, 20, 21. reclaim them; according to that rule, *If it be possible, as much as in you lies, live peaceably with all men. Dearly beloved, revenge not yourselves, but rather give place unto wrath; therefore, if thine enemy hunger, feed him, if he thirst, give him drink; for in so doing, thou shalt heap coals of fire on his head: be not overcome of evil, but overcome evil with good.* Whilst they manifest no signs of repentance, I am indeed to remember that vengeance belongs to God, and must not avenge myself with my own hand; but it is impossible, under the violence of that wicked temper, that I should take any pleasure in such people. Nor does religion oblige me to do a thing so gross and foolish, as to put myself into their hands, in whom I see no disposition Psal. lv. 6, 7, 8. to peace. We should rather wish for *wings like a dove, that we may fly away, and be at rest, wander far off, and remain in the wilderness.* If an enemy reproaches

reproaches me, I muft hide myfelf from him: *God himfelf fhall hear and afflict them, even he that abides of old.* But then,

Secondly, Several of thofe who have curfed and hated us are afhamed of it; they confefs their faults, and defire to be reftored into that favour which either their imprudence or our impatience has made them lofe. Now here, *loving* thefe, and doing them good, takes into it a great deal more. We are to act to them as God does to us. He may *fpare* without repentance, but he never *pardons* without it. There may be *forbearance* and long-fuffering, but there is no *forgivenefs;* and in this he is a pattern to us.

Charity to thofe who have been injurious, and continue fo, is doing them no harm; but the charity that we fhould ufe to one who humbles himfelf, and is afflicted with a fenfe of the wrong that he has done, is of a more benevolent temper: *Let the righteous fmite me, and it fhall be a kindnefs; let him reprove me, and it fhall be an excellent oil, which fhall not break my head.* Praying for the former fort, is only that God may convince them, *fhew them their error that they have exceeded,* and grant them repentance. But when all this is done in them, praying for them is the fruit of brotherly love. A friendfhip thus reftored, is like a bone fet anew after it has been broken. Some fay it is ftronger and firmer than it was. Whether that be fo or no, I cannot tell; but thus it is in the cafe before us.

Two perfons whom the grace of God has reconciled, who have felt the bitternefs of quarrelling, and who come to underftand one another in a true light, are like to be more ufeful and endeared than ever they have been; becaufe the friendfhip rifes from a mortification of luft, from a fenfe of God's love to us, and fome exercife of ours to him. It is all godlinefs; and I can never think that Chriftians

stians either feel or shew a greater power of religion, than in their obedience to that command, *Confess your faults one to another,* **and** *pray one for another, that ye may be healed.*

Job and his friends had lived in a prosperous acquaintance for some years; high words pass between them, when his affliction had brought them together; and perhaps a great deal of crime in the conversation on both sides. He charges them with cruelty, they him with unbelief. *Elibu's wrath was kindled against Job, because he had justified himself rather than God; and against his three friends was his wrath kindled, because they had found no answer, and yet had condemned Job.* But observe how this ends: *God turns Job's captivity when he prays for his friends,* and he tells them that it was his prayer that should be accepted for them. What a happy close was this, of a debate that seemed to be strengthened on both sides, and never like to expire! they come to see that the man whom they accused of denying Providence, of speaking atheistical language, and uttering rebellion against God, must be their advocate at the Throne of grace; and he who complained of injuries by these people, must not have a blessing upon himself, till he has begged one for them.

This advantage can the grace of God teach us to make of the wiles of Satan. The friendship which piety restores, is a thousand times better than that which mere acquaintance begun. Onesimus was a relation to Philemon, and also a servant; but very ungrateful to the former character, and very disobedient to the latter: he runs away from his kinsman and his master; but the grace of God follows, and finds him when he was lost: a principle of religion sets all his thoughts in a toil to go back again. The Apostle, who had been his spiritual father, must be also his temporal peace-maker. The person by whom he was brought to God, is the
same

same that restores him to Philemon; and a noble [SERM. 60. Philemon, 15, 16.] argument he has in his pacific design: *Perhaps he therefore departed for a season, that thou shouldst receive him for ever; not now as a servant, but above a servant, a brother beloved, especially to me, but how much more unto thee, both in the flesh and in the Lord?* What the issue of this proposal was, we are not told; but I think the Apostle has given us ground for our confidence, in what he saith of his own: *Having confidence in thy obedience, I wrote* [ver. 21.] *unto thee, knowing that thou wilt also do more than I say.*

(4.) Charity is often used to signify no more than liberality or external beneficence, upon which I would desire you to take one observation, That though this is a needful part of charity, it is far from being the greatest thing in it. That it is necessary we are plainly told: *If any man have this* [1 John iii. 17.] *world's goods, and sees his brother have need, and shuts up his bowels of compassion from him, how dwells the love of God in that man?* there must be outward kindness to demonstrate inward compassions: *If a brother or sister be naked, and destitute* [Jam. ii. 15, 16.] *of daily food, and one of you say to them, Be thou clothed, and be thou warmed, and give them not those things that are needful to the body, what shall it profit?* It profits neither you nor them. *As you have* [Gal. vi. 10.] *opportunity, do good to all men, especially to the household of faith. It is a faithful saying,* and what [Tit. iii. 8.] we are to *affirm constantly, that they who believe in God be careful to maintain good works, which are good and profitable to men.* Rich men are not to be [1 Tim. vi. 17, 18, 19.] allured, desired, and importuned, but *charged to do good, to be ready to distribute, willing to communicate, laying up in store a good foundation for the time to come, laying hold on eternal life.*

Thus you see these external favours are necessary; but yet they are far from being the main thing in our charity, as you will soon find, if you do but consider, that the poor, who are *rich in faith, and heirs of the kingdom*, would be deficient in the best of all graces, if there was no charity but in *giving:* And, on the other hand, the Apostle has laid down a text, which ought to strike an awe quite through our souls: *Though I bestow all my goods to feed the poor, and give my body to be burned, and have not charity, it profits me nothing.*

What a tremendous proposition is here! that a man shall bestow all his goods on the poor, and yet not have charity! He may do this, as superstitious people have often done, without any love to God; he is only frighted into it by the darkness of an unsanctified conscience. This shews, that the grace we speak of lies within, and takes its name, not from what is in the *hands*, but from what is in the *heart*. Paul was as charitable as David or Solomon, not in what he gave, but in what he felt.

(5.) Charity, in this place, signifies that temper of mind that we should have to the people of God, considered in their religious character. It is more than a meekness to all the world, and a patience under injury: In the former, we regard people as men; in the latter, we strive to conquer them as enemies; but here we look upon them as *holy brethren, partakers of the heavenly calling*, as those *who have obtained like precious faith with us, through the righteousness of God our Saviour.*

If a person is no Christian, or no friend, we are to do him no harm; but he is not within the reach of that charity which the Apostle is writing of; for he lays it upon the ground of our Lord's own rule: *By this shall all men know that ye are my disciples, if ye have love one to another.* Certainly by this love to one another, he means a great deal more than the love of courtesy to mankind in general, or the love of pity to enemies. These would never shew them to be his disciples; that is, not *loving*

ving the brotherhood, loving as brethren. *Love one another, and this is love, that we walk after his commandments; and this is the commandment, that, as ye have heard from the beginning, ye should walk in it.* {SERM. 60. 1 Pet. ii. 17; —iii. 8. 1 Joh. 5, 6.}

Such a charity as this, is what the Holy Ghost produces in us; nor can we have it any other way than by an Almighty creation. It is not the peculiar of certain schemes, nor the prerogative of some opinions, but a personal grace. I may think as another does about the doctrines of the Gospel, and yet want his charity. If he has this grace, he is as much born to that as to any other principle. As his faith is of the operation of God, as he is filled with hope by the power of the Holy Ghost; so *the fruit of the same Spirit is love, joy, peace, gentleness, meekness, and patience.* It is only as *the elect of God, holy and beloved, that we put on bowels of mercies, humbleness of mind, meekness, long-suffering, forbearing one another, and forgiving one another; and above all, putting on charity, which is the bond of perfectness.* {Gal. v. 22. Col. iii. 12.}

It is the vanity of some schemes to make men talk of charity; but God leaves them deficient in that, on purpose to let all the world see, that none but he can give it. It is not engrossed by a party, as we cannot but own by observing, that where it is most talked of, it is least practised; like the people who were always bawling out, *The temple of the Lord, the temple of the Lord, the temple of the Lord are these,* who seemed in their disposition to be farthest from the temple; for they *swore, and killed, and committed adultery, and served Baal, and burned incense to other gods, and came into that holy place, saying, We are delivered to do all these abominations.* The Scripture has recommended no other charity than that which *suffers long and is kind, envies not, vaunts not itself, is not puffed up, does not behave itself unseemly, seeks not her own, is not easily provoked,* {Jer. vii. 4. 9, 10. 1.Cor. xiii. 4, 5, 6.}

provoked, thinks no evil, rejoices not in iniquity, but rejoices in the truth.

(6.) This grace, like all the rest, is imperfect in us now; and therefore that we may abound in it, we should use the means that are appointed. There must be a caution over our own hearts, *looking diligently, lest any man fail of the grace of God, and a root of bitterness spring up. Putting off the old man, which is corrupt according to the deceitful lusts, which are bitterness, wrath, anger, clamour, and evil-speaking;* these are to be *put away, with all malice; be kind to one another, tender-hearted, forgiving one another, even as God for Christ's sake has forgiven us.* Believe that the opposite to this is a lust of the flesh, and that Satan will do all he can to hinder us in it. He will allow us to make our boast of charity, or any other grace, provided we do not live in the practice.

(7.) Charity is never to be separated from other graces, much less opposed to them. A man who says, You are for faith, and I for charity, is as ridiculous as if he should say, You are for feeding, and I am for breathing. They are both necessary, not only to us, but to one another. He will make but poor work with his criticism, who advances the lungs above the stomach, so as to employ all his care about the former, and none about the latter. We read of *purifying our hearts by obeying the truth unto an unfeigned love of the brethren,* and are ordered to *love one another with a pure heart fervently:* where you may observe these four things,

First, That all brotherly love begins in conversion, with *purifying the soul.* An unregenerate person may have a good temper, a civil deportment, and from lower considerations take delight in the company of God's people; but he has no more charity than he has faith or hope: *Love is of God; every one that loveth is born of God, and knows God.*

Secondly,

Secondly, The Spirit is the author of this grace. Though it is spoken of as your act, *You have purified your souls*, yet it is *through the Spirit*. As it is said in another place, *Ye are taught of God to love one another*. There is as great a work needful upon your souls to love one whom you have seen, as one whom you have not seen: *We know that we have passed from death to life, because we love the brethren*. No other than the Almighty arm, that gives us a look into heaven, can dispose our minds to a right esteem of the saints: **He that makes them** *the excellent of the earth*, **must** make *them all our delight*.

Thirdly, It was by *obeying the truth*, (which supposes hearing and believing it), that their souls were thus purified to *an unfeigned love of the brethren*. They were not left in error or in darkness; charity comes, as faith does, by hearing, and hearing by the word of God. A man that does not know the truth, cannot obey it; and a man who does not obey it, can have none of this brotherly love. He may have what *he* calls charity, and what *he* calls faith; but they are false, and will be thrown out at the first payment. It signifies nothing what we give religious names to; God knows his own work, and will approve of no other. He has made a love of the brethren to be the effect of obedience to the **truth**; and if we make it any thing else, it is no plant that our heavenly Father has planted, but shall be **rooted up, and thrown into** the fire.

Fourthly, He exhorts them upon the ground of what the Holy Spirit had already given them, that as in obedience to the truth their souls were purified to an unfeigned love of the brethren, they ought *to love one another with a pure heart fervently*. This is but acting up to their nature; I do not mean their first, but their second nature, which they are made partakers of through the influence

of

of those exceeding great and precious promises that are given to them.

(8.) As the result of all these observations, I would farther tell you, that a belief of this mystery in my text, HIS *Deity*, who was manifest in the flesh, and *received up into glory*, is a belief of *the truth*, by which the Holy Spirit has purified the souls of men to an unfeigned love of the brethren. This is a doctrine of charity, as well as all other godliness, as I think will appear from these following particulars: It gives us the greatest tenderness for those that are in error, it is a foundation of esteem for those that love the truth, and it lays before us the best arguments for a brotherly kindness.

1. Our belief of any mystery, but especially of this, is the ground of forbearance and meekness to them who are yet in error; and the reason is plain, because as a mystery is what none but God can reveal, and what none but God can impress, so it employs my pity, and not my anger, to them who will not own it.

People who advance the schemes which they call *rational*, are impatient with any who have more or less light than themselves. What a strait path has a certain author cut out for his charity! exposing, censuring, and condemning those who say, that the Son of God was *not derived*, and doing the same, by a back stroke, against them who say, *there was any moment of the derivation*. He thinks it is very clear from nature, that there can be but one person who is the Supreme God; and yet it is clear from Scripture, that more than one person is spoken of under that title. He is sensible the Socinians were quite wrong in making Christ no more than a man; the Arians were as bad in making him a creature; and the Christian Church, in so many ages and places, is most of all condemned for saying, he is *the same with the Father in substance, equal in power and glory.*

So

So that it is very hard, when a man has got a scheme of his own, to keep him in temper with any one else; because he does not pretend this doctrine is revealed to him; it is the glory of *his* opinion, that it is void of mystery, and therefore every one who does not come into it, must be slothful, or ignorant, an *enthusiast*, or a *tritheist*, of an unpolite and confused head. That these are the effects of man's wisdom when it pretends to measure God's, is notorious from the sad experience of our day. It has brought among us *debates, envyings, wraths, strifes, backbitings, whisperings, swellings, tumults.* Hence we have had *evil surmisings, and perverse disputings of men, who suppose that gain is godliness.*

_{2 Cor. xii. 20.}
_{1 Tim. vi. 4, 5.}

This seems to be the natural consequence of such proceedings. For, if I say, as these authors do in their title pages, ' that here is a scheme of the ' Trinity, not only agreeable to Scripture, but no ' ways repugnant to the old philosophy, or to hu-' man reason;' a man that does not come into it represents me as mistaking the Scripture, and saying what is contrary to reason; and therefore in this dissent the charge of folly is insinuated on both sides. He thinks there is no reason in my opinion, and I must think there is as little in his opposition. We are charged *to beware, lest any man spoil us through philosophy and vain deceit, after the traditions of men, after the rudiments of the world, and not after Christ.* Let us not heed those who *intrude into things that they have not seen, vainly puffed up in their fleshly mind, and not holding the head.*

_{Col. ii. 8.}
_{ver. 18, 19.}

But they who say, that great is the mystery of godliness, leave no room for persecution; for the very title we give our doctrine, intimates that flesh and blood cannot make it known. And it is an absurdity of the darkest, as well as the vilest nature, to punish men for not believing what is above them, as much as not seeing what is behind them.

The

SERM. 60. The Apostle directs us to leave people in the hands of Christ: *If any man be otherwise minded, God will reveal even this to him.* It is an argument for the meekness that should be used in *the instruction of those who oppose themselves, that peradventure God will give them repentance to the acknowledgment of the truth.* They never can acknowledge the truth without repentance, and they never can have that till God gives it.

2 Tim. ii. 25.

Indeed a good man looks upon an error in this point to be of a dangerous nature, because Christ himself has said, *If ye believe not that I am he, ye shall die in your sins.* But though this is a powerful argument for us to endeavour *the turning of a sinner from the error of his way,* yet the transcendency of these things to human reason ought to banish all external force and violence from our ways of promoting them. A mystery is never conveyed into the mind by a punishment upon the body; and he that allows a man no other choice than a church or a jail, to be a proselyte or a prisoner, has given a mortal wound to the very cause he contends for.

I would also farther observe to you, that it is no persecution, nor the least degree of it, to exclude persons from what they are not fit for. You do no injury in keeping those from the table who are not of the family. There is a happy *medium* between forcing them to enter in, and plaguing them for staying out. Neither of these are lawful; but it is no harm to keep those out that should not be in. It was the glory of an Asian church, that she *tried and could not bear those who said they were Apostles, and were not, and had found them liars.*

Rev. ii. 2.

If a man does not believe the great truths of the Christian religion, he is neither fit for my communion nor for my abhorence. We are to *receive one another as God has received us all;* but where there

there are no *marks* of God's receiving, there can be no *rule* for ours. He that denies the mysteries of religion may be pitied, and ought not to be punished for his error; but there is no more harm in keeping him out of the church, than there is in denying the bread of a child to the clamour of a stranger.

2. The noblest foundation for charity is a mutual acknowledgment of the truth that is after godliness: *Our hearts are comforted, being knit together in love, to the acknowledging of the mystery of God, and of the Father, and of Christ.* We *follow righteousness, faith, charity, and peace, with them that call on the Lord Jesus out of a pure heart.* Do but enquire into a late scheme of peace, and what a strange mixture is comprehended in it. Some have their standing there, who are for the truth, because they choose to conceal it: *They stand on the other side, when strangers carry us away captive, and foreigners enter into our gates. They should not have looked on in the day of their brethren, nor have rejoiced in the day of our destruction, nor spoken proudly in the day of our distress.*

Others make up the number who oppose themselves to the doctrine of the Gospel, and these are of different sorts. Some run into the Sabellian *scheme*, as *they* do who cannot give the title of Supreme God to the Son, because they say it belongs only to the three persons considered together. Others are tinctured with unsublimated Arianism: they tell us the Son is co-eternal with the Father, and yet *derived* from him; that he is of an inferior nature; and that the Spirit is not called God at all, nor has any title to our worship.

Some will give adoration to Jesus Christ, and others will not; and though it is but a few years since the opposition to our Lord's Divinity was managed by the Socinians, yet now they are spoken and written against with contempt. Socinus himself faith, the Arians are not Christians; and they are out of his debt, by declaring they would not admit a Socinian to baptism.

Besides, an union upon concealment of principle is nonsense. What sort of a charity is that, which makes us agree with people we know not why, and run after them we know not where, and own them as brethren for we know not what? But when persons *hold the head,* and are visibly concerned for the common salvation and the glory of Jesus Christ, *both their Lord and ours,* it throws a vail over our lower divisions. Aristarchus, Paul's *fellow prisoner,* Marcus, sister's son to Barnabas, and Jesus, called Justus, *were of the circumcision; and yet these only were his fellow-workers to the kingdom of God, and were a comfort to him.* We are neither in temper nor at leisure to attend the disputes that have been stretched out with violence. We can, then, conceal the faith that we ought to have, *to ourselves,* on purpose to maintain that which ought to *be spoken of throughout the world.*

3. This doctrine gives us the best argument for charity, because God has revealed himself to others upon these articles that have been of importance to us. They have obtained the like precious faith with us: *Grace and peace are multiplied through the knowledge of God, and of Jesus our Lord.* And it gives us ground to hope we shall meet in a better world, and sing over that doctrine in eternal praises, which now fills us with a silent wonder. The temple of God was opened in heaven, and there was *seen in his temple the ark of his testament.* This is the great provocation to love and good works, that we see the day approaching, the day of knowledge and glory, when *the sun shall no more be our light by day, nor the moon by night, but the Lord himself will be an everlasting glory.* As for a *faith* we know not, we are not like to *follow* it, nor can we have any thoughts about the *end of their conversation,*

verſation, whoſe works are in the dark. When men ſee not the glorious Goſpel of Chriſt, whether it is the god of this world who has blinded their eyes we cannot tell; but the knowledge of the truth is our preparative for heaven, and we look upon thoſe that have it, as our fellow-travellers thither. And it ſtrikes a life through all our converſation to think we are going to a place where thoſe doctrines will be no more denied, but *the myſtery of heaven be opened* to ſwell and delight our ſouls for ever.

SERMON LXI.

October 5. 1725.

I SHALL now diſmiſs this glorious text that gives us the main branches of our religion, or, as it is here called, *the myſtery of godlineſs;* a doctrine that is revealed from heaven, and promotes a divine purity upon earth, that employs our faith and animates our practice. All that I need to do at parting with ſuch a ſubject, is only to look back upon the road over which we have gone. The diſtribution of what I have to ſay at the cloſe of this great work, you may take under the following heads:

1. I would give ſome friendly advice to thoſe who are not convinced either of the truth or importance of this doctrine, which I have laid before you in ſuch an abundant way.

2. I

2. I shall make some little application to such whose hearts God has touched with the knowledge of the truth as it is in Jesus. And,

3. I would give you a short account of myself, with relation to this *glorious Gospel of the ever blessed God, which has been committed to my trust.*

(1.) We may suppose, after all that has been said, that there are yet gainsayers amongst us, to whom the word of the Lord is a reproach, and who are *weary of hearing it. Our Gospel is hid from them.* The Spirit speaks expressly, that in the latter times *some shall depart from the faith, giving heed to seducing spirits, and doctrines of devils, speaking lies in hypocrisy, and having their conscience seared with a hot iron.* But as they are still within the joyful sound, as it is not too late to call after them, so I would, from a hearty concern for their welfare, leave these few admonitions with them.

1. Though you cannot believe this doctrine, do not indulge yourselves to a profane contempt of it: *Be ye not mockers, lest your bands be made strong. Surely He scorns the scorners.* A very little wit will serve to ridicule the mysteries of the Gospel, and make you agreeable to those that *walk after their own ungodly lusts.* But what do these sports of infidelity end in? they may tend to harden conscience in others, but they will wofully soften it in yourselves.

This is the way to a double darkness upon a sickbed, and to make death a thousand times more the king of terrors than he is in himself: *What will ye do in the day of visitation, and in the desolation that shall come from far? to whom will ye flee for help, and where will ye leave your glory?* What do you get by tossing out a jest upon the great salvation, but only to be stung with despair, when you come to find that there is no hope for you, and no spirit in you?

People

People may have their doubts about any doctrine of religion. The beft of God's children have complained of *a wicked heart of unbelief;* but there is a wide difference between thofe principles of oppofition to the truth which are our burden, and thofe that a corrupt nature will efteem to be our glory. I remember a paffage in the works of Mr Ifaac Ambrofe, to this purpofe, that one told him he had attended a long time upon Mr Richard Vines, an eminent preacher in this city, who had managed the controverfy between us and the Jews with great learning and piety: And when he had gone through his arguments, he addreffed himfelf to the people in fuch words as thefe: ' Now, faith
' he, perhaps many of you will think that I have
' fully confuted the Jews, and given them fuch
' an evidence of our religion, as they will not be
' able to anfwer; and indeed I do take the rea-
' fons to be above the oppofition of gainfayers;
' but yet I would embrace the feet of that man
' who could affure me, that I fhould never again
' queftion in my own foul, whether Jefus was the
' Mefliah or no. Upon which, faith the hifto-
' rian, a general groan went through the congre-
' gation, as if every perfon fhared in the concern
' that a minifter fo eminent fhould complain of an
' unbelief that would hazard the foundation of our
' moft holy faith.'

Indeed there is no truth in all religion that Satan will not tempt us to blafpheme, and to which our own corrupt hearts will not fupply the feeds of infidelity: *The tranfgreffion of the wicked fpeaks in our hearts, that there is no fear of God before his eyes.* Luther complains that his mind was filled with *horribilia de Deo, et terribilia de fide:* fuch thoughts of God as were horrible, and fuch of faith as were dreadful.

But

But how vile and dangerous must the case of that sinner be, who does not mourn over this unbelief as his burden, and keep it all concealed within himself as that which is not fit to be ventured abroad; but rather *glories in his shame*, and throws out the filth of a heart that is desperately wicked in raw and rude arguments of blasphemy; like *raging waves of the sea, foaming out their own shame!* Have a care of *increasing to this ungodliness.* Do not make light of that which the Holy Spirit has delivered with all the solemnity that words can have.

And, in particular, let me warn you against one sleight of these men that *lie in wait to deceive;* and that is this; they endeavour to break your concern for a doctrine by telling you, ' It is possible you ' may disbelieve it, and not be damned; that sure- ' ly none will dare to say, that they who deny ' this opinion are all vessels of wrath fitted to de- ' struction.' What low reasoning is this! how mean in so great an argument as the Divinity of Christ! how trifling in so great an affair as the salvation of souls! We see that they who perished in the wilderness *entered not in because of unbelief. Let us therefore fear, lest a promise being left us of entering into his rest, any of you should seem to come short of it; for to us was the Gospel preached as well as to them, but the word preached did not profit them, not being mixed with faith in them that heard it. We who have believed do enter into rest.*

It is nothing to me how many errors may be consistent with a state of pardon, I can have no hopes of being *saved* but by *the love of the truth.* God has joined together *a sanctification of the Spirit, and a belief of the truth,* as the way of my salvation; and I have no authority to drop the one any more than the other. When I desire a person to go in a safe road, and not to travel upon a precipice

cipice that may turn his head, and make him lose his life, I act a friendly part; and if another persuades him to run the hazard, because it is possible he *may* escape, he that talks at this rate, if he is not an enemy, must be looked upon as a trifler; for though others have gone secure through these dangers, yet what recompence is that to a man who by venturing is dashed in pieces? therefore do you *build up one another in your most holy faith,* and have compassion on those that differ.

We are not called to determine the state of Mahometans, Jews, or Pagans, who can scarce say they have *heard the fame of Jesus with their ears.* Nor is it our business to say of any who are cut off without giving a testimony to the truth, what is become of them: *Secret things belong to God: Judge nothing before the time.*

But is my charity to make me an infidel? must I either pronounce sentence on one who has denied the Lord that bought him, or be indifferent to what the Scripture itself has called *damnable heresies?* is there no medium between censuring another and guarding myself? There are *strange delusions* that some are given up to, who have *no pleasure in the truth, but in unrighteousness.* Several people *believe a lie, that they all may be damned:* and these things are written not for us to point out the men, but to fence against the opinions. Whilst we *follow peace with all men,* we must *look diligently lest any man fail of the grace of God.*

2. Let me farther beseech you not to run into the common extravagance of those who deny the Deity of Christ: *Shun profane and vain babblings, for they will increase unto more ungodliness, and their word will eat as does a canker. In a great house there are vessels to dishonour.*

One would think it very possible for people to be in that error without going any farther; but as

SERM. 61. as God has told us, so we find it, that *evil men and*
2 Tim. iii. *seducers shall wax worse and worse, deceiving and*
13. *being deceived.*

  The only question is, and ever must be, whether this doctrine is revealed in Scripture or no. If it is not, there is no other evidence that we can possibly bring in as the ground of your faith; and therefore he that opposes it fairly, has nothing to do with its conformity to reason and the maxims of philosophy. These we are warned against as
Col. ii. 8. so much *vain deceit: The rudiments of the world*
1 John iv. *and the traditions of men* are *not after Christ. False*
5. *teachers are of the world, and therefore speak they of the world.* It may be a truth, and yet appear in none of that light; it is of a superior nature. If God has told us it some other way than by the understanding that his Spirit has given to all man-
1 Cor. ii. 6, kind, it is certain their cause is lost. For *we speak*
7. *not the wisdom of this world, nor of the princes of this world, which come to nought; but the wisdom of God in a mystery, even the hidden wisdom which God ordained before the world unto our glory.*

  If He has said it in his word, the man who thinks he reads it there is never to be convinced but by one of these ways; either that what he takes for a divine revelation is not so, or that he has mistaken the sense of the words. The controversy of our day runs fast into the former question; though, as some of their writers own, the matter is not yet ripe. Now, observe what danger people are entangled with by departing from the truth.

  First, Some take refuge for this error in another that is more general, that there can be *no certainty in matters of faith.* This makes a Christian's hope to be no more than a silly dream, and his practice no better than a perpetual ramble. This is one
2 Tim. iii. reason why we *continue in the things that we have*
14, 15. *learned, and been assured of,* because *we know of whom we have learned them, and have known the*

Holy

Holy Scriptures that are able to make us wise to sal- SERM. 61.
vation. Believers have *an unction from the Holy* 1 John ii.
One, and know all things. We must *continue in the* 20.
faith grounded and settled, and not be moved away Col. i. 23.
from the hope of the Gospel, which we have heard;
rooted and built up in him, and established in the —— ii. 7.
faith, as we have been taught. When we talk to
the Jews, we *fight uncertainly, as those that beat*
the air, if there is no certainty in matters of faith:
And when the martyrs *overcame by the word of*
their testimony, as they lived they knew not how,
so they died they knew not why. Here is the seal
of blood given to mere *enthusiasm!* but they were
supported with the hope, that the Spirit witnessed
with their spirits, that the cause for which they
suffered was of God. Yet,

Secondly, All this mighty and gracious work of
the Holy Ghost is profaned with contempt; so
that, though he has done so much in giving us the
Scriptures, and is promised to lead us into the way
of all truth, yet we are told there is no such thing
as *the way of truth,* and therefore it is a jest to
speak of his leading us thither. These are men
blaspheming what they know not. But *he that over-* Jude 10.
comes the world is he that believes that Jesus is the 1 John v.
Son of God; and the Spirit bears witness, because the 5, 6.
Spirit is truth.

Thirdly, This brings them either to deny the divine revelation, or to curtail it. Some are at work
to tear out single verses, others run away with entire books, though plagues are threatened to the
man who either *adds to these things, or takes away* Rev. xxii.
from the words of the book of this prophecy. Some 18, 19.
will make the words of Scripture not to be a declaration of the truth, but a cover of heresy;
handling it deceitfully, and walking in craftiness.

Fourthly, This runs into a contempt of God's
people, who have not only professed the doctrine
in words, but believed it in the whole course of

VOL. II.   3 F   their

their experience: their steadiness is abhorred, their seriousness is laughed at. We cannot but see that divine grace has made a public difference between some and others, and therefore it is never safe to refuse the precious, and choose the vile. The man who gives up himself to prayer, who reads the Scriptures, and with a devout importunity fetches light from above, *may be* in an error; but whatever I may think of his notions, it would be wrong in me to disdain him, and admire those who take the name of God in vain. I ought to *purge myself from these, and follow charity with those who call on the Lord out of a pure heart. These are spots in our feasts of charity.*

2 Tim. ii. 21, 22.
Jude 12.

Fifthly, Take heed that these things do not ruin practical religion. No new opinions concerning Christ can be your protection in the neglect of his worship. I fear it may be observed of some families, that as these doctrines have come in, prayer has gone out. Now, whatever light people get, yet if their zeal for holiness is lost, if the Sabbath is defiled, the name of Jesus treated with no reverence, and his worship attended with no fervour, your *hearts* are not right in the sight of God, and it is a dreadful sign that your *heads* are wrong too.

3. Another advice I would give you is this, Be open to conviction. Let the truth be its own recommendation. Do not struggle against evidence; there is nothing got by stifling that, but a reproach of conscience. No agreements or acquaintance are of so much value as the doctrines of the Gospel. What do you get by depriving Christ of his Deity, but a floating faith, a misgiving hope, and an undetermined practice? *Search the Scriptures daily, whether the things be so or no.*

Acts xvii. 11.

What is the advantage of having a Saviour who is not God? what are your souls afraid of in supposing that He who paid your ransom was equal to Him who received it? to say that this is a contradiction, is only to involve the wisdom of God in a slander; for if he has revealed it, it must be true and right; if he has not, why are his own people ensnared? How come men, that have always shewn a true regard about happiness, to mistake it in the dependence of their faith, in the direction of their prayer, and the comforts of a death-bed?

Is it likely that they who live as without God in the world, whatever other advantages they have, do know the deep things of God, the wisdom that lies in a mystery; and that the humble praying Christians, the generation that have sought his face, are suffered to live and die in an error? Whatever you may make of *politeness*, it is never to be set upon a level with *piety* in matters of pure revelation: *The meek will he guide in judgment, the meek will he teach his way. If any man do his will, he shall know of the doctrine whether it be of God. He has hid these things from the wise and prudent, and revealed them unto babes.*

Your danger comes from those who care not whether there is any other world or no, *men that rebel against the light, and abide not in the paths thereof.* It is all one to them whether Christ be God or a creature, because they are unconcerned whether he is a Saviour or an enemy. Such as are *incontinent, fierce, despisers of them that are good, that have scarcely a form of godliness, but certainly deny the power thereof; lovers of pleasures more than lovers of God.* Whom would you resemble in your latter end; those that live in pride, and die in darkness, or such as walk humbly with their God, and go off rejoicing in hope of his glory? *Remember those that have taught you the word of God, whose faith follow, considering the end of their conversation.*

4. Beg the Divine teachings; do not despise His admonitions who has promised to *guide our feet.* I fear the naming of this direction in these

terms

SERM. 61. terms will be a disadvantage to it: and as our age are more afraid of *enthusiasm* than of *atheism*, they do not like some phrases that the Scripture has used. If that is the case, till He who *convinces the world of sin*, even of their *unbelief*, does his office, and tries his power, it is in vain for us to argue; we call after the winds, press the rocks, and court the waves.

But I hope there may be some among you, who though you have doubts, yet you do not despise Him who alone can give you the victory. You may be sure, on which side soever the truth lies, it is upon no other ground than the testimony of the Spirit in Scripture, and with no other evidence than the testimony of the Spirit to Scripture; and therefore it is no begging the question to send you to your knees. Whatever party laughs at this, and makes a jest of the witness that is given in answer to humble prayer, they are either opposite to Eph. i. 16, the truth, or unworthy of it. Pray that the *God of our Lord Jesus Christ, the Father of glory, may give to you the Spirit of* **wisdom** *and revelation in the knowledge of him*.

(2.) I would address myself to those that are convinced of this doctrine.—If these sermons have been blessed to the opening of your eyes, or the settling of your faith, you and I have reason to be thankful for them. I would hope there is one argument, that these labours are not altogether in vain; because, though the continuance of this subject has been unexpected, and by me I am sure undesigned, yet they were always delivered to very great assemblies. And, notwithstanding the curiosity there is in our nature to be entertained with variety, yet I have not observed any abatement of your numbers, or your zeal to receive the love of the truth.

The uneasiness of some, who could either be *drowsy* upon design, or *angry* without it, has been no farther my trouble than for their sakes. For
whether

whether they care for it or no, they have heard what in a little time they shall feel, that He whom they despise is God, and *it is hard for them to kick against the pricks.* However, these examples of sleepy, lolling, and discontented hearers, have been very few. I have had the satisfaction to see, that there are some whom the truth of God has not drawn, but it has driven them; and as they did not like to hear what they did not love to admire, so they were afraid to meet what they could not answer.

The insinuations that this doctrine is *enthusiasm*, and the manner of promoting it too violent, are only desperate vollies of those that quit the field, who, when they are broken for disputants, set up for railers. But to you, my brethren, who have not been ashamed of Christ and his words, in this corrupt and untoward generation, let me apply with these two directions.

1. See that you feel in your own souls the influence of what you believe. To what purpose is *the manifestation of a God in the flesh*, if He who took upon him your nature is not allowed to have any concern in your happiness? Why is he *justified in the Spirit*, if your spirits are an exception to that honour? if he there meets with nothing but unbelief, rebellion, and darkness? To what purpose does the Holy Ghost give him a testimony which you will not receive; but, instead of that, suffer yourselves to be guided by a reason that is vile and cloudy? What a conviction will that be, that He who is *seen of Angels*, to be admired and adored, should not be seen by you, so as to discover any form or comeliness in him!

Why is He who is *preached to the Gentiles* mentioned with any abatement of his character? why must not they who are his witnesses to mankind, own him to be a God? if he is *believed on in the world*, what will become of those who, in contempt

tempt of these examples, *will not come unto him, that they may have life?* and what an aggravation will his being *received into glory* leave upon your refusal, your infidelity, and impenitence? Therefore see to it, that your experiences strike to this doctrine, that they are both to one key. When you hear of his being God, feel that your faith is employed in the deepest adorations, in a continual homage, in all the fervour and duty of life. As he is preached to you Gentiles, so endeavour to see, that you are part of the world that believe in him. Follow the glory that he is received up to, with breathings after it, and a dependence upon him to bring you thither.

2. Consider your obligations to *own* what you have believed: *Hold forth the word of life, that I may rejoice in the day of Christ, that I have not run in vain, nor laboured in vain. Yea, and if I be offered upon the sacrifice and service of your faith, I joy and rejoice with you all; for the same cause also do ye joy and rejoice with me.* It was a great deal of opposition that Christ went through for your sakes, and resolve that you will run all dangers for his.

Phil. ii. 16, 17, 18.

Is a God manifest in the flesh, a God lost in that flesh? Must his taking upon him *your nature* be an argument why you will not be witnesses to *his?* This condescension is what he designed both for your happiness, and his own glory. Do you pretend to secure the one, and be unconcerned about the other? It is true, he does not want your assistance in another world, nor indeed in this. He that formed the mouths of men can set the voices of the universe a-going. He needs none of your learning, but is able to ordain *strength out of the mouths of babes and sucklings, to still the enemy and the avenger.*

Psal. viii. 2.

Nevertheless, he puts it to the trial, what you think his honour is worth; whether it is not set at too great a rate, if your reputation is to suffer in the service of this glorious cause. Can you deny those that deny him? It will be impossible to *believe, if you receive honour from one another.* This is given as the reason why *many that believed in Christ,* i. e. were thoroughly convinced of his title and his perfections, yet *did not confess him; because they were afraid of being put out of the synagogue, for they loved the praise of men more than the praise of God.*

If this is your case; if you think to maintain the honour of Christ, and the favour of those that oppose it, it is a desperate attempt; you are striving to do what our dear Lord tells us no man can do, *serve two masters.* This coalescence can succeed but a very little while, for in time you must hold to the one, and despise the other. Let me therefore beg of you, not to be afraid of men, or *fear their revilings, but sanctify this Lord of hosts in your souls, and make him to be your fear and your dread.*

This is a courage that may in one sense be said to bear its own charges. The more you use, the more you will have. A man's cowardice begins from himself; it is an indulged carnality; we make it our crime, and God makes it our judgment. He that fears a Redeemer, fears nothing else; he that does not fear him, fears every thing. A person who dare not let go the deity of his Saviour, dare do every thing to promote it. But he that is unconcerned about that, will be always a burden to himself: fear will be on every side.

It is a sweet hazard that you run in this cause, and a glorious infamy that the malice of men has clothed you with: *To them it is an evident token of perdition, but to you of salvation, and that of God: to you it is given on the behalf of Christ, not only to believe, but to suffer for his sake.* If you suffer the reproach of Christ, which the fearful and unbelieving reckon the greatest mischief in the world,

happy

SERM. 61.
1 Pet. iv. 14.

happy are ye, for the Spirit of God and of glory shall rest upon you. On their part he is evil spoken of, but on yours he is glorified.

(3.) I promised to give you some little account of myself, which you know I do not use to trouble you with; nor should I have done it now, were it not in duty to the glorious doctrine for which God has honoured me, both as a witness and a sufferer: *I am not ashamed of the Gospel of Christ*; and, *I thank the Lord who has enabled me, counting me faithful, and putting me into the ministry.*

Rom. i. 16.
1 Tim. i. 12.

The text I have been now upon, is what my thoughts were turned to above twenty years ago. And I cannot but regard that hand of Providence that orders all our steps, that I have so long been kept off from engaging in a subject that gave me many pleasing views at a distance. He that fixes the bounds of our habitation, settles also *the times before appointed*, and he makes every thing *beautiful in its season*. It is by his over-ruling counsel that these designs should never be brought into life till they were most needful.

I must farther observe to you, that we were actually engaged upon this text above eleven months before our contentions broke out, that are now become like *the bars of a castle*. I little thought, at my entrance upon the Mystery of Godliness, that I should be driven into the field of battle, or that a zeal for those doctrines would make me the abhorrence of friends, and the contempt of strangers. But a wise and gracious God had thus appointed it, to try whether in the service and defence of the truth, we could live upon the *honour that comes from him only.*

It is two years and seven months since I began these sermons. I had no more in view than about ten or twelve discourses; but I have found myself refreshed and enlarged in these studies beyond what I have been conscious to, upon any other subject. And

And therefore, though I could not be untouched with *the defaming of many*, and especially considering how unexpected and undeserved it was, yet the doctrine was so much the joy of my soul, that the ill usage of men is what I could both neglect in the closet, and despise from the pulpit.

I had thought to have insisted only on three or four texts in maintenance of our Lord's divinity, and I am apt to think they have rather grown to so many hundreds; which I endeavoured to lay before you, not under the interpretations of men, not as driven in with the authority of councils and synods, but in their own light; *by a manifestation of the truth, commending myself to every man's conscience in the sight of God.*

And I do now with the greatest solemnity affirm to you, and appeal to the Searcher of hearts, that I have not perverted one scripture to serve a cause which I did not think the Holy Spirit had designed it for. I am sensible some are grown weary of the subject, and are gone out from us, and by these we are charged with heat and fury about a needless debate.

If people are angry that the truth is defended, it is well if they do not want some concern about its being opposed. But I am so sure that this doctrine is of God, and so persuaded that it is fundamental to all your hopes, that I think my work and my life can never be closed with any thing of more importance.—I will therefore conclude with a doxology, that is to be understood of Christ: *Now to the King eternal, immortal, invisible, the only wise God, be honour and glory for ever and ever,* Amen. [1 Tim. i. 17.]

A

COLLECTION

OF

SOME SCRIPTURES

That are EXPLAINED, IMPROVED, or RESCUED in the foregoing Sermons; relating to the Myſtery of Religion, the Deity of Chriſt, the Neceſſity of Revelation, and the Danger of Unbelief.

GEN. iii. 15. The ſeed of the woman ſhall bruiſe the ſerpent's head, vol. i. page 13.
EXOD. vii. 1. I have made thee a God to Pharaoh, vol. ii. 36.
xxiii. 20. I ſend an angel before thee to keep thee in the way.——Beware of him, and obey his voice, provoke him not, for he will not pardon your tranſgreſſions, for my name is in him. If thou wilt indeed obey his voice, and do all that I ſpeak, I will be an enemy to thy enemies, i. 174.
2 CHRON. vi. 30. Thou, even thou only, knoweſt the hearts of the children of men, ii. 188.
JOB xv. 15. He puts no truſt in his ſaints, i. 397.
ix. 33. There is no days-man between us, who may lay his hand upon us both, i. 396.
xii. 2, 4. No doubt ye are the people, and wiſdom ſhall die with you. I am as one mocked of his neighbour, who calls upon God, and he hears him: the juſt upright man is laughed to ſcorn, ii. 332.
PSAL. ii. 1, 2. Why do the heathen rage, and the people imagine a vain thing? the kings of the earth ſet themſelves, and the rulers take counſel together againſt the Lord, and againſt his Anointed, ii. 272.
——6. I have ſet my King upon my holy hill of Zion, ii. 274.
——7. I will declare the decree the Lord has ſaid unto me, Thou art my Son, this day have I begotten thee, ii. 274, 314.
xxii. 1, 2. My God, my God, why haſt thou forſaken me? why art thou ſo far from helping me? i. 280.
——30. A ſeed ſhall ſerve him, and be accounted to the Lord for a generation, ii. 78.
xxxi. 5. Into thy hands do I commit my ſpirit, for thou haſt redeemed it, O Lord God of truth, i. 159. ii. 61, 64, 269.
xxxvi. 5, 6. Thy mercy, O Lord, is in the heavens, and thy faithfulneſs reaches to the clouds. Thy righteouſneſs is like great mountains, thy judgments are a great deep, i. 31, 45.
xlv. 6. Thy throne, O God, is for ever and ever, i. 300. ii. 90.
lxviii. 4. Extol him that rides upon the heavens, by his name JAH, i. 181.
——17. The chariots of God are twenty thouſand, even thouſands of Angels; the Lord is among them, i. 181, 317. ii. 229.
lxxxiii. 18. Thou whoſe name alone is JEHOVAH, art the Moſt High, i. 181. ii. 43.
xcvii. 7. Worſhip him all ye gods, i. 138, 141. ii. 174.
cii. 25. Thou, Lord, in the beginning haſt laid the foundations of the earth, and the heavens are the work of thine hands, ii. 211, 212.

a   PSAL.

PSAL. cx. 1. The Lord said unto my Lord, Sit thou at my right hand, ii. 130, 236.
cxviii. 26, 27. Bleſſed is he that comes in the name of the Lord: God is the Lord who has ſhewn us light, ii. 25.
PROV. viii. 22. The Lord poſſeſſed me in the beginning of his ways: I was ſet up from everlaſting; when there was no depth I was brought forth, ii. 216.
xix. 27. My ſon ceaſe to hear the inſtruction that cauſes to err from the words of knowledge, ii. 353.
xxx. 11. There is a generation which curſes their father,——how lofty are their eyes, &c. ii. 332.
ISAIAH vi. 1. I ſaw the Lord upon a throne high and lifted up, and his train filled the temple. Above it ſtood the Seraphims,——and cried one to another, Holy, holy, holy, Lord God of hoſts,——the poſts of the door moved, i. 121, 294, 341, 342, 343. ii. 206.
———5. Mine eyes have ſeen the King, the Lord of hoſts, ii. 24.
ix. 6. To us a Child is born, to us a Son is given, and his name ſhall be called Wonderful, Counſellor, The mighty God, The everlaſting Father, i. 14, 150, 213. ii. 256.
xl. 6, 7. Prepare ye the way of the Lord, make ſtraight in the deſert a high way for our God; comfort ye my people, ſaith your God, ii. 192, 193.
———9. Say to the cities of Judah, Behold your God, i. 370, 403. ii. 32, 194.
xlii. 8. I am the Lord, that is my name, and my glory I will not give to another, ii. 98.
xliv. 5. Subſcribe with the hand to the Lord God of Iſrael, ii. 379.
xlv. 23. Look unto me, and be ye ſaved, all the ends of the earth, for I am the Lord, and there is none elſe: to me every knee ſhall bow, and every tongue ſhall ſwear, i. 351, 397.
———24. In the Lord ſhall one ſay I have righteouſneſs and ſtrength, i. 169. ii. 233.
l. 2, 3, 4. Is my hand ſhortened at all, that I cannot redeem? at my rebuke I dry up the ſea.——The Lord has given me the tongue of the learned.——I gave my back to the ſmiters, ii. 191, 192.
liii. 8. Who ſhall declare his generation? ii. 42.
JER. ix. 3. They bend their tongue like their bow for lies, and are not valiant for the truth, i. 29.
xvii. 12. A glorious high throne from the beginning, is the place of our ſanctuary, i. 95.
xxiii. 6. This is the name whereby he ſhall be called, JEHOVAH our Righteouſneſs, i. 181, 268, 400. ii. 42, 386.
xxxiii. 15, 16. She ſhall be called, the Lord our Righteouſneſs, ii. 43.
DAN. ix. 26. The Meſſiah ſhall be cut off, but not for himſelf: he ſhall finiſh tranſgreſſion, make an end of ſin, and bring in an everlaſting righteouſneſs, i. 180. ii. 42.
MIC. v. 2. Thou Bethlehem Ephratah, though thou be leaſt among the thouſands of Judah, yet out of thee ſhall he come forth to me, that is to be the ruler in Iſrael, whoſe goings forth of old have been from everlaſting, i. 152, 153, 154. ii. 217.
HAG. ii. 9. In this place will I give peace, ſaith the Lord of hoſts, i. 403.
ZECH. xiii. 7. Awake, O ſword, againſt the man that is my fellow, i. 336, 400.
MAT. i. 18. She was found with child of the Holy Ghoſt, i. 213.
————23. His name ſhall be called Immanuel, God with us, i. 161.
ii. 2. We have ſeen his ſtar in the eaſt, and are come to worſhip him, ii. 21.
iv. 10. Thou ſhalt worſhip the Lord thy God, and him only ſhalt thou ſerve, i. 449. ii. 55, 221.
v. 44. Bleſs them that curſe you, &c. ii. 390.
xi. 6. Bleſſed is he who ſhall not be offended in me, ii. 7.

MAT.

MAT. xi. 26. I thank thee, O Father,——that thou haſt hid theſe things from the wiſe and prudent, and haſt revealed them unto babes. All theſe things are delivered to me of my Father: no man knows who the Son is but the Father, and who the Father is but the Son, and he to whom the Son will reveal him, i. 426, 427. ii. 182.

xviii. 20. Where two or three are met together in my name, I am in the midſt of them, i. 271. ii. 56, 269.

xix. 17. Why calleſt thou me good,? there is none good but one, that is God, i. 447.

xxvii. 46. My God, my God, why haſt thou forſaken me? i. 279, 280.

xxviii. 17. They worſhipped him, but ſome doubted, ii. 24.

————19. Baptize them in the name of the Father, Son, and Holy Ghoſt, ii. 25.

————20. I am with you always to the end of the world, i. 434. ii. 82, 83, 269.

MARK ii. 10, 11. That ye may know that the Son of man has power on earth to forgive ſins, he ſaith to the ſick of the palſy, Ariſe, ii. 108.

xii. 10, 11. The ſtone which the builders rejected is made the head of the corner. This is the doing of the Lord, and it is marvellous in our eyes, i. 416.

xiii. 32. Of that day and hour knows no man, nor the angels, nor the Son, but the Father, ii. 185, 188.

LUKE i. 16. Many of the children of Iſrael ſhall he turn to the Lord their God, and he ſhall go before HIM, i. 300. ii. 193.

————33. Of his kingdom there ſhall be no end, ii. 215.

————35. The Holy Ghoſt ſhall come upon thee, and the power of the Higheſt ſhall overſhadow thee; therefore the holy thing that ſhall be born of thee ſhall be called the Son of God, ii. 204, 314.

————68. He has viſited and redeemed his people, i. 200.

————76. Thou child ſhalt be called the Prophet of the Higheſt, and go before the face of the Lord, to prepare his way, i. 309, 310. ii. 193.

ii. 52. He grew in wiſdom and ſtature, ii. 285.

v. 8. Depart from me, for I am a ſinful man, O Lord, ii. 23, 24.

ix. 26. Whoever ſhall be aſhamed of me, and of my words, of him ſhall the Son of man be aſhamed, i. 354.

xix. 7. He is gone to be a gueſt with a man that is a ſinner, i. 419.

xxiv. 52. He was parted from them, and they worſhipped him, ii. 24.

JOHN i. 1. In the beginning was the Word, and the Word was with God, and the Word was God, ii. 212.

————3. All things are made by him, and without him was not any thing made that was made, ii. 35.

————4. In him was life, and that life was the light of men, ii. 47, 93.

————10. He was in the world, and the world was made by him, ii. 9, 34.

————13, 14. The Word was made fleſh, and dwelt among us, and we beheld his glory, (the glory as of the only begotten of the Father), full of grace and truth: and to them that received him gave he power to become the ſons of God, even to them that believe on his name, i. 199.

————18. No man has ſeen God at any time; the only begotten Son, who is in the boſom of the Father, he has declared him, i. 208.

————49. Thou art the Son of God, thou art the King of Iſrael, ii. 23.

ii. 25. He did not commit himſelf to men, becauſe he knew what was in man, ii. 186.

iii. 13. No man has aſcended into heaven, but he that came down from heaven, even the Son, who is in heaven, i. 211, 271. ii. 227.

— 36. Whoever believes not is condemned already, the wrath of God abideth on him, i. 175.

iv. 10. If thou kneweſt the gift of God,——thou wouldſt have aſked of him, and he would have given thee living water, i. 20.

v. 18. He ſaid that God was his Father, thereby making himſelf equal with God, i. 140. 216. ii. 249, 250.

JOHN v. 23. That all men may honour the Son, as they honour the Father: he that honours not the Son, honours not the Father who has sent him, i. 296, 297. ii. 223, 384.

―――― 26. As the Father has life in himself, so has he given to the Son to have life in himself, ii. 49.

vi. 46. He that is of God has seen the Father, i. 208. ii. 182.

―――― 57, 58. As the living Father has sent me, and I live by the Father, so he that eats me shall live by me, ii. 251, 252, 253.

―――― 65. No man can come unto me, except it were given him of my Father, ii. 252.

―――― 68. Thou hast the words of eternal life, ii. 252.

―――― 69. We believe and art sure, that thou art the Christ, the Son of the living God, ii. 253.

―――― 71. Jesus knew from the beginning who they were that believed not, and who should betray him, ii. 186, 187.

viii. 32. Ye shall know the truth, and the truth shall make you free, i. 15.

―――― 56. Before Abraham was, I am, ii. 254.

x. 15. As the Father knows me, I know the Father, I lay down my life for the sheep, ii. 161.

―――― 27. I give to them eternal life, ii. 255.

―――― 28. My Father is greater than all, and none shall pluck them out of my Father's hands, i. 188, 274.

―――― 30. I and my Father are one, i. 152, 188. ii. 255.

―――― 31. Believe the works, that ye may know and believe that the Father is in me, and I in him, i. 190, 275.

―――― 33. Thou being a man, makest thyself God, i. 189, 274.

―――― 34. If he called them gods to whom the word of God came; say ye of him whom God has sanctified and sent into the world, Thou blasphemest, because I said, I am the Son of God? i. 189, 274.

―――― 38. I am in the Father, and the Father in me, i. 19, 275.

xii. 42. Many of the Pharisees believed in him, but they did not confess him, lest they should be put out of the synagogue, ii. 207.

―――― 43. These things said Esaias when he saw his glory, and spake of him, i. 121, 344. ii. 207.

xiv. 1. Ye believe in God, believe also in me, i. 191, 196, 451. ii. 201.

―――― 3. I will come again and receive you to myself, that where I am you may be also, ii. 63.

―――― 6. I am the way, the truth, and the life, ii. 201.

―――― 8. If ye had known me, ye should have known my Father also, and henceforth ye have known him and seen him, i. 209. ii. 63, 183.

―――― 17. My Father is greater than I, ii. 30, 296.

―――― 18. Because I live, ye shall live also, i. 271. ii. 18, 53.

xvi. 8, 9. When the Spirit shall come, he shall convince of sin, because they believe not on me, i. 260, 261. ii. 113.

Of righteousness, because I go to the Father, and ye see me no more, i. 268. ii. 245.

―――― 14, 15. He shall take of mine, and shew it unto you. All that the Father has is mine, therefore I said he shall take of mine, i. 156, 243, 244, 275. ii. 202, 269.

―――― 16. Yet a little while, and ye see me no more: and again, yet a little while, and ye shall see me, ii. 53.

―――― 22. I will see you again, and your heart shall rejoice, and your joy shall no man take away from you, ii. 17, 18.

―――― 30. We are sure thou knowest all things and needest not that any man should ask thee, ii. 191.

xvii. 1. Father the hour is come, glorify thy Son, that thy Son also may glorify thee, ii. 163.

―――― 5. Glorify me with the glory I had with thee before the world war, ii. 169, 170, 171, 172, 173.

JOHN xvii. 10. All mine are thine, and thine are mine, and I am glorified in them, i. 406.
———— 23. I in them, and thou in me, i. 183, 184.
———— 24. I will that they whom thou haft given me, be with me where I am, that they may behold my glory, ii. 264, 265, 266.
xviii. 37. For this caufe came I into the world, that I might bear witnefs of the truth, i. 19.
xix. 7. We have a law, and by that law he ought to die, becaufe he made himfelf the Son of God, ii. 149.
xx. 22. Receive ye the Holy Ghoft, i. 266.
——28. My Lord, and my God, ii. 76, 320.
——31. Believe that Jefus is the Son of God, and believing have life in his name, ii. 75.
xxi. 17. Thou, Lord, knoweft all things, thou knoweft that I love thee, ii. 187.
ACTS ii. 33. Being by the right-hand of God exalted, and having received of the Father the promife of the Holy Ghoft, he has fhed forth that which ye fee and hear, i. 259, 390.
iii. 15. Ye have killed the Prince of life, ii. 110.
iv. 23. They took knowledge of them, that they had been with Jefus, i. 429.
vii. 59. Lord Jefus receive my fpirit, i. 127, 159, 160. ii. 61, 62, 63, 64, 269.
ix. 6. Lord what wilt thou have me to do? i. 170, 171.
——11. Behold he prays, i. 111.
——15. He is a chofen veffel to bear my name before the Gentiles, i. 171.
xvii. 11. They received the word with all readinefs of mind, and fearched the Scriptures daily, whether the things were fo or no, i. 11. 99.
———— 23, 24. Him whom ye ignorantly worfhip declare I to you, the God who made the world, ii. 306.
xix. 17 Many that believed came and confeffed their deeds, i. 95.
xx. 28. The church of God which he has purchafed with his blood, i. 182, 246, 247, 400. ii. 243.
xxii. 24. Be baptized, calling on the name of the Lord, i. 171.
xxvi. 17, 18. I have made thee a minifter and a witnefs to people,——from whom I will deliver thee; having therefore obtained help from God, i. 172, 435. ii. 52.
———— 19. Sanctified by faith in me, ii. 106.
ROM. i. 4. Declared to be the Son of God with power, ii. 314.
iii. 4. Let God be true, and every man a liar, i. 57.
iv. 4, 5. To him who works not, but believes on him that juftifies the ungodly, to him faith is imputed for righteoufnefs, ii. 12.
——24. Who was delivered for our offences, and raifed again for our juftification, ii. 164.
vi. 3, 4. We are buried with him in baptifm, i. 68.
viii. 3, 4. What the law could not do in that it was weak in the flefh, God fent forth his Son in the likenefs of finful flefh, &c. i. 179, 203.
——7. The carnal mind is enmity againft God, and is not fubject to the law of God, neither indeed can be, ii. 376.
ix. 4. To them pertained the adoption, the glory, the fervice of God, i. 78, 162, 378, 379.
——5. Over all God bleffed for ever, i. 218, 350.
——33. I lay in Zion a ftumbling ftone, and rock of offence, ii. 255.
x. 4. They fubmitted not to the righteoufnefs of God, i. 180.
——6,——10. What faith the righteoufnefs of faith? the word is nigh thee in thy mouth, and in thy heart: if thou believe with thy heart that Jefus died, and confefs with thy mouth that God raifed him from the dead, thou fhalt be faved, i. 87. ii. 84, 85.
xi. 34. Who has directed the Spirit of the Lord, and who has been his counfellor? i. 413.

ROM.

ROM. xiv. 7, 8, 9. No man lives to himself, and no man of us dies to himself. Whether we live, we live unto the Lord, or whether we die, we die unto the Lord: whether therefore we live or die we are the Lord's: For to this end Christ both died and rose again, and revived, that HE might be the Lord both of dead and living, i. 67, 68, 298, 438, 439. ii. 53, 54, 384.

———11, 12. We shall all stand before the judgment seat of CHRIST; for it is written, As I live, faith the Lord, every knee shall bow to ME, and every tongue shall confess to GOD; so then every one of us shall give an account of himself to GOD, i. 352. ii. 234.

xvi. 17. I beseech you mark them that cause divisions and offences, contrary to the doctrine that ye have heard, and avoid them, ii. 351.

———25, 26. The revelation of the mystery which is manifest to all nations, i. 67.

1 COR. i. 2. Call on the name of the Lord Jesus, both theirs and ours, i. 299.

———17. I will bring to nought the wisdom of the wife, and destroy the understanding of the prudent. Has not God made foolish the wisdom of this world? ii. 309.

———21. Where is the wife? where is the scribe? where is the disputer of this world? i. 427.

ii. 2. Not with wisdom of words, lest the cross of Christ should be of no effect, ii. 310.

———7. We speak the wisdom of God in a mystery, which none of the princes of this world knew, i. 36.

———9. Eye hath not seen, nor ear heard, nor has it entered into the heart of man, what God has laid up for them that love him, i. 40.

———12. We have received not the spirit of this world, but the Spirit which is of God, that we may know the things that are freely given to us of God, ii. 376.

———14. The natural man receives not the things of the Spirit of God, for they are foolishness to him, because they are spiritually discerned, i. 37. ii. 113.

vi. 19. Ye are not your own, but bought with a price, and therefore glorify God in your spirits and bodies which are God's, i. 439.

x. 29. Do ye provoke the Lord to jealousy? are ye stronger than he? i. 106.

xii. 3. No man can say that Jesus is Lord, but by the Holy Ghost, i. 128. ii. 73, 114.

xiii. 4. Charity suffers long, and is kind; envies not, vaunts not itself, is not puffed up, ii. 353.

———11. When I was a child, I thought as a child, i. 36.

———13. The greatest of these is charity, ii. 388.

xiv. 9. Except ye utter by the tongue words easy to be understood, how shall it be known what is spoken, &c. ii. 324.

———34. God is among you of a truth, ii. 270.

xv. 24. He shall give up the kingdom to the Father, that God may be all in all, ii. 215.

2 COR. i. 3, 4. We are comforted of GOD, our consolation abounds in CHRIST, ii. 52.

ii. 17. We are not as many who corrupt the word of God, ii. 325.

iv. 2. Not walking in craftiness, nor handling the word of the Lord deceitfully, ii. 325.

———4. The god of this world has blinded their eyes, ii. 86.

——4. Christ is the image of God, i. 209. ii. 259.

———6. The light of the knowledge of the glory of God in the face of Jesus Christ, i. 45, 209. ii. 33.

———8. We believe, therefore we speak, ii. 100.

v. 10. We must stand before the judgment seat of Christ, i. 173.

———15. The love of Christ constrains us, i. 123, 221, 450. ii. 54.

———19. God is in Christ Jesus reconciling the world to himself, i. 65.

ix. 21. Under the law to Christ, i. 170.

x. 5. Casting down imaginations, and every high thing that exalts itself against the knowledge of God, ii. 89.

2 COR.

2 COR. xiii. 8. We can do nothing against the truth, but for the truth, ii. 351.
GAL. ii. 20. The life I live in the flesh, I live by faith in the Son of God, ii. 48.
iv. 4. When the fulness of time came, God sent forth his Son, made of a woman, made under the law, i. 20.
——29. He that is born after the flesh, persecutes him who is born after the Spirit, i. 129.
EPH. i. 22. He is head over all things to the Church; the fulness of him that fills all in all, i. 272. ii. 44, 270.
iii. 4. Ye may understand my knowledge in the mystery of Christ, i. 32.
——8, 9. The unsearchable riches of Christ; to make all men see what is the fellowship of the mystery, i. 93, 372. ii. 237, 238.
iv. 10. He ascended up far above all heavens, that he might fill all things, ii. 53.
——11. He gave some Apostles, Evangelists, Prophets, and Teachers, i. 99.
——16. Be not children, tossed to and fro with every wind of doctrine, ii. 114, 115.
PHIL. i. 17. Stand fast in one spirit, with one mind, striving together for the faith of the Gospel, ii. 351.
ii. 7, 8. He was in the form of God, and thought it no robbery to be equal with God, i. 146. ii. 256.
——10. Every knee shall bow to Christ, and every tongue confess that Jesus is Lord, to the glory of God the Father, i. 351, 352.
iii. 20. We look for a Saviour, Christ Jesus the Lord, i. 247.
——21. He shall change our vile bodies,——according to the power whereby he is able to subdue all things to himself, ii. 124, 135.
COL. i. 15. The first born of every creature, ii. 123.
——16. By him were all things created in heaven and in earth: thrones, dominions, principalities, and powers, all are created by him, and for him, i. 339, 448. ii. 218, 219.
——19. It pleased the Father, that in him should all fulness dwell, i. 356.
——20. By him to reconcile all things, ii. 241.
——26. The riches of the glory of this mystery, i. 23.
ii. 2. That our hearts may be comforted, being knit together, to the riches of the full assurance of understanding, to the acknowledgment of the mystery of God, and of the Father, and of Christ, i. 124.
——3. In him are hid all the treasures of wisdom and knowledge, ii. 186.
——10. Complete in him, who is the head of all principality and power, ii. 27.
——19. Increase with the increase of God, ii. 47.
1 THES. ii. 5. As we are allowed of God to be put in trust with the Gospel, even so we speak, not as pleasing men, but God, who searches the hearts, i. 445. ii. 100.
2 THES. ii. 11. He gave them up to strong delusions to believe a lie, i. 60.
iii. 2. That I may be delivered from wicked and unreasonable men, for all men have not faith, ii. 83. 300.
1 TIM. i. 17. The King eternal, immortal, invisible, the only wise God, i. 46. ii. 180.
vi. 10. The love of money is the root of all evil, which whilst some have coveted after, they have erred from the faith, ii. 354.
——15, 16. Keep the commandments to the coming of Jesus Christ, who in his own times shall shew that he has immortality, and dwells in light, i. 208. ii. 181, 182, 189.
——21, 22. Avoid opposition of science falsely so called, which some professing have erred from the faith, ii. 310, 331.
2 TIM. i. 12. I know in whom I have believed, and am persuaded that he is able to keep what I have committed to him, i. 127, 128, 157. ii. 190, 191.
ii. 13. He abides faithful, he cannot deny himself, ii. 203.
——16. They increase unto more ungodliness, i. 59.
——16, 17. Their words do eat as a canker; if a man purge himself from these, he shall be a vessel of honour, ii. 353.

2 TIM. i. 25. In meekness instructing those that oppose themselves, if peradventure, God may give them repentance to the acknowledging of the truth, ii. 351, 352.
iii. 13. Evil men and seducers shall wax worse and worse, deceiving, and being deceived, i. 60.
iv. 3, 4. The time will come that they will not endure sound doctrine, but after their own lusts shall heap to themselves teachers, having itching ears, and they shall turn away from the truth, and be turned to fables, i. 59, 60.
TIT. i. 1. Acknowledge the truth which is after godliness, ii. 361.
——— 15. To the unbelieving nothing is pure, but their mind and conscience are defiled, i. 38.
ii. 13. Adorn the doctrine of God our Saviour, ii. 95.
—14. Looking for the glorious appearance of our great God and Saviour, ii. 96.
HEB. i. 1. God spake to us by his Son, i. 161, 176, 177. ii. 63, 260.
——— 2. By whom he made the worlds, ii. 243, 260.
——— 3. Being the brightness of his glory, and the image of his person, upholding all things by the word of his power, i. 269. ii. 41, 243, 259.
——— 4. He by himself purged away our sins, ii. 244.
——— 6. Let all the Angels of God worship him, i. 138, 140, 141, 318, 330, 331. ii. 174, 261.
——— 7. He makes his Angels spirits, i. 308, 336.
——— 8. Thy throne, O God, is for ever and ever, i. 337. ii. 223.
——— 9. God, even thy God has anointed thee, i. 338.
——— 11, 12. Thou, Lord, hast laid the foundations of the earth, ii. 212.
——— 14. Are they not all ministring spirits sent forth to minister to the heirs of salvation? i. 325, 326.
ii. 2. The great salvation began to be spoken by the Lord, i. 198.
—5. He has not to the Angels put in subjection the world to come, i. 458.
—8. He was made lower than the Angels, i. 347.
—11. He that sanctifies, and they who are sanctified, are all of one, ii. 91.
—14, 15. As the children were partakers of flesh and blood, he took part of the same, that through death he might destroy him that had the power of death, i. 210, 271, 278. ii. 122, 123.
iii. 2. Moses was faithful, as a servant in all his house, ii. 36.
——— 3. This man was counted worthy of more honour than Moses, ii. 38, 39.
——— 4. Inasmuch as he who builded the house has more honour than the house, ii. 38, 39.
——— 8. An evil heart of unbelief in departing from the living God, ii. 39.
—16. Whose house we are, if we hold fast the confidence of our hope to the end, i. 175.
iv. 14. Let us hold fast our profession, ii. 227.
— 15. He was in all things tempted as we are, i. 201.
— 16. Come with boldness to the throne of grace, i. 119, 120.
vi. 18. By two immutable things, in which it is impossible for God to lye, we have strong consolation, i. 13.
vii. 24. Because he continues for ever, he has an unchangeable priesthood, ii. 245.
— 25. He is able to save to the uttermost, ii. 26.
ix. 17. Moses sprinkled the book, &c. ii. 40, 41.
— 23. The heavenly things are purged with better sacrifices, ii. 41.
— 26. He put away sin by the sacrifice of himself, i. 246.
x. 14. He has for ever perfected them that are sanctified, i. 398.
— 19. He has consecrated a new and living way, i. 118, 375.
xi. 27. He endured as seeing him who is invisible, i. 50.
xii. 2. Jesus the author and finisher of our faith, i. 127, 160, 161. ii. 60.
xiii. 7. Whose faith follow, considering the end of their conversation, ii. 358.
——— 8, 9. Be not carried about with divers and strange doctrines: Jesus the same yesterday, to-day, and for ever, i. 13. ii. 214, 215, 336.
JAM. v. 19, 20. If any man err from the truth, and one convert him, let him know that he who turns a sinner from the error of his way, shall save a soul from death, and hide a multitude of sins, ii. 352.

1 PET.

1 PET. i. 10. Of which salvation the prophets prophesied,———the sufferings of Christ, and the glory that should follow, i. 174, 254.
——— 11. Which things the Angels desire to look into, i. 333, 334.
——— 21. By him we believe in God who raised him from the dead and gave him glory, that our faith and hope may be in God, ii. 29, 107.
——— 22. You have purified your hearts through a belief of the truth to an unfeigned love of the brethren, ii. 396, 397.
ii. 3. Having tasted that the Lord is gracious, i. 184, 185. ii. 44.
2 PET. ii. 13. Spots are they, and blemishes in your feasts of charity; sporting themselves with their own deceivings, ii. 311.
——— 18, 19. They speak great swelling words of vanity, and allure through the lusts of the flesh those who were clean escaped from error: whilst they promise them liberty, they themselves are the servants of corruption, i. 59. ii. 316, 356.
iii. 10. 12. The day of the Lord comes, ii 189, 190.
1 JOHN i. 1. Our hands have handled of the word of life, i. 208, 209. ii. 213.
ii. 18, 19. There are many antichrists; they went out from us, but they were not of us, for had they been of us, they would no doubt have continued with us, i 22.
— 21. No lye is of the truth, i. 22.
iii. 1. When he shall appear we shall be like him, for we shall see him as he is, i. 186. ii. 51.
iv. 2, 3. Every spirit that confesses Jesus Christ, is of God, i. 22.
— 4. Ye are of God, little children, and have overcome them, ii. 51.
v. 7. There are three that bear record in heaven, the Father, the Word, and the Holy Ghost, and these three are one, ii. 329.
— 9, 10. He that believes has the witness in himself. If we receive the witness of men, the witness of God is greater, i. 12.
— 11. This life is in his Son: he that has the Son of God has life, ii. 47.
2 JOHN 7. Many deceivers are entered into the world, who confess not that Jesus Christ is come in the flesh. This is a deceiver and an antichrist, ii. 22.
——— 9. He that abides not in the doctrine of Christ has not God, ii. 227.
JUDE 1. Preserved in Christ Jesus and called, ii. 386.
——— 4. Contend earnestly for the faith that was once delivered to the Saints, i. 21.
——— 21.———25. Look for the mercy of the Lord Jesus to eternal life: to him who is able to keep us from falling, and to present us faultless before his glory with exceeding joy: to the only wise God our Saviour, be dominion and praise for ever, i. 158, 275. ii. 58, 387.
REV. i. 5, 6. To him that loved us and washed us from our sins in his own blood, and has made us kings and priests to God and his Father, be glory, ii. 240.
——— 8. I am Alpha and Omega, the beginning and the end, ii. 197.
——— 18. He has the keys of death and eternity, ii. 61.
ii. 23. I search the hearts and try the reins, i. 172, 173. ii. 188.
v. 1. I saw a book written and sealed, &c. ii. 157, 158, 159, 160.
xiv. 12. Here is the patience and faith of the Saints; they keep the faith of Jesus, i. 322.
xvi. 11. He is faithful and true, ii. 202, 203.
xx. 11, 12. I saw a great white throne, and him that sat upon it.———I saw the dead small and great stand before God, i. 173. 174.
xxi. 3. The tabernacle of God is with men,———and God himself shall be with them, and be their God, ii. 270.
xxii. 2. The throne of God, and the Lamb, ii. 267.
——— 9. Worship thou God, i. 447.
——— 13. I am Alpha and Omega, ii. 197.
——— 20. He that testifies these things saith, I come quickly: Amen, even so come Lord Jesus, ii. 197, 387.

THE END.

ADVERTISEMENT.

BESIDE thefe two Volumes, fome other Works of equal merit, and feveral detached Pieces, written by Mr Bradbury, were publifhed at different times, and were all well received, and highly efteemed by ferious Chriftians.— Thefe excellent Productions being thus fo much difperfed, and now become fo very fcarce as not to be found complete in the hand of almoft any individual, the Editors intend to proceed in the publication of the Author's *Whole Works*, on a uniform plan; and they are hopeful, that fuch a Collection will by many be deemed a valuable acquifition.— The Sermons for the 5th of November, and thofe on Baptifm, were formerly in two volumes, but will now be comprifed in one, which fhall be the volume next publifhed.

The ever bold and unaffected, yet often lofty ftyle, in which the Myftery of Godlinefs is written, may be confidered as a fpecimen of the Author's general manner; and the fame zeal for evangelical Truth, and practical Holinefs, which is fo confpicuous in it, may be looked for in the ftrain of all his other Writings.

☞ To prevent miftakes, it is requefted, that Subfcribers for the Myftery of Godlinefs, who do not mean to continue for the reft of Mr Bradbury's Works, will pleafe fignify their intention to J. Ogle, bookfeller, Edinburgh, as otherwife the fubfequent volumes, as publifhed, will be forwarded to them.

www.ingramcontent.com/pod-product-compliance
Lightning Source LLC
Chambersburg PA
CBHW020535300426
44111CB00008B/680